D1215187

Brendon J. Cannon

Legislating Reality and Politicizing History
-
Contextualizing Armenian Claims of Genocide

With an Introduction by Michael M. Gunter

Offenbach am Main/Germany
Cover design: A. Franklin W., Frankfurt am Main
Type: Manzara Verlag Bölge & Avşar
Font: Garamond font size 10/11
Print and binding: SOWA Sp. z.o.o,
Piaseczno / Polska
Printed in Poland

www.manzara-verlag.de

Brendon J. Cannon

LEGISLATING REALITY AND POLITICIZING HISTORY

~

CONTEXTUALIZING ARMENIAN CLAIMS OF GENOCIDE

Manzara Verlag
Offenbach am Main

Cannon, Brendon J.:

Legislating Reality and Politicizing History – Contextualizing Armenian Claims of Genocide
Brendon J. Cannon. - 1. Edition

Offenbach am Main/ Germany: Manzara Verlag 2016

ISBN: 3-939795-67-4
978-3-939795-67-4

www.manzara-verlag.de

PREFACE

The fact remains that the vast majority of people who have been made aware of the events of 1915 now term them as a genocide; the Armenian Genocide. Most of the countries that have recognized the Armenian Genocide, however, are in the West, if one includes Russia, and more particularly in Europe. This is a reflection of the political efforts of a strong, highly-mobilized and relatively wealthy Armenian diaspora in countries such as France and the United States. Efforts at genocide recognition are also assisted by some in the West, particularly Europeans, who are consumed by historical guilt and keen to make amends for the European excesses – colonialism, genocide, ethnic cleansing, two World Wars – that characterized most of the nineteenth and twentieth centuries. American liberals, if they are aware of it, offer their full support for recognition of the events of 1915 as the Armenian Genocide because it is the "right" thing to do. The logic of their actions is also informed by the idea that recognition of the Armenian Genocide is a magnanimous gesture and one that partially assuages the guilty conscience of the West for its centuries-long catalogue of murder, slavery, rape and pillage. Recognition is also beguilingly cheap and easy, especially when all that is asked for is a piece of legislation or some official proclamation that the events of 1915 constituted the Armenian Genocide. These *ad hoc* acts are thought, often with the best of intentions, to assist in honoring the Armenian victims and survivors of 1915. They also avoid the rather more difficult, expensive and politically sensitive demands of reparations and rights of return, issues that inherently require addressing in any acts deemed to be genocide by a proper court of law. Yet, because recognition of the events of 1915 as genocide only adversely affects outsiders (Turks), and correspondingly "helps" insiders (Armenian-Americans, for example), many unquestioningly support such *ad hoc* legislative moves. It should be pointed out, however, that many of these same supporters become squeamish when issues such as reparations for slavery or colonial excesses are raised. These issues are closer to home, so to speak, and therefore the historical record and accompanying narratives appear more complicated, involved and potentially very expensive.

This is one of the salient points of this book. Narratives based on historical documents and "facts" can be construed differently depending on multiple variables, to include time and space. Therefore, the issue of Armenian Genocide recognition becomes more complicated in Turkey than it would be in Marseille, La Paz or Portland precisely because the costs are high and the narrative appears more complicated. Based on historical texts, and unlike slavery in the United States or Brazil, the events of 1915 and the discourse surrounding them are not only more complicated but carry direct and high costs to those who are wrongly implicated, as this book demonstrates. The act of genocide recognition, particularly vis-à-vis the events of 1915, is a profoundly symbolic act, but it is one that is informed by politics and political calculations. In this particular case, the act is highly politicized and based on egregious efforts to legislate history.

This politicization bleeds into operational modes and methods of the Armenian campaign. The Armenian diaspora operates in and focuses on regions where it has natural strengths and natural allies. For example, lobbying efforts and lobbying organizations are strongest in countries such as France and the United States because of the large number of French-Armenians and Armenian-Americans. Countries with the proverbial axe to grind with Turkey are also a target. Greece, with Turkey and the Ottoman Empire as its historical "Other" to the Greek "Self," is a prime example. Russia is another. When countries such as these reach economic or political impasses with Turkey, the recognition of the Armenian Genocide becomes a very handy cudgel.

What of the rest of the world? Is this truly a global campaign for genocide recognition? According to the current Armenian campaign, the events of 1915 constituted the Armenian Genocide, the world's first genocide or, at very least, the first genocide of the twentieth century. This has truly universal implications and arguably calls for a global campaign. However, from my current vantage point in East Africa, the subject and the campaign for Armenian Genocide recognition is neither seen nor heard. This can partially be explained by the Armenian diaspora's lack of resources and natural allies in a place like Sub-Saharan Africa, for example. This understandably makes it difficult for Armenians to lobby for genocide recognition, should this be desired. Yet, the fact remains that regardless of resource issues or other variables, Armenians have largely ignored Africa and other parts of the globe, to include East Asia and South Asia. Herein reside over half of the world's population. If a critical mass of support and recognition is behind the Armenian diaspora's logic that informs their campaign for recognition of a truly universal crime, it would be logical for the diaspora to focus their efforts on regions other than the West. Yet, the issue of recognition of the Armenian Genocide remains a largely Western, mostly northern hemispheric and, therefore, "white" affair. This is not surprising on one level, given that the Armenian campaign and lobbying effort are rooted in and informed entirely by events that occurred over a century ago in the crucible that forged modern Europe and the Middle East. The campaign also continues to rely on racist images of the Asiatic, swarthy and bloodthirsty "terrible Turk." This means that the "white," successor states of the Great Powers in 1915 still matter now and, indeed, are the only states that matter. As such, a truly global recognition of the events of 1915 as the Armenian Genocide is not part of the agenda, either because of resource constraints or because the diaspora still looks at recognition through racial lenses and, as such, it remains a largely European, or Western, affair.

Regardless of the campaign's veracity, tenacity and success, this book does not classify what happened to Ottoman Armenians as genocide. This is because the term does not apply to the horrific massacres, slaughters, injustices and murders of 1915. This is an uncomfortable position to take and one that is unpopular in places ranging from Los Angeles to Paris to Beirut. Though the events of 1915 are not, and indeed (legally) cannot be referred to as genocide, this book does not shy away from the need to describe, fully acknowledge and therefore, in some small, way honor all of the victims (Muslims and Christians) who suffered unspeakable horrors, shame, disgrace, and injustice in 1915. The Armenian victims who survived such calamities received no compensation or acknowledgment of any wrongdoing for their suffering from either the Ottoman authorities or their Turkish successors, thus adding insult to grave injury. Though verifiable proof of a genocidal blueprint by the Ottoman state has never been found, the records do demonstrate, time and again, ample proof of the monstrous inhumanity of man to man. Yet, this book strives to take a holistic and nuanced view, positing the Armenian historical trauma against the backdrop of equally horrific slaughters and forcible relocations of Ottoman Muslims in the Balkans, the Crimea, the Caucasus and Anatolia. It is only by understanding the perfect storm that was eastern Anatolia in 1915 that one can appreciate the magnitude of the calamity, as well as how and why it occurred.

Since the publication of my original dissertation (the inspiration for this book) in 2009, numerous books have been published by historians, sociologists and political scientists who have grounded works such as this through the utilization of historical methods, quantitative population studies, political science theories and archival records. It is hoped that this book adds to these previous scholarly works, works that examine and re-examine the events of 1915 - events that take on a particular poignancy given that they occurred just over one century ago.

This book is the product of over a decade of intellectual engagement and conversations. I have incurred many debts during this time period. First, I would like to thank Michael M. Gunter for his willingness to write the book's introduction and for providing the genesis of the book's prescient title. His scholarly works precede him and they are amply quoted and referenced throughout. This is also true of the articles and books of M. Hakan Yavuz, my friend and doctoral advisor at the University of Utah. I thank him for his patience, his vital input and germane edits. The pioneering works of Justin McCarthy, Edward J. Erickson and Jeremy Salt need no introduction here, suffice to say that I am indebted to their cogent political thoughts and works based on archival research. Though I cannot possibly thank them all individually, I am deeply indebted to my many friends and colleagues in Istanbul, Nairobi, Hargeisa, Tashkent, Salt Lake City and Washington, D.C. for their insights, support and contributions to this book. I also thank the publishers at Manzara Verlag for their willingness to consider this book for publication and offering to do so in English, German and Turkish-language versions. Lastly, I must thank my dear friend and consummate scholar, Bosire Maragia, for our continuous and continuing conversations, his unflagging interest and unfailing attention to detail. They made this book possible.

Nairobi
April 2016

TABLE OF CONTENTS

LIST OF MAPS

"There is no present or future, only the past, happening over and over again, now."

– Eugene O'Neill

A Moon for the Misbegotten

"The past is never dead; it's not even past."

- William Faulkner

Requiem for a Nun

INTRODUCTION

There is another side to the Armenian interpretation of the tragedy they suffered during World War I, and Brendon J. Cannon tells it well. In an academically clear and scholarly manner, Cannon articulately analyzes what he terms the wanton application of the term genocide to these events of 1915 that resulted in such a huge loss of life. This study should be read by anyone interested in these tragic events. It should also be read by those who would object to what Cannon calls an elastic definition of genocide, one that undermines its legal definition and thus complicates the courts' ability to punish actual genocide perpetrators.

Much confusion exists about what is meant by the term genocide because the word has come to have at least two different meanings, a precise international legal one and a non-legal popular one. The two different meanings have been conflated by some, either by mistake or on purpose, to confuse the world and accuse Turkey of being legally guilty of genocide for the Armenian massacres that occurred more than 100 years ago in 1915. Given this confusing situation a brief analysis of these two different meanings of the term genocide is in order.

Legally genocide is defined by the Genocide Convention that was signed in 1948 and then ratified in 1951 when it went into effect. The Genocide Treaty, in part, legally defines genocide as "acts committed with intent to destroy, in whole or in part, a national, ethnical, racial or religious group." Therefore, for genocide to have legally occurred, there must have been intent on the part of the perpetrators to wipe out an entire ethnic group and this act must have been committed since 1951 after the Genocide Treaty went into effect. Neither requirement has occurred in regards to the Armenians.

Despite what many Armenians and their supporters claim, there is no authentic document that proves that the Ottoman authorities intended to wipe out the Armenians. Indeed, many Armenians living in western Anatolia who were deemed no threat to Ottoman supply lines and security were not relocated in 1915. Is it possible to imagine Hitler sparing any Jews from his genocidal rampage because they were not threatening his supply lines or security? Therefore, without proven intent, legally there can be no genocide.

In addition, of course, even if intent could be demonstrated (which it has not), genocide legally could not have occurred before the Genocide Treaty was ratified and went into effect in 1951 because it would constitute an *ex post facto* law expressly prohibited by Article 11 of the Universal Declaration of Human Rights, Article 15 of the International Covenant on Civil and Political Rights, and Article 1/Section 9 of the U.S. Constitution. An *ex post facto* law of course makes some action a crime which, when it was originally committed, was not a crime.

Furthermore, as Cannon points out, for the U.S. Congress or any other legislative body to pass any resolution declaring that the Armenian tragedy was a genocide (itself a highly political and politicized act) would be analogous to a bill of attainder. This is a legislative act which punishes somebody without a fair judicial trail. This is also specifically prohibited by Article 1, Section 9 of the U.S. Constitution. Therefore, applying the Genocide Treaty to the Armenian tragedy by using an *ex post facto* law or bill of attainder would be a clear violation of due process of law which is specifically prohibited by the Fifth and Fourteenth Amendments to the U.S Constitution as well as through implication by Article 7 of the Universal Declaration of Human Rights, and Articles 14 and 26 of the International Covenant on Civil and Political Rights.

As Cannon's book demonstrates, the Armenians, particularly the Armenian diaspora, and their supporters are trying to get around these major international legal and U.S. constitutional safeguards by confusingly conflating the legal definition of genocide with the more general popular one. This popular definition equates genocide loosely with any large-scale killings that have ever occurred either before 1951 or after that date when the Genocide Treaty went into effect. By this second, non-legal definition of genocide, of course, the Armenians suffered from large-scale killings or genocide. However, as Cannon points out, so did the Turks and other Muslims who were killed by ethnic violence during World War I and earlier in the Balkans. By this non-legal definition of genocide both Muslims and Armenians committed genocide against each other. To accuse only one side for this situation ignores what happened to the other and is patently unfair, as this book cogently illustrates.

However, the many Armenians and their supporters who accuse Turkey of genocide—either through simple lack of the complete facts or on purpose to malign Turkey for their own reasons—continue to try to piggy back these two different definitions of genocide. It is time for governments, scholars, and the intelligent lay public to stop conflating these two different definitions of genocide and get their facts straight so we will not continue to dishonor the memory of those who so tragically died on both sides during World War I.

Professor Michael M. Gunter
Tennessee Technological University

CHAPTER 1

UNDERSTANDING THE EVENTS OF 1915 AND THE ARMENIAN GENOCIDE CAMPAIGN

The ongoing, vitriolic campaign for Armenian Genocide recognition is perhaps framed at its tragic best by the cold-blooded murder of Hrant Dink. Dink, an Armenian-Turk, was shot and killed in broad daylight outside the office of his newspaper in Istanbul on January 19, 2007. Dink's murder committed by a Turkish nationalist revealed alternating currents in the Turkish psyche: revulsion by some, coupled with shameful, nationalist pride by others. His murder also stirred up waves of resentment and painful memories amongst Armenians in Armenia, Turkey and the Armenian diaspora.

Dink was an activist newspaper editor and one of Turkey's most prominent ethnic Armenian citizens. His sin, according to some Turkish nationalists, was that he had argued for dialogue and debate regarding the tragedy that befell his Armenian ancestors in the waning days of the Ottoman Empire. Because of his openness and forceful statements regarding the issue, he was repeatedly threatened and eventually killed.

Hugh Pope, an author of numerous books generally favorable to Turkey and the Turks, pointed to deeper, historical problems in attempted to explain Dink's murder.

He posited that it was the "…bad laws, malevolent prosecutions and a growing nationalist hysteria [that] helped create a lynch mob atmosphere [in Turkey]..." Pope added that Turkey has never been able to deal with what he termed "the Armenian issue," referring to the 1915 massacres and exile of thousands of ethnic Armenian citizens of the Ottoman Empire; the predecessor state to the Republic of Turkey.[1] In other words, Pope directly links *and* blames Dink's tragic and untimely murder in 2007 on events that occurred over one hundred years ago in the waning days of the Ottoman Empire.

This "Armenian issue," this tragic event or series of events that occurred mainly in 1915 and the years surrounding it, begs that certain questions be asked. Namely, why would a series of events– painful as they were – regain or continue to hold such salience that they affect not just Armenian and Turkish relations, but even have the potential to disrupt Turkey's economic and strategic ties globally?[2] What would lead the foreign minister of Turkey in 2007 to argue that if the United States Congress adopted a resolution labeling the massacres of Armenians in the Ottoman Empire in 1915 as

---

[1] Hugh Pope. "Armenia Haunts Turkey Again." *Los Angeles Times*, January 23, 2007. http://www.latimes.com/news/la-oe-pope23jan23-story.html

[2] Turkey has repeatedly warned multiple countries considering recognition of the events of 1915 as Genocide with various penalties affecting bilateral strategic, economic and political ties. See Angelique Chrisafis. "Turkey Warns France over Armenian Genocide Bill." *The Guardian*, October 11, 2006. http://www.theguardian.com/world/2006/oct/11/turkey.eu. See also A.A. "Fransız markaları boykot edilecek." *Hürriyet*, October 12, 2006. http://www.hurriyet.com.tr/fransiz-markalari-boykot-edilecek-5246217. See also Jonathan Lis. "Foreign Ministry: Israel's Recognition of Armenian Genocide Could Threaten Turkey Ties." *Haaretz*, April 12, 2016. http://www.haaretz.com/israel-news/foreign-ministry-israel-s-recognition-of-armenian-genocide-could-threaten-turkey-ties-1.403687. See also Julian Pecquet. "Turks link Armenia to US Foes in bid to derail Genocide Nod." *Al-Monitor*, April 16, 2014. http://www.al-monitor.com/pulse/originals/2015/04/turkey-armenian-genocide-congress-recognition-anniversary.html#.

"genocide," Turkey's strategic relationship with its North Atlantic Treaty Organization (NATO) partner of 50 years would suffer "lasting damage?"[3] What century-old events, depending on the semantics used to describe them, have the potential to economically and strategically strangle the Republic of Armenia? Finally, what contested events have defined the Armenian diaspora's identity and nurtured the development of a powerful transnational campaign to recognize the events of 1915 as the "Armenian Genocide," the world's first genocide?[4]

The primary aim of this book is to properly define Armenian and, more particularly, Armenian diaspora identity and its relationship to and reliance on the events of 1915. This book posits that Armenian diaspora communities, in large part, rely on and gain sustenance from the traumatic events of 1915 because these tragic events provide the only glue that bonds disparate linguistic, religious and geographically atomized communities. Thus, the common perception of the Armenian diaspora as a cohesive force speaking with a unified voice quickly falls apart when issues are broached outside the purview of the campaign for Armenian Genocide recognition. Though views of how genocide recognition should be achieved and what should come afterward vary, little dissent exists or is tolerated – at least publicly - within the diaspora. This is particularly true in regards to relations between individual ethnic Armenians and ethnic Turks, regardless of their citizenship. Because contact is discouraged and, very likely, unwanted by the diaspora, relations between the two groups at almost every level remain non-existent outside of Turkey and, importantly, the Republic of Armenia.

---

[3] "Waving Ataturk's Flag," *The Economist.* March 8, 2007: 45.

[4] This has been quietly amended in recent years, and the campaign for Armenian Genocide recognition now refers to the Armenian Genocide as "the first genocide of the twentieth century." See Peter Balakian. *The Burning Tigris: The Armenian Genocide and America's Response.* New York: HarperCollins, 2003: 1-2.

In order to fully comprehend the campaign to recognize the events of 1915 as the Armenian Genocide, it is absolutely essential to understand contemporary and historical issues surrounding the identity construction and transmission of diaspora Armenians and their Armenian counterparts in the Republic of Armenia. This can only be accomplished, in part, through a corollary consideration of the centuries of Ottoman Turkish rule in Anatolia and to a slightly lesser extent, the southern Caucasus – the ancestral home of many Armenians. This, in turn, must be posited against the dilatory and troublesome demise throughout the decades of the nineteenth and early twentieth centuries of what was once one of the most powerful empires in the world.

Synopsis

The events and historical record catalogued in this book have been subject to an egregious amount of politicization by the Armenian diaspora campaign for genocide recognition and correspondingly, but less so, by the government of Turkey. As such, an attempt to deconstruct the highly polemical and vitriolic debate surrounding the events of 1915 is in order. It is hoped that by providing a firm foundation, no matter how cursory, readers will be better able to frame the concepts and definitions of genocide, crimes against humanity, memory, trauma, ethnic cleansing and time collapse. The book also explicates and frames how and why the Armenian diaspora communities, through lobbying organizations and other interest groups, have used and reified the definition and conceptualization of genocide, particularly in the United States. Furthermore, it explores how Turks and Armenians in Turkey as well as Armenians in the Republic of Armenia have reacted to the Armenian diaspora's reconstructed memories, the campaign it has spawned and the policy aims the diaspora nurtures and produces. As such, this first chapter attempts to highlight the salient features and nuances of this complicated debate, deconstruct the campaign for

Armenian Genocide recognition, and provide the structure required for further exploration of historical and political data. A survey of the literature regarding theories of identity, construction of Self and Other, chosen trauma and glories, ethnic conflict, diaspora politics and globalization as well as the collapse of time is discussed in a necessarily lengthy chapter 2.

It is hoped that the firm historical foundation available in chapter 3 will provide readers with the ability to frame the concepts and definitions of genocide, crimes against humanity, memory, trauma, ethnic cleansing and the time collapse and how the Armenian diaspora communities, through lobbying organizations and other interest groups, have used and reified the definition and conceptualization of "genocide," particularly in the United States, and how Turks and Armenians in both Turkey and Armenia have reacted to the Armenian diaspora's reconstructed memories of what they term genocide and the policy aims they nurture and produce.

Chapter 4 identifies the Armenian diaspora's major lobbying groups, paying particular attention to in the United States and France and how these groups' efforts are direct products of mutually constitutive and self-reinforcing Armenian diaspora identity.

A broad discussion of genocide theory, law and legislation in chapter 5 leads to a deconstruction of the goals and nature of the Armenian diaspora's campaign of genocide recognition. Specifically, this book asks and attempts to answer exactly what genocide recognition would entail? Who exactly would benefit from recognition and how? The book looks at the subject of genocide recognition and the campaign by members of the Armenian diaspora through a critical lens asking whether this is a simple yet highly symbolic act of commemoration, a public apology, material for educational curricula or something else entirely. Specifically, this book delves into the final aim or aims of genocide recognition. Does recognition of the events of 1915 as genocide necessarily engender something more tangible such as reparations or territory, for example? If so, how would this be achieved?

The official stance of successive Turkish governments, broadly speaking, and Turkish public opinion are discussed in chapter 6. This is novel in that the views of Turks regarding this volatile, highly emotional and profound issue and campaign are rarely, if ever taken, into account. Public opinion surveys in Turkey and the development of Turkish diaspora lobbying groups all point to a more multi-faceted approach to countering the Armenian diaspora campaign of genocide recognition, internal societal changes within Turkey and the realization that events the occurred over one century ago still profoundly affect Turkey's past, present and future.

Chapter 7 details and explores the often pronounced and deep-seated divergence that exists between Armenian diaspora and Armenian "native" memories, with particular emphasis on the differences of memories, chosen trauma, time collapse and the attempts at homogenization of diaspora Armenian and Armenian historical narratives and identities.

A discussion of the broad differences between Armenian and Armenian diaspora memories, policy goals and respective futures necessarily leads to a discussion of the effects the Armenian diaspora's campaign of genocide recognition have on Armenia and Armenians. As such, chapter 8 details Armenia's development or decline as an independent nation-state over the past few decades, with special attention paid to diaspora investment or lack thereof, political influence and diaspora attempts to dictate or at least influence Armenia's domestic and foreign policy agendas.

Chapter 9 discusses different theoretical and operational approaches to pressure – vertical, horizontal and diagonal – as applied by and to the Armenian Genocide campaign and how this affects the diaspora, the Republic of Armenia and the Republic of Turkey. It also highlights option available to all parties for potential resolution of this emotive subject and the issues surrounding it.

The events of 1915 and the Armenian diaspora's campaign for recognition of those events as the Armenian Genocide are necessarily part of a larger human need to deal with atrocities. As such, chapter 10 discusses attempts at coming to terms with historical atrocities within the legal framework of the UN Convention on Genocide and, perhaps more importantly, the international human rights regime. In essence, by positing the Armenian question against the background of the human rights regime as it has developed over the course of the last century and in terms of human rights, a number of useful questions are automatically raised. By doing so, the potential of allowing all parties involved the opportunity to view the issue from novel vantage points is achieved. Perhaps this offers the potential for a breakthrough and escape from the status quo? It is from this vantage point that real and lasting progress may be possible – not just for Armenians.

The concluding chapter attempts to analyze the current situation for reconciliation and closure from the perspectives described in the preceding chapters: the historical record, the Armenian campaign, definitional elasticity and the human rights regime. Given the nature of Armenian diaspora identity and its direct opposition to its Turkish "Other," it appears that a state-to-state solution (Turkey-Armenia) may be amenable or, at very least, in the realm of the possible. However, given the vitriol and sheer emotiveness of the issue and campaign as defined by the identities involved, the future looks rather bleak indeed.

Armenians and Turks: From Benign Symbiosis to Perpetual Enmity

The historical record of the Caucasus and Anatolia demonstrates that Armenians and Turks are not age-old enemies. Neither are Armenians the enemy of Muslim peoples inhabiting the region, such as the Kurds, Persians, Chechens, Laz and others. This is not to say that all was bliss. Scholars have listed the multiple destructions of ancient Armenia by numerous marauding armies, including

Persians and Mongols, although the Ottoman Turks are not part of this list. However, rather than seeing this destruction as motivated by religious or cultural biases, scholars ascribe it to the nature and realities of war, pillage and conflicting empires. In short, there was no real intent to destroy the Armenians, their culture or their livelihood.[5]

From its earliest beginnings, but particularly after the conquest of Istanbul (Constantinople) in 1453, Armenians played important roles in the Ottoman government, trade and manufacturing and were often described as the most loyal community in the Empire by Ottoman court historians.[6] Armenians and Muslims rarely suffered effects of inter-communal violence until well into the nineteenth century. When conflict arrived, it did so largely because of the advent and wide dissemination of outside ideas, the promulgation of a new Ottoman constitution that was favorable to minority communities in the Empire and the increasingly forceful meddling in Ottoman affairs by foreign powers.[7] Indeed, their coexistence throughout the vast majority of Ottoman rule has been characterized as one of "benign symbiosis."[8] Yet, as the years of the nineteenth century passed, the forces of nationalism and imperialism and the rise of major military and economic powers, such as Russia, led to cracks, splits and fissures in a fragile vase, one that symbolically held and displayed a generally symbiotic and benign relationship between ethnic and religious communities in the Ottoman Empire. Eventually, the cracks deepened to the point where the vase shattered, never to be reassembled.

---

[5] Richard G. Hovannisian. *The Armenian People from Ancient to Modern Times, Volume II: Foreign Dominion to Statehood: The Fifteenth Century to the Twentieth Century.* Vol. 2. (Macmillan, 2004), 10-11 and 48-49.

[6] Guenter Lewy, *The Armenian Massacres in Ottoman Turkey* (Salt Lake City, UT: University of Utah Press, 2005), 3.

[7] Şerif Mardin. *The Genesis of Young Ottoman Thought: A Study in the Modernization of Turkish Political Ideas.* (Syracuse University Press, 2000), 19.

[8] Ronald Grigor Suny, *Looking Toward Ararat: Armenia in Modern History* (Bloomington: Indiana University Press, 1993), 101.

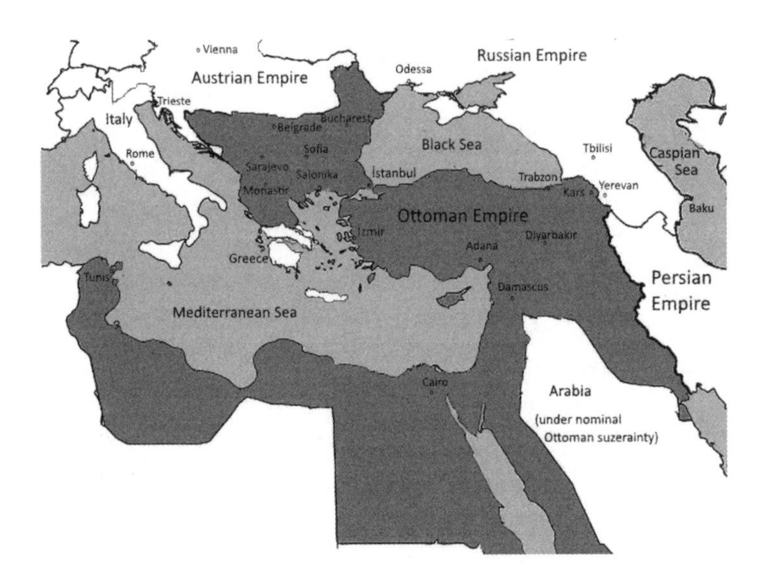

The Ottoman Empire in 1862

The first cracks occurred with imperial Russia's forays into formerly Muslim and Ottoman territories such as the Crimea and the Caucasus and the arrival of radical ideas regarding nationalism and self-determination from Europe and via Russia and Istanbul. These ideas led to the genesis of an Armenian nationalism and led many Armenians to view Russian rule as a positive alternative to Ottoman rule and an eventual stepping-stone towards an independent Armenia. Russian power, influence and actions made it clear that it wished for nothing more than outright control of Istanbul and the Bosphorus and Dardanelles Straits and the dissolution of the Ottoman Empire.[9]

As colonial powers such as Great Britain, France and Russia chipped away at Ottoman power and hegemony from the outside, the empire was slowly disintegrating internally with the birth of national societies with the violent intent of overthrowing the empire and the establishment of national states. Greece, with the support of Britain and

[9] Mardin, 24-26.

other powers, broke away first. Egypt, Bosnia and Romania followed with the significant support from Britain, Austria-Hungary and Russia, respectively. Secret political societies were created to advocate, often using violence, for a greater Greek kingdom that would span the Aegean Sea, or an independent Armenia in eastern Anatolia, or an independent Bulgarian nation. Acts of sabotage and the murder of Ottoman officials became increasingly common.[10] Reports of abuse by Christian minorities at the hands of Ottoman authorities also became more prevalent, as the desperate and perennially bankrupt Ottoman state lashed out against threats to its survival. The 1880s and 1890s were particularly violent, culminating with the seizure of the Ottoman Bank in Istanbul by a group of Armenian nationalists armed with dynamite and firearms. Violence and massacres, sabotage and counter massacres convulsed the empire and largely poisoned relations between Christian Armenians and Ottoman Muslims, with relative calm and a return to the "way things were," making a second debut only after the turn of the century. Yet the die had been cast and relations between the empire's multi-confessional citizens were now viewed through the new prisms of nationalism and the right of self-determination.[11] However, it took the worldwide conflagration of World War I to lead to events that still haunt and inform relations between Turks and Armenians to this day and provide the basis and bond for a common and politically powerful Armenian diaspora identity.

Forging a Durable Armenian Identity in the Diaspora

Events that occurred during World War I in the fateful year 1915 are at the heart of the issue of Armenian diaspora identity: the massacres, deportations, rapes, forced

---

[10] Sam White. *The climate of rebellion in the early modern Ottoman Empire.* Cambridge University Press, 2011.

[11] Tigran Akopian. *Political Violence in Armenia (Sources, Public Perception, Ways to Overcome the Problem).* Central Asia and the Caucasus Press. No. 5 (17), 2002.

migrations and murder of many Ottoman Armenians. These tragic events culminated in the disappearance of the vast majority of Armenians from their ancestral homeland of Anatolia. This traumatic set of events is central to group cohesion and identity formation. The Armenian diaspora continues to relive the tragedy that befell them in 1915 through memories, commemorations and, most importantly, their high-profile campaign to gain recognition; an eventually global recognition that the trauma and wounds suffered by Armenians in 1915 constituted not just the "Armenian Genocide, but the world's *first* genocide."[12]

Armenian Political Identity

In discussing Armenian large group identity, the term "identity" is most often a reference to "political identity," and this book is necessarily an attempt, in part, to deconstruct this highly politicized identity. Political identity, for the purposes of this book, refers to the process of Armenians becoming conscious of the political and social effects of a unique historical memory and the frames of reference associated therewith. These fames of reference are then utilized by the Armenian diaspora, in particular, as political means to fulfill a highly politicized agenda: recognition that the events of 1915 constituted the Armenian Genocide.

Though Armenian large group identity, vis-à-vis the events of 1915, is unique, Armenians are certainly not alone in utilizing - consciously and strategically - shared conceptions of history, ethics, justice and community for advancing large group goals.[13] Identities "... are not things we think *about*, but thing we think *with*. As such, they have no existence beyond our politics, our social relations, and our

---

[12] Balakian. 1-2.

[13] M. Hakan Yavuz, *Islamic Political Identity in Turkey* (New York: Oxford University Press, 2003), 6-7.

histories."[14] Crawford Young noted that identity "... at the bottom is a subjective self-concept or social role; it is often variable, overlapping and situational... 'We' is defined in part by 'they;' the relevant other in a social setting is central in shaping the role selection."[15]

Young noted the variable and situation-specific nature of identity, yet what is fascinating in regards to Armenian large group identity is the stunning power and longevity of the campaign for genocide recognition. This campaign is almost entirely shaped and prosecuted via the high degree of politicization of this same identity as informed by the events of 1915. Though Armenian political identity is a frame of reference that is unconsciously internalized through socialization, as demonstrated in the proceeding pages, it is an identity that maintains an unusually high degree of politicization and objectification in direct relation to the desired ends of the campaign for genocide recognition. Armenian large group identity demands that the West, Russia and, in particular, Turkey officially recognize that the events of 1915 constituted the Armenian Genocide. In order to do so, Armenians - as their political identity demands and this book will demonstrate - have blatantly politicized history and attempted to legislate reality, regardless of changing social, political or economic circumstances.

In this book, Armenian identity or, more specifically, Armenian political identity is viewed as relational and contingent. It is relational in that the social forces that assist in the construction of Armenian political identity are constructed through opposition or "oppositional moments." In essence, Armenian identity and the campaign for genocide recognition exhibit such power and cohesive force precisely because of the existence of opposition, strenuous at times, to the aims of the campaign. In other

---

[14] John R. Gillis (ed.). *Commemorations: The Politics of National Identity* (Princeton: Princeton University Press, 1994), 5.
[15] Crawford Young. *The Politics of Cultural Pluralism* (Madison: University of Wisconsin Press, 1976), 65.

words, Armenian political identity thrives on and is galvanized by real or perceived opposition to the campaign.

Armenian identity is not only relational, but contingent in that it is dependent on the construction of difference vis-à-vis its perceived, historical "Other." In the case of Armenian large group identity, the "Self" is necessarily constructed in opposition to the its Other; i.e. the "terrible Turk." In this, Armenian political identity only differs from other large group identity in ingredients rather than form. "Every identity, by definition, carries its "other" within it as a constituting element. The 'significant other' is not only an oppositional 'other' but also a constitutive part of identity. No identity has its own self-referential standpoint."[16] In the case of Armenian political identity, confrontations with internal others are limited. In essence, the proverbial wagons are circled and internal, large group differences are subsumed to face the external Other, the Turk. It is the events of 1915 that inform this oppositional identity. In essence, the suppurating wounds inflicted in 1915 are now suffered and lived with collectively through the transmission of distilled and redistilled memories on societal, familial and individual levels within the Armenian diaspora. The trauma that occurred in 1915 for Ottoman Armenians now constitutes *the* glue that cements and grounds the Armenian diaspora community. In other words, the reimagined trauma of 1915 forms the cornerstone of their identity. Correspondingly, the goal of international recognition of the events as the world's first genocide, the Armenian Genocide, disputed and thwarted for valid reasons by the Ottoman Empire's successor state Turkey, continues to stoke the flames of anger, hurt and hostility that constitute the rubric of transnational Armenian diaspora identity.

Having established that the events of 1915 claim the central role in the identity of the Armenian diaspora,[17] this

---

[16] Yavuz. *Islamic Political Identity in Turkey*, 22.

[17] The Turkish-Armenian activist Hrant Dink concurred, noting that Armenians had formed an unhealthy identity not as themselves but rather in opposition to Turks. Dink's comments offended not just

identity, in turn, has developed a central narrative - based on shared memories - that has been assembled, reassembled and disseminated as historical fact: *over 1.5 million Armenians were slaughtered by Ottoman Turks with the intent to eradicate Ottoman Armenians in accordance with a rigid plan and in an organized fashion with the express approval of the Ottoman government.* This planned and executed campaign resulted in the world's first genocide, according to the diaspora narrative. According to a 2007 statement on the website of a prominent Armenian-American interest group strongly involved in the campaign of Armenian Genocide recognition, "This April marked the 92nd anniversary of the cataclysmic events that occurred in the Ottoman Empire from 1915-1923, where 1.5 million Armenians were killed and over half a million survivors were exiled... Despite the overwhelming evidence, Turkey continues to deny its genocidal legacy, ignoring what U.S. Ambassador to the Ottoman Empire, Henry Morgenthau, called 'a campaign of race extermination...' as well as the public declaration in 2000 by 126 Genocide and Holocaust scholars which affirmed the incontestable *historical fact* of the Armenian Genocide and accordingly urged the governments of Western democracies to likewise recognize it as such."[18]

It is true that the "Armenian Genocide," referred to on the interest group's website, is recognized as historical fact by the Armenian diaspora, the Republic of Armenia, much of the North American, Russian and European news media, many politicians and some important scholars. It is also a fact that the government of the Republic of Turkey and numerous, prominent historians and scholars dispute this reading of history as biased, incomplete and mischaracterized. Importantly, the vast majority of scholars who dispute the Armenian Genocide narrative do *not*

Armenians but also Turks. Thomas De Waal. *Great Catastrophe: Armenians and Turks in the Shadow of Genocide.* Oxford University Press, 2015: 191.

[18] AAINC. "Issue Brief: Armenian Genocide Affirmation." *Armenian Assembly of America.* http://www.aaainc.org/index.php?id=114

dispute the tragedy and deaths that occurred beginning in 1915. It is the number of deaths and the circumstances surrounding the murders, massacres and deportations that are in question. The historical fact that the Armenian citizens of the Ottoman Empire were deplorably killed, forcibly deported and massacred, *en masse* in certain instances, is not in dispute. Rather the dispute revolves around the circumstances surrounding those events, why they happened, and the semantics used to describe them. To wit, what is in question is the *narrative* informed by Armenian diaspora identity and disseminated via the highly political campaign for genocide recognition.

A Quest for Identity; An Identity-Driven Campaign

The memories engendered by these blood-soaked and tragic events - the very real deaths of thousands of Ottoman Armenians over one hundred years ago - have defined and sustained an identity that has empowered Armenian diaspora communities worldwide, galvanizing them to popularize and promote their *chosen* identity, in perpetuity, as a nation of victims and survivors of genocide. International recognition of the events of 1915 as the "Armenian Genocide" is the lofty goal that this identity has come to demand. Achievement of that coveted recognition, in turn, validates the central Armenian diaspora narrative and formally places Armenians in the world's collective memory in the tragic and revered camp of genocide victims and survivors.

However, and of utmost importance, simple recognition of the events of 1915 as "genocide" through official and unofficial statements of commemoration, educational curriculum or apology is not an end goal for the Armenian diaspora for two reasons. First, the campaign explicitly posits that the events of 1915 should be recognized not only as the "Armenian Genocide," but as constituting the "first" genocide in human history or, at very least, the first genocide of the twentieth century. Second, and much less explicitly, recognition of these events as an Armenian

Genocide constitutes the first step towards the end goals of recognition: indemnity payments and right of return of property and land in Turkey.

In the promotion of their identity via the transmission and reconstruction of memories that occurred at the turn of the twentieth century, the Armenian diaspora communities and their interest groups have procured *ad hoc* legislation and symbolic statements of commemoration from a number of townships, municipalities, states, provinces and nation-states, recognizing the events of 1915 as genocide.[19] Furthermore, the diaspora's chosen role as partial creator and protector of "Armenian" identity has led to the development of interest groups that maintain goals - beyond Armenian genocide recognition – that include the mobilization of support for and the procurement of large amounts of development aid and assistance to the Republic of Armenia. However, as will be demonstrated in a later chapter, Armenian diaspora interest and assistance to the nation-state of Armenia often come at a steep price.

Although the constitution of the Republic of Armenia makes explicit reference to the events of 1915 as the Armenian Genocide, thus furthering the diaspora's goal of worldwide genocide recognition, many Armenians in Armenia *and* Turkey have grave misgivings regarding the semantics employed by the diaspora and their allies in Armenia's governments over the years. Specifically, the act of genocide recognition, though highly symbolic, is also legal in nature and carries with it the possibility of

---

[19] As of early 2016, 27 sovereign nation-states (UN member states) recognized the events of 1915 as the Armenian Genocide in one form or another. These sovereign states are all located in Europe (if Russia is included) and the Americas (North and South). Though the US has not recognized the events of 1915 as the Armenian Genocide, all but six US states recognize the same in one form or another. See "Countries that Recognize the Armenian Genocide." *Armenian National Institute.* http://www.armenian-genocide.org/recognition_countries.html. See also "International Affirmation of the Armenian Genocide." *Armenian National Institute.* http://www.armenian-genocide.org/current_category.11/affirmation_list.html

reparations to and the return of survivors to lands and properties lost in events deemed genocidal in nature. Furthermore, a serious rapprochement between the Republic of Armenia and Turkey is unthinkable, whilst the campaign's demands for reparation, return of territory and properties continue.

Armenian diaspora communities' memories of the events of 1915 construct and sustain their self-identification, as mentioned previously. This particularly important facet will be explained and deconstructed in detail, as it is critical to any understanding of the insistence on semantics and the all-consuming campaign. This Armenian diaspora identity, based on the events of 1915, in turn drives their efforts, as victim and survivor nation of the world's first genocide, to characterize and gain worldwide and thereby, Turkish recognition of the events of 1915 as the Armenian Genocide. This goal, regardless how noble or flawed, has ultimately hurt and continues to hinder the overall economic, political and strategic development of the nation-state of Armenia. Furthermore, this book will illustrate the disconnectedness and distance between the Armenian diaspora and the Armenian homeland, not only in terms of physical separation, but in terms of memories and trauma. This has had the effect of leading to an acute rift in identities, which has exacerbated the difference in aims and goals of groups, thereby pitting, at times, the Armenian diaspora against Armenians in Armenia vis-à-vis certain policies and goals. The very physical distance that has separated the diaspora from their perceived homeland has also led, in most cases, to greater wealth and freedoms, which in turn has led to the development of interest groups whose main aims are legislation, recognizing the events of 1915 as genocide and through this, the promotion of a unified Armenian identity: that of a nation of genocide victims *and* survivors.

In short, the Armenian diaspora continues to relive through memory, commemorations and, most importantly, their campaign for genocide recognition the trauma and wounds of 1915. These deep, unhealed wounds are suffered and lived with collectively as a group through the transmission of distilled and redistilled memories at both a societal and familial level. The trauma that was 1915 for Armenians is now *the* bond that unites worldwide Armenian diaspora communities. Their holy grail, constituted as the goal of genocide recognition, constantly disputed and thwarted by the Ottoman Empire's successor state Turkey, continues to stoke the flames of mistrust, hurt and antipathy that constitute diaspora identity.[20]

This memory-based nationalism bolstered by horrific trauma, rather than the more common form nationalism that is territorially-based, has supported the development and continues to sustain the fecund nature of Armenian diasporic nationalism and the main cause it espouses: that of consolidation of the diaspora's version of "Armenian" identity through global recognition of Armenians as one, united nation. The identity is, however, chameleon in nature; both powerless as a victim of genocide and powerful as a survivor of genocide.

This quest for identity consolidation has led to the development and maintenance of strong Armenian diaspora ethnic lobbies.[21] In turn, the ethnic interest groups' survival

---

[20] As the successor to the Ottoman Empire, the Turkish state's reaction to diaspora and Armenian government claims of genocide in 1915 have been reactive, plodding and, for a variety of reasons both political and historical (most notably Armenia's occupation of the Azeri territory of Nagorno-Karabakh in the early 1990s), Turkey has effectively blockaded land-locked and resource-poor Armenia in concert with Azerbaijan. This handicap that cuts off significant trade and infrastructure development coupled with Armenia's continued economic and military reliance on Russia has left it in the relatively unenviable position of being the "odd-man-out" in the Caucasus, having been by-passed by the major oil, gas and rail links connecting Central Asia with, via Azerbaijan and Georgia, with Turkey and points further west. For more on Russia's presence in Armenia and troop numbers see Emil Danielyan. "Putin Visit Highlights Russian Interest in Armenia," *The Jamestown Foundation*, Eurasia Daily Monitor, 2, no. 62, (2007).

[21] In the United States alone, Armenian diaspora lobby groups include the Armenian American Political Action Committee

is guaranteed through continued mobilization of the target ethnic group, which in turn mobilizes support and funding for their "own" lobbying group's efforts, both inside and outside the Armenian communities. This is not a simple tautology that varies from state to state depending on the political climate. Rather, this book demonstrates how and why Armenian diaspora interest groups, particularly in the United States, survive, multiply and wield power and influence much greater than their share of the population. This book also explains the force or forces motivating and mobilizing Armenian diaspora communities, whose members then provide critical sustenance and support for the survival of Armenian diaspora lobbying groups and the very issues they promote.

(AAPAC), the Armenian National Committee of America (ANCA) and the Armenian Assembly of America (AAA). In Europe, lobbying efforts are spearheaded by two main groups: European Armenian Federation for Justice and Democracy (EAFJD) and European Friends of Armenia (EFA).

CHAPTER 2

MEMORY TRANSMISSION AND IDENTITY

Armenians, regardless of location, freely admit to deep-seated divisions within their communities. From language to religion to politics Armenians still struggle with divisions inherited from the nineteenth century and earlier.[22] However, divisions between Armenians in the Republic of Armenia and diaspora Armenians, particularly in North America and Western Europe, are less understood by outsiders. Accordingly, an exploration of these divisions and the corresponding importance of the chosen trauma of 1915 and its centrality to Armenian large group identity (diaspora and non-diaspora) will be discussed. This will be posited against the backdrop of the Armenian diaspora's campaign of genocide recognition and the campaign's aim of tying Armenian identity formation and large group trauma to that of

[22] See Bahar Baser and Ashok Swain. "Diaspora design versus homeland realities: case study of Armenian diaspora." *International Journal on World Peace* 25 (2008): 7-28. See also Lev Freinkman. "Role of the Diasporas in Transition Economies: Lessons from Armenia." *Cuba in Transition-ASCE* (2001). See also Samim Akgönül. "The Armenian Community of France and Turkey: Propaganda and Lobbyism." *Review of Armenian Studies*, Vol. 1, No. 3, 2003.

another: Europe's Jews and the large group trauma instigated and largely carried out by Nazi Germany.

It can be argued – and is vehemently argued by the Armenian diaspora – that the events of 1915 that harmed Armenians and those occurring roughly between the years 1939-1945 that harmed Europe's Jews share similarities, particularly as to their large group effects. Yet a discussion of some very stark differences in events as well as various lobbying and campaign strategies conducted by both groups is absolutely necessary. This is done with a three-fold aim: first, in order to demonstrate key differences between the events. Second, in order to contextualize the Turkish governmental response to the Armenian diaspora campaign for genocide recognition. Third, such a discussion will formulate an understanding as to how important semantics remain to the Armenian diaspora campaign. Lastly, this chapter contains an explanation of theories from various social science disciplines and include relevant comparative examples of trauma, memory and collective identity transmission.

Ethnicity as Power: Division and Hypermobilization

Amongst Armenian diaspora communities, organizational and lobbying differences coupled with emphasis by all groups on key themes such as recognition of the events of 1915 as the "Armenian genocide" have led to a *hypermobilization* of the ethnic group's resources. That is, competition for resources amongst competing interest groups within finite Armenian diaspora communities has resulted in the hypermobilization of these communities in a profound and effective way.[23] To put it another way, the ethnic group's mobilization is hypermobilized vis-à-vis other ethnic groups. When compared to other diaspora and ethnic groups in America, France, Sweden and elsewhere,

[23] Michael M. Gunter. "Politicizing History." In *Armenian History and the Question of Genocide*. Palgrave Macmillan US, 2011; 75-97. See also Heather S. Gregg. *Divided They Conquer: The Success of Armenian Ethnic Lobbies in the US*. Precis, 2001; 16, 41.

Armenian diaspora communities tend to exhibit a higher degree of interest, vocal and financial support for certain issues over long periods of time. It is hypothesized that the reason behind this is the development of a multiplicity of lobbying and interest groups that compete for and speak out on behalf of a relatively small community, population-wise. This is also because Armenian diaspora interest groups possess the tools of a common and powerful discourse that revolves around shared, traumatic memories and the very identity these memories have produced in their constituency. That is, Armenian diaspora interest groups "hypermobilize" their communities' support for their actions and primary goal, that of gaining recognition by nation-states, provinces and/or municipalities that the events of 1915 constitute the world's first genocide.

Recognition of these events as genocide is the central mission of Armenian diaspora interest groups and herein exists their fecundity and corresponding ability to hypermobilize their fellow Armenians. Not only is the issue of genocide recognition substantive on an emotional and political level, it is perhaps most prescient and powerful on an identity level. In other words, Armenian diaspora identity (though not necessarily Armenian identity) is fundamentally shaped and defined by the horrendous events that took place in the waning days of the Ottoman Empire over 100 years ago.[24] The constructed memories of events and the narrative they have produced becomes the rallying force that unifies diverse Armenian groups within the diaspora communities themselves. Indeed, with strong religious, political and linguistic differences, it is posited that there is no alternative outside the genocide narrative to rally and mobilize the Armenian diaspora community.[25] An

---

[24] Khachig Tölölyan and Taline Papazian. "Armenian Diasporas and Armenia: Issues of Identity and Mobilization. An interview with Khachig Tölölyan." *Études Arméniennes Contemporaines* 3 (2014): 83-101.

[25] Rachel Anderson Paul. "Grassroots mobilization and diaspora politics: Armenian interest groups and the role of collective memory." *Nationalism and Ethnic Politics* 6, no. 1 (2000): 24-47.

Armenian diaspora lobby or group of lobbies is therefore able to generate much wider and more vocal support for their primary cause - that of genocide recognition - than say the much larger Chinese diaspora community in the United States, for example, in promoting the memory of the Nanking massacres as genocide.[26] In essence, the goal of recognition for events that are thought to have been ignored and also disputed, calls for a mobilization and modicum of support from ordinary Armenian diaspora members in ways that other remembered traumas, such as the Irish Potato Famine of 1848 or the Rape of Nanking, do not. This is because these tragedies do not play a central role in Irish diaspora and Chinese diaspora identities in the way the events of 1915 do for the Armenian diaspora. Indeed, it is the centrality of this remembered trauma at the intersection of identity and the corresponding need for recognition and affirmation, coupled with outright opposition from Turkey to recognition, which have created the perfect arena for long-term, grassroots mobilization of the Armenian diaspora.

As salient as the memories of 1915 and the subsequent quest for recognition of the events as genocide may be, it is, however, hypothesized that one organization presenting a unified voice would not have the same effect as a multiplicity of competing voices: that is, mobilization would be achieved, rather than hypermobilization.[27] This competition for survival among competing Armenian diaspora interest groups, both ideological and political, has led to a more powerful lobbying outreach and mobilization of resources, which in turn has magnified the presence and

---

[26] David B. MacDonald. "America's Memory Problems: Diaspora Groups, Civil Society and the Perils of 'Chosen Amnesia'" in Jing-Bao Nie, Nanyan Guo, and Arthur Kleinman (eds), *Japanese Wartime Medical Atrocities: Comparative Perspectives on Science, History and Ethics* (Routledge: 2010) pp. 166-182.

[27] For more on hypermobilization and the Armenian-American community see Benjamin F. Alexander. *Armenian and American: The Changing Face of Ethnic Identity and Diasporic Nationalism, 1915-1955* (Ph.D. diss., The City University of New York, 2005).

lobbying clout of the Armenian diaspora in places like Washington, D.C. and Paris. The strength of the competition among diaspora groups has also had major repercussions in regards to relations with the Republic of Armenia.

Linguistic, Political and Religious Divisions

Political, religious, linguistic and geographic divisions within Armenian diaspora communities may hold the answer, in part, to the high level of competition and corresponding singular aim of purpose, as mentioned above. For many immigrants and their descendants - not just Armenians in Argentina, Lebanon or Mexico - conflicts that originated in the "old country" often persist and deepen, but in new socio-cultural contexts in countries the world over. For example, linguistic commonalities or differences may serve as a natural bridge or barrier. Similarly, ethnic churches, such as the Greek Orthodox Church, have customarily served as bridges, linking the past with the present; the old world with the new. These (possible) bridges, however, can be shaken by and disintegrate in conflicts where the fundamentals of an ethnic community - manifested by differences in generation, socioeconomic status, and ethnicity - are strained by the forces of tradition and conservatism on one hand and the pressure for change and assimilation on the other.

In the case of the Armenian diaspora, language has served to divide rather than unite communities. Those of the diaspora community who hail from the pastures and farms of Anatolia or the large cities of İzmir and Istanbul speak (or their ancestors spoke) Western Armenian or *Arevm'tahayeren*. Western Armenian is a language or dialect that has undergone several phonetic mergers, possibly reflecting the close proximity of its speakers in the past to Turkish and Arabic-speaking communities. Western Armenian is thus distinct from Eastern Armenian or *Arevelahayeren*, spoken by Armenians in the nation-state of Armenia and their diaspora counterparts who originated from the Caucasus region. In addition, both languages can be subdivided into numerous sub-dialects. Although Western and Eastern Armenian share almost identical vocabularies, "… the important divergences in pronunciation and the grammatical differences between the two varieties are so significant that they may be considered two different languages."[28]

Members of Armenian diaspora communities tend to feel strongly about their differing, deep and historical ties to religion. They also feel the same in regards to their allegiance to one of two political societies or groups of societies. These groups, dating from the nineteenth century, were strong advocates of Armenian autonomy or outright independence from Russian, Persian and/or Ottoman rule. The first group will be referred to as *Dashnaks* (variant "Tashnag") for reasons that will become apparent. The second, more amorphous grouping of various political societies will be referred to as *non-Dashnaks,* for lack of a better term.[29] Though admittedly a simplification, it can be said that for over half a century, many diaspora Armenians (and this is particularly true of Armenian-American diaspora members) have identified themselves with the Armenian National Committee (ANC), a lobbying and interest group which was originally founded by members of the Dashnak party. Alternatively, many diaspora Armenians have identified themselves with affiliated interest groups traditionally tied to non-Dashnak parties, organizations, charitable groups and churches. In the case of Armenian-Americans, non-Dashnaks would align themselves with and support the Armenian American Assembly of America, generally referred to as "The Assembly."

The two groups differ in many respects. For example, internationally, the ANC cooperates and coordinates actions and campaigns with regional offices located in Russia,

---

[28] Andrzej Pisowicz. "Armenian Language." *Enyclopedia Brittanica.* http://www.britannica.com/EBchecked/topic/35305/Armenian-language#tab=active~checked%2Citems~checked&title=Armenian%20language%20--%20Britannica%20Online%20Encyclopedial

[29] Hovannisian, *The Armenian People, vol. II*, 402-406.

Armenia, France, Canada, Australia and the United States, among others. The Armenian Assembly maintains a lower profile outside the United States, though it maintains a presence in Yerevan, the capital of the Republic of Armenia.

In addition to deep linguistic and political divisions, diaspora Armenians are divided along religious lines. Secularization can be said to be slowly undermining the binding role of religion and "the Church" within various communities.[30] This has had a corresponding effect of lending greater emphasis to the role "the Armenian genocide" plays. That of the glue that binds and the center of gravity of Armenian identity. However, even with secularization proceeding naturally apace in Europe and, to a lesser degree, North and South America, most diaspora Armenians and Armenians from Armenia still consider themselves Catholics, Protestants or members of the Apostolic Armenian Church, which is itself divided.[31]

Jenny Phillips' study of a community of diaspora Armenians in the state of Massachusetts in the United States provides snapshots and vignettes of factional divisions within the Armenian Apostolic Church. Phillips categorizes one of these factions as the Armenian National Church of America, which is composed of diaspora Armenians who support the ANC and are therefore referred to as Dashnaks. The Armenian National Church of America owes its allegiance to the Catholiscosate of Cilicia in Antelais, Lebanon. The second faction is the Armenian Apostolic Church in the United States, which owes its allegiance to the Catholiscosate of Echtmiadzian in Armenia and is largely supported by supporters of the Assembly and is thus referred to as non-Dashnaks.[32]

---

[30] Robin Cohen. *Global diasporas: An Introduction*. Routledge, 2008, 55.

[31] Susan Pattie. "At home in diaspora: Armenians in America." *Diaspora: A Journal of Transnational Studies* 3, no. 2 (1994): 185-198.

[32] Jenny Phillips, "Symbol, Myth, and Rhetoric: The Politics of Culture in an Armenian-American Population," *Immigrant Communities and Ethnic Minorities in the United States and Canada,* no. 23 (1989).

Phillips notes that diaspora Armenians show a proclivity and attachment to certain symbols and myths that "play a critical role in the expression of Armenian identity."[33] These same myths and symbols, as well as institutions such as the Armenian Church may exacerbate political conflict. In essence, Phillips argues that the church is an arena where competing versions of Armenian identity are presented as a language of claims by Dashnaks and non-Dashnaks.

Tension and conflicts between these two, basic, competing groups and their identities manifest themselves in the form of different readings of major events and developments in Armenian history and in differing symbols of Armenian identity.[34] Often these interpretations dispose of painful, humiliating or complex events, while others are preserved and altered into symbols that "have major impact on collective identity and channel reactions to contemporary situations."[35] Similarly, in the wake of violence, such as that which occurred during the events of 1915, communal groups like the geographically dispersed Armenian diaspora are likely to have broadly divergent views about the "truth" of certain past events. Daniel Bar-Tal notes that these views are developed to "make sense of the present reality," but adds that "in order to fulfill this function, the past is reconstructed and re-appropriated to serve current needs and attitudes of society's members."[36] In fact, an

---

[33] Ibid, 17

[34] For example, Hunchaks and those allied with their point of view accepted Soviet Armenia as the legitimate Armenian homeland whereas Dashnaks refused to accept any homeland that did not encompass both Soviet Armenian lands and territory in Anatolia. This viewpoint continues to exist to this day in regards to the Republic of Armenia and territory controlled by Turkey that is thought to be "Western Armenia." See Armine Ishkanian, "Diaspora and Global Civil Society: The Impact of Transnational Diasporic Activism on Armenia's Post-Soviet Transition," *Central Asia and the Caucasus: Transnationalism and Diaspora* (New York: Routledge, 2005), 120.

[35] Phillips, 34.

[36] Daniel Bar-Tal. "Collective memory of physical violence: Its contribution to the culture of violence." In E. Cairns & M. D. Roe

individual's connection to a particular group or commune plays a large part in shaping the nature of that individual's beliefs about the past. "Members of [like] ethnic groups in contexts of conflict are likely to share accepted ways of seeing history… Members of different groups are likely to have significantly different beliefs about the past."[37]

This is true not just of diaspora Armenians and their extended Armenian family, but of many other groups with a real or imagined historical memory of mutual animosity such as Poles and Russians, Somalis and Ethiopians or Palestinians and Israelis, regardless of when or under what circumstances these memories were formed. That is, each group can be broadly said to base its interpretations of history and Self versus Other identification on its own collective narratives, memories and ideological representations of those memories of history.

At a more local level, Phillips illustrates the deep divides that can occur in ethnic and/or diaspora communities by relating two social dramas that occurred in Armenian diaspora communities and churches. The first conflict occurred when members of the community used the specter of a "Dashnak takeover" of a particular church to rally support among non-Dashnak elements and maintain control of *their* church. The second conflict involved a couple and their plans for a wedding. The parents of the bride and groom were from different churches, respectively and the neither set could agree where the marriage should be performed, no doubt the cause of great angst and alarm for the prospective couple.[38]

While broad differences persist that may be generalized to a certain degree between Dashnaks and non-Dashnaks and those who belong to different "Armenian" churches, many

(eds.). *The Role of Memory in Ethnic Conflict.* (Houndmills, England: Palgrave Macmillan, 2003): 85.

[37] Patrick Devine-Wright. "A Theoretical Overview of Memory and Conflict," *The Role of Memory in Ethnic Conflict* (New York: Palgrave, 2003): 243.

[38] Phillips, 18.

diaspora Armenians belong to neither group nor are they affiliated religiously. Benjamin Alexander, writing specifically about Armenian diaspora communities in America and emphasizing the importance of the events of 1915 to Armenian diaspora identity noted, "Of course, not all Armenian-Americans identify themselves with any partisan leaning at all. There have always been the *chezoks,* or "neutrals," and in the present era a considerable number of persons of Armenian lineage are not familiar with the Tashnag and (other) party labels… or for that matter with the word *chezok*. Armenianness for them may well consist of attending an occasional service, if even that, at their local church; of being vaguely familiar with a few culinary specialties associated with the Mediterranean world; or merely of noticing an Armenian name in a new article or in the credits of a cultural event. However, virtually *all persons of Armenian descent* know the date 1915, and associate it with a horrifically potent set of syllables: "the genocide.""[39]

What Alexander, Phillips and others have posited through their scholarship is that it is "the Armenian Genocide" rather than any other variable that acts as the unifying glue binding the Armenian diaspora; a diaspora composed of geographically-diffuse communities that are in turn further divided along the lines of church, politics and language. The cement utilized to seal deep fissures and cracks and inform the Armenian diaspora Self is the remembered trauma of "the genocide." This Self is necessarily accompanied by the genocide-perpetrating Other: the Turk. Otherizing Turks as genocidal people in 1915 and genocide deniers now functions as an alternative unifier in a way the Armenian churches, languages and politics cannot.

However, otherizing the Turk as the basic building block for Armenian diaspora identity has all sorts of consequences, among them self-victimization. Though this facet will be discussed in detail in later chapters, it is useful to highlight some of the pitfalls of this otherization. For example, the "self-victimization of the [Armenian] diaspora

---

[39] Benjamin F. Alexander, "Armenian and American," 4.

creates impediments for the normalization of the relations between Armenia and Turkey. It also continues to divide the Armenians into Western and Eastern ones with their own homelands, languages and traditions."[40] Adding a further twist, the Armenian diaspora otherization of the "terrible Turk" may correspond little to reality and often relies on dated and racist Orientalist sources. As the political scientist M. Hakan Yavuz highlighted, "the Armenian genocide narrative revives the racist rhetoric that justified the forcible resettlement of millions of civilians, both Christians and Muslims, in the Balkans and the Middle East before, during and after World War I. Furthermore, those who write and think in terms of Orientalist categories tend to turn the concept of genocide into a platform for perpetuating the stereotype of the 'Terrible Turk.'"[41] The fact that very few members of the Armenian diaspora actually know Turks complicates the issue further.[42]

Despite secularization and often over a century of domicile in places other than Istanbul, Van and Diyarbakır, diaspora Armenians collectively remember and identify with the severe trauma that occurred over one hundred years ago. This is precisely because the events that occurred in 1915 comprise what has been remembered and become a unifying group identity as well as a culture of victimization and that of survival. Diaspora Armenians have reconstructed and re-appropriated the events of 1915 to serve current needs and identities. As Bar-Tal posited regarding societal conflict and associated trauma, "These beliefs are one-sided and selective. They serve the needs of

[40] Bagramyan, Kristina. *Diaspora –Enforced Identity: Construction of the Victim Identity in the Film "Ararat."* PhD diss., Central European University, 2006, 64.

[41] Yavuz, M. Hakan. "Orientalism, the 'Terrible Turk' and Genocide." *Middle East Critique* 23, no. 2 (2014): 113.

[42] Illustrating the position of Dashnaks, in particular, to avoid all contact with Turks, Thomas De Waal quotes the deceased Hrant Dink as stating, "I became more active in finding solutions instead of adopting extremist attitudes of no contact with Turks, like the Dashnaks do." De Waal, Thomas. *Great Catastrophe:* 13.

the society's members to view themselves as just, righteous, humane, and moral, and provide explanations of the present situation."[43] As such, the collectively remembered trauma of 1915, referred to within the diaspora communities as "the Armenian Genocide," is what sustains and unifies the diaspora. That is, though deeply divided by language, geography, religion and political persuasion, diaspora Armenians do share a historical commonality that tends to supersede their differences: the deportations, massacres and humiliation of 1915.

Collective Trauma

Numerous and ongoing attempts by certain interest groups, scholars and politicians to posit these traumatic events as the Armenian Genocide have led some to compare the events to the shared trauma inflicted by the Nazis on Europe's Jews before and during World War II. However, regardless of key and crucial differences between the two events, it is precisely the genocide of Europe's Jews during the Nazi Holocaust, which occurred 20-30 years after the trauma remembered by the Armenian diaspora, that has lent its definitions and nomenclature to the events of 1915. As such, a theoretical discussion of collective trauma - as suffered, remembered and transmitted through generations and communities - is instructive.

The merits of collective trauma have been debated by a variety of scholars. The debate possesses some similarities to arguments regarding collective memory and identity; though these are not necessarily mutually exclusive. As a term, collective trauma can apply "… to any society, ethnic group, social category or class which has been exposed to extreme circumstances of traumatization, such as natural disasters, technological catastrophes, and social, political, cultural, gender, ethnic, or religious persecution."[44]

---

[43] Bar-Tal, 88.

[44] Robben, Antonius CGM, and Marcelo Su'arez-Orozco. *Cultures under siege: Collective violence and trauma*. Vol. 11. Cambridge University Press, 2000, 24.

Relatedly, collective political trauma is a concept utilized in political psychology. Collective political trauma is "… a shattering, often violent event that affects a community of people (rather than a single person or a few members of it) and that results from human behavior that is politically motivated and has political consequences. Such an event injures in one sharp stab, penetrating all psychological defense barriers of participants and observers, allowing no space for denial mechanisms and thus leaving those affected with an acute sense of vulnerability and fragility."[45] The Armenian diaspora can be said to suffer from both collective trauma and collective political trauma, as highlighted below.

Scholars such as Cathy Caruth argue that trauma cannot be represented adequately, because it escapes the bounds of intelligibility. However, she argues that ideas, memories, representations of ideas and memories and thus identities are still transmissible through and via generations and society, much like an infectious disease. That is, it can be transmitted not only between people, but also across generations and cultures.[46] This is instructive in that even though most survivors of the events of 1915 have died, their trauma, or rather their mental representations and reconstructions of that trauma, have been transmitted to and across generations of diaspora Armenians.[47] This

---

[45] Alexander L. Veerman and R. Ruard Ganzevoort. "Communities Coping with Collective Trauma." *International Association for the Psychology of Religion*. Soesterberg, The Netherlands. 2001. Conference Presentation, 3.

[46] See Cathy Caruth, *Unclaimed Experience: Trauma, Narrative, and History* (London: Johns Hopkins University Press, 1996). See also Cathy Caruth, "Introduction: Trauma and Experience," *Trauma: Explorations in Memory* (Baltimore, MD: Johns Hopkins University Press, 1995).

[47] As of mid-2015, Yevnige Salibian, at 101, is among the last remaining survivors of the forced deportation of Ottoman Armenians that began in 1915. See Benjamin Gottlieb. "101-year-old Armenian genocide survivor tells her story." *PRI,* April 27, 2015. http://www.pri.org/stories/2015-04-27/101-year-old-armenian-genocide-survivor-tells-her-story

collective trauma, built on the memories of survivors of 1915, has been transmitted to and transplanted in the various cultures and geographically diverse communities of diaspora Armenians.

Vamık Volkan, a Turkish Cypriot Emeritus Professor of Psychiatry at the University of Virginia, argues along similar lines as Caruth, positing that "The influence of a severe and humiliating calamity that directly affects all or most of a large group forges a link between the psychology of the individual and that of the group. In the wake of such an event, a metal representation of it, common to all members, begins to take shape. This mental representation is the consolidated collection of shared feelings, perceptions, fantasies, and interpretations of the event, as well as the images of relevant characters, such as a fallen leader."[48] Volkan adds that when this mental representation becomes too burdensome and people who have suffered are unable to mourn and cast away these humiliations, they pass it on to later generations. This is done in the hope that "…others may be able to mourn and resolve what the prior generation could not."[49] However, because the images of trauma are passed on, possibly surfacing in works of art, literature or music or through socialization into one's respective community's discourse and culture, they become part of a group identity; a marker of ethnicity and the definition of a people.

In this area, the Armenian diaspora continues to develop, possess and support a veritable cottage industry dedicated to producing books, films and artwork whose primary subjects and objects are the events of 1915 and the people associated therewith. Overt, graphic, yet ultimately imagined depictions of the starvation, forced marches and murder of Ottoman Armenians in 1915 are instilled and crystallized not only in the minds and memory of diaspora Armenians, but all others who witness films such as Atom Egoyan's

---

[48] Vamık D. Volkan, *Blood Lines: From Ethnic Pride to Ethnic Terrorism* (Boulder, CO: Westview Press, 1997), 45.
[49] Ibid.

2002 film “Ararat” or the vivid and disturbing posters of Ruben Malayan.

While trauma may remain dormant for generations, memories of trauma and the identities they may spawn can virulently emerge again under certain conditions, to be used as tools and political blunt objects. This could be politically motivated, as when the president of the former Yugoslavia, Slobodan Milosevic recalled and revived memories of the past greatness of the Serbian people *and* their loss of power and prestige under the Ottoman Turks. Milosevic opened these old, imagined wounds and grievances in order to maintain his own tenuous grip on political power – even expand it - by deflecting popular agitation against his rule and a dire economic situation toward the perceived historic “Other” of the Serbs: Muslim Bosnians. Indeed, Milosevic’s particular brand of “Serbian” propaganda creatively sought to denigrate Bosnians as “marauding Turks,” thereby constructing an image of Bosnians as foreigners, oppressors and the direct descendants of the “terrible Turk.” In Milosevic’s Serbia, Bosnians were no longer individuals; they were a foreign, dangerous group to be resisted at all costs and ultimately exterminated.[50]

New enemies or those from an historically antagonistic ethnic group - perceived or literal - may be looked at as extensions of an old enemy from the past. Though not referring to the historical memory of the Serbs and their collectively remembered trauma suffered at the hands of the Ottoman Turks, Volkan presciently noted “Although the original event was no doubt humiliating, the function of the mental representation of it changes, now serving to bond the individuals in the group, paradoxically raising their self-

---

[50] Roger Cohen, “To His Death in Jail, Milosevic Exalted Image of Serb Suffering,” *New York Times*, March 12, 2006. http://www.nytimes.com/2006/03/12/international/europe/12assess.html?pagewanted=1

esteem and fueling their attempt to reverse their ancestors' humiliation."[51]

This is instructive vis-a-vis occurrences in Bosnia in the early 1990s and Kosovo in 1999. It is also illuminating in regards to diaspora Armenians and their collective memories of 1915. That is, how a collective trauma defines, informs and ultimately politicizes an identity. In the case of diaspora Armenians, the ties that bind the large group are not language, religion or even a commonly perceived territorial "homeland." Rather, the events of 1915 - commemorated, memorialized, remembered and "survived" again every April 24th - have become the *chosen* identity of diaspora Armenians, whether they reside in Canada, Mexico or the United Kingdom.[52]

Why a "chosen" identity? First, the tragic events of 1915, as memorialized in books, stories, memorials, commemorations and, more recently, legislation, have become the shared mental representation of not only what is perceived to have happened, but what has created and sustained the Armenian diaspora. Second, the identity informed by the collective trauma experienced in 1915 has been chosen over other, often more divisive linguistic, territorial, religious or political identities. This is because none of these variables are shared by the whole group; indeed, they often exhibit a polarizing effect. As such, the Armenian Genocide, as imagined collectively by the Armenian diaspora, plays the pivotal role.

---

[51] Volkan, *Blood Lines,* 46-47. Armenian discourse regarding survival did not change after the occupation of Nagorno-Karabagh: The exterminators (Turks) need to be exterminated. Azeris were treated as extensions of Ottoman Turks. Indeed, it was strengthened. See Paul Quinn-Judge, "Zhirinovsky vs. the Turks," *Middle East Quarterly* 1, no. 2 (1994).

[52] The single date of April 24th has been chosen by the Armenian diaspora and the Republic of Armenia to encompass and commemorate the momentous and tragic events of 1915-1923. April 24, 1915 is considered by Armenians to be the day the "Armenian Genocide" began. On this date, 235 to 270 Armenian leaders and intellectuals were arrested in Istanbul by the Ottoman government and relocated to various parts of the Ottoman Empire.

The consensus among diaspora Armenians is that historically, via the events of 1915, Armenians worldwide share the same identity: they comprise a nation of genocide victims *and* genocide survivors.[53] The diaspora's shared mental representation of the traumas suffered by many of their collective ancestry in 1915 has been altered in such a way as to create an overarching narrative; an ideological representation of events that is collectively taught, remembered and repeatedly commemorated. As demonstrated in greater detail in the proceeding pages, their stories and memories of the humiliation and shock of the victims who were murdered or deported commingles with stories that celebrate, in imagined forms, the violent resistance of Armenians on Musa Dagh and the siege of Van.

In continuing the exploration of collective trauma, scholars such as Jeffery Alexander move beyond psychological details and argue that trauma is actually a social construct. "Events are not in themselves inherently traumatic. Traumas occur when individuals and groups feel they have been subjected to a horrendous event that leaves indelible marks upon their consciousness, will mark their memories forever, and will change their future in fundamental and irrevocable ways."[54] In other words, trauma should be ascribed to "real or imagined phenomena, not because of their actual harmfulness or their objective abruptness, but because these phenomena are believed to have abruptly and harmfully affected collective identity."[55]

---

[53] This manifests itself worldwide in a variety of disparate press releases and other announcements. An internet search for "Armenian genocide survivors and victims," found numerous results, including a press release by a California district assemblyman, an announcement from Moncton, New Brunswick, Canada commemorating the 20th century's first genocide with an Armenian Festival, and a press release from the office of the president of the Republic of Armenian.

[54] Jeffrey C. Alexander. "Towards a Theory of Cultural Trauma." *Cultural Trauma and Collective Identity* (Berkeley, CA: University of California Press, 2004), 1.

[55] Ibid, 8 and 10.

Alexander uses this approach to create a so-called trauma process model and thereby usefully outlines the materialization of a particular Holocaust discourse in the years after 1945.[56] Similarly, Duncan Bell highlights the role the Nazi Holocaust has played in helping to create a new moral code for the globe. "The project of renaming, dramatizing, reifying and ritualizing the Holocaust contributed to the moral remaking of the (post) modern, (western) world."[57]

In this light, the Armenian diaspora's dramatizing and reifying the events of 1915, and Turkey's refusal to accept responsibility for what the diaspora refers to as the Armenian Genocide, have contributed to shaping the current international dynamics and dilemma faced by Turkey, Armenia and the Armenian diaspora. The Armenian diaspora - viewing the power of the Nazi Holocaust narrative of victimhood, victim nation and survival and the outpouring of monetary and strategic resources it has brought Israel – specifically tailors its campaign for Armenian Genocide recognition based on a specific argument: the incidents of ethnic cleansing, deportation, exile and massacres that befell Ottoman Armenians in 1915 were *the* precursor to the Nazi Holocaust. In other words, the events of 1915 constituted the template or blueprint containing the instructions, means and methods that were later used by the Nazis in their attempted extermination of Europe's Jews.[58] According to this interesting yet

---

[56] Ibid.

[57] Duncan Bell. *Memory, Trauma and World Politics. Reflections on the Relationship between Past and Present*, London: Palgrave Macmillan (2006), 17.

[58] For more on the necessity of the "Armenian Genocide" as a blueprint for the Nazi Holocaust, see Helen Fein. "A Formula for Genocide: Comparison of the Turkish Genocide (1915) and the German Holocaust (1939-1945)." *Comparative Studies in Sociology* 1 (1978): 271-294. See also Wolfgang Gust. "Die Verdrängung des Völkermords an den Armeniern-Ein Signal für die Shoah." In *Der Völkermord an den Armeniern und die Shoah*. Kieser, Hans-Lukas and Schaller, Dominik J. Schaller, eds. (Zurich: Chronos, 2002): 463-80. See also Robert F. Melson. "The Armenian Genocide as Precursor

unsubstantiated narrative, the Nazi Holocaust would not, indeed could not have occurred without being first informed by the events of 1915.

The connecting of two disparate tragedies that occurred within 25 years of one another is significant in that it demonstrates the willful ignorance and blatant politicization of the Armenian campaign for genocide recognition. The two events were unconnected.[59] It also demonstrates the absolutes of Armenian collective trauma and the importance of this trauma in the development of Armenian large group identity. Though not speaking directly about the Armenian diaspora campaign, Jeffrey C. Alexander illustrates what has occurred through the wholesale appropriation of terms such as "genocide" and "The Holocaust" by those, such as Armenians, who were never affected by these events:

"How did a specific and situated historical event, an event marked by ethnic and racial hatred, violence, and war, become transformed into a generalized symbol of human suffering and moral evil, a universalized symbol whose very existence has created historically unprecedented opportunities for ethnic, racial, and religious justice, for mutual recognition, and for global conflicts to become regulated in a more civil way? This cultural transformation has been achieved because the originating historical event, traumatic in the extreme for a delimited particular group, has come over the last fifty years to be redefined as a traumatic event for all of humankind. Now free floating rather than situated – universal rather than particular – this traumatic event vividly 'lives' in the memories of

---

and Prototype of Twentieth-Century Genocide," *Is the Holocaust Unique?* (Boulder, CO: Westview Press, 1996), 87-99.

[59] See Michael M. Gunter. *Armenian History and the Question of Genocide*. Palgrave Macmillan US, 2011.See also Yücel Güçlü. *The Holocaust and the Armenian case in comparative perspective*. University Press of America, 2012.

contemporaries whose parent and grandparents never felt themselves even remotely related to it."[60]

Revision and Representation of Atrocities

Regarding the memories of survivors of trauma and the ideological representations of those memories, Norman Finkelstein argues that even in the case of the attempted extermination of Europe's Jews by Nazi Germany, there is a difference between the events of the Nazi Holocaust and what is popularly referred to today as "The Holocaust."[61] His iconoclastic thesis never takes issue with the brutal reality of the death and destruction visited upon Jews the Third Reich's henchmen and allies. Rather, what Finkelstein questions are present-day popular representations and mythologies of "The Holocaust" in contrast with what occurred during the actual Nazi Holocaust. He argues that these representations and mythologies are constantly used and misused by numerous individuals and groups for a variety of aims, some rather unsavory.

Finkelstein's main argument is that "The Holocaust," the popularized and thus popular version of events, is nothing more than an ideological representation of the very real horror and tragedy that was Nazi Holocaust. Importantly, this does not mean that the representation is entirely false. Similar to most ideologies, this representation does bear a connection with reality - however tenuous that connection may be. For example, "The Holocaust is not an arbitrary, but rather an internally coherent construct. Its central dogmas sustain significant political and class interests. Indeed, The Holocaust has proven to be an indispensable ideological weapon."[62]

---

[60] Jeffrey C. Alexander. "On the Social Construction of Moral Universals: The Holocaust from War Crime to Trauma Drama." In *Cultural Trauma and Collective Identity* (Berkeley, CA: University of California Press, 2004), 197.

[61] Norman G. Finkelstein. *The Holocaust Industry: Reflections on the Exploitation of Jewish Suffering.* (London: Verso, 2000).

[62] Ibid, 3.

Finkelstein's diatribe against successive Israeli governments and their "collaborators" in the United States and elsewhere is polemical and purposely provocative. Yet his arguments regarding the role Israel has chosen to cast for itself - that of a victim state – are lucid, prescient and cogent. That is, Finkelstein successfully demonstrates that considerable dividends can be accrued by states such Israel, as well as other entities, groups and individuals who have achieved victim status in popular memory and perception - regardless of how justified or unjustified the status. Importantly, Finkelstein does not question the worthiness of the victim status of Jews, but rather demonstrates the abuse of that same victim status by various entities.

In Israel's case, Finkelstein argues that its status as a victim state and nation has largely led to its immunity from criticism by the international community. Yet those in power who enjoy this immunity have not escaped the moral corruptions that often attend said immunity.[63] Here he is referring specifically to Israel's occupation of territories largely populated by Palestinians.

How do Finkelstein's arguments relate to Armenians? The Armenian diaspora and Armenia, taken together as a "victim nation" that suffered and survived the events of 1915, have been rather immune to criticism (however muted) of their occupation of Nagorno-Karabakh in Azerbaijan.[64] By portraying both Armenia and ethnic

---

[63] Ibid.

[64] Nagorno-Karabakh is internationally recognized as part of Azerbaijan, but most of the region is governed by the Nagorno-Karabakh Republic. This *de facto* independent, but unrecognized state was established in 1991 by Armenians in Nagorno-Karabakh in cooperation with the Republic of Armenia. It can be argued that much of the world's population has never heard of Nagorno-Karabakh and could never place it on a map. While this is true, it is hard to argue against the geographic and strategic importance of the region as a whole, especially in light of Azerbaijan's seemingly inexhaustible oil and gas reserves and the wealth generated therefrom. See Svante E. Cornell. "Turkey and the conflict in Nagorno Karabakh: a delicate balance." *Middle Eastern Studies* 34, no.

Armenians as victim nation and victims who are continuously affected by the events of 1915, opprobrium of Armenia's conduct in Nagorno-Karabakh (and the diaspora's clamorous support for its continued occupation) has been muted. Though parallels between the two countries and groups are slim at best, Israel and Armenia as well as Jews and Armenians are considered to be victims of historical atrocities. As such, attempts to tie the Nazi Holocaust to the events of 1915 by the Armenian diaspora, though flawed, are a centerpiece of the diaspora campaign for genocide recognition. For example, the Knights of Vartan Armenian Research Center (Center for Armenian Research and Publication at The University of Michigan-Dearborn), among others, has attempted to establish not only the similarities between the events of 1915 and the Nazi Holocaust, but also Armenians, Jews and their common history of brilliant civilization in the face of sustained oppression. "Both people adhere to an ancient religion. Both were religious minorities of their respective states. Both have a history of persecution. ... Both are talented and creative minorities who have been persecuted out of envy and obscurantism."[65]

How relevant is this argument, as put forward repeatedly by members of the Armenian diaspora? First, the Nazi Holocaust represents the paradigm of genocide – a crime without reason executed in a deliberate, often mechanized fashion. The Nazi attempt to exterminate Europe's Jews was based entirely on identity. Its stated aim and sole purpose were the destruction of every Jewish man, woman and child. Documents exist that lay out in chilling detail Hitler's plan for a "Final Solution" to the "Jewish Problem."

---

1 (1998): 51-72. See also Svante E. Cornell. *The Nagorno-Karabakh Conflict.* Inst. für Osteuropastudien, 1999.

[65] Center for Armenian Research and Publication is dedicated to documenting the Armenian Genocide and current Armenian issues. See Adam Jones. "Case Study: The Armenian Genocide, 1915-17." *Gendercide Watch*, 2002.
http://www.anca.org/assets/pdf/armenian_genocide_reference/Case%20Study%20-%20The%20Armenian%20Genocide.pdf.

In contrast, the events of 1915 that occurred in the Ottoman Empire were discriminate in nature. Simply put, there was no attempt on the part of Ottoman authorities, their henchmen or other societal groups to exterminate *all* Ottoman Armenians or even most of them. Documents do not exist that demonstrate either the desire or the will of the Ottoman government to exterminate its Armenian citizens.[66] Massacres and instances of ethnic cleansing that were at once savage, brutal and likely incomprehensible to many of the victims occurred. It would be incorrect and unconscionable for historians or other scholars to say otherwise. However, these were neither general massacres of Ottoman Armenians nor can they be referred to as a genocidal slaughter. Rather, as the research will demonstrate, the killings of Ottoman Armenians were localized in nature and occurred mainly in eastern and southern Anatolia.[67] Importantly, they were also a reaction

---

[66] Yücel Güçlü. "Will untapped Ottoman archives reshape the Armenian debate?." *Middle East Quarterly* (2009).

[67] Though limited deportations occurred in İzmir (Smyrna) and Istanbul (Constantinople), most Armenians in these locations remained untouched throughout the war. Scholars such as Lepsius and Hovannisian argue that the large number of foreign diplomats and personnel were the reason Armenians were largely left in peace. See Richard G. Hovannisian, ed. *The Armenian Genocide in Perspective* (New Brunswick, NJ: Transaction Books, 1986), 29. Yet Lewy argues, "Whatever the real reasons for the decision to spare this large group of Armenians, it is certainly significant in regard to the alleged intent of the Young Turks to destroy and exterminate the entire Armenian population." See Lewy, 204. Similarly, Michael Gunter, noting the differences between the Nazi Holocaust and the events of 1915 notes, "Could anyone conceive Hitler allowing the Jews of Berlin to continue living in Berlin while he implemented his genocide against them elsewhere?" See Michael M. Gunter, "*Pursuing the Just Cause of Their People:" A Study of Contemporary Armenian Terrorism* (New York: Greenwood Press, 1986), 23. For a glimpse at evolving Ottoman policies towards non-Turks in İzmir, the noble actions of Ottoman Governor Rahmi Bey during World War I and the terrible massacres and reprisals that befell the cities minorities in the last days of the Greco-Turkish War, see Giles Milton, *Paradise Lost: Smyrna 1922, The Destruction of a Christian City in the Islamic World* (New York:

to the widespread armed insurrection of Ottoman Armenians in support of invading Russian troops and the widespread atrocities committed by Armenians against Ottoman Muslims, particularly following the departure of Russia from the war in 1917.[68] The evidence and reality of these atrocities are blatantly ignored by the Armenian diaspora. Indeed, it is possible that many Armenians are either entirely unaware or remain blatantly ignorant in regards to the sheer scale of intercommunal violence that engulfed the Ottoman Empire both before and after the deportation of many Ottoman Armenians in 1915.

In stark contrast to the premeditated, proactive and exhaustively planned and executed capture, deportation and extermination of Europe's Jews, the deportation of Ottoman Armenians was performed as part of a reactive strategy on the part of the Ottoman government in the face of massive insurrections and almost certain defeat during World War I. Intercommunal violence, pitting Christians against Muslims, had become endemic in eastern Anatolia since the outbreak of the war in 1914. Coupled with a massive invasion of Russian troops and the loss of significant amounts of territory, the Ottoman government reacted by deporting what had become a largely traitorous Armenian population from the front lines. These details and the reasons behind the events of 1915 will be discussed in greater detail in the proceeding chapters. However, in order to lay a proper foundation, it is worth highlighting one of the few unbiased and, more importantly, eyewitness accounts immediately following World War I. This was performed by two Americans charged by the United States

---

Basic Books, 2008), especially 69-88. The reprisals were revenge for the slaughter of Turks at the hands of Ottoman Christians and invading Greek troops during Greece's occupation of İzmir (1919-1922). See Justin McCarthy. *Death and Exile: The Ethnic Cleansing of Ottoman Muslims, 1821-1922* (Princeton, N.J: Darwin Press, 1995): 261-266.

[68] McCarthy. *Death and Exile*, 196-202.

government to investigate the situation in eastern Anatolia.[69] Their report detailed the incredible scale of the atrocities committed by Armenians against Muslims, thus turning the popular narrative paradigm on its head. "In the entire region we were informed that the damage and destruction had been done by Armenians, who, after the Russians retired [in late 1917], remained in occupation of the country, and who, when the Turkish army advanced, destroyed everything belonging to Musulmans [Muslims]. Moreover, the Armenians are accused of having committed murder, rape, arson and horrible atrocities of every description upon the Musulman population. At first we were most incredulous of these stories, but we finally came to believe them, since the testimony was absolutely unanimous and was corroborated by material evidence… Villages said to have been Armenian were still standing, whereas Musulman villages were completely destroyed."[70] Given the postwar eyewitness accounts coupled with population records from the time showing the precipitous drop in both the Muslim and Armenian populations during World War I, the idea that Ottoman Armenians were innocently rounded up for murder in a manner similar to that performed by the Nazis on Europe's Jews is utter nonsense. Ottoman actions against a significant portion of its Armenian populace were provoked and defensive in nature rather than proactive and unprovoked, as in the case of the Nazi Holocaust.[71]

Despite diaspora Armenians perception and designation by many as a victim nation akin to Jews residing in Israel and elsewhere, and despite the concerted attempts of many scholars and lobbyists to draw similarities between the Nazi Holocaust and the events of 1915, Armenian diaspora efforts to gain the support of Israel as well as powerful

---

[69] Justin McCarthy. "The Report of Niles and Sutherland: An American Investigation of Eastern Anatolia after World War I." *XI. Türk Tarih Kongresi, Ankara: 5–9 Eylül 1990* (1994): 1809-53.
[70] Niles and Sutherland Report, as quoted in McCarthy. *Death and Exile*, 224-225.
[71] Ibid, 193-196.

Jewish lobbying interests, particularly in the United States, have been fraught with tension and controversy. In the recent past, the lack of cooperation and inaction on the part of Jewish lobbying and special interest groups vis-à-vis the issue of Armenian Genocide recognition was chalked up to Israel's strategic relationship with Turkey. This has changed precipitously over the past decade, as ties between Tel Aviv and Ankara have become strained almost to the breaking point. Yet this has not resulted in a corresponding amount of action on the part of Israel either to recognize or support Armenian diaspora resolutions labeling the events of 1915 as the Armenian Genocide. Indeed, in a blow to Armenians and their campaign's narrative, Israel does not formally recognize that the events of 1915 constituted the Armenian Genocide, nor are the details, as desired by the Armenian diaspora, taught in Israeli schools.[72]

While Armenian diaspora interest groups see the passage of resolutions and laws that recognize the events of 1915 as the Armenia Genocide as moral and necessary, it would seem that some Jewish interest groups mirror that of the official position of the state of Israel. They express sympathy for the victims and survivors of the horrific massacres, starvation and deportations suffered by many Ottoman Armenians in 1915, but prefer to tacitly support the idea and policies the Turkish government loudly promotes: that of leaving "history to the historians."

It is true that victims of tragedies are naturally given an unabashedly large and deserving degree of sympathy by most people, even though the historical situations and circumstances surrounding these same tragedies can vary greatly. One could argue that it is human nature to succor,

---

[72] While Israel's ties with Turkey are currently strained, Israel's relationship with Azerbaijan has grown in strategic importance. For example, Israel imports 40 percent of its oil from Azerbaijan and exports Israeli weapons and defense systems to Baku. See Ishaan Tharoor. "Why Israel does not recognize the Armenian 'genocide.'" *The Washington Post*, April 24, 2015.
https://www.washingtonpost.com/news/worldviews/wp/2015/04/24/why-israel-does-not-recognize-the-armenian-genocide/

attend to and ultimately believe the stories and memories of those who are victims of atrocious circumstances or claim to be. Yet, as Finkelstein demonstrated, even in the case of the largely unquestioned Nazi Holocaust, a collective tool has been forged from altered and distorted memories in the form of "The Holocaust." This political and politicized tool was forged from the arguably Machiavellian standpoint of the "calculation of advantages and disadvantages."[73]

A Critique of Ideological Representations of Memory

Criticism of ideological representations of memory, such as that performed by Finkelstein, should not be construed as denial of tragic events such as the Nazi Holocaust. Rather, a critique raises the possibility that these ideological representations of important historical events may not only be explored, but openly researched, deconstructed and discussed. If the memories of 1915 and their ideological representations have the power to shape Armenian identity, attitudes, prejudices and policies over one century after their occurrence, they are necessarily of a very sentient and germane nature. Yet it is precisely those who harness their political objectives to such ideological representations of memory who also brook no opposition to their version of events. That is, their version of the events of 1915 in the way they were taught to remember them and the political and highly politicized goals encapsulated and defined therein. It is difficult to capture in words the tragic nature of the events that occurred, whether they happened and were perpetrated in the year 1915 or the years 1939-1945. That these events occurred is not in question. What requires our attention, questions and answers is whether these events and others are properly grounded in the historical record with all that entails.

Honoring victims of horrific events – whether they occurred as part of a genocide or not – does not require everyone to agree with a particular ideological

[73] Finkelstein, 5.

representation of the events. It does require the events and actions be acknowledged. Yet, in the case of the events of 1915, the historical record is contested – and justifiably so. Furthermore, it is the particular semantics or nomenclature used to describe the events that can and should be the object of healthy debate. Indeed, one can argue that the very ideological representations of what occurred, as passed on to popular memory thereby attaining an unquestionable status, do not honor the memory of the victims of these tragedies, but possibly denigrate and degrade them. This is a shocking conclusion, but one that is arrived at by observing the almost continuous usage of ideological representations of tragic events by various interest groups and states as political cudgels. The watchwords of "denial" and "victimhood" are ever-present and act as gatekeepers to deflect criticism, stymie critical thinking and discourage further research.[74]

Finkelstein, as a child of parents who survived the Nazi Holocaust, in no way denies the validity and reality of those events. Instead, he highlights the cottage industry and mythology surrounding the popular representation of those same events. In a similar fashion, the refusal by certain scholars, interest groups and states to use the term "genocide" in relation to the forcible deportations of many Ottoman Armenians in 1915 does not constitute the denial of the events. Rather, acknowledgment of these events as something more nuanced and more descriptive, more tragic and life-like - more human - may actually validate their connections to a tragic reality that was over one century in the making. Doing so may also exhibit the more nuanced, human and individual realities that make up the events of 1915: Armenian individuals as victims and survivors; Armenian individuals who fought against Ottoman rule; Armenians who collaborated with invading Russian armies; Armenian individuals who were Armenian nationalists and

---

[74] For example, see Richard G. Hovannisian. "Denial of the Armenian Genocide 100 Years Later: The New Practitioners and Their Trade." *Genocide Studies International* 9, no. 2 (2015): 228-247.

thus traitors in the eyes of the Ottoman government; Armenian murderers, rapists and brigands; Armenians who fought in defense of the Ottoman Empire; Armenians who were massacred, raped and slaughtered by Ottoman Muslims, be they Turks, Kurds or Circassians; and Armenians who were rescued or given succor by Ottoman Muslims.

The Armenian diaspora position regarding the events of 1915 is that they constituted not only the Armenian Genocide, but the world's first genocide or, at very least, the first genocide of the twentieth century. On the other hand, the official position of successive Turkish governments is that the deaths and deportations of Ottoman Armenians occurred as part of the wider war effort. "The removal of the Armenians from certain regions, it is argued, was a measure dictated by the imperative of military necessity. The Armenian revolutionaries threatened the rear of the Turkish army in all parts of the empire and were supported and fed by the local population. In these circumstances it was impossible to limit the relocation to one area or to sort out the guilty from the innocent."[75]

One of the many problems with both the "official" Turkish and "official" Armenian theses regarding the events of 1915 is that they are often nothing more than beliefs informed by ideological representations of memories. The Armenian position, in particular, contains only rather vague and tenuous ties to the realities of the situation as it actually occurred in 1915. In essence, both the Armenian and Turkish narratives exist outside of history; they are simply positions taken up by players of opposing teams who only care about their side "winning." Correspondingly, these ideological narratives brook no opposition and allow little if any nuance, thus denying, in part, the victims and survivors of these murderous events - Christians and Muslims, Armenians and Turks - of their humanity and individuality.

Individual acts that run the gamut of humanity from sadistic brutality to self-sacrifice to compassion are

[75] Lewy, 248.

eschewed for overarching narratives that often serve short-sighted political aims or nurture constructed identities based on ideological representations of history and memory. The Armenian campaign narrative is particularly politicized, political in nature and composed of sound bites meant to convince the world of public opinion of their validity. Memory, if it were a mirror, is thus tarnished and reflects only distortions in black and white.

Referring to the one-sided nature of the Armenian ideological representation of the events of 1915, Ara Baliozian wrote, "Nothing could be more naïve than to think if you read only Armenian sources, you can form a more or less balanced view of our history, culture and identity, on the grounds that no one knows and understands Armenians better than an Armenian. My own impression is that when Armenian scholars write or speak publicly about Armenians, they stress only half of what they know and cover up or ignore the other half. But then, this is true not only of Armenians but also of all nations… No nation is known for its love of truth… When Turks and Armenians paint themselves all white and their adversaries all black, *odars* [non-Armenians] may be justified in suspecting that both sides are guilty of misrepresentation."[76]

Because conformity is encouraged, and the very building blocks of Armenian diaspora identity are at risk of crumbling, the campaign to classify the events of 1915 as the Armenian Genocide has taken to portraying anyone who acknowledges the events but refuses to utilize the required nomenclature as "genocide deniers." Respected scholars and historians such as Michael Gunter, Bernard Lewis, Ezel and Stanford Shaw, Justin McCarthy and others who have long been critical of the Armenian ideological narrative because it does not correspond to what they have uncovered in their research, are marginalized, reviled and in

---

[76] Ara Baliozian. "On Controversies." *ARA Home Page*, March 19, 2008. http://baliozian.blogspot.com/

some cases and countries arrested and convicted for their crime of denial.[77]

Yet a similar problem exists in Turkey, where scholars and individuals who deviate from "acceptable" readings of history are upbraided and accused of being traitors to the Turkish state and charged with the nebulous and therefore easily applicable crime of "insulting Turkishness." National security is often cited as the reason for this stance. It has also been used to inform court decisions. Indeed, in 2007, Sarkis Seropyan and Arat Dink, the son of assassinated Armenian-Turkish journalist Hrant Dink, received suspended sentences of imprisonment for using the term "genocide" in reference to the events of 1915. The Turkish court in Istanbul that delivered the ruling explained, "Talk about genocide, both in Turkey and in other countries, unfavorably affects [Turkish] national security and the [Turkish] national interest. The claim of genocide… has become part of and the means of special plans aiming to change the geographic [and] political boundaries of Turkey… and a campaign to demolish its physical and legal structure." The ruling stated further that the Republic of Turkey is under "a hostile diplomatic siege consisting of genocide resolutions… The acceptance of this claim may lead in future centuries to a questioning of the sovereignty rights of the Republic of Turkey over the lands on which it is claimed these events occurred." Due to the national security concerns cited by the Turkish court, reference to the events of 1915 as genocide by the accused was deemed, unequivocally, a crime.[78] The irony, if there is one, is that the opposing Armenian and Turkish camps - the Armenian camp utilizing its chosen historical narrative as a political

---

[77] See Richard G. Hovannisian. "Denial of the Armenian Genocide 100 Years Later." See also Richard G. Hovannisian. "Denial of the Armenian Genocide in Comparison with Holocaust Denial." *Remembrance and Denial: The Case of the Armenian Genocide* (1999): 201-236.

[78] Court Decree, *2nd Penal Court of First Instance for The District of Şişli*, File Number: 2006/1208, Decree Number: 2007/1106, Prosecution No.: 2006/8617.

tool and the Turkish camp clumsily attempting to utilize the historical record for the same purpose – both attempt to criminalize the usage, or lack thereof, of the term "genocide,"

Measures passed by various governing and legal bodies regarding the denial of the Nazi Holocaust and various events termed as genocide are likely well-intended. However, they are not necessarily wise or just. Numerous writers, politicians, legal experts and scholars have pointed out that such laws limit free expression, "...a unique and primary good in free societies."[79] Furthermore, rather than combating xenophobia, racism and - in the case of the Nazi Holocaust - anti-Semitism, the court cases and show trials of scholars and other individuals have offered precisely the "nimbus of persecution" that many far-right groups and ultra-nationalists crave.[80] But the real problem with blanket bans on the denial of the Nazi Holocaust or other historical atrocities is that they would not stop there. Would discussions and debates of prickly and polarizing subjects such as the Japanese "Rape of Nanking," Saddam Hussein's *Anfal* campaign against the Kurds and, of course, the forced relocation and massacres of thousands of Ottoman Armenians in 1915 - all labeled unequivocally by some as genocide - be banned? This is precisely the type of unquestioned, ideological representation encapsulated in the ideological representation of "The Holocaust" that Finkelstein argues against. Similarly, the Jewish-American lawyer Alan Dershowitz complained, "I don't want the government telling me that [the Nazi Holocaust] occurred because I don't want any government ever to tell me that it didn't occur."[81]

---

[79] Timothy Garton Ash. "A Blanket Ban on Holocaust Denial would be a serious Mistake." *The Guardian,* January 18, 2007. http://www.theguardian.com/commentisfree/2007/jan/18/comment.secondworldwar

[80] Ibid.

[81] R. J. Evans. "History, Memory, and the Law: The Historian as Expert Witness." *History and Theory*, 41 (2002), 342.

The history of the events of 1915 and the ideological representations of the "Armenian genocide" beg discussion, if only to encourage unofficial dialogue between Armenians and Turks and correspondingly official dialogue between Armenia and Turkey. Indeed, nine activists and scholars, including Hrant Dink and Etyen Mahcubyan along with the Turkish author Elif Shafak, issued a joint statement in 2006 condemning a proposed law before the French National Assembly that would criminalize denial of the "Armenian Genocide." The activists, authors and scholars argued that the French law would not only curb free speech in France but elsewhere, including Turkey. Dink was so opposed to the proposed law that he stated, "If this law goes into effect, I'll be the first to travel to Paris to violate it."[82]

What is interesting is that these Turkish citizens were well-known for their opposition to the officially obtuse Turkish narrative of the events of 1915 and some had even called for Turkey's outright acknowledgement that these events constituted the Armenian Genocide. Sadly, Dink and Shafak, in particular, were painfully aware of what bans on free discussion meant. Both had previously been charged for crimes under Turkey's notorious Article 301, which, as noted above, criminalizes "insulting Turkishness." Shafak was acquitted by a group of judges after they found insufficient evidence to prove she "denigrated Turkish national identity."[83] Dink, however, was convicted and given a six-month suspended sentence.

Perhaps the lesson learned by Shafak and Dink, who ended up paying for his unpopular stance and activism with his life, is that individuals should be able to characterize and discuss historical events freely with the understanding that

---

[82] Jürgen Gottschlich. "Dispute over Mass Killings of Armenians: French Law Outrages Turks." *Der Spiegel*, October 13, 2006. http://www.spiegel.de/international/dispute-over-mass-killings-of-armenians-french-law-outrages-turks-a-442422.html

[83] "Top Novelist acquitted in Turkey." *BBC*. September 21, 2006. http://news.bbc.co.uk/1/hi/world/europe/5366446.stm

those characterizations, discussions and the campaigns they may spawn will likely attract a great deal of scrutiny.

Highlighting the strange politico-legal nature of "denial" and the passage of genocide recognition laws and legislation, historian and previous Academic Research Director of the Holocaust Educational Trust, Donald Bloxham, aptly pointed out that "The notion of states passing resolutions on the character of historical events is undoubtedly an odd one in any circumstances [sic]. Whether in [sic] something qualifies as an instance of genocide is a matter for scholars of history and the law, not politicians acting as politicians. The fact that genocide is the quintessential state crime only adds piquancy to the issue."[84]

Regardless of the protests by Dink, Shafak and others, the French National Assembly passed a bill in October 2006 criminalizing the denial of what it termed the "Armenian Genocide." However, the law could only come into effect if approved by the French Senate. This occurred six years later when the French Senate adopted the law on January 23, 2012. However, just one month later, on February 28, 2012, the Constitutional Council of France invalidated the law, noting that it would curb freedom of speech in France.[85]

Armenian groups in France have argued that a French law passed in 2001 recognizing the events of 1915 as the "Armenian Genocide" have normative applications equal to that of the Gayssot Act or Gayssot Law (French: *Loi Gayssot*). However, the 2001 law is a declarative law with no legally binding effect; it is purely political in nature. This differs markedly from the Gayssot Act, passed to 1990, which makes it illegal to question the existence of crimes that fall in the category of crimes against humanity as defined in the London Charter of 1945, on the basis of

---

[84] Donald Bloxham, *The Great Game of Genocide: Imperialism, Nationalism and the Destruction of the Ottoman Armenians* (Oxford: Oxford University Press, 2005), 226.

[85] "La loi contre la négation du génocide arménien est censure." *Liberation*, February 28, 2012. http://www.liberation.fr/planete/2012/02/28/la-loi-contre-la-negation-du-genocide-armenien-est-censuree_799353

which Nazi leaders were convicted by the International Military Tribunal at Nuremberg in 1945–46. In practice, it is illegal in France to deny that the Nazi Holocaust occurred. Armenians inside and outside of France have argued that the Gayssot Act should be extended to cover what they term as denial of the Armenian Genocide. Yet this was struck down in 2012 in the French court ruling referenced above. Undeterred, Armenian interest groups and their French-Armenian lawyers allied themselves with a convicted Nazi Holocaust denier, French citizen Vincent Reynouard, in challenging the Gayssot Act. Indeed, they asked for its repeal! In what can only be termed a confused stance, it was argued that it should be a proper exercise of free speech to deny the Nazi Holocaust because the French Constitutional Court had previously ruled, in 2012, that questioning the Armenian allegation of genocide was covered under freedom of speech. The French-Armenian lawyers present in the case wanted to replace the Gayssot Law with a more inclusive law criminalizing the denial of all crimes against humanity and genocides. In essence, they argued in the alternative that the Nazi Holocaust and the events of 1915 were historical equivalents and, therefore, that denial of both ought to be criminalized.[86]

Not to be outdone, a Turkish interest group, the *Association pour la Neutralité de l'Enseignement de l'Histoire Turque dans les Programmes Scolaires* (ANEHTPS), argued that since the Constitutional Council of France in 2012 had invalidated the French Senate law criminalizing the denial of the Armenian Genocide, it should now issue a decree nullifying the 2001 law recognizing the events of 1915 as the Armenian Genocide. As noted above, this law is purely declarative, political, and not legally binding.

In the end, the French court ruled against all parties, to include Reynouard, the Holocaust denier and his Armenian

[86] Fatih Gökhan Diler. "What does French court's 'genocide decision' mean? *Agos*, January 13, 2016. http://www.agos.com.tr/en/article/14004/what-does-french-court-s-genocide-decision-mean

allies.[87] The Court ruled that international law had established the Nazi Holocaust as a genocide. As such, denial of the Nazi Holocaust can be punished in France. This contrasts with Armenian allegations that the events of 1915 constituted the Armenian Genocide precisely because this "fact" has never been established by a court of law, as noted by the French court.

Speaking about the ruling, Philippe Kalfayan, an international law scholar and former Secretary General of International Human Rights Federation, noted "It is quite easy to understand [the court's ruling]: genocide is a crime, and only a judge can form a decision on the nature and the qualification of a crime."[88]

Similar laws in Switzerland regarding the denial of the Armenian Genocide have played out over the past decade. Turkish politician Doğu Perinçek was the first person convicted in a Swiss court of law in March 2007 in Lausanne for the crime of denial and being guilty of racial discrimination. Perinçek defended himself by claiming that it was impossible to deny the Armenian Genocide because what occurred in 1915 did not constitute genocide.[89] Perinçek appealed the verdict, but in late 2007, the Swiss Federal Court confirmed the sentence given to Perinçek. He duly appealed to the European Court of Human Rights and was vindicated. The Court ruled in 2013 that Perinçek's freedom of expression, as enshrined in Article 10 of the

---

[87] See Turgut Kerem Tuncel. "Searching for the Right Approach to Solve the Turkish-Armenian Controversy." *Historians Without Borders: The Use and Abuse of History in Conflicts, Helsinki, 19-20 May 2016*, 8.

[88] Ibid. See also Taha Akyol. "The 'genocide decision' of France's Constitutional Council." *Hürriyet*, January 12, 2016. http://www.hurriyetdailynews.com/the-genocide-decision-of-frances-constitutional-council-.aspx?PageID=238&NID=93720&NewsCatID=458. See also "Anti-Armenian Aspirations of Turkey toppled in France." *Armenpress*, January 8, 2016. http://armenpress.am/eng/news/831385/anti-armenian-aspirations-of-turkey-toppled-in-france.html

[89] "Turkish politician fined over genocide denial." *SWI*. March 9, 2007. http://www.swissinfo.ch/eng/turkish-politician-fined-over-genocide-denial/977094

European Convention on Human Rights, had been violated.[90] The Grand Chamber of the European Court of Human Rights again ruled in favor of Perinçek on October 15, 2015.[91]

In another instance, in 1993, renowned historian of the Middle East, Turkey and the Ottoman Empire, Bernard Lewis, stated in an interview that Ottoman Armenians were not the subject of deliberate or planned annihilation and thus were not the victims of genocide. In 1995, Lewis was sued by the French Forum of Armenian Associations and a French court found him at fault for the crime of doing harm to a third party. He was ordered to pay a symbolic fine of one franc.[92]

After successive, though conflicting, rulings by French and Swiss courts, which were then superseded by the European Court of Human Rights, Phillipe Kalafyan noted his pessimism that any law could be successfully drafted that would criminalize denial of the Armenian Genocide. He added, however, that "French Armenian organizations are still able to institute civil proceedings for denial cases. This is what the European Court [of Human Rights] encouraged in its 15 October [2015] judgment, basing its argument as

---

[90] The Court ruled that "(l)aws that penalize the expression of opinions about historical facts are incompatible with the obligations that the Covenant imposes on States parties in relation to the respect for freedom of opinion and expression. The Covenant does not permit general prohibition of expressions of an erroneous opinion or an incorrect interpretation of past events." See Dirk Voorhoof. "Perinçek Judgment on Genocide Denial." *ECHR Blog*, January 7, 2014. https://biblio.ugent.be/publication/4227441/file/4227442. See also "Case of Perinçek v. Switzerland (Application no. 27510/08): Judgement." *European Court of Human Rights*, December 17, 2013. http://hudoc.echr.coe.int/eng?i=001-139724

[91] Celia Luterbacher and Urs Geiser. "European Court confirms Perinçek's right to freedom of speech." *SWI*. October 15, 2015. http://www.swissinfo.ch/eng/do%C4%9Fu-perin%C3%A7ek_european-court-confirms-perin%C3%A7ek-s-right-to-freedom-of-speech-/41720676

[92] Jason Harris. *Stumbling blocks: Geopolitics, the Armenian Genocide, and the American Jewish community*. Brandeis University: PhD diss., 2008: 96.

such: the Armenian genocide is a component of the Armenian identity. To deny the reality of the genocide amounts to insulting Armenian dignity and its right to be respected is then violated."[93]

Given the gloomy situation in the courts, it appears as if Armenian diaspora groups will need to continue their push for *ad hoc*, declarative and purely political legislation for the time being, as a court of law has yet to rule the events of 1915 constituted genocide. However, the very rulings by various courts call into serious question the Armenian campaign's argument of the "established truth" of what they term the Armenian Genocide. It should be remembered that the Second Chamber of the European Court of Human Rights in its verdict on Perinçek v. Switzerland case on December 17, 2013 stated "It is even doubtful that there could be a 'general consensus', in particular a scientific one, on events such as those that are in question here, given that historical research is by definition open to debate and discussion and hardly lends itself to definitive conclusions or objective and absolute truths."[94]

Forging a Collective Identity through Memories of Trauma

Reflecting Jeffrey Alexander's germane passage regarding traumatic events and memory, other scholars have noted that it is not just the Nazi Holocaust or the events of 1915 that can be conceived of as "free floating rather than situated – universal rather than particular – [a] traumatic event [that] vividly 'lives' in the memories of contemporaries," but a whole series of events.[95] For example, Neil Smelser has written about September 11, 2001 as the quintessential cultural trauma, an event that constituted and was experienced as a collective violation, a trauma that was "simultaneously shocking and fascinating,

---

[93] Diler.

[94] Tuncel, 12.

[95] Jeffrey Alexander. "On the Social Construction of Moral Universals." 197.

depressing and exhilarating, grotesque and beautiful, sullying and cleansing – and leaving [America] feeling both bad and good about itself."[96] Piotr Sztompka argues that trauma occurs "when there is a break, a displacement, or disorganization in the orderly, taken-for-granted universe."[97] W.G. Sebald posits that the "experience of terror… dislocates time, that most abstract of all human homes."[98]

In other words, the study of trauma may well be illuminating in the study of politics in a situation where the past is no longer considered the past; certain events, especially tragic ones cannot be left behind and, as such, have profound effects on identity. Thus, answers are available, as evidenced below, regarding the social construction of past events with jarring relevance today and the future, such as the 1915 deportations of thousands of Armenians, the Serbian loss of Kosovo to Ottoman forces in 1389 or the importance of the Greek betrayal, fratricide and defeat at Missolonghi in 1826. For example, K.M. Fierke writes "political trauma can be understood as a state in which fear and hypervigilance become habitual."[99] She uses examples of contemporary Israeli society and post-9/11 America to note "… it is less censorship or repression, in and of itself… than the *assimilation* of a past context of trauma such that it comes to structure identity within a linguistic world of action and interaction vis-à-vis others. It is less the existence of a repressed memory than the habitual acting out of the life world of the past in the present,

---

[96] Neil J. Smelser, "Epilogue: September 11, 2001 as Cultural Trauma," in *Cultural Trauma and Collective Identity*. Berkeley, CA: University of California Press, 2004: 264 and 266.

[97] Piotr Sztompka. "Cultural Trauma." *European Journal of Social Theory*, no. 3 (2000): 449-67.

[98] W.G. Sebald. *On the Natural History of Destruction*. trans. Anthea Bell (New York: Modern Library, 2004), 154.

[99] K.M. Fierke. "Bewitched by the Past: Social Memory, Trauma, and International Relations." In *Memory, Trauma and World Politics. Reflections on the Relationship between Past and Present*. Duncan Bell, ed. London: Palgrave Macmillan (2006), 132.

mirroring a past experience of humiliation and destruction."[100]

Mainstream political science is suspicious of employing concepts such as memory and trauma. Many political scientists simply consider the concepts too vague and nebulous to be of much theoretical use. However, the political scientist Duncan Bell has suggested three methods of mapping out the causal relationship between trauma, memory and world politics: the characterization of national identity, the possible globalization of memory and the ethics of memory.[101] Ideas regarding exactly how methods used by various groups of people in the past may shape the nature of political communities are quite old, according to Bell. Both John Stuart Mill in *Consideration on Representative Democracy* (1861) and Alexis de Tocqueville in *L'Ancien Regime* (1856) wrote, respectively, of the importance of a "community of recollections" and the inclination of the French to "put an abyss between what they had been and what they wished to become."[102]

Most studies of trauma, memory and politics have been carried out by historians or sociologists, but a number of constructivist International Relations (IR) scholars "have investigated the formation of collective identities in order to explain the configuration of national interests, the development of foreign policy positions, and the evolution of international norms and institutions."[103] Consuelo Cruz, a scholar of comparative politics in Latin America, has argued that collective identity is "a robust declarative statement that a group makes, under the pressure of collective memory and contextual forces, to itself and to others about its normative constitution and its practical competence when facing the world."[104] Constructivist

---

[100] Ibid.

[101] Bell, 11.

[102] Ibid.

[103] Ibid, 12.

[104] Consuelo Cruz. "Identity and Persuasion: How Nations remember their Pasts and Make their Futures." *World Politics*, no. 52 (2000), 310.

scholars also compellingly dispute the idea that comprehension of "national" interest is not viable without first understanding the way in which these are grounded and fashioned by the ideals and norms of societies.[105] For example, understanding the response of the United States after the trauma of 9/11 can perhaps only be understood through the lens of other experienced traumas: Pearl Harbor and even memories of Vietnam. Indeed, then-President George W. Bush invoked references to the past – particularly World War II and the traumatic Japanese assault on Pearl Harbor – in an attempt to further legitimate U.S. actions in Iraq and Afghanistan with what Americans remember as a "just war."[106]

In a similar fashion, the Republic of Armenia's national interests and present stance vis-à-vis Turkey may best be understood in the context of the ideals, norms and identity developed by Armenian diaspora communities and centered around the traumas suffered in 1915. This central theme resonates, as demonstrated previously, because it is the only cohesive bond shared, or popularly thought to have been shared, by all Armenians. Unlike the Republican Irish, for example, Armenians have no common religion. Unlike the Cuban diaspora, Armenians possess no common language. And unlike Jews, Armenians do not possess a common homeland to return to if they so wished. Indeed, many diaspora Armenians argue that "their" Armenia is not centered in and around Yerevan or Gyumri; i.e. within the confines of today's Republic of Armenia, but in Van or Malatya in what is the Republic of Turkey. One diaspora Armenian, speaking of what was formerly the Soviet Republic of Armenia noted, "This Armenia held little interest for me. My heritage, the land I thought of as

---

[105] See Martha Finnemore and Kathryn Sikkink. "International norm dynamics and political change." *International Organization* 52, no. 04 (1998): 887-917.

[106] Parmar, Inderjeet. "Catalysing Events, Think Tanks and American Foreign Policy Shifts: A Comparative Analysis of the Impacts of Pearl Harbor 1941 and 11 September 2001." *Government and Opposition* 40, no. 1 (2005): 1-25.

'Armenia,' was the region that today is part of the modern Turkish state."[107]

In regards to the emergence of an undifferentiated "victim" culture, the historian Joanna Bourke has argued - mirroring Finkelstein's ideas - that this culture has arisen precisely because of the pervasive use of trauma discourse in Western societies, and the accompanying abandonment of individual and political accountability.[108] Interestingly, Bourke writes that trauma has been utilized in a variety of ways to justify biased, political agendas on one end of the spectrum and brutality, revenge - even torture, on the other. She writes that this first occurred in the 1980s in an attempt to absolve and explain the brutality of U.S. soldiers in Vietnam. By labeling the soldiers opaquely as "victims" who suffered from an illness known as post-traumatic stress disorder (PTSD), their actions, while not legitimated entirely, were largely excused and could be ignored. Similar actions occurred after the U.S. invasion of Iraq in 2003. American, British and other members of the occupying coalition force were not only traumatized by what they had "witnessed" in the prison complex of Abu Ghraib and the cities of Fallujah, Baghdad and Ramadi, it was indeed the very act of witnessing brutality and horror that was used, in turn, to justify their torture or mistreatment of others.[109]

Bourke presciently writes that "one effect of the trauma trope has been to create a universal suffering subject *outside of history*. Individuals are reduced to bodies-in-pain. Yet pain is always local. To universalize it is to remove the specifics of an individual's history; it is to situate torture in the realm of moral edification."[110] In essence, what Bourke has argued is that the universalization of trauma leads to a corresponding trivialization of the trauma suffered by the individual. This holds true whether or not that individual suffered alone or as a member of a large group: ethnic,

---

[107] Ishkanian, 120.

[108] Joanna Bourke. "When Torture Becomes Humdrum." *Times Higher Educational Supplement*, February 10, 2006.

[109] Ibid.

[110] Ibid.

religious, political, economic or social. Thus, the individual's suffering is not forgotten, but rather it is subsumed and, ultimately consumed by a wider interpretation of the individual's trauma as that of a collective trauma experienced and felt by an entire people or nation.

This interpretation may lead to what could be termed immoral absolutes, absolutes that paint the perpetrators of a collectively imagined trauma in black and the victims of this trauma in white, allowing for little or no gray area. This not only holds out the possibility that an entire nation, state or group will be demonized as a monster because some (perhaps most) were perpetrators of a crime, but also neuters and silences the individual victims of that same crime. This has the effect of rendering the victims as helpless individuals who were only acted upon, depriving them of agency, thoughts and a voice. In doing so, nuance is erased and stories of kindness and compassion and/or victimization of the "perpetrating people" - no matter how rare or common - are forgotten or relegated to the realm of the merely trivial. In the case of the Armenian diaspora's collective memory, actions of one's own group (the Self) and the actions of the perpetrators (the Other) are mythologized. In this scenario, all Armenians – regardless of location or station in life - were and continue to be victims; innocent and blameless. Correspondingly, in this mythology all Turks were, and continue to be, barbarians who perpetrated genocide.

In a study of communal conflict, James Waller, a psychologist and the Cohen Professor of Holocaust and Genocide Studies at Keene State College, noted the polarizing nature inherent in collective memories of violence. "Instead of judging people across a broad spectrum running from good to bad, we make extreme categorical judgments based on the polar opposites of 'good us' versus 'bad them.' Our cause is sacred; theirs is evil. We are righteous; they are wicked. We are innocent; they are guilty. We are the victims; they are the victimizers. It is rarely *our* enemy or *my* enemy, but *the* enemy – a usage of the definitive article that hints of something fixed and immutable, abstract and evil."[111]

Nuance offers a method of combating the effects of polarization inherent in collective memories of violence. At the very least, a nuanced understanding or conscious thoughtfulness regarding a particular trauma holds out the possibility of reconciliation, apology and even forgiveness through the reconstitution of victims as individuals rather than faceless members of nations, groups or states. The same holds true for the individuals responsible for perpetrating the crime, those who populate or populated atrocity-perpetrating nations, states or other entities. That is, only certain members (in some cases the majority) committed atrocities. From this vantage point and perhaps because the Nazi Holocaust is broadly accepted and unquestioned as a historical fact, the Western historical view of Nazi Germany, its extermination of Jews and the occupation of Europe is in some respects quite nuanced. That is, only certain Germans, Italians, Poles and Hungarians actively defended or attempted to save Jews. Only certain people rebelled or sacrificed themselves in their struggle against Nazi tyranny and occupation. Indeed, in Germany, these numbers were infinitesimal. Most non-participants, if they can be defined as such, simply watched and were silent.[112] However, those who did risk their lives to save their fellow human beings and attempted to combat the atrocities being committed around them - regardless of motivation - are remembered as heroes and, most importantly, as individuals.

If, as Waller posits, collective memories of trauma are polarizing, how are these emotions, memories and feelings - this trauma and the identity it creates - transmitted beyond the generation of individuals who actually experienced the trauma?

---

[111] James Waller. *Becoming Evil: How Ordinary People Commit Genocide and Mass Killings* (Oxford: Oxford University Press, 2002), 243.
[112] Michael J. Cohen. "When Did They Know and What Could They Have Done? More on the Allies' Response to the Holocaust." *Israel Journal of Foreign Affairs* 7, no. 1 (2013): 127-133.

Shared Trauma and the Transmission of Identity

The Armenian immigrants who emigrated to the United States, France, Argentina and elsewhere after 1915 generally settled into cities and villages with previously existent, if rather small, Armenian communities.[113] The influx of large numbers of immigrants from the Ottoman Empire with vivid memories of the tragic events of 1915 and beyond led to a sense of shared trauma that time has neither erased nor eased with the passage of time. It was precisely this large group of migrants that defined, to a large degree, the discourse regarding what it means to be Armenian, regardless of geographic location, language or religion. Yet, how was this trauma-defined identity transmitted?

Scholarly works regarding identity construction, paying particular attention to childhood years, have done much to illuminate the cultural and social worlds of children and their innate importance to the process of identity construction and transmission. Scholars have volubly challenged more traditional studies of childhood, socialization, identity transmission and development, which depicted children as largely passive. Instead, newer studies have focused on the important role of a child in his or her identity development.[114] Alison James, a renowned professor of sociology, examined the development of identities in children by positing children as social actors and emphasizing their often-complex social relationships and experiences as they occur in different milieus.[115] On another level, scholars contributed groundbreaking research

---

[113] Robert Mirak. *Torn between two lands: Armenians in America, 1890 to World War I*. No. 7. Harvard University Press, 1983.
[114] See B. Mayall. *Children, Health and the Social Order* (Buckingham: Open University Press, 1996). See also H. Morton. *Becoming Tongan: An Ethnography of Childhood* (Honolulu, HI: University of Hawaii Press, 1996). See also I. Hutchby and J. Moran-Ellis, eds. *Children and Social Competence: Arenas of Action* (London: Falmer Press, 1998).
[115] Allison James. *Childhood Identities: Self and Social Relationships in the Experience of the Child* (Edinburgh: Edinburgh University Press, 1993).

to the study of the role culture and politics play in childhood.[116] Even more recently, scholars studying identity and childhood have shown an interest in nationalism as a social phenomenon.[117] The role of education in defining the political sense of the Self in relation to the Other is of particular importance. Studies of education have begun to focus on actual cultural production rather than reproduction, thus demonstrating the intricacy and dynamism of the process of identity development in schools and extra-curricular activities.[118] Hatcher and Troyna, in particular, illustrate the evolution of the racialization process in childhood identity development. These scholars posit that children aid in the reproduction of large group prejudices and/or racism, because these attitudes provide the children with an important construct in understanding their own lives.[119]

Scholars such as Frederik Barth have contributed a great deal to the understanding of identity construction in interethnic contexts. According to Barth, ethnic boundaries are social and cultural differences that are only of importance insofar as they help maintain ethnic boundaries through social interaction between groups.[120] This approach

---

[116] S. Stephens, ed. *Children and the Politics of Culture* (Princeton, NJ: Princeton University Press, 1995).

[117] See C. Cullingford. *Prejudice: From Individual Identity to Nationalism in Young People* (London: Kogan Page, 2000). See also D. Koester. "Childhood in National Consciousness and National Consciousness in Childhood." *Childhood*, 4, 125-142. See also S. Spyrou. "Education, Ideology, and the National Self: The Social Practice of Identity Construction in the Classroom." *The Cyprus Review*, 12, 61-81.

[118] See B. Levinson, D. Foley and D. Holland, eds. *The Cultural Production of the Educated Person: Critical Ethnographies of Schooling and Local Practice* (New York: State University of New York Press, 1996). See also A. Lukyx. *The Citizen Factory: Schooling and Cultural Production in Bolivia* (New York: State University of New York Press, 1999).

[119] R. Hatcher and B. Troyna. "Racialization and Children." In *Race, Identity and Representation in Education,* eds. C. McCarthy and W. Crichlow (New York: Routledge), 1993.

[120] Fredrik Barth. *Ethnic groups and boundaries: The social organization of culture difference.* Waveland Press, 1998, 9-10.

is instructive vis-à-vis the maintenance of boundaries resulting from interaction between groups, but less so when there is an almost utter absence of social interaction between groups. This is the case of diaspora Armenians and Turks and, on the divided island of Cyprus, Greeks and Turks.[121]

In the case of Cyprus, Turks and Greeks have been separated by a physical barrier or wall, manned by troops under the aegis of the United Nations, that runs the length of the island. Cyprus has been divided since 1974 when Turkey invaded in response to a military coup on the island, which was backed by the Greek government in Athens. According to the social anthropologist Spyros Spyrou, "The boundary that separates the two communities is not only physical but also a psychosocial. It is a relational boundary, which is constantly created and recreated by members of the two communities in the process of making sense of who they are."[122] Spyrou argues that the Cypriot boundary is, in essence, an ethnic boundary. However, it is a boundary that was constructed and sustained through a process that constitutes "…ethnic socialization; that is, the cultural learning that allows members of one ethnic group to construct their self-identities as distinct from those of others."[123] In Cyprus and in the case of diaspora Armenians and Turks, the utter lack of physical inter-ethnic contact "implicates both individual and collective imagination in the process."[124]

Volkan noted the decisive importance of trauma and the dynamics of group cohesion. "When people are attacked by an enemy group and suffer, they also feel shame and humiliation. Such traumas are also accompanied by a combination of great emotional (abstract) and concrete

---

[121] Spyros Spyrou. "Images of 'the Other': 'the Turk' in Greek Cypriot Children's Imaginations" *Race, Ethnicity and Education* Vol. 5, No. 3, (2002), 255-272.
[122] Ibid, 258.
[123] Ibid.
[124] Ibid.

losses. Sometimes these people only lose their sense of security and dignity, but other times such emotional losses are accompanied by concrete losses… In the case of shared trauma, reactions to being hurt by the enemy at individual, familial, and regional levels spread over the entire large group. If the shared trauma creates a refugee problem, those who are not directly affected show empathy for the refugees from their own side. But when refugees… become a burden or are perceived to be a burden to other people of the same group, we may see splits in the large group. Renewed hostility with the outside enemy, however, can easily erase such splits."[125] This has been the case of the Armenian, Iranian, Vietnamese, Bosnian and Kurdish diasporas, particularly in the United States. All groups not only experienced a loss of dignity, but many suffered the utmost of concrete losses, i.e. loss of family members, homes and ways of life. In many cases, only those who became refugees internally or made the harrowing journey to a host country survived. Furthermore, and mirroring Volkan's theories regarding the perception of burden, diaspora Armenians experienced deep splits along political and sometimes religious lines in the form of political party affiliation (Dashnak vs. non-Dashnak). Indeed, many diaspora Armenians freely admit that the only uniting factor is their identification with the events of 1915 and their subsequent quest for recognition of these events as the Armenian Genocide. As one Canadian-Armenian author and critic half-jokingly noted, "Armenians are united by little except mutual contempt."[126]

Furthering the discussion, it should be stressed that the transmission of collective memory and communal mythology occurs and is reinforced for subsequent generations through the socialization of violence and trauma via the media of stories, documentaries, photos, museums and works of art. These disseminate appropriately

---

[125] Vamık D. Volkan. *Killing in the Name of Identity* (Charlottesville, VA: Pitchstone Publishing, 2006): 50.

[126] Ara Baliozian. "Resurrection." *ARA Home Page,* March 23, 2008. http://baliozian.blogspot.com/

communal memories and myths that demonize the actions of the enemy group (the Other) and reinforce collective identity (the Self). Furthermore, it is important to note that dislocation and dehumanization do not necessarily cease when overt violence stops. The violence and atrocities, perceived or real, expand and intensify social divides among opposing groups. Furthermore, violent acts lead to the formation of memories and mythologies that, in turn, lead to a subjective communal narrative whereby the threatened or once-threatened group defines itself narrowly, distinguishing sharply its Self and its Other.[127]

Events such as those of 1915 occur to the sad accompaniments of death and destruction and produce unintended and long-lasting results. Daniel Bar-Tal posits that the greater the number of human losses - a subject of some debate in competing Armenian and Turkish historiographies - the greater the possibility that societies will develop firm and unshakeable beliefs regarding their victimization by those they perceive as their Other.[128] These beliefs focus exclusively on the memories and myths of loss, death, violence and atrocities committed by the perpetrators as they assign the blame for the violence exclusively to their Other. This self-perception focuses intensely on the gloomy and miserable fate of the group - ignoring other circumstances - and frames all victims as martyrs. The fate of dead and wounded, as represented, imparted and mythologized by survivors and their children, becomes the solid, formidable evidence of the group's victimhood status.[129]

---

[127] John E. Mack. "The Psychodynamics of Victimization Among National Groups in Conflict." In *The Psychodynamics of International Relationships, Volume 1: Concepts and Theories*, eds. Vamık D. Volkan, Demetrios A. Julius and Joseph V. Montville (Toronto: Lexington Books, 1990), 124.

[128] Bar-Tal, 86.

[129] Ibid.

Group Identity Formation

No matter how small or large they are, groups, by their very nature, are defined and shaped by their similarities and interests. These commonalities, perhaps a shared affinity for food or clothing, perhaps shared historical experiences, perhaps a common homeland, are what constitute some of the more simplistic but durable bonds of shared, group identity. Yet how these ties are formed, transmitted and perpetuated from generation to generation within the group is the subject of much discussion.

It has been argued that there are three important "building blocks" in the formation and longevity of large-group (i.e. ethnic) identity and the role that the mental representation of historical memories plays in shaping this identity. "First, every person's core individual identity is inextricably intertwined with his or her large-group identity. Second, the study of mental representations of historical events is a key link between individual and large-group psychology. Third, and finally, when an individual's symptomatic expressions are inflected by large-group historical experience, the psychopathology itself connects the individual to his or her large group with a profound sense of belonging which, in turn, creates a resistance to relinquishing the psychopathology. To these individuals, giving up the large-group relationship, object-relations conflicts, symptoms, and/or character traits is a threat to the comforting identification that has closely bound them to the large group."[130]

Though core-identity formation begins as early as infancy, Volkan argues the formation of identity more accurately begins "…when the integration of early identifications is solidified."[131] Just as individual identity is the "persistent sense of sameness within himself or herself," so large-group identity is a subjective experience of hundreds, indeed

---

[130] Vamık D. Volkan. "Large group identity and chosen trauma." *Psyche. Zeitschrift für Psychoanalyse und ihre Anwendungen,* no. 9-10 (2000): 931.

[131] Ibid.

millions of people. This is pervaded by a sense of similitude while at the same time sharing a large number of the characteristics found in "foreign" groups.[132]

Because the internal and external worlds of all children are tied together from an early age by material things that may be cultural, they become permanent containers of externalized "good" images for the children. These material things may include certain types of food, toys, music, dance or types of dress. It is precisely because these material items are stable and not subject to change over the years that they achieve the status of permanency and are viewed as good, comforting and remembered fondly.

Children at first are not fully conscious of their "we-ness" and sense of belonging to a large group. As such, most of the mechanisms involved in creating this sense of membership in a larger group are formed unconsciously. However, as a child's conscious self matures, and his/her mental faculties expand, interactions with adults of the same large-group increase. Various levels of identification with these same adults' images and beliefs regarding large-group membership also increase. Thus, the child is able to structure more refined ideas about his/her place in, and the importance of, group membership. "The child slowly becomes conscious of more abstract concepts of Scottishness, Finnishness, Jewishness, or Germanness associated with the suitable reservoirs which are, indeed, at the foundation of large-groups' identity: A Scottish child becomes aware that a kilt or bagpipe represents and is associated with many issues: manhood, clan and national history, specific heroes, battles for independence won and lost, songs and poems, language and dialect, and other specific facets of the large group."[133] Accordingly, what is crucial to a child's investment, development and membership within the large-group is what adults around them identify as most important: ethnicity (I am Greek),

---

[132] Ibid.

[133] Ibid.

religion (I am Mormon), nationality (I am Chinese) or any combination of these.

Mapping Memory in the Armenian Diaspora

As an example of the formation and consolidation of large-group membership and identity, Donald and Lorna Touryan Miller's research involving terrorists who hail from the Armenian diaspora demonstrates that one can make generalizations from the broader Armenian experience of memory transmission through the generations. From this, an expansive theory of identity of descent is possible.[134]

First, the Millers note the importance of trauma and traumatic events – be they massacres, floods, earthquakes, military defeats or epidemics. This particular trauma is the pivotal point around which groups and generations base their self-understanding and ultimately, their identity. A traumatic event or series of events become the guide and blueprint whereby generations relate to each other: they become the means through which group identity and self-identification progresses. "These events are the objects of interpretation, reinterpretation, dispute, rejection, embrace,

---

[134] Donald E. Miller and Lorna Touryan Miller. "Memory and Identity across the Generations: A Case Study of Armenian Survivors and Their Progeny." *Qualitative Sociology* Vol. 14, no. 1 (1991), 13-38. The Millers borrowed a methodological principle form from William James and his 1961 study *Varieties of Religious Experience*. In his study, James mapped the terrain of religious life by studying those for whom religion was a passion, not by sampling a cross-section of religious people. James believed that study of "extreme" cases led to a better understanding of the experience of persons for whom religion may be a much more banal experience. Similarly, the Millers aimed to elaborate the "extreme" case histories of several Armenian terrorists, "…for whom the Armenian cause, and the genocide in particular, has been a commitment for which they were willing to die" in order to "embody the many issues and conflicts that are present more generally in the Armenian population, although to a lesser degree."

and/or denial. But whatever else they may be, *they are not ignored.*"[135]

Second, the supreme importance of grandparents as the main conveyors and transmitters of collective group memories and identities cannot be overstated. The Millers also noted the corresponding desire of grandchildren for roots that define who they are and where they come from; i.e. a firm identity. "Identity is the story we tell others – as well as ourselves – about who we are."[136] And the story is just that: a catalog of what is remembered or thought to have happened rather that what actually occurred. The story is - unwittingly at times - necessarily expanded, invented, embellished and repackaged for the consumption of oneself and others.

Amongst diaspora Armenians, the scholars found that an introduction to, and primary education of, the events of 1915 more often than not came from grandparents – some of whom had experienced the events first-hand. According to the Millers, this pattern was reinforced because of the strong extended family network that exists among diaspora Armenians. It was also informed and strengthened from the outset by Armenian diaspora settlement patterns. As noted previously, diaspora Armenians tended to settle in groups, living in the same quarters or neighborhoods and favoring certain geographic regions such as the Fresno, Detroit or Watertown, Massachusetts in the United States or Marseilles in France.[137] Indeed, the hometown of an individual in the

---

[135] Ibid, 36; my emphasis

[136] Ibid.

[137] For more information on Armenian settlement patterns and history in the United States, see Harold Takooshian. "Armenian Immigration to the United States from the Middle East." *Journal of Armenian Studies* III, (Winter 1986-1987), 133-156. See also Marc A. Mamigonian, ed., *The Armenians of New England.* (Belmont, MA: ArmenianHeritage Press/NAASR, 2004). See also Berge Bulbulian, *The Fresno Armenians: History of a Diaspora Community* (Fresno, CA: The Press at California State University, Fresno, 2000). See also Joan Bamberger, "Family and Kinship in an Armenian-American

Ottoman Empire largely dictated where that individual would settle as an emigrant – particularly in the United States. Those from present-day Elazığ (referred to in Armenian as Kharberd/Kharpert) tended to settle in Worcester, Massachusetts; Armenians from Van favored Pawtucket, Rhode Island; and those from Silvan (Dikranagerd/Tikranakert in Armenian) found their way to Jersey City, New Jersey.[138] In this way, Armenian immigrants managed to share and recreate with one another a more homogeneous and hegemonic version of the events of 1915. However, though the overall narrative is the same, the interviews conducted by the Millers exhibited a complex pattern among grandparent survivors of the 1915 deportations, which directly affected the way in which their children and grandchildren may interpret the same events. This, in turn, highlighted a third finding of great interest. That is, the Millers research demonstrated that when memories and tales of origin proved contradictory in a moral sense, reactions varied from rejection because of paralysis to fulmination. Thus, if stories conflicted they were homogenized to fit the version based on the "victim" Armenian (Self) versus the "barbaric" Turk (Other), thereby leading to an internalization of this narrative.

The authors noted that some diaspora Armenians sought to "correct" the past through efforts aimed at achieving healing or outward actions such as legislation or violence against perceived perpetrators. In the case of Armenian survivors of the events of 1915, a small but significant group appeared to be reconciled with their past and to have forgiven the perpetrators of the violence and trauma they had experienced. Others appeared resigned to their past; though the Millers described this group as "clinically depressed."[139] Another significant group turned their anger and frustration outward. "They were vocal about the injustices of the past, with some survivors limiting their rage

---

Community." *Journal of Armenian Studies* III, (Winter 1986-1987), 77-86.

[138] Benjamin F. Alexander, 95.

[139] Miller and Miller, 28.

to verbal expression, while others suggested specific political goals related to reclaiming their homeland in Turkey."[140] Still others objected to political violence and put their trust in God to avenge their "Turkish oppressors," while other struggled with what they believed should be their Christian response to the event and their perpetrators rather than their baser human feelings.[141] Some diaspora Armenian survivors were wary of transmitting their painful memories and therefore, their trauma. One woman in particular noted that she had asked her husband to refrain from telling their children about his experiences in the Ottoman Empire, but "… nothing would stop him. Now my sons are filled with revenge. Even my grandchild comes and asks him questions."[142]

Despite the differences exhibited among those interviewed, the Millers noted a near universal desire among diaspora Armenian survivors for their grandchildren to maintain their Armenian identity. Many defined this identity as a combination of language and allegiance to the Armenian Apostolic Churches. However, those interviewed also affirmed the supreme importance of maintaining, transmitting and knowing the history of the Armenian people, placing particular emphasis on what they termed the Armenian Genocide.

The research conducted by the Millers found that the children of survivors also played a complimentary, complex and important role in mediating between the generations and ensuring the trauma of 1915 and the identity it has

---

[140] Ibid.

[141] Importantly, the Millers never questioned the dominant and paradigmatic Armenian diaspora narrative that the events of 1915 constituted the Armenian Genocide. Nor did they question their research subjects regarding the same. It is possible, though unsubstantiated, that some Armenian grandparent survivors of 1915 were equivocal in their desire for revenge precisely because of their first-hand experiences and understanding of Christian-Muslim atrocities, Armenian uprisings and collaboration with invading Russian armies.

[142] Miller and Miller, 29.

created is passed on to their own children. "Children of survivors often feel responsible to not betray 'the cause,' realizing that they serve as the bridge to 2,500 years of Armenian history which they feel it is their obligation to perpetuate."[143] Yet the identity of grandchildren also depends heavily on the physical proximity between grandparents and grandchildren and whether extended family traditions are maintained, thereby ensuring the exposure of grandchildren to the memories and stories of their grandparents and past generations. Parents of these grandchildren either choose to maintain this vital link between their children and their own parents or eschew it in favor of a more atomized nuclear family.

The Millers found that grandparents and parents play vital and complex roles in the transmission of identity and trauma to their children. They also uphold the responsibility (or lack thereof) for generating and preserving the institutions that foster identity awareness and the perceived values of the group.[144] In their study, the Millers found broad, but often shallow support for the preservation of the group's "Armenianness." On the one end of the spectrum, there exist certain individuals who many diaspora Armenians refer to pejoratively or jokingly as "shish kebab Armenians," those whose only ties to Armenian identity is their predilection for their ancestors' cuisine. For example, Armenian may not be spoken in these shish kebab Armenian homes, children are often sent to mainstream public schools and their religious ties may be non-existent, weak or something other than Armenian Apostolic. On the other end of the spectrum, there are those who insist on Armenian being spoken at home and whose children are only sent to Armenian schools. These families most likely attend yearly genocide commemorations held on April 24th and whose social life, discourse and identity are based around their extended Armenian family and Armenian diaspora community. Interestingly, families from almost the

143 Ibid, 30.

144 Ibid, 32.

entire spectrum actively fund and support what they view as *their* Armenian diaspora lobby's campaign to recognize the events of 1915 as the Armenian Genocide. These actions highlight yet again just how vital ideological representations of memories and the reconstructed trauma suffered in 1915 are to Armenian diaspora large-group identity.

While parents and grandparents lay the foundation for identity development, the roles played by socializing institutions are also crucial. Armenian diaspora schools, clubs, churches and institutions are heavily funded and supported by the more overtly "Armenian" families mentioned above. These socializing institutions aim to preserve cultural memory, baptize (literally and figuratively) and socialize each proceeding generation in practicalities and meaning of being an Armenian in the diaspora. As such, these schools and clubs play an extremely important role in the transmission and maintenance of Armenian diaspora group identity. Indeed, it was in Armenian schools both in the United States and abroad that subjects of the Millers' case study were first exposed to graphic images and documentaries of the events of 1915, rather than the stories and memories of ancestors. In their interviewees' experiences, schools served to affirm, reinforce and universalize the stories they had heard at home from their parents and grandparents. That is, pupils at schools and institutions - particularly those who were heavily attended by ethnic Armenians with an emphasis on Armenianness - came to the realization that their immediate ancestors were not the only ones who had suffered. They came to understand through the socializing institution's curricula that *all* Armenians throughout history had suffered at the hands of the Other, particularly at the hands of the Turks. Thus, a child's psychological development is influenced and shaped by the group's identity. "Just as Armenian identity cannot be understood apart from the particular historical and cultural circumstances within which it is negotiated, so also the personal struggle for identity may be understood within a framework of psychological development."[145]

Regarding education and the development of large group identity, anthropology professor Ana Maria Alonso argued, "It is through epic discourses, broadly conceived, that the nation is particularized and centered, imagined as eternal and primordial, and that nationalist love becomes a sacralized and sublime sentiment, indeed, a form of piety."[146] Similarly, Spyros Spyrou noted, "It is to nationalistic discourse that teachers have often turned to in the classroom in their efforts to explicate self-identity."[147]

Schools emphasizing Armenianness utilize tools such as nationalistic folklore, emotional language, imagery and stories of loyalty and bravery in depicting the history of Armenians, thereby transmitting, in part, the foundations and structure of Armenian diaspora identity. This is no different than, broadly speaking, curricula found in French and Greek schools, for example. Precisely because the construction of national or group identity is predicated on a Self/Other frame of reference and because one's Self is considered essentially good – the opposite of one's Other – it necessarily follows that the Self is posited as superordinate to the Other. "It is a kind of logic that seeks to define the 'self' in terms of the 'other' but in the process both 'self' and 'other' emerge as two polarized opposites that cannot exist (in that form) but in relation to one another. To put it another way, *there are Greeks because there are Turks.*"[148] Alternatively, there are diaspora Armenians because there are Turks. Indeed, a cornerstone of diaspora identity holds that if it were not for the events of 1915 there would never have been an Armenian diaspora.

---

[145] Ibid, 33.

[146] Ana Maria Alonso. "The Politics of Space, Time and Substance: State Formation, Nationalism, and Ethnicity." *Annual Review of Anthropology*, 23 (1994), 388.

[147] Spyrou. "Images of 'the Other': 'the Turk' in Greek Cypriot Children's Imaginations." 259.

[148] Ibid, author's emphasis.

It is interesting to note that there is almost nothing mechanical about the transmission of memory from one generation to another. Because the struggle for identity is potentially very individual and idiosyncratic, it appears that regardless of circumstance, children exercise considerable control in what they accept or reject as identity markers. In a community or large group where memory and the myth of trauma are powerful identity markers and makers of the Self, the Other is vilified and revenge or some other form of compensation for the chosen trauma becomes a powerful motivator. In some groups scarred by atrocity and violence, avenging the victimization of one's group – whether that victimization occurred yesterday, one hundred or one thousand years ago - may become something akin to a social obligation; a moral requirement.[149] Thus, some members of the group may support violent activities to gain acceptance or settle old scores. Others may support legal and political goals aimed at achieving legislation, territory or financial compensation to avenge victimization.

It is along these lines of inquiry that scholars discovered that many Armenians in their diaspora communities, including children, suffered from the feeling of being uprooted and a profound sense of loss for a particular homeland.[150] These feelings did not seem to dissipate over time and were transmitted from generation to generation. Other group members voiced a sense of impotence and rage at what they saw as Armenian weakness in the face of historic and continuing aggression by Turks and the Republic of Turkey. "This feeling was compounded by a perception that Armenians are always on the losing side. For a young adolescent to feel that his people are weak, that he is a loser, surely runs counter to at least the stereotypical male notions of strength and independence…"[151]

---

[149] Bar-Tal, 82.

[150] Miller and Miller, 33.

[151] Ibid, 34.

Acts of Terror and Armenian Identity Formation

Beginning in 1975, certain members of Armenian diaspora communities – mostly from Lebanon – began a campaign of terrorism targeting Turkish diplomats, businesses and military personnel. The aptly named Armenian Secret Army for the Liberation of Armenia (ASALA) and its rival group, the Justice Commandos for the Armenian Genocide (JCAG), operated until the mid-1980s and demanded Turkish recognition of the events of 1915 as genocide, payment of reparations and the creation of what they termed "Wilsonian Armenia." Wilsonian Armenia encompassed the territories in eastern Anatolia promised by U.S. President Woodrow Wilson to the Armenians in the never-implemented Treaty of Sèvres that sought to dismember the Ottoman Empire.

A wave of assassinations of Turkish diplomats, military figures and innocent civilians was perpetrated members ASALA and JCAG.[152] In all, there were 27 attacks carried out against Turkish diplomats. Shock reverberated through the Armenian diaspora communities and many were astonished because they simply felt that Armenians were incapable of killing. Diaspora Armenians felt they did not possess the capacity to kill, according to their imagined identity and bolstered by an accompanying, perceived, historical "weakness." Even though this assumption regarding their identity is patently false - Armenians proved themselves capable killers of Muslims and even fellow Armenians time and again in the waning days of the Ottoman Empire[153] - the killing of Turks was a way of countering perceived group weakness. According to one terrorist, "There was almost a festive atmosphere in the Armenian community after each of the assassinations [of

[152] For more on Armenian acts of terrorism and its causes, see Michael M. Gunter, *"Pursuing the Just Cause of Their People": A Study of Contemporary Armenian Terrorism* (Westport, CT: Greenwood Press, 1986). See also Francis P. Hyland. *Armenian Terrorism: The Past, The Present, The Prospects* (Boulder, CO: Westview Press, 1991).

[153] See McCarthy. *Death and Exile*, 187-230.

Turks]… this celebration of these terrorist acts revealed that Armenians were no longer helpless and impotent."[154]

Yet the perpetrators did not necessarily connect the assassinations to feelings of weakness amongst Armenians dating to 1915. One arrested terrorist, when interviewed, noted that the assassinations were something cathartic and contemporary; something needed by the Armenian communities to counter the feelings of powerlessness they were feeling in the face of what they viewed as close to a century of Turkish intransigence and propaganda. In particular, there was anger at what was perceived as the Turkish denial of what the terrorists and the Armenian diaspora considered not only the Armenian Genocide, but the world's first genocide; the blueprint for all other genocides that followed.

This reference to awakening and catharsis mirrored the thoughts of a leading Armenian-American lobbying representative,[155] though the representative was by no means referring to or condoned the terrorist acts referenced above. Rather, the lobbyist highlighted an Armenian diaspora genocide awakening; an event or series of events that happened to occur and coincide with other awakenings that included the racial, sexual and ethnic awakenings in the 1960s and 1970s. According to this narrative, the Armenian-American diaspora had previously focused inward and therefore resources and passions were distributed in a rather insular, community-centric manner. At around the same time of the referred-to awakening, many of the survivors of the tragic events of 1915 began to die. Feelings of tragedy and impotence were transformed into legends and, correspondingly, organizational strength through the money of wealthy members of the Armenian-American diaspora

---

[154] Miller and Miller, 34.

[155] Excerpts from an interview with an Armenian-American lobbying representative, conducted at USAPAC Headquarters, 1518 K St., N.W., Ste. M, Washington, D.C. on 08 June 2007. As of 2016, USAPAC is no longer in existence. Information is sparse and it is unclear what led to USAPAC's demise or when it occurred.

community and a dedication to the perceived cause of their forebears. Through this awakening, the real possibility and importance of Armenian-American interest groups became apparent, which quickly evolved into an agenda that continues to be partly contemporary and partly historical.

The Dynamic Nature of History: Chosen Glories and Chosen Trauma

All large groups possess memories and myths. These form the central building blocks of communal identity. Rituals, commemorations, school curricula and stories are all central features in the cycle of affirmation and reaffirmation of group identity. In protracted conflicts and conflicts that are considered unresolved by one group or the other, memories are mythologized as beliefs, sayings and identities and, as referenced above, become socialized and institutionalized within groups. They are transmitted and maintained through political, social and cultural channels. These are passed on to future generations, ultimately becoming a central element of communal identity. This, in turn, leads to what scholars refer to as the rigidification of identities. In cases where there is communication with members of "the Other" group, the communication will only serve to corroborate the negative image of the Other in the Self's mind. If the Self's Other was not perfidious and murderous before the advent of the distortions of memory and myth, the behavior of the Other demonstrates that they certainly are now.[156] In other words, the bad feelings and premonitions a group feels towards its opposite, the Other, often serve as self-fulfilling prophecies.

Volkan coined the term *chosen trauma* in order to precisely define the shared mental representation of an ill-starred and ruinous event or events. Correspondingly, Volkan notes that *chosen glories* are composed of ritualistic remembrances of

[156] Terrel A. Northrup. "The Dynamic of Identity in Personal and Social Conflict." *Intractable Conflicts and Their Transformation* (Syracuse: Syracuse University Press, 1989), 75-76.

events and heroes whose mental representations contain feelings of shared triumph and ascendancy among large group members.[157] Understanding chosen glories and chosen traumas, in particular, is crucial to understanding the trans-generational dissemination of historical events as outlined in the Millers' study of diaspora Armenians.[158] The remembrance and constant commemoration of these glories and traumas includes a combination of historical facts, fiction, fantasies of what may have occurred or will occur again, intense emotions that include pleasure and a defensive mechanism against undesirable feelings and painful memories.

All large groups ritually celebrate and commemorate memories of heroes and events. These commemorations and their mental representations conjure up shared feelings of success, triumph, patriotism and pride. These chosen glories - what can be referred to as group history or histories - simply change over time and have the possibility of becoming heavily mythologized. For instance, Robert Furman cites the example of what many people in the United States believe to be historical facts regarding the Pilgrims who settled Massachusetts Bay Colony.[159] Yet, the history of the Pilgrims' first years has been significantly altered or even replaced over the centuries by what have become myths. Thus, the celebration of the Thanksgiving Holiday every November by Americans is nothing more than an idealized account and retelling of what "our common American ancestors" accomplished; one in a long list of American chosen glories.

In essence, the Pilgrims, regardless of their bravery, perfidy or otherwise have become mythologized and their actions exaggerated in popular history to highlight what are now considered core values, ideals and principles of

---

[157] Vamık D. Volkan. "Large group identity and chosen trauma." 938-939.

[158] Miller and Miller.

[159] Robert A. Furman. "The Pilgrims: Myth and Reality." *Mind and Human Interaction,* 9 (1998), 5-17.

American large group identity.[160] These chosen glories, these ostensibly historical accounts – what children are taught in schools - are passed on to succeeding generations through commemorations and "…transgenerational transmissions made in parent/teacher-child interactions and through participation in ritualistic ceremonies recalling past successful events. Chosen glories link children of a large group with each other and with their large group, and the children experience increased self-esteem by being associated with such glories."[161]

Regardless of when events happened or individuals lived and died, the shared importance of such events sustains group identity and binds individuals together who form the large group. A leader, or cadre of leaders, of a large group may choose to recall already accepted and commemorated chosen glories and thereby stimulate the large group's self-esteem and sense of worth. For example, Russian President Vladimir Putin's decision in 2000 to reinstate the anthem of the Soviet Union, albeit with new words, could be viewed as calculated bid to recall the past glories and political power of the defunct USSR.[162] It also signaled a symbolically and stylistically abrupt departure from the humiliating and rudderless previous decade under the leadership of Boris Yeltsin. Putin's highly symbolic move also coincided with legislation that officially made the white, blue and red, pre-Soviet Union tricolor Russia's state flag and the tsarist-era, two-headed eagle the state symbol.[163] In one swift move, Putin managed to fuse the chosen glories of Soviet victories, global power and the nostalgia people felt for it with the pre-Communist, imagined glories of Russia's czarist rule, Orthodox Christianity and Russian nationalism.

---

[160] See Elizabeth Pleck. "The making of the domestic occasion: The history of Thanksgiving in the United States." *Journal of Social History* (1999): 773-789.

[161] Volkan. "Large Group Identity and Chosen Trauma," 939.

[162] Jane Henderson. "Rapports: Russia: Signs and Portents." *European public law* 8, no. 3 (2002): 321-332.

[163] J. Martin Daughtry. "Russia's new anthem and the negotiation of national identity." *Ethnomusicology* 47, no. 1 (2003): 42-67.

The impact on large group self-esteem is more complicated in cases where chosen trauma is valued, mythologized and commemorated in a large group identity over chosen glories. Chosen trauma can be defined as a shared mental representation of an event or series of events in which a large group is victimized by another group, thus causing it to experience feelings of helplessness and weakness through significant loss and death.[164] Thus, the large group collectively shares a massive injury, which, in turn, may become a deep and suppurating wound. Understanding chosen trauma is necessary to gain an understanding of the act of transgenerational transmission of past events.[165] Some may take offence to the use of the word "chosen" when paired with "trauma" since a large group cannot generally be said to consciously choose humiliation, exile, murder, rape and victimization. However, Volkan defends the term, explaining that "…large groups do make the unconscious choice to include mental representations of shared events as experienced and remembered by a past generation to their own identity."[166] Indeed, over the centuries, most large groups can be said to have experienced numerous traumatic events, yet only certain events remain alive in the shared psyche of the large group. That is, only some events, through their mental representations, remain visceral and "alive" over the years. "A chosen trauma reflects the traumatized past generation's incapacity for or difficulty with mourning losses connected to the shared traumatic event as well as its failure to reverse the injury to the group's self-esteem ("narcissistic injury") and humiliation inflicted by another large group, usually a geographical neighbor."[167]

As described in the Millers' study, there is far more to the transgenerational transmission of shared mental

---

[164] Vamık D. Volkan and Norman Itzkowitz. *Turks and Greeks: Neighbors in Conflict* (Cambridgeshire, England: Eothen Press, 1994)
[165] Ibid.
[166] Volkan, "Large Group Identity and Chosen Trauma," 940.
[167] Ibid.

representations than the process of children simply hearing stories from their parents, feeling acute transgenerational sympathy, mimicking their forebears' behavior and then transmitting these same stories, sympathies and behavior, in turn, to their own children.[168] "Rather, it is the end result of mostly unconscious psychological processes by which children's core identities are flooded with and therefore influenced by the injured self- and internalized object-images and associated affects that rightfully belong to the original victims, caregivers or parents."[169]

It is important to understand that people do not transmit "memories" of their experiences to their descendants; they only can transmit aspects of themselves – their own deposited self- and object-images. This is reason that the effects of chosen trauma are so intense; the representation of history in the chosen trauma is intimately bound up with the very foundations that support the identity of group members as individual human beings. This is also why chosen traumas are much more powerful as large group identity markers than are chosen glories. Chosen glories merely raise a large group's collective self-esteem. Chosen trauma necessarily includes complicated tasks such as mourning and attempts to reverse feelings of humiliation. However, like chosen glories, chosen traumas are often ritualistically commemorated.

The single date of April 24th has been chosen by the Armenian diaspora and the Republic of Armenia as Armenian Genocide Remembrance Day. Commemorations on this date are meant to encompass, in one day, a series of events that stretched from 1915-1923. Speeches are given, candles are lit, events are organized in order to re-establish and affirm group identity, cohesion and a sense of belonging. The events also galvanize political and material support to address the trauma that is daily lived and experienced by members of the diaspora community. As one young Armenian diaspora author wrote, "There are no

---

[168] Miller and Miller, 34.

[169] Volkan, "Large Group Identity and Chosen Trauma," 944.

limitations, no quantification to how much I care in regards to the Armenian Genocide and massacres committed by the Young Turk Government and Ottoman Empire in 1915... The fact remains that we have been robbed of our land. Robbed of our potential. Robbed of our ancestral integration. I, and like-minded individuals, have no resignations in mediocrity in regard to our nationality...As a half-breed and direct bi-product of the genocide's end result, I have never held a belief quite as close as this one and cannot imagine that I could."[170]

Mirroring this overwhelmingly important identity that is the driving force in the Armenian diaspora's campaign for genocide recognition, the commentator and journalist, Christian Garbis noted, "The horrors of 1915 continually plague the Armenians. They cannot be escaped because they cannot be forgotten... The Armenian Genocide has become their albatross, the anchor of their ancient ship at bay. They are so blinded by their torment that they cannot lay a course for their own future, a tranquil one that bears the fruit of a free nation, emerging as a phoenix from depressive darkness."[171]

It should be re-emphasized that the fateful and horrific events of 1915 constitute the defining characteristic of Armenianness, particularly that of the diaspora, often subsuming other forms of Armenianness. This is arguably detrimental as this chosen trauma form of Armenianness ignores thousands of years of Armenian history, empire, Christianity, language and art. These important and brilliant facets still survive and flourish in varied shapes, forms and locations across the globe. Armenians are truly an international people, inhabiting six continents. However, the events of 1915 brought the millennia-long evolution of collective identity formation in defined geographical locales

---

[170] Steve Tateossian. "April 24: Commemorative Date of Armenian Genocide." *Associated Content.*

[171] Christian Garbis. "The 'Religion' of Genocide: A Uniting Force Stronger than the Armenian Church and Language." *The Armenian Weekly: Armenian Genocide Insert*, 73, (16), April 12, 2007.

to an abrupt end. According to Razmik Panossian, the director of Rights and Democracy in Canada and author of *The Armenians: From Kings and Priests to Merchants and Commisars*, it is impossible to understand Armenian consciousness and identity without situating the events of 1915 front and center.[172] Accordingly, Panossian outlined six key factors that emerged directly from this tragedy and how they deeply affect what it means to be Armenian.

- Every Armenian is a victim. "Being Armenian meant being a survivor of Genocide, and therefore a member of a community of sufferers."
- The transformation of the diaspora into a community of Genocide victims. "Diaspora by definition was always associated with exile and hardship, but after 1915 these notions were magnified and reinforced. It was no longer a diaspora of merchants, laborers, fortune seekers, intellectuals and political exiles. Rather, it was of refugees, starving survivors and deeply scarred people."
- After 1915, the Armenian cause was territorialized and the focus came to be one of regaining the Armenian homeland; i.e. Anatolia. "Post-Genocide Armenian identity (especially in the diaspora) … came to be associated with a 'lost homeland' and the need to regain it."
- The Muslim and Turk, the historical Other for Armenians, came to represent evil after 1915. The wounds opened in 1915 have never healed and the concept of the "terrible Turk" was popularized and perpetuated in Armenian diaspora culture. "Turkishness was considered immoral, dirty and violent. Anti-Turkishness was therefore accepted as a 'natural' and inherently 'good' attitude."
- The politics of genocide recognition deeply affect Armenian diaspora political identity. The majority of

---

[172] Razmik Panossian. "The Impact of the Genocide on Armenian National Identity." Armenian Weekly 73, no. 16 (2007).

the work done by the diaspora lobbies centers on recognition of the events of 1915 as genocide in an effort to put pressure on Turkey. "Part of the Armenian effort has to do with the terminology used to refer to the events of 1915. Armenians insist on the use of the word genocide by the world community rather than the less forceful term massacres (which does not necessarily imply intent to eliminate a people)."

- The events of 1915 brought about a division that continues to this day in the evolution of eastern and western Armenian identity. Though the events wounded all Armenians symbolically, they physically only affected western Armenians, or those residing in the Ottoman Empire.[173]

Panossian's observations are illuminating and thought-provoking. Namely, two thousand years of brilliant Armenian history play a decidedly second tier role in the development and maintenance of diaspora Armenian identity. The events of 1915 are the key to understanding the Armenian diaspora's large group identity. These events also explain the divisions - symbolic and physical - between western and eastern Armenians, the former the descendants of Ottoman Armenians who inhabited what is now the Republic of Turkey and the latter inhabiting the Republic of Armenia. Yet perhaps the most prescient point Panossian makes is the sheer interconnectedness with the events of 1915 and diaspora attitudes, identities, history, prejudices, sorrow, anger and hatred. In contradistinction to what numerous scholars have attempted to demonstrate regarding centuries of Turkish tyranny and oppression of Armenians in the Ottoman Empire, Panossian identifies 1915 as the *beginning* of the development of the distinct Armenian Self and the Turkish Other. In other words, Turks and Armenians are not age-old enemies. The enmity felt by Armenians for Turks that has characterized the past

[173] Ibid.

one hundred years since 1915 were preceded by a largely amicable period that stretched over at least five centuries. Though enmity and mutual suspicion developed throughout the latter half of the nineteenth century and Ottoman Christians were always ultimately subservient to their Ottoman Muslim (Turkish) rulers, Armenian diaspora identity that posits the Self versus a "terrible Turk" Other was undeniably forged in the conflagration and demise of the Ottoman Empire and what had become an archaic and anachronistic Ottoman order in 1915.

On account of this conflagration, vast ideological, historic, linguistic and religious differences between Armenians were forgotten and often remain thus. This is because it was the Turk - via memories transmitted regarding the trauma of 1915 - who essentializes the Other for the Armenian Self. In this context, the word *Turk* is pejorative and references to "the Turks" are efforts to encapsulate an entire race throughout time and space as the opposite of what it means to be Armenian. In this vein, *"'If his ancestors were barbarians, he must be too; if his ancestors had expansionist tendencies, he too must have the same tendencies,'* and so on. Through this process of illustrating the 'other' historically, an eternal enemy is constructed; an enemy who, like 'us,' is immutable, unchanging, primordial. By collapsing time and historical contingency, identity is fully essentialized."[174]

Thus, the diaspora Armenian Self is not fully realized, indeed does not exist in its present state, without a fully essentialized Turkish Other. As will be demonstrated, this has and will continue to have major implications vis-à-vis the uncompromising nature of the diaspora campaign for genocide recognition, relations with Armenia, Turkey-Armenia relations, the intransigence of the official Turkish government position and any hope of reconciliation between these large groups: Turks, Armenians and diaspora Armenians.

---

[174] Spyrou. "Images of 'the Other': 'the Turk' in Greek Cypriot Children's Imaginations," 261. Author's emphasis.

Defining and Mobilizing Identity

A dialectic has emerged in the literature between a deterministic, primordialist and essentialist understanding of identity and one that, in being constructivist or modernist, sees in identity the possibility of reinvention and regeneration. In other words, the issue was and remains as follows: Do we exist as a nation (or large-group in Volkan's parlance)? If so, why are we the way we are? Is the nation or large-group simply a construct? Can we therefore construct our national or large-group identity in a particular, even tailored fashion?

Peter Lambert, a professor of Latin American politics, posits that the belief in a collective identity "… represents a way of thinking about the world, a framework from which others both within and outside the nation are viewed, providing people with an explanation both of what unites us, culturally, socially and politically, and what divides us from others outside the nation."[175] As such, national and, to some extent, ethnic identity both represent a symbolic, imagined community. Yet, regardless of how one approaches the issue, the question remains, where does fiction begin and where does it end?

Anthony Smith, an ethnicist working within the modernist framework, highlighted five concepts of crucial importance to the development and maintenance of an *ethnie,* or ethnic community: form, identity, myth/memory, symbol and communication. Smith noted that "form" is akin to style in that though symbolic content and meanings of communal creations may morph over time, their characteristic mode of expression remains the same. "Identity" refers to a sense of community based on history and culture rather than any conceptualization of collectivity or the concept of ideology. "The need for identification with a community in order to

---

[175] Peter Lambert, "Myth, Manipulation and Violence: Relationships between National Identity and Political Violence." *Political Violence and the Construction of National Identity in Latin America* (New York: Palgrave, 2006), 2.

achieve individual identity and self-respect, is in part a function of socialization experiences in the historic culture-community; and the modes and goals of identification are given by the group and its past experiences as they coalesce into a collective 'tradition.'"[176]

Smith argued that the core of ethnicity is composed of the closely inter-related concepts of myths, memories, values and symbols. Special emphasis should also be paid to the ethnie's "myth-symbol" complex and particularly the *mythomoteur* or constitutive myth of the ethnie. "Both indicate the vital role of myths and symbols as embodying the corpus of beliefs and sentiments which the guardians of ethnicity preserve, diffuse and transmit to future generations."[177] Smith noted that one must look at historical memories rather than ecological locations, class configurations or military and political relationships to understand the special qualities and durability of a particular ethnie. "One has to look at the nature (forms and content) of their myths and symbols, their historical memories and central values, which we can summarize as the 'myth-symbol' complex, at the mechanisms of their diffusion (or lack of it) through a given population, and their transmission to future generations, if one wishes to grasp the special character of *ethnic* identities."[178] Smith cited Greeks, Armenians, Jews, Persians, Chinese and Japanese as examples of ethnic continuity, since, despite massive cultural changes over the centuries, certain key identifying components - name, language, customs, religious community and territorial association - were broadly maintained and reproduced for millennia.[179]

Though Smith's primordialist theories have been justifiably criticized,[180] they are instructive regarding the way

---

[176]Anthony D. Smith. *The Ethnic Origins of Nations* (Cambridge, MA: Blackwell Publishing, 1996), 14.
[177] Ibid, 15.
[178] Ibid.
[179] Ibid, 191.
[180] See Montserrat Guibernau. "Anthony D. Smith on nations and national identity: a critical assessment." *Nations and Nationalism* 10, no.

diaspora Armenians view themselves and correspondingly, their identity, ethnicity and quest for genocide recognition. Vokan's theories of what he termed "time collapse" are also instructive. Time collapse is described as a large group's conscious and unconscious connections to a past trauma and an imagined or real, current threat, whereby a chosen trauma has been reactivated. "The reactivation of shared anxieties, expectations, fantasies, and defenses associated with the chosen trauma naturally magnifies the image of the current enemies and current conflicts. If the large group is now in a powerful position, the sense of revenge may become exaggerated, even ennobled. If the large group is in a powerless position, a current event may reanimate a shared sense of victimization."[181] Time collapse can lead to irrational or even sadistic decision-making by those in positions of power in the large group, which, in turn, can lead to the perpetration of irrational and cruel acts by members of the large group on individuals who they perceive to constitute the opposite of the Self; i.e. the Other. The conscious or unconscious aim of such decision-making and the acts they engender is a form of protection of the large group's shared identity.

An example of time-collapsed trauma and its reactivation is the history of ethnic Serbs in the late 1980s and early 1990s. In addition to the mobilization of popular Serbian opposition to and hatred of Muslim Bosnians, as highlighted previously, Serbian president Slobodan Milosevic, with help from key state and church ministers, was also able to popularly reactivate large group memories of the chosen trauma experienced by Serbs at the battle at *Kosovo Polje* (Field of Blackbirds). Indeed, the two are linked and hatred of Muslim Bosnians was transferred to hatred of Muslim Kosovars. The time-collapsed trauma in this case was the defeat suffered by Serbs on the battlefield in 1389,

---

1-2 (2004): 125-141. See also Timothy Baumann. "Defining ethnicity." *The SAA archaeological record* 4, no. 4 (2004): 12-14.

[181] Volkan. "Large-Group Identity and Chosen Trauma."

which resulted in the loss of Serbian sovereignty to invading Ottoman forces for the next five hundred years.

Milosevic and his cadre, by insisting on the re-entombment in Kosovo of Lazar, the Serbian leader killed at *Kosovo Polje*, reactivated collectively-held mental images of Lazar, the Serbian defeat at *Kosovo Polje* via the symbolism of Lazar's embalmed body. At the same time, Milosevic made an overtly, political statement that the province of Kosovo, regardless of ethnic constitution, was and would remain an integral part of Serbia.[182] In doing so, Milosevic unwittingly or wittingly provoked age-old grievances and opened the floodgates of collectively learned grief at their large group's defeat and humiliation in Kosovo in 1389.[183] Lazar's ritualistic re-entombment in Kosovo, for many Serbs, symbolized a return to imagined Serbian greatness. The perceived and real ability of Serbs to exact revenge and right past injustices, reversed feelings of loss, helplessness and shame that were a key fact of Serbian large group identity for centuries. "Mourners appeared to feel afresh affects appropriate to traumatized self-images, bonding the modern-day Serbs more closely together; individual Serbs' self-images became suffused with a new sense of common entitlement for revenge."[184]

Milosevic's reactivation of chosen trauma and the time collapse it produced arguably have played a large part in consolidating present-day, large-group identity among Serbs. It also firmly demarcated the Serb Self from its perceived

---

[182] Lazar's body was embalmed and originally entombed in Kosovo after his death on the battlefield in 1389. Later, as Ottoman troops advanced on Serbia proper, his mummified remains were moved to a monastery north of Belgrade. At the same time, the Battle of Kosovo's role as the Serb's chosen trauma crystallized and stories of the Serbs' glorious defense and defeat at the hands of the invading Muslim Ottoman were passed from generation to generation.

[183] See Agneza Bozic-Roberson. "Words before the war: Milosevic's use of mass media band rhetoric to provoke ethnopolitical conflict in former Yugoslavia." *East European Quarterly* 38, no. 4 (2004): 395-409. See also Thomas Emmert. "The Kosovo Legacy." *Serbian Studies* 5, no. 2 (1989): 5-32.

[184] Volkan, "Large-Group Identity and Chosen Trauma."

Other: Muslim Bosnians, Albanians and Kosovars. There is a direct link between the reactivation of a chosen trauma, time collapse and the atrocities subsequently committed against the Other large groups by Serbs. The Serbs, with their renewed sense of humiliation, entitlement and the capability to exact revenge for a military defeat that occurred a full seven centuries in the past, perceived Muslims in the region not as neighbors or compatriots (even though they had also been so for centuries), but as extensions of their eternal enemy and Other: Ottoman Muslim Turks.[185]

Correspondingly, an imagined, shared traumatic history is the strongest tie - the glue that bonds diaspora Armenians together. This, in turn, has become their strongest identity and thus *the* mobilizing force in their campaign for Armenian Genocide recognition. The chosen trauma of diaspora Armenians can be collapsed in the year 1915 and the tragic, murderous events that spanned the years 1915-1923. There are two events, in particular, that precipitated time collapses for Armenians: the wake-up call of terrorist acts targeting Turks that were perpetrated by diaspora Armenians in the 1970s and 1980s as discussed previously, and the independence of the Republic of Armenia in 1991. Both events had the cathartic effect of reawakening the humiliation and helplessness of 1915. Yet both events also allowed space for large group grief, thus enabling the reversal of that same humiliation, shame and pain.[186] While it could be argued that time collapse has not occurred because diaspora Armenians face no current threat, it could also be argued that the perceived threat from Turks or, rather, the reality of Armenian disappearance from Anatolian Turkey has never ceased since 1915, at least in

---

[185] Lynda E. Boose. "Crossing the River Drina: Bosnian rape camps, Turkish impalement, and Serb cultural memory." *Signs* 28, no. 1 (2002): 71-96.

[186] Tsypylma Darieva. "“The Road to Golgotha”: Representing Loss in Postsocialist Armenia." *Focaal* 2008, no. 52 (2008): 92-108.

diaspora minds.[187] The fact is that there are few to no Armenians in eastern Anatolia today – a vast region that hosted countless, vibrant Armenian communities for centuries.[188] Yet the reasons for this situation vary markedly from the Armenian campaign's narrative paradigm, as will be demonstrated in later chapters.

The diaspora Armenian narrative of what occurred in 1915 also revolves around the notion that complete annihilation was in store for the Armenians of the Ottoman Empire and it was only by the grace of God, luck, skill, fortitude, or a combination of all the above that some escaped. Furthermore, the independence of the Republic of Armenia in 1991 from the Soviet Union and the subsequent Armenian annexation of the Azeri territory of Nagorno-Karabakh awakened largely unfounded fears in the Armenian diaspora of renewed Muslim, Turkic aggression.[189] The traumatized self-image and the unconscious/conscious mental representations of reimagined events that were perpetrated in 1915 against their collective ancestors have morphed over time. These changes that have occurred along with accompanying, acute feelings of humiliation and shock have resulted in the Armenian diaspora's attempts to characterize the Ottoman Turks and their present-day offspring, the Turks, as genocidal agents capable of perpetrating the horrific events of 1915 - as reimagined in the diaspora's chosen trauma - over and over again.[190]

The Turkish government has pointedly refused to recognize the legitimacy of the Armenian diaspora's

---

[187] Michael M. Gunter. "The Historical Origins of the Turkish-Armenian Animosity." In *Armenian History and the Question of Genocide*, pp. 1-26. Palgrave Macmillan US, 2011.

[188] Tessa Hofmann. *Armenians in Turkey today: A critical assessment of the situation of the Armenian minority in the Turkish Republic*. Forum of Armenian Associations of Europe, 2003, 6.

[189] Svante E. Cornell. "Turkey and the Conflict in Nagorno Karabakh: A Delicate Balance," 66.

[190] Maral N. Attallah. *Choosing silence: The United States, Turkey, and The Armenian Genocide*. PhD diss., Humboldt State University, 2007, 67.

campaign of genocide recognition. Indeed, many scholars of Ottoman history have never accepted the diaspora's version of the events. The Armenian diaspora, in turn, views this Turkish "denial of historical and established facts" as further proof of Turkish perfidy and insincerity. In other words, the Turkish Other did, does and will continue to act as the Armenian Self's conscious and unconscious mental representations mirror; a self-fulfilling prophecy, so to speak. Thus, denial by the Turkish government and, by proxy, the Turkish population, of the events of 1915 as the Armenian Genocide is consistent with the diaspora's view of the Turkish Other. Indeed, Turkish denial is expected and is simply a by-product of the historical atrocities and the engendered trauma as remembered and mythologized by the Armenian diaspora.[191]

The ongoing fight for genocide recognition serves to reinforce the chosen identity of the many diaspora communities with their shared trauma serving as the cohesive bond that ties the communities together. In an article published in the *Armenian Weekly*, Christian Garbis wrote, "The Armenian Genocide has beat out the church and language as the key uniting force of Armenian nationhood in diasporan communities, for they are comprised mainly of families whose extended members have suffered during the tragedy as well as its aftermath…"[192] Garbis added "Armenians currently present themselves as being the victims of the first genocide of the twentieth century, rather than for their possession of a rich cultural legacy and a distinct, ancient language. The Genocide's acceptance is worshipped in the sense that people still struggle in coming to terms with the understanding that a tragedy occurred of some magnitude and thus still search for limitless knowledge to prove that the events did take place, not to mention the overwhelming desire to spread the gospel of the Armenian Genocide.

---

[191] Aida Alayarian. *Consequences of Denial: The Armenian Genocide.* Karnac Books, 2008, 34.
[192] Garbis.

Armenians are clearly obsessed—many live with the Genocide every day of their lives, imagining the horrors in their minds, studying it, finding modern comparisons to it, sifting through news articles daily for references to it. Others toil relentlessly at finding strategies for politically promoting the Genocide's recognition by government bodies."[193]

As alluded to, this potent and powerful identity – what Garbis termed as an obsession for some – is strengthened and, indeed, invigorated by the official stance of successive Turkish governments regarding the Armenian diaspora's campaign for genocide recognition. Turkey argues that massacres occurred in 1915, but that they were mutual massacres in a time of war. Many Turks feel the issue has been overtly politicized and is an historical matter better left to historians. "The Turkish government and the overwhelming majority of Turks, as well as other governments and many scholars or experts, reject the qualifying of the tragic events of 1915 as genocide, because the legal conditions incorporated in the 1948 Genocide Convention which are a *sine qua non*, especially the *dolus specialis*, the intent to destroy as such, were not fulfilled."[194]

Turkey's subsequent blockade of Armenia over its forceful annexation of the Azerbaijani province of Nagorno-Karabakh further kept alive diaspora memories of the trauma suffered at the hands of their Other, the "terrible Turk," past, present and future.[195] Indeed, "…the politicization of the Genocide had served, wittingly or unwittingly, to create the mentality and psychology that

---

[193] Ibid.

[194] Pulat Tacar and Maxime Gauin. "State Identity, Continuity, and Responsibility: The Ottoman Empire, the Republic of Turkey and the Armenian Genocide: A Reply to Vahagn Avedian." *European Journal of International Law* 23, no. 3 (2012): 825-826.

[195] R. G. Suny. "Writing Genocide: The Fate of the Ottoman Armenians." In *A Question of Genocide: Armenians and Turks at the End of the Ottoman Empire*. Suny, R.G., Göçek, F.M., and Naimark, N.N. (eds.) New York: Oxford University Press, 2011: 20-21.

Turkey, through its non-recognition of the Genocide, is likely to repeat it, that Turkey is the eternal enemy."[196]

The idea that Turkey's denial of the events of 1915 as genocide is tantamount to the Turks committing the atrocity all over again was echoed by a representative of a now-defunct Armenian-American lobbying group.[197] According to this representative, Turkey's recognition of the atrocities committed in 1915 as the Armenian Genocide would serve as an explicit barrier to Turkey and the Turks - as heirs to the Ottoman Empire - from ever perpetrating genocide again (presumably against anyone, but necessarily against Armenians). Accordingly, the security of Armenia would be advanced and recognition by Turkey that the events of 1915 constituted the Armenian Genocide would then liberate the two communities. They would then be able to deal constructively with each other and discuss the consequences of this crime. The Armenian-American lobbying group representative noted that this would be a true discourse as opposed to what was clearly deemed to be the present, Turkish denial of genocide and Turkey's demands regarding the return of Nagorno-Karabakh to Azerbaijan. For the representative and presumably other diaspora Armenians, recognition by Turkey of the events of 1915 as genocide is a zero-sum game. Without Turkey's explicit admission of its guilt through recognition, Armenians feel as though they necessarily face the possibility of another massacre at the hands of Turks.[198]

---

[196] Gerard Libaridian. "The New Thinking Revisited." *Libaridian speaks at Princeton University*, May 9, 1998.

[197] Excerpts from an interview with an Armenian-American lobbying representative, conducted at USAPAC Headquarters, 1518 K St., N.W., Ste. M, Washington, D.C. on 08 June 2007. As of 2016, USAPAC is no longer in existence. Information is sparse and it is unclear what led to USAPAC's demise or when it occurred.

[198] Ibid.

Diasporic Nationalism

The related concepts of diaspora and diasporic nationalism add further definition and nuance to the conceptualization of an individual's or group's ethnicity. For example, "The prevailing definition of diaspora seems to be a group that recognizes its separateness based on common ethnicity/nationality, lives in a host country and maintains some kind of attachment to its home country or homeland."[199] In addition, the definition of diaspora may also include references to overt or latent tendencies towards political action. Indeed, some have argued that diasporas are difficult to catalog as the term applies to groups with different origins; i.e. migrants, refugees, expatriates and exiles.[200] Furthermore, diasporas overlap and individuals can belong to more than one diaspora group. Yet, like nationalities, diaspora members self-identify and, as such, are capable of exhibiting dynamic behavior. This means that events - past or present – that affect their country of origin may cause a diaspora member living in a host country to self-identify with other diaspora members hailing from the same country of origin when they may not necessarily have considered themselves as such previously. When this occurs, the same diaspora member may become active politically, personally and financially in causes that are deemed to affect their country of origin. Analogously, certain events may lead presently active diaspora members to halt their political, personal or financial support for initiatives affecting the country of origin.[201]

A study carried out by the World Bank on the potential power of diaspora groups found that "…by far the strongest effect of war or the risk of subsequent war works through diasporas… the risk of renewed conflict is around six times higher in the societies with the largest diasporas in

---

[199] William J. Lahneman, *Impact of Diaspora Communities on National and Global Politics: Report on Survey of the Literature* (College Park, MD: CISSM, University of Maryland, 2005), 1.
[200] Ibid, 3.
[201] Ibid, 6-7.

America than in those without American diasporas..."[202] This is by far the most startlingly bellicose indication of the powerful impact diasporas may exhibit on the international scene, yet it is not necessarily the most indicative. Multiple studies as well as media reports have highlighted the influence of Vietnamese, Greek, Chinese, Indian, Tamil, Kurdish and Cuban diaspora groups on international behavior.[203]

The impact of diaspora groups on social, economic and political processes and pressures is felt as part of a wider process of migration and refugee dilemmas in a host country. Diasporas can also open political channels for conflict prevention, causation and/or intervention in a host country precisely because they are national minorities. Diasporas may provide the pretense for state or non-state acts of irredentism – the effort by a group or actor to "recover" territory either peopled by ethnic kin or perceived

---

[202] Paul Collier and Anke Hoeffler. *Greed and Grievances in Civil War.* Policy Working Paper 2344 (Washington, D.C: World Bank, 2000).
[203] For example, see Terrence Lyons and Peter Mandaville. *Politics from afar: transnational diasporas and networks.* (2013). See also Maria de los Angeles Torres, "Encuentros y Encontronazos: Homeland in the Politics and Identity of the Cuban Diaspora," *Diaspora*, vol. 4, no. 2 (Fall 1995). See also Monika Hess and Benedikt Korf. "Tamil diaspora and the political spaces of second-generation activism in Switzerland." *Global Networks* 14, no. 4 (2014): 419-437. See also Singh, Milan, and Anita Singh. "Diaspora, Political Action, and Identity: A Case Study of Canada's Indian Diaspora." *Diaspora: A Journal of Transnational Studies* 17, no. 2 (2014): 149-171. See also Berkowitz, Lenka, and Liza M. Mügge. "Transnational Diaspora Lobbying: Europeanization and the Kurdish Question." *Journal of Intercultural Studies* 35, no. 1 (2014): 74-90. See also Kieu-Linh Caroline Valverde. *Transnationalizing Viet Nam: Community, Culture, and Politics in the Diaspora*. Philadelphia, PA: Temple University Press, 2012. See also Michael Fullilove. "Chinese Diaspora carries Torch for Old Country." *Financial Times* August 29, 2008; http://www.brookings.edu/opinions/2008/0519_china_fullilove.aspx?rssid=china. See also Manos Tsilimidis. "A Life in the Service of the Greek Diaspora." *Ekathimerini, English Edition*, September 21, 2006, http://www.ekathimerini.com/4dcgi/news/content.asp?aid=74476.

to be historically part of homeland. Some scholars have argued that diaspora groups often challenge the traditional state institutions of citizenship and loyalty.[204] Others have demonstrated that they are a salient feature of the relationship between international and domestic politics.[205] Because diasporas reside outside their kin-state, but claim a licit interest in it, they defy the conventional meaning of the state. Diaspora groups "… are therefore defined as the 'paradigmatic Other of the nation-state,' as challengers of its traditional boundaries, as transnational transporters of cultures and as manifestations of 'de-territorialized communities.'"[206]

Once politicized, actual mobilization characteristics vary widely among diaspora communities. Some, including the Chinese and Indian diasporas, have been able "… to exert sufficiently focused, organized and powerful influence to make them significant actors in international affairs."[207] Many diasporas use networks to coordinate activities. These diaspora networks often take the form of civic organizations, associations and interest groups, some without ties to host country or homeland governments. In some cases, diaspora networks may be government-sponsored (predominantly by the homeland government rather than the host government) and may be based in the homeland, host country/countries, or both. In the case of many networks, including that of the Armenian diaspora, they promote public works projects in the homeland by utilizing contributions made from members of the diaspora

---

[204] See Charles King and Neil J. Melvin. "Diaspora Politics: Ethnic Linkages, Foreign Policy and Security in Eurasia," *International Security* 24, no. 3 (1999/2000): 108-38. See also Michael Mandelbaum, ed. *The New European Diasporas: National Minorities and Conflict in Eastern Europe* (New York: Council on Foreign Relations Press, 2000).

[205] Yossi Shain and Barry Bristman. "The Jewish Security Dilemma." *Orbis* 46, no. 1 (2002): 47-72.

[206] Yossi Shain and Aharon Barth. "Diasporas and International Relations Theory." *International Organization* 57 (Summer 2003): 449-479.

[207] Ibid, 8.

community as well as lobbying for funds from the host country government. In some instances, networks may operate as independent variables. That is, the network may seek to further the agenda of its members rather than those of the diaspora large group.[208]

A specific type of diasporic nationalism occurs when citizenship in a worldwide diaspora, for example the Indian or Chinese diasporas, resonates with immigrants and their offspring. This citizenship often places emphasis on the "home" country, whether or not the home country exists, *de facto* or *de jure*. These phenomena are not just products of homesickness or simple sentimentality, rather diasporic nationalists care deeply about specific issues and conditions in the homeland, especially regarding regime-type. Instances of strong diasporic nationalism are particularly prevalent among groups whose homeland is felt to be neither fully autonomous nor secure.[209]

The discussion and conceptualization of diaspora and diasporic nationalism necessarily leads to a further term and theory, that of transnationality. Instances of transnationality are apparent in a particular diaspora group when these groups exhibit "the ability and willingness… to participate simultaneously in their homelands and in their receiving societies."[210] Investment is a major form of participation in the diaspora's homeland. Investment is increasingly easy for diaspora groups and high-speed travel as well as the ability of many groups to continue voting in their homeland's elections ensures their continued participation, pressure and presence.[211]

---

[208] Ibid, 9.

[209] Matthew Frye Jacobson. *Special Sorrows: The Diasporic Imagination of Irish, Polish and Jewish Immigrants in the United States* (Berkeley, CA: University of California Press, 2002), 16-18.

[210] David A. Gerber and Alan M. Kraut, eds. *American Immigration and Ethnicity: A Reader*, (New York: Palgrave, 2005), 58.

[211] See Eliud Githiga Muchiri. *Impact of remittances inflows on economic growth in Kenya*. PhD diss., University of Nairobi, 2014. See also Jean-Michel Lafleur. *Transnational politics and the state: The external voting rights of diasporas*. Routledge, 2013.

Several diverse paths of influence exist when it comes to diaspora involvement in politics. They include:

• A diaspora tries to affect home country government policies.

• A diaspora tries to affect host country government policies.

• Home country government tries to tap into diaspora resources for its own purposes, usually for economic gain or to sway host country government or popular opinion.

• Host country government tries to tap into diaspora resources for its own purposes, which can include policies to reduce the diaspora's influence.

• Diaspora supports rebel movements.

• Rebel movement exploits diaspora (element of extortion).

• Diaspora supports criminal activity.

• Ethnically-based criminal network exploits diasporas (element of extortion).

• Diasporic civic associations play an increasingly important role in managing agendas to bring about desired outcomes.[212]

The possibility of a generational difference or divergence should be noted when addressing the issue of influence wielded by diaspora communities. In some cases, politically-active diasporas may consist entirely of first- and second-generation immigrants. In other cases, such as that of the Armenian and Jewish diasporas, political activism has proven much more resilient and has transcended several generations. One explanation for the activism exhibited by these particular groups may be the diasporic nationalism brought on by the lack of a viable, autonomous, secure state over the course of several centuries. Even after the birth of

---

[212] Lahneman, 9.

Israel and the Republic of Armenia, a siege mentality remains and is a powerful marker of identity, for residents of these states and, to a lesser extent, their diaspora cousins.[213]

The characteristics of the host country's assimilation dynamics, which may heavily shape a diaspora's durability, represent another variable in diaspora transnationalism. Even in immigrant communities such as the Irish and Armenians with long histories in host countries, "...there are many examples from the distant past of transnationalism among immigrants, when travel and communication were more challenging. There is also evidence of the continuing interest among immigrants in their past, not only in maintaining ties with family, kin, and friends in their homelands, but also in being involved in homeland politics and social affairs."[214] Indeed, personal identities largely rest on a continuity between one's past and present. Rarely do people break from their past completely, nor do they "... banish familiar relationships and memories from the heart or mind."[215]

There is evidence that certain immigrant communities lose touch with their homelands or, at the very least, certain generations emphasize assimilation in the "receiving society." If this occurs, later generations may reify and breathe new life into their ethnic identity with a corresponding interest in the politics of that identity.[216]

Certain studies and their corresponding terms and concepts may shed some light on the "sliding scale" of ethnic identity amongst immigrants in receiving societies. An example is Herbert Gans' model of *symbolic ethnicity*.

---

[213] See Neta Oren. "The Jewish–Israeli Ethos of Conflict." In *A Social Psychology Perspective on The Israeli-Palestinian Conflict*. Springer International Publishing, 2016: 115-131. See also Dennis Sammut. "Armenia–Stuck between a rock and a hard place." *The South Caucasus* (2015): 48.

[214] Gerber and Kraut, 58-59.

[215] Ibid.

[216] Jessica Muñoz. "Mexican Identity Beyond Labels, Beyond Borders." *Sociology Honors Projects*. Paper 46, (2014): 5.

Awash in a relentlessly homogenizing mass culture, Gans argues that third and fourth-generation diaspora members or *ethnics* can "…find their identity by affiliating with an abstract collectivity which does not exist as an interacting group. That collectivity… can be mythic or real, contemporary or historical."[217] These embraced identities are expressed only intermittently, as most people "…refrain from ethnic behavior that requires an arduous or time-consuming commitment."[218] For example, ethnic expression is largely a leisure time pursuit in the case of white European ethnics.[219]

The concept of symbolic ethnicity may explain the reification and salience amongst various ethnic and diaspora communities living in host countries of language, types of dress, food and cultural norms. However, it does little to provide insight into the high degree of diasporic nationalism and transnationality exhibited by certain diaspora groups, such as that of the global Armenian diaspora.[220]

The diasporic nationalism of late-nineteenth-century Polish, Irish and Jewish immigrants to the United States, as discussed by Matthew Frye Jacobson, whose homelands were either colonized or not yet established is instructive and shares a similar set of factors that contributed to the development of Armenian diasporic nationalism.[221] A nation-state for Armenians did not come into existence, except for a brief interlude in the late nineteen-teens, until the fall of the Soviet Union in 1991. And while diaspora Armenians, regardless of political persuasion, continued to advocate for the independence of an eastern Armenian state from Russian and then Soviet domination, the memories held by most diaspora members in Lebanon, France and

---

[217] Herbert J. Gans. "Symbolic Ethnicity: The Future of Ethnic Groups and Cultures in America," *Ethnic and Racial Studies,* 2:1 (January 1979), 8.

[218] Ibid.

[219] Mary C. Waters. *Ethnic Options: Choosing Identities in America* (Berkeley: University of California Press, 1990), 1-15.

[220] Gregg, 5-16.

[221] Jacobson.

elsewhere - and those they transmitted to their offspring - involved geography to the west of what constituted Soviet Armenia and today's Republic of Armenia. Diaspora Armenians in Fresno, Marseille and Mexico City remembered the trauma suffered in 1915 at the hands of the Ottoman Turks in Anatolia, in what is today the Republic of Turkey. Thus, diaspora Armenians who hail from what is today's Turkey – what they refer to as western Armenia - possess an identity, memories and traumas different from those of their cousins living further east under Russian and then Soviet rule. For diaspora Armenians, their lost homeland was and remains under Turkish domination, not Russian or Soviet. Their memories, distilled and re-fashioned in diverse locales far from the homeland, were of Ottoman Turkish massacres and rape, not Russian and Soviet exile, starvation, massacres and purges. Given these contingencies, diaspora Armenians have developed a highly emotional, powerful and perhaps insoluble nationalism, focused not so much on territory, but memory. The area referred to as "Armenia" on today's map is not *their* Armenia.[222]

Just as the Irish had and continue to have reimagined memories of the potato famine, humiliation and colonization, the Jews also remember and "never forget" the many centuries of discrimination, theft and pogroms. The Armenian diaspora communities brought memories and experiences to various host countries, and subsequently distilled and transmitted these shared memories to their offspring of Ottoman humiliation, discrimination and massacres.

The memories of collectively experienced traumas shared by all three large groups have been codified and reified over the years. In the Armenian case, the memories are encapsulated as The Genocide; for the Jews it is The Holocaust; for the Irish it is The Famine. The stories

[222] Susan P. Pattie. "Longing and belonging: Issues of homeland in Armenian diaspora." *PoLAR: Political and Legal Anthropology Review* 22, no. 2 (1999): 80-92.

transmitted by grandparents, parents and social structures within diaspora communities to children and grandchildren tell of horror and helplessness in the face of unrelenting cruelty and brutality. The memories are also punctuated with images and examples of bravery, self-sacrifice and resistance against the odds in the face of evil oppressors. There is also an element of the David versus Goliath narrative shared by these three large groups that is lionized in commemorations, education, stories and histories, thus informing their identities and what can be termed the collective, large group soul.

Myth, memories and time combine with the stark reality of events to form an overarching and, ultimately, simplified narrative; an ideological representation. The popular Irish narrative therefore emphasizes how the fledgling Irish nation bravely battled the most powerful empire in the world and, against all odds, succeeded in finally establishing the Republic of Ireland.[223] The overarching Jewish narrative describes and documents the pogroms, massacres and finally the Nazi Holocaust, suffered only by European Jewry but now remembered and commemorated collectively by all Jews. Some survived these tragedies and eventually assisted in the establishment of a Jewish homeland in the form of the state of Israel. The Armenian narrative, divorced from the historical record, emphasizes how the smaller Armenian nation suffered centuries of oppression and domination under the "Turkish yoke" culminating in massacres, deportations, ethnic cleansing and starvation through an exhaustively planned and well-organized campaign of extermination.[224]

Importantly, and somewhat problematic for the framed, historical picture of victimhood framed for public

---

[223] See Cormac Ó. Gráda. *Black '47 and Beyond: The Great Irish Famine in History, Economy, and Memory*. Princeton University Press, 2000.
[224] Vahakn N. Dadrian. *The History of the Armenian Genocide: Ethnic Conflict from the Balkans to Anatolia to the Caucasus*. New York, Oxford: Berghahn Books, 2003. See also Vahakn N. Dadrian. *Warrant for Genocide: Key elements of Turko-Armenian Conflict*. Transaction Publishers, 1999.

consumption by the diaspora as part of its campaign for genocide recognition, the Armenian diaspora narrative also places special emphasis on armed resistance, siege and combat.[225] This narrative highlights acts of brave – even suicidal – revolt and resistance against a perceived Turkish, Muslim horde. Exploits of Armenians characterized variously as revolutionaries or freedom fighting guerrillas are remembered in stories and myths with Robin Hood-like qualities while patently ignoring the very real atrocities committed by Ottoman Armenians.[226] For example, James Mandalian wrote in the 1960s of Armenian guerrillas who were popularly known as *Fedayee.*

"[They] roamed the hillsides and the plains defending the hard-pressed peasants and redressing wrongs, executing revolutionary justice and inflicting punishment on the tormentors of their people…It might be truthfully said that the Fedayee was the finest and noblest creation of the Armenian revolution. Dedicated to the cause of his people, fearless in battle, chivalrous toward women, generous to his foes and yet terrible in his vengeance, the Armenian Fedayee renounced the comforts and pleasures of life, gave up his family and loved ones, endured the privation and suffering of a wanderer's life, and became a living Madagh [sacrificial offering] for the liberation of his people."[227]

Historical memories such as those of the Armenian Fedayee, the Irish rebel or the Filipino freedom fighter – the foundational texts that set one diaspora group apart from natives and other large groups alike – lead to the continued salience of a group's diasporic nationalism, distinctiveness and, ultimately, their organizational power. Correspondingly, and writing specifically about diaspora communities in the United States, Jacobson noted "… the

---

[225] Gerard Chaliand and Yves Ternon. *The Armenians, from Genocide to Resistance.* Zed Press, 1983.

[226] McCarthy. *Death and Exile*, 179, 187-193, 196-208.

[227] James G. Madalian, ed. and trans. *Armenian Freedom Fighters: The Memoirs of Rouben der Minasian* (Boston: Hairenik Association, 1963); 19-20.

ebb and flow of ethnic identification itself may usefully be examined in the transnational context of America's many diaspora communities and the turbulent politics of their overseas homelands. The so-called Troubles in Ulster, that is, may be part of what keeps the Irish in America, Irish."[228]

Issues related to the homeland, particularly the issue of foreign domination, seem to act as mobilizers of diasporic nationalism and activism more than what could be termed more bread and butter issues that may be tied to the more personal or familial. However, are the Irish in America still Irish though the Troubles in Ulster are, in large part, over? Are Armenians in France or Canada any less Armenian because the events of 1915 are long past? The answer is unequivocally no. This is because the reimagined and relived traumas have become part and parcel of both the Irish and Armenian diaspora large group identities.

Marilyn Halter, a professor of history and American Studies, has attempted to explain ethnic awakenings, pride and the longevity of memory amongst various ethnic groups in the United States. She noted that though nostalgia shapes a large amount of the emotional consistency of movements for ethnic heritage retention, another profound factor among certain groups has been a perceived history of oppression as a basis of shared identity. "An important element of a renewed ethnic consciousness can be the revelations of the hardships and indignities that one's ancestors may have suffered."[229]

Utilizing the cases of Irish-Americans and Armenian-Americans, Halter demonstrates the importance of shared trauma and its definitional effects on diaspora identity. For Irish-Americans, St. Patrick's Day has a special meaning and pride of place, regardless of aggressive marketing in the United States that casts everyone as "Irish for a day," encourages the wearing green, the drinking of green beer and plasters images of hapless leprechauns everywhere. The

---

[228] Ibid, 5-6.

[229] Marilyn Halter. *Shopping for Identity: The Marketing of Ethnicity* (New York: Schocken Books, 2000), 87-88.

irony of all this good humor and good luck, at least for many Irish-Americans, is that their large group memories and constructed identity are largely composed of remembered sorrows, hardships and their status as the perennial underdog. For example, a piece in the *New York Times* occasioned by an annual St. Patrick's Day commemoration, told the stories of Irish-Americans who worked in the copper mines of Butte, Montana at the turn of the twentieth century, replete with themes of sorrow, loss, underdog status and, ultimately, triumph.

"Butte was a hard-edged, dirty, dangerous town on the crest of the Continental Divide, and if a single man lived to his 30th birthday he was considered lucky. Yet entire [Irish] parishes left the emerald desperation of County Cork for the copper mines of Butte, fleeing a land where British occupiers had once refused to let mothers educate their children, and where famine had killed a million people in seven years' time."[230]

An Irish-American man tending graves in a cemetery in Butte stated, "The thing about the Irish is that we have always been there for the little guy. We go through life as underdogs. We die as underdogs. There is no other way for the Irish."[231]

Jim Berry, a third-generation Irish-American who founded the Boston Police Gaelic Column in 1992, "awakened" to the importance of Irish history, oppression and the centrality of his Irish roots only later in life. When his brother-in-law lost his house and business, Berry cast about for what to say to someone who had lost "everything."

"I sat down and said that you are two generations away from people that have suffered through having their farms taken away. They were tenants on their own land. Even though they were farming it, they were paying rents to other people. And those rents had to be paid. If they weren't paid,

---

[230] Timothy Egan, "True Irish," *New York Times,* March 12, 2008.
[231] Ibid.

they starved. They were thrown off. Their buildings were taken down, and the land went to someone else."[232]

By using this example, Berry compared his brother-in-law's desperate situation with that of their real or imagined Irish ancestors. Berry drew inspiration from his identity and drew strength from the idea that previously his Irish forebears had come through tough times, survived and even thrived.

Armenian-Americans also tend to emphasize their historical oppression, victimization and their current victimhood status. A twenty-three-year-old resident of Watertown, Massachusetts, Christine Manavian, explained the centrality of the century-old event to her identity as well as that of the Armenian diaspora, writ large. "It's because we were challenged and there was a chance for our language and lives to be lost. From day one you're taught to learn your language and preserve your culture. If I don't speak Armenian with my brother, my parents just start [speaking Armenian] with us."[233]

An Armenian-American attending college explained that the older he became, the more he valued his Armenian identity. "The more education one receives, the easier it becomes to see the value of one's ethnic identity… there are very few Armenians on this [college] campus, yet rather than view that fact as negative, I thrive on it. I jump at every chance I can get to talk about being Armenian, Armenia, or the genocide… ethnicity is a vital part of a person's identity. For Armenians in particular, this struggle for [genocide] recognition and distinction is vital. The genocide shattered the Armenian community into fragmented populations worldwide. The remembrance of these events, as for the victims of the Nazi Holocaust, is critical to the survival of the Armenian people."[234]

Timothy Egan, in writing about the Irish of Butte, Montana, argued that every family and thus, every ethnic

---

[232] Halter, 88.
[233] Ibid, 90.
[234] Ibid, 90-91.

group must possess a "…guiding narrative – sometime more mythic than real. For the Irish, *misery* is our currency, and the key to all Irish story-telling."[235]

Victimhood as Identity

Despite the real or imagined exploits of Ottoman Armenians against the Ottoman state and Ottoman Muslims and their importance as a facet underpinning Armenian diaspora identity, the trauma of 1915 and its terrible legacy take primacy. As such, for diaspora Armenians, an even stronger sense of diasporic national consciousness has developed, that of victim. Victimhood can be said to haunt as well as define the identity of Armenians. Yet they are by no means alone. According to Ian Buruma, the idea of victimhood also "… haunts Hindu nationalists… African-Americans, American Indians, Japanese-Americans, and homosexuals who have adopted AIDS as a badge of identity."[236] In the diaspora Armenian case, this victimhood is reflected in literature, histories, film and art. The idea of victimhood is further entrenched and perpetuated on a yearly basis through commemorations of the Armenian Genocide held on April 24th.

The events of 1915, whether they will ever be classified legally as constituting genocide or not, "Became the defining moment – the founding 'moment' – of contemporary Armenian identity."[237] Post-1915 Armenians, particularly in the diaspora, now see themselves in terms of historical "firsts." The Armenian large group constitutes the first Christian nation and members of the large group were first victims of genocide.[238]

---

[235] Egan. My emphasis.
[236] Ian Buruma. "The Joys and Perils of Victimhood." *New York Review of Books* 46 (1999): 4.
[237] Razmik Panossian. "The Impact of the Genocide on Armenian National Identity." *The Armenian Weekly: Armenian Genocide Insert*, 73, (16), April 21, 2007.
[238] Ibid.

Victimhood is problematic, however. Referring to the public discourse about genocide and victimhood in Europe in the early 21st century, the historian Pieter Lagrou presciently noted, "... victims of contemporary crimes and human rights violations occupy only a modest place on the political agenda. They seem increasingly marginalized by the claims for public attention for crimes belonging to a distant past – crimes for which no redress is possible and no political action prescribed to stop or prevent them. This discourse is exclusively retrospective and is increasingly ritualized to strengthen communal bonds and assert identity claims."[239]

Referencing actions by the Armenian diaspora and others to legislate genocide commemoration and recognition, Lagrou added, "A commemorative discourse of victimhood is very much the opposite of a constructive and dynamic engagement with the present, but rather a paralyzing regression of democratic debate."[240] Indeed, "the notion of victimhood is non-partisan. It does not tolerate contradiction and operates a consensual and inclusive partitioning between a suffering humanity of victims on the one hand, and a minority of unredeemable perpetrators who have set themselves beyond the pale of humanity, on the other."[241] The notion of victimhood is, at its core, about establishing and cementing a sense of identity, community and belonging. It is also exclusionary, particularistic and largely aimed at communitarian recognition. It is no surprise then that the identity-driven campaign to recognize the events of 1915 as the world's first genocide demonizes Turks as unreformed "genocidal agents" capable of committing genocide again and again. This is a direct reflection of the exclusionary nature of victimhood. One that, while claiming to rest on reality and history, fully and

---

[239] Pieter Lagrou. "Europe as a Place for Common Memories? Some Thoughts on Victimhood, Identity and Emancipation form the Past." In Muriel Blaive and Christian Gerbel. *Clashes in European Memory: The Case of Communist Repression and the Holocaust*. Studienverlag, 2011: 283.

[240] Ibid.

[241] Ibid.

willfully ignores the complex situations, conditions and events that heralded and directly produced the horrendous events that occurred in the year 1915.

The massacres, deportations and ethnic cleansing that occurred in 1915 took place in eastern Anatolia, just one of many corners in the vast Ottoman Empire. Yet by focusing solely on localized events, the Armenian diaspora and the scholars who support diaspora assertions that the events constituted the Armenian Genocide necessarily isolate the events from any sort of wider context. In reality, a series of extremely interconnected and complicated events occurred at the intersection of Great Power politics and a world war that resulted in the demise of at least three, centuries-old, agrarian empires: Russian, Ottoman and Austro-Hungarian. These events occurred, perhaps only could have occurred, after close to one century of regional and national political revolutions, population exchanges, ethnic cleansing inspired by rabid nationalism and the advent of modernity resulting in cataclysmic, violent changes. Armenians of the Ottoman Empire were both players and pawns at the dawn of a new age and the birth of the bloodiest century, to date. As such, they are neither wholly innocent nor wholly guilty of what befell them. Yet, "reducing the international debate on the dissolution of the Ottoman Empire to the Armenian genocide… generates a partly legitimate sense of injustice and frustration [among scholars, historians etc]. This is potentially a debate that engages with some of the most urgent challenges of international politics today, both in the Middle East and South Eastern Europe (Sykes-Picot and Balfour, Sèvres and Lausanne, internationally endorsed ethnic cleansing, Islam and secularism, the creation of Iraq and Lebanon, Arab nationalism and Zionism…) - a process in which historical responsibilities for catastrophic outcomes are largely shared by all the major players of the time and not only the issue of the Turkish State admitting or denying the legal definition of genocide to qualify one specific set of crimes."[242]

---

[242] Lagrou, 285.

Internal Conflict and Symbiotic Marketing Relationships

As mentioned earlier, the importance of both ethnicity and diasporic nationalism are key and crucial for scholars in understanding immigrant communities and their offspring. Benjamin Alexander notes that two further points of emphasis may be useful for scholars of ethnic groups in the future. The first of these is internal conflict. That is "the dynamics by which members of an ethnic population disagree and debate over what perceptions and aspirations the groups should collectively express."[243] Arguably when a large portion of an ethnic group's identity revolves around struggle and a particular emphasis on the status of the "mother country," it may be assumed that multiple ideas regarding the definition of the vision and goals of the group will be exhibited.[244] This helps explain on one level why there are multiple Armenian-American lobbying organizations, as discussed below.

Benjamin Alexander highlights a second point of emphasis, that of a *symbiotic marketing relationship*. In this type of marketing, "visions of peoplehood" or nationhood as well as certain political ideologies coupled with goals are marketed along with items that are actually marketable: print and non-print media, membership to organizations and admission to events that promote an ethnic group's cultural exceptionality through food, music, dress and continued use of the homeland's vernacular.

"The concept of a symbiotic marketing relationship requires some clarification. Most importantly, it does not imply passivity or reluctance on the part of the general

---

[243] Benjamin F. Alexander, 7.

[244] See Victor Greene. *For God and Country: The Rise of Polish and Lithuanian Ethnic Consciousness in America, 1860-1910* (Madison, WI: The State Historical Society of Wisconsin, 1975). See also June Granatir Alexander. *Ethnic Pride, American Patriotism: Slovaks and Other New Immigrants in the Interwar Era* (Philadelphia, PA: Temple University Press, 2004).

ethnic population. Nor does the use of the phrase connote a value judgment against (or for) the legitimacy of the ideas being circulated, the institutions that are circulating them, or the group consciousness being maintained. Finally, it does not mean to suggest that the sense of identity or the attachments to matters of group or homeland originate with the institutions, the 'marketers.' Rather, it seeks to provide a way of understanding the dialogue between the editorials, speeches, and sermons of the ethnic leadership and the thought and actions of the broader populace, a task made harder by the fact that, much of the time, it is only the leadership's part of the dialogue that has been preserved to 'listen to.'"[245]

The dialogue between constituency and leadership automatically assumes that the leadership wants to influence or gain influence with the constituency. However, in order to establish dialogue, it is also assumed that the leadership is answering or wedded to some pre-existing needs of the constituency. Alexander offers the model of a newspaper purchase to illustrate this. When a person purchases a newspaper, it is understood that the newspaper should or will meet at least some of the needs of the purchaser. The symbiotic marketing relationship model provides the framework to track negotiations between leadership and their constituency, the dependency of the leadership on their constituency, and the power the leadership exerts over their constituency. From the newspaper example, Alexander highlights the added dimension associated with more conventional marketing situations among Armenian-Americans: the intense competition between two political parties, which vie for their own market share amongst their constituency. "Each [political party] had its own press, peddling not only competing visions of peoplehood, but bitter castigations and recriminations of each other. The constancy of these recriminations certainly shows that the advocates of each party found the ideas and actions of the other party offensive, but perhaps more importantly it

[245] Benjamin F. Alexander, 8.

shows a fear on the part of each party of its rivals' persuasive powers. The notion that to be a good Armenian meant to listen to the ideas of this party and this newspaper rather than that one pervaded the editorial discourse…"[246]

Theories of Ethnic Conflict

Why did Turks, Kurds and other Muslims kill Christian Armenians in the waning days of the Ottoman Empire? What caused Hutus to kill millions of Tutsis in Rwanda in 1994? Why has conflict along tribal or ethnic lines engulfed and continues to engulf states, localities and entire regions? Lake and Rothchild argue that ethnic conflict is not a product of age-old hatreds, differences between groups or the stresses of modern or post-modern life in the age of globalization. Rather, they argue that the most common cause of ethnic conflict is collective fears of the future.[247] As any number of security dilemmas arises, individuals or groups begin to fear for their physical safety. "As information failures, problems of credible commitment, and the security dilemma take hold, the state is weakened, groups become fearful, and conflict becomes likely. Ethnic activists and political entrepreneurs, operating within groups, reinforce these fears of physical insecurity and cultural domination and polarize society. Political memories, myths, and emotions also magnify these fears, driving groups further apart. Together, these between-group and within-group strategic interactions produce a toxic brew of distrust and suspicion that can explode into murderous violence, even the systematic slaughter of one people by another."[248]

Viewing ethnic conflict through the process of *ethnic dissimilation* is also instructive. According to the political scientist and economist, Timur Kuran, ethnic dissimilation

---

[246] Ibid, 9.

[247] David A. Lake and Donald Rothchild, eds., *The International Spread of Ethnic Conflict: Fear, Diffusion, and Escalation* (Princeton, NJ: Princeton University Press, 1998), 4.

[248] Ibid.

occurs when, for any number of reasons, one ethnic group (g1) begins to coalesce and emphasize commonalities.[249] Members of a second ethnic group (g2) may feel excluded and perform maneuvers similar to g1. This results in stronger intercommunal bonds and a stress on g2 commonalities. These maneuvers are termed "dissimilation" because the behaviors exhibited by the two groups grow less common. Yet, ethnic dissimilation does not necessarily result in mistrust or violence. Rather, it frequently "...heightens ethnic antagonisms and facilitates ethnic collective action. In extreme forms... it causes states to become unglued, even to fall prey to ethnic warfare."[250]

Kuran argues on two, broad levels. First, he demonstrates how individuals who seem indifferent to ethnicity may ethnically dissimulate because of reactions and counter-reactions. "The crux of the reasoning is that people's ethnically meaningful behaviors shape the perceptions and incentives that drive the choices of others. Specifically, such behaviors pressure others into making frequent displays of their ethnicity, and they also raise the perceived advantages of ethnic solidarity."[251] Second, ethnic activities of other states or entities may be the motivation for the beginning and continuation of ethnically meaningful behaviors.

At the primarily state level, Kuran argues that "Ethnic strife within one state sensitizes people elsewhere to their own ethnic particularities, possibly raising their expectations of ethnic conflict at home."[252] A bandwagon effect may then develop as promoted by international interdependencies that give certain states or regions disproportionate significance vis-à-vis others. Under certain conditions, a bandwagon effect that results in ethnic dissimulation within one country may ignite a

---

249 Timur Kuran, "Diffusion of Ethnic Dissimilation." In *The International Spread of Ethnic Conflict: Fear, Diffusion, and Escalation.* David A. Lake and Donald Rothchild, eds., (Princeton, NJ: Princeton University Press, 1998).

250 Ibid, 36.

251 Ibid.

252 Ibid.

"superbandwagon," which would heighten the role of ethnicity in other states successively.

Kuran's model, "accommodates the existence of conditions that accord ethnic relations within a particular country some immunity to ethnic dissimulation elsewhere; it is consistent with a persistent state of low ethnic activity."[253] Because of *ethnic preference falsification*, or the act of misrepresenting one's ethnic needs under real or imagined social pressures, there is imperfect predictability and difficulty in observation. As such, ethnic dissimilation may only be observable at the outbreak of conflicts and ethnic dissimilation is never a given.

Kuran's approach and model are important not only to the study of the events of 1915 - as will be demonstrated in the next chapters – but hold the explanatory power necessary to at least partially understand the fault lines that lead to ethnic cleansing and genocide. Kuran's work also explores the common need to feel that one is cared for and not alone in this world. This desire is as old as human civilization and represents a form of Parkinson's Law: "Group identity tends to expand or contract to fill the political space available for it expression… As the importance of a given political unit increases so does the importance of the highest level of identification immediately *beneath* the level of that unit."[254]

Concepts of trauma, ideas of victimhood, diasporic nationalism and activism, and ethnic dissimilation are crucial when looking at the historical narrative of what occurred in the waning days of the Ottoman Empire. These events did not occur in a vacuum. By ignoring events that occurred before and after, context is lost or, at very least, greatly diminished. As will be demonstrated in the following chapter, the slaughter and exile of Armenians of eastern Anatolia occurred against the backdrop of a cataclysmic world war and the mutual massacres that accompanied it as

---

[253] Ibid, 37.

[254] Donald L. Horowitz. "Ethnic Identity." In Nathan Glazer and Daniel Patrick Moynihan. *Ethnicity: Theory and Experience.* No. 109. Harvard University Press, 1975; 137. Author's emphasis.

multiple empires collapsed. To ignore this as well as the fundamental impact of Great Power policies vis-à-vis the Ottoman Empire, particularly those of Russia, France and Great Britain, is tantamount to divorcing the events from the contextual history of which they were part. The retreat of the Ottoman Empire over the previous two centuries, the ethnic cleansing of Muslims and the mass influx of Muslim refugees from the Crimea, Balkans and elsewhere, as well as the Balkan Wars are of extreme importance in understanding the context in which the expulsion and murder of Armenians occurred.[255] "History is not about the reification of events, but about processes, causation, integrating events in what came before and what followed. If using legal concepts to define crimes become the only valid language with which to discuss the past, we not only deny ourselves historical understanding but, moreover, make any reciprocal debate impossible by creating a huge and partially legitimate sense of injustice."[256]

---

[255] See McCarthy. *Death and Exile*, particular chapters 2-5.

[256] Lagrou, 285.

CHAPTER 3

A COMPLICATED GENESIS: ARMENIANS AND THE OTTOMAN EMPIRE

Armenians and the Ottoman Empire to 1850

Armenians possess a history and culture that stretches back in time over 2,000 years. Armenians claim to be the first people to have accepted Christianity *en masse*, in either 301 C.E. or 314 C.E. The Holy Apostolic and Orthodox Church of Armenia (also referred to as the Gregorian Church) was arguably a significant force in sustaining a strong sense of Armenian identity even as they were sandwiched between or ruled by non-Armenians for much of their history.

After their conversion to Christianity, Armenians were ruled variously by the Byzantines, Persians and Arabs until 886, when they achieved a large measure of self-rule for two centuries under the Armenian Bagratid dynasty. This empire fell in 1045 to the Byzantines and then to the invading Seljuk Turks (*Selçuklular* or *Selçuk Türkleri*). The independent Armenian-ruled Kingdom of Cilicia remained autonomous until 1375 when it fell under Persian and, subsequently, Ottoman Turkish rule.[257]

---

[257] See Seta B. Dadoyan. *The Armenians in the Medieval Islamic World, Volume Three: Medieval Cosmopolitanism and Images of Islam. Vol. 3*. Transaction Publishers, 2013. See also Eduard L. Danielyan.

Compared to the Armenians, the Ottoman Turks were relative newcomers to Anatolia, the Caucasus, the Middle East and the Balkans and synthesized the many legal, religious and civic traditions of former empires and their subject peoples. "The Ottoman Empire took the religious traditions of the Middle East and the Balkans and codified them into law. Each religious group was named as a *millet* (literally 'nation')."[258] Under this system, the Christian Armenians (Orthodox and Catholic), along with the Orthodox Christian Greeks and the Jews, were granted a high degree of cultural, social and religious autonomy. Each group's spiritual leadership was granted the authority by the Ottoman government to manage the communities' civil and legal affairs. For example, most Armenians living in the Ottoman Empire were subject to the authority of the Armenian Patriarch of Istanbul. In essence, the millets of the Ottoman Empire were subservient to and taxed by the larger Muslim majority, but enjoyed a degree of autonomy unheard of by their contemporaries in Europe.[259]

When the Ottoman sultan, Mehmet II, conquered Istanbul in 1453, the city was largely decimated and depopulated. Indeed, Istanbul's huge population and storied wealth could never be recovered after the sacking it received at the hands of the Latin Crusaders in 1204. It was in 1204, not 1453, that the great library was burned and most of the great art treasures of Byzantium were plundered and removed, many finding a new, permanent home in a vastly enriched Venice. To further complicate matters, the Byzantines lost control of the hinterlands surrounding Istanbul in the preceding centuries to both Christian Latin and Muslim Turkic forces, keeping them from properly financing a significant urban revival. "The fact that there were some 8,500 men to defend

---

Armenian Statehood and Governance through Millennia: History and Modernity. 21st Century 1 (17) (2015).

[258] Justin McCarthy, *The Ottoman Turks: An Introductory History to 1923*. (London and New York: Longman, 1997), 128.

[259] Ronald Grigor Suny, *Looking Toward Ararat: Armenia in Modern History* (Bloomington: Indiana University Press, 1993), 100-101. See also Halil Inalcik, *Osmanli Toplumu* (İstanbul: Eren, 1993).

the city against an Ottoman army of some 50,000 [in 1453] reveals not only the self-sacrificing futility of the effort, but also how inconsequential the Byzantine entity had become… The immediate consequences of its fall were symbolic. The practical significance lay in the future rather than in the present, for control of the city was eventually to bring the Ottoman dynasty enormous wealth, prestige and power."[260]

In order to repopulate the new Ottoman capital, Sultan Mehmet II forcibly moved large groups of Armenians and Greeks from the countryside to the city. This forced movement soon became the preference for many, as life in the Ottoman capital often meant advancement and inclusion in the Ottoman state apparatus, the possibility of economic advancement, access to royal power, goods and services and security.[261] Thus many Armenians, Jews, Greeks and non-Muslim foreigners, such as the Catholic Genoese and Venetians, settled in Istanbul or other garrison towns governed by the Ottomans because of the opportunities afforded. Indeed, the status and prestige of the Armenian Church grew as a direct result of the Ottoman conquest of Istanbul. In fact, the Greek Orthodox Byzantines had refused to allow the Armenian Church to operate in Istanbul, as it viewed Armenian Christians as heretics.[262] Armenian church leaders were even imprisoned on the Princes' Islands in the Sea of Marmara by the Byzantines for committing "heresy."[263]

When Sultan Mehmet II invited Hovagim I to relocate to Istanbul from Bursa, he created the office of the Armenian patriarch and made Hovagim I the first Armenian Patriarch of Istanbul. The Patriarch of Istanbul was recognized as the

---

[260] Daniel Goffman. *The Ottoman Empire and Early Modern Europe* (Cambridge: Cambridge University Press, 2002), 52.
[261] Mesut Uyar. "The Ottoman Empire and the Early Modern World." *Agora* 50, no. 4 (2015): 22.
[262] Speros Vryonis. "Byzantium: The Social Basis of Decline in the Eleventh Century." *Greek, Roman and Byzantine Studies* 2, no. 2 (1959): 169-171.
[263] Ibid.

religious and secular leader of all Armenians in the Ottoman Empire and carried the title *Milletbaşı* (literally "head of the millet"), ethnarch and patriarch.[264]

While it is true that non-Muslims could not hold office in the Sultan's household, in the Muslim religious classes or the Ottoman administration, they generally thrived in other areas. "Outside of these cadres… there were few professions within the empire that imposed such religious limitations. In profound contrast to the rest of the European world, agriculturalists, merchants, bankers, mariners, herders, and hawkers might be Muslim, or Armenian, Greek Orthodox, or Jewish."[265]

The vast majority of Armenians continued to live as peasants in the eastern provinces and in the district of Cilicia along the Mediterranean. Unlike Istanbul, where non-Muslims were the majority, "…there is general agreement that by the latter part of the nineteenth century the Armenians constituted a minority even in the six provinces usually referred to as the heartland of Armenia…"[266] This was the result of a combination of factors: the willing conversion of Christian Armenians to Islam,[267] boundary changes to the Ottoman Empire, and a massive influx of Muslims expelled from the Caucasus and the Balkans in the wake of independence struggles in former Ottoman territories in the Balkans and Russian expansion and conquest of former Ottoman territories in the Crimea and Caucasus. It should be noted that demography studies have conclusively shown that these areas all possessed majority Muslim populations prior the massacres and ethnic cleansing that occurred in the wake of Christian nationalism

---

[264] Osman Sezgin and Ramazan Biçer. "Foundations of tolerance in Turkish culture." *Kalem Eğitim ve İnsan Bilimleri Dergisi* 2012, 2 (1), 27-31.

[265] Ibid, 83.

[266] Lewy, 3.

[267] See Selim Deringil. *Conversion and apostasy in the late Ottoman Empire.* Cambridge University Press, 2012.

in the Balkans and Russian imperial expansion into the Black Sea region and the Caucasus.[268]

Though Armenians did possess a large degree of autonomy within the Ottoman millet system, as noted, some Muslims referred to them - along with the other non-Muslim minorities in the Empire - as *gavurs* or *kafirs*, a pejorative term meaning unbeliever or infidel. Armenians, like Jews and Greeks, often suffered discrimination, occasional abuse and frequent taxation. Despite discrimination and instances of abuse, Armenians were regularly referred to as "the most loyal millet" by Ottoman officials in court documents, highlighting the importance of Armenians within the Empire. Armenians were famous for their skills as translators, financiers, administrators, and traders across the Ottoman Empire. "The church remained at the head of the nation; Armenians with commercial and industrial skills were able to climb to the very pinnacle of the Ottoman economic order; and a variety of educational, charitable, and social institutions were permitted to flourish"[269] For over four centuries, the harmony that characterized Muslim and Armenian relations within the Empire can be described as one of "benign symbiosis."[270]

On the eve of major Russian incursions into Ottoman and Persian territories in the Caucasus and eastern Anatolia, Armenians were divided vertically by geography and politics, and horizontally by social class and intellect. Geographically, the Armenians were divided by the frontier of the Persian and, later, the Russian Empire to the east and the Ottoman Empire to the west. Broadly mirroring these geographical and political divisions, Armenians developed into speakers of western and eastern Armenian. Armenians

---

[268] See Justin McCarthy. *Death and Exile*, chapters 1-3.

[269] See Ronald G. Suny. *Looking Toward Ararat: Armenia in Modern History*, 101. See also Benjamin Braude and Bernard Lewis, eds., *Christians and Jews in the Ottoman Empire: The Functioning of a Plural Society*, 2 volumes (New York and London: Holmer & Meyer Publishers, Inc., 1982).

[270] Suny. *Looking Toward Ararat: Armenia in Modern History*, 101.

inhabiting eastern Anatolia in the Ottoman Empire were generally poorer and less educated than Armenians residing in Russian Armenia.[271] Furthermore, they were separated by hundreds of miles from their much wealthier, educated and urban, Ottoman Armenian compatriots residing in Istanbul, İzmir (Smyrna) and elsewhere. Armenians living in eastern Anatolia had little contact, if any, with their more cosmopolitan and wealthier Armenian cousins in the Ottoman Empire.[272] They were closer geographically to their cousins in Russian Transcaucasia and this proximity and ease of travel across the porous and fungible borders that separated the Russian and Ottoman Empires would have a profoundly damning effect on Muslim/Christian relations leading up to and culminating in the year 1915.

Intellectually, there existed vast differences between urban and rural Armenians as well as differences of Armenians under Persian and then Russian rule and those under Ottoman rule. Whether one was urban or rural imposed the greatest difference in exposure to education and exposure to intellectual currents percolating in Europe. Vast differences persisted into the twentieth century between urban elites and their rural counterparts. "One can say without exaggeration that while urban Armenians lived in nineteenth century surroundings, Armenian villages still lived as they had a hundred years earlier."[273]

Armenians living in cities under Russian rule often traveled to St. Petersburg and Moscow as well as Germany in order to gain their education, thereby exposing them to ideas of nationalism and the European enlightenment. Likewise, Ottoman Armenians inhabiting the Empire's coastal cities were exposed to European ideas and literature and were educated in more liberal locations than their Russian counterparts, such as France and Italy. This led to

---

[271] Justin McCarthy has made a forceful argument that the entire region of eastern and western Armenia should be recognized geographically and culturally as one region regardless of political divisions. See *Death and Exile*, 23-29.
[272] Suny, 18.
[273] Ibid, 19.

the development of a liberal streak that differed from their counterparts in Russian-ruled Transcaucasia. Indeed, the development of the western Armenian intelligentsia was rather at odds with that of their contemporaries in the Caucasus, precisely because of the vertical and geographical differences cited above, as well as the different realities and developmental space available under Russian versus Ottoman rule.

Reacting to the rural poverty that characterized the life of the rural peasantry in eastern Anatolia, many Armenians relocated, most often to western Anatolia and the cities of Istanbul and İzmir. Alternatively, they moved to the burgeoning frontier garrison town of Tiflis - today's Tbilisi, Georgia – in what was then the Russian Empire.

Armenians are said to have left eastern Anatolia in order to escape the brutality and arbitrariness of Ottoman rule for the relative freedom and wealth of the Russian-controlled Caucasus, though many later returned to former Ottoman territories.[274] Regardless of the false promise of more freedom and wealth, "Russia, despite its autocratic government and failure to fulfill the promises of an autonomous *Armianskaia oblast* (Armenian district), was regarded as a liberator by many Armenians. Hopes had been laid on the Russians for centuries…"[275] This, too, would lead to the conflagration that destroyed both empires and peoples in 1915.

Interestingly, studies have demonstrated that life greatly improved for Armenians whenever they simply absconded from the poverty and misery of eastern Anatolia. This points to the fact that migration, if one possessed the means to do so, had less to do with Ottoman rule and more to do with a search for better living conditions. "The question was not one of escaping *to* Russia, but of escaping *from* eastern Anatolia."[276]

---

[274] McCarthy. *Death and Exile*, 29-32.

[275] Suny, *Looking Toward Ararat*, 23.

[276] Justin McCarthy. *Death and Exile: The Ethnic Cleansing of Ottoman Muslims, 1821-1922*, 122. Author's emphasis.

Attempts at Reform and the Genesis of Armenian Nationalism

Much of the status quo that had characterized the relationship between Ottoman Muslims and non-Muslims changed in 1856, when Sultan Abdülmecid I (Abdulmajid or Abdul Mejid), under diplomatic and military pressure from European powers as well as vocal support for reforms within the Empire, issued the *Hatt-ı Hümâyun,* or Imperial Rescript. This imperial directive ordered that tax laws be formalized and regularized in order to put an end to widespread irregularities and abuse.[277] Tax farms were to be abolished, justice was to be dispensed equitably through a new and codified legal system and the religious millets were ordered to draw up constitutions and submit them to the Ottoman government. In essence, political power was devolved and, *de facto*, rested in the hands of the people. "The significance of this within the Armenian millet was considerable: It reduced the Apostolic Patriarch to a spiritual figurehead while shifting governance of the millet to a broader base of urban bourgeoisie. The condition of the majority peasant population remained unchanged."[278]

These legal changes and pronouncements meant that the centralized power the Armenian patriarch had enjoyed during the previous four centuries of Ottoman rule, was abruptly and permanently undermined by notions as well as the actual practice of popular representation, rule of law and nationalism. However, this was not the first time the patriarch's authority had been curtailed. After 1830, Protestant missionaries from the United States, England and Germany achieved considerable success among the Orthodox Armenian community in the form of converts. American Protestant missionaries opened up their first school in 1834 in Istanbul, which was soon followed by Robert College in the early 1840s. By 1845, there were an

---

[277] Adrian Boldişor. "Human Rights in Orthodoxy and Islam: A Comparative Approach." *Review of Ecumenical Studies Sibiu* 7, no. 1 (2015): 125.

[278] Benjamin F. Alexander, 23.

estimated 8,000 Armenian Protestants and the Ottoman government granted them the status of separate millet as early as 1847 against strenuous opposition from the Armenian patriarch and the Armenian Apostolic Church hierarchy.[279] Indeed, before the creation of a separate Armenian Protestant millet, Armenian converts to Protestantism were often jailed - not by Ottoman authorities - but by Armenian apostolic authorities under orders from the Armenian patriarch in Istanbul, as this fell under their jurisdiction as per the Ottoman millet system and the large amount of autonomy it granted.[280]

Though Sultan Abdülmecid's edict had the immediate effect of devastating the centuries-old Ottoman millet system and curtailing some of the temporal power of religious authorities, his 1856 imperial rescript was never fully implemented. Intransigence by a well-entrenched Ottoman bureaucracy and the various *Milletbaşı* such as the Armenian patriarch who were intent on maintaining the status quo, imperial dithering and a weak civil society all led to its demise. The imperial edict, however, raised a variety of hopes among non-Muslim groups within the Empire – particularly those of the Armenian, Jewish, and Greek Orthodox urban elite. And though a program of comprehensive reforms was never initiated, the non-Muslim populations of the Empire were granted legal equality with Muslims, to include equal access to public office. It was under these conditions that the non-Muslim commercial and professional elite gained a position of significant advantage in the socioeconomic life of the late Ottoman Empire.[281]

As a result of the preeminent position occupied by many Armenians, Greeks and Jews, the Ottoman Muslim elite –

[279] Ibid, 33.

[280] Nicola Migliorino. *(Re) constructing Armenia in Lebanon and Syria: Ethno-cultural Diversity and the State in the Aftermath of a Refugee Crisis.* Vol. 21. Berghahn Books, 2008: 38; footnote 49.

[281] Deniz T. Kılınçoğlu. *Economics and Capitalism in the Ottoman Empire.* Vol. 174. Routledge, 2015. 195.

along with the more traditional *Milletbaşı* - increasingly defended their declining status within the Ottoman Empire.[282] According to the historian Fikret Adanır, after the 1850s, non-Muslims elites – particularly the Armenian elite - dominated the cultural scene. Armenians introduced modern theater and opera, in the Ottoman Turkish language, to the public. By 1876, some 47 newspapers were published in Istanbul, of these only thirteen were in Turkish and a total of nine were in Armenian. By the end of the nineteenth century, thirty-two of the ninety printing houses in Istanbul were controlled by Armenians; twenty-three were owned by Muslims. During the same time period, in Istanbul, Ottoman Muslims controlled only twenty-five percent of the retail trade, fifteen percent of wholesale businesses and a miniscule three percent of transportation companies.[283]

In light of their professional success, it would seem that at least a significant portion of Ottoman non-Muslims were successfully integrated in the Ottoman social, economic and political fabric. As such, what constituted the dramatic shift from coexistence to the confrontations, massacres and instances of ethnic cleansing in 1915? Numerous scholars agree that the major, even decisive, factor was the development and then upsurge of ethnic nationalism that occurred within the Ottoman Empire during the second half of the nineteenth century.[284]

---

[282] Mardin, 19.

[283] Fikret Adanır. "Nicht-muslimische Eliten im Osmanischen Reich." *Eliten in Südosteuropa: Rolle, Kontinuitäten, Brüche in Geschichte und Gegenwart.* (Munich: Südosteuropa-Gesellschaft, 1998), 49-68.

[284] See Ronald Grigor Suny. *Looking Toward Ararat*: 18-30; Richard G. Hovannisian. *The Armenian People*: 203-238. See also Fikret Adanır. "Armenian Deportations and Massacres in 1915." In *Ethnopolitical Warfare: Causes, Consequences, and Possible Solutions*, eds. Daniel Chirot and Martin E. P. Seligman (Washington, D.C: American Psychological Association, 2001): 71-82. See also Richard G. Hovannisian. "Caucasian Armenia Between Imperial and Soviet Rule: The Interlude of Independence." In *Transcaucasia, Nationalism and Social Change: Essays in the History of Armenia, Azerbaijan and Georgia*, ed.

Theories of Nationalism and the Development of Non-Muslim Nationalisms in the Ottoman Empire

The study of nationalism is often contentious and much nonsense has been written about the subject, particularly in relation to ethnic groups in the Balkans and the Middle East, to include Armenians. Accordingly, this book focuses on two major schools of thought regarding the development of nationalism, though it is hoped that the brief discussion of primordial nationalism as posited by Anthony D. Smith in chapter 2 provides a broader contextual framework.[285]

Scholars such as Ernest Gellner, a social anthropologist and scholar of nationalism, argue that nationalism developed in tandem with industrialization and the advent of modernity. According to Gellner, the general and central features of industrial society including, but not limited to, literacy, mobility, the ability to communicate on a massive scale and an education system that guarantees literacy allow nationalism to develop and prosper. "Nationalism is essentially the general imposition of a high culture on society, where previously low cultures had taken up the lives of the majority, and in some cases the totality, of the population. It means that generalized diffusion of a school-mediated, academy-supervised idiom, codified for the requirements of reasonably precise bureaucratic and technological communications. It is the establishment of an anonymous, impersonal society, with mutually substitutable atomized individuals held together above all by a shared culture of this kind…"[286]

While agreeing with the basics of Gellner's premise, other scholars such as Benedict Anderson take the argument a step further, arguing that nationalism is largely an imagined

---

Ronald Grigor Suny (Ann Arbor, MI: University of Michigan Press, 1999): 261-294.

[285] Anthony D. Smith, particularly 64-65, 115-117.

[286] Ernest Gellner. *Nations and Nationalisms* (Ithaca, NY: Cornell University Press, 1983): 57.

construction. "The nation is an imagined political community – imagined as both inherently limited and sovereign."[287] It is imagined because individuals of nations will never meet or even know of the existence of other individual members of their nation. This is because even the largest nations, sometimes encompassing a population of millions or even billions, have finite boundaries. As such, the nation is imagined as limited. Furthermore, even though inequality exists, the nation is always conceived as a deep, horizontal comradeship.[288]

Using the theories of both Gellner and Anderson, it can be said that rather than possessing some primordial ethnic and national consciousness, the rise of Armenian, Jewish and Greek nationalisms in the Ottoman Empire occurred and coincided with outside events, mainly in Europe. This explains why they were *not* a significant factor in Ottoman Muslim and non-Muslim relations until the latter part of the nineteenth century.

The rise of industrialization, access to education and the wide dissemination of European notions of ethnicity and the nation-state in the Ottoman Empire, exacerbated and encouraged the further development of separate and distinct identities among non-Muslim Ottomans. It should be noted that the Ottoman millet system, by its very nature, offering inclusivity yet encouraging separateness, provided the fertile soil in which Greek and Armenian nationalisms and identities could grow. For example, the Armenian millets possessed and operated Armenian schools, welfare systems and courts and had done so for centuries under Ottoman rule. They often lived in separate neighborhoods or districts, such as Beşiktaş, Kuruçeşme and Üsküdar in Istanbul.[289]

---

[287] Benedict Anderson. *Imagined Communities* (London: Verso, 1983): 6-7.

[288] Ibid, 50.

[289] See E. Ümran Topçu. "The significance of neighborhood in Istanbul." *Conference Paper; 51st Congress of the European Regional Science Association: "New Challenges for European Regions and Urban Areas in a Globalised World", 30 August - 3 September 2011*, Barcelona, Spain, 5. Also see Jelena Trkulja and Christopher Lees. "Armenians in

Armenians also possessed and often spoke a distinct language from their surrounding Greek and Turkish neighbors, though interestingly, many in Cilicia spoke Turkish as their first language.[290]

Armenian traders, famous for their linguistic and trading skills, maintained ample contact with Europe, Europeans and European philosophies of the nation-state and nationalism. This contact with Europeans and their ideas, particularly after 1789, the radical, French ideas of nationalism and the rights of man, acted as a catalyst. What was once considered the simple linguistic and religious separation inherent in the Ottoman millet system changed into Armenian nationalism.

Another possibly more important catalyst for change and the confrontation it engendered, was that the Empire's Armenians, Greeks and Jews "…saw that members of their own ethnic group were not the ones that ran the [Ottoman] Empire. This was undoubtedly a cause of resentment. There was a natural human desire to run their own affairs. Separation and resentment made the adoption of nationalism easier."[291]

Just as the Sultan Abdülmecid's 1856 imperial rescript had a major impact on the status minorities previously held in the Empire, the Ottoman constitution of 1876 was a further effort to foster inclusivity and the notion of "Ottomanness" for all the Empire's subjects, Muslim and non-Muslim alike. The constitution proclaimed the equal treatment of all nationalities within the Empire and made allowances for the representative government. From 1876-1878, a parliament met in Istanbul composed of representatives of the empire's nationalities. "Every Ottoman male above the age of thirty with ability in Turkish and enjoying civil rights could be elected deputy, unless he had accepted citizenship or employment in the service of a foreign government, was

---

Constantinople", 2008, *Encyclopaedia of the Hellenic World, Constantinople.* http://www.ehw.gr/l.aspx?id=12208.

[290] Lewy, 183.

[291] McCarthy. *The Ottoman Turks*, 205.

bankrupt or a domestic servant, or was stigmatized by 'notoriety for ill deeds.' A caveat to the language requirement was that after four years (i.e., 1880), candidates would be expected to read and 'to the extent possible' write Turkish."[292]

In 1878, the constitution was abruptly suspended by Sultan Abdülhamid II (Abdulhamid or Abdul Hamid). His thirty-year reign (1876-1909) is often described as autocratic, bloody and paranoid, largely on account of misleadingly lurid and racist stories in the European and American yellow press.[293] His reign coincided with thirty years of territorial losses, erstwhile modernization efforts within the Empire, multiple bankruptcies, increasingly bold meddling in Ottoman affairs by the Great Powers, as well as numerous insurrections and rebellions. Yet during Abdülhamid's reign, further intellectual awakening occurred in the Empire, informed by European ideas of nationalism that revolved the concept of the *Volk:* an organic community with a shared destiny and collective soul, which articulated itself through the medium of a national language. Intellectuals within and without the Empire busied themselves, promoting national awakenings amongst their own *Volk.*[294]

These ideas along with almost constant wars of national liberation by Ottoman subjects, coupled with a string of Ottoman military defeats and the dissolution of the 1876 constitution, dealt a serious blow to the idea - however tenuous - of Ottoman fraternity and Ottomanness. In the process of these upheavals, hundreds of thousands of Muslims were uprooted from their homes in former Ottoman territories in the Caucasus and the Balkans by a combination of Russian military might and new, "Christian" nation-states, such as Romania. Matters reached a boiling

---

[292] Hasan Kayalı. "Elections and the Electoral Process in the Ottoman Empire, 1876–1919." *International Journal of Middle East Studies* 27, no. 03 (1995): 266.

[293] See Nadine Lange-Akhund. *The Macedonian Question, 1893-1908: From Western Sources.* NY: Columbia University Press, 1998.

[294] Adanır. "Armenian Deportations and Massacres in 1915," 72.

point in 1876, when Bulgaria revolted against Ottoman rule with Imperial Russia's support. It was at this time that many in the Ottoman government began to overtly voice concern over the loyalty, or lack thereof, of the Empire's non-Muslim minorities.[295] The very survival of the centuries-old Empire was at stake.

Armenians between Two Empires

Contrary to the general re-imagination of historical relations within the Armenian diaspora, the Russian Empire was not necessarily a source of succor, strength or escape for Ottoman Armenian subjects. Indeed, Armenian and Russian relations had been fraught with difficulty and mistrust long before the Bolsheviks rose to power.[296] The historian Paul Werth deconstructs a complex, historical relationship in his masterful study, detailing Imperial Russia's control of eastern Armenia and the Armenian Catholicos at Echmiadzin.[297] Werth demonstrates how Russian officials used the office of the Catholicos at Echmiadzin, the chief bishop of the Armenian Apostolic Church, to influence and gain leverage over Armenian subjects residing in the Ottoman Empire. Furthermore, far from being overly eager to throw off the Ottoman yoke, Werth explicitly acknowledges the overwhelming loyalty of Ottoman Armenians - particularly those in Istanbul - to the Ottoman state. This led to Russia's initial irritation with and overwhelming fear of Armenian nationalism. This was the case both within in its own borders; i.e. eastern Armenia, and the potentially disastrous effects Armenian nationalism

---

[295] See Markus Dressler. "Historical Trajectories and Ambivalences of Turkish Minority Discourse." *New Diversities* (2015): 13. Also see Samim Akgönül. *The Minority Concept in the Turkish Context: Practices and Perceptions in Turkey, Greece and France*. Vol. 13. Brill, 2013: 69.
[296] McCarthy. *Death and Exile*. 29-31.
[297] Paul Werth. "Imperial Russia and the Armenian Catholicos at Home and Abroad." *Reconstruction and Interaction of Slavic Eurasia and Its Neighboring Worlds* (2006): 203-235.

could have on the Russian rule in the region, should it take root in the Ottoman Empire.[298]

Russia annexed eastern Armenia (broadly the area constituting the present Republic of Armenia) in 1828, during a period of Russian expansion into the Caucasus and Crimea, taking territory at the expense of the Ottoman and Persian Empires. Officials in St. Petersburg were keen to annex this portion of the Caucasus because it placed the seat of the Armenian Catholicos at the monastery at Echmiadzin within Russia's borders, thereby making the Catholicos a subject of the Russian Empire.

For purposes of clarity, at present, the Catholicos of the Armenian Apostolic Church in Echmiadzin is an office that is separate and distinct from that of the Armenian Patriarchate of Istanbul, that is presently under the authority of the Catholicos in Echmiadzin. However, this was not always the case. The Armenian Patriarch in Istanbul was originally deemed by the Ottoman rulers to be the head of the Armenian *millet*. The officeholder eventually became the head of the Apostolic (Gregorian) or Orthodox Armenian Church as opposed to the Armenian Catholic Church, which pledged allegiance to the Pope in Rome.

The Russians, through their control of Echmiadzin via conquest, acquired an unprecedented opportunity to influence the Armenian communities in both Persia and the Ottoman Empire, since the Catholicos claimed spiritual authority over all adherents of the Armenian Apostolic confession, regardless of geographical location. Accordingly, over the course of the nineteenth century, the Russian government made strenuous efforts to uphold and enhance the prestige of the Catholicos as a way of broadcasting Russian power to the Ottoman Empire. It also did so in order to maximize its leverage in manipulating Ottoman Armenian relations with their Ottoman rulers.[299]

St. Petersburg's influence over Ottoman subjects was rather dependent on its own relations with the Sublime

---

[298] Ibid., 217, 230.

[299] Werth, 204.

Porte in Istanbul. For example, ties were severed between Istanbul and Russia and, by proxy, Russian-controlled Armenia as a result of the Crimean War (1835-1856).

Ottoman statesmen feared the continued expansion of Russia and the growth of Russian influence in the Ottoman Empire, to include eastern Anatolia. European powers, such as Great Britain and France, also attempted to stop Russian advances at the expense of the Ottoman Empire. Worried about seeming Ottoman impotence in the face of alarming events in eastern Anatolia ostensibly orchestrated by Russia, European powers actively courted the Armenian population, urban and rural, through missionary work, attempting to convert Ottoman Armenians to Protestantism and Catholicism, thereby removing them from Echmiadzin's and Russia's purview.[300]

The Ottoman government protested against the actions of European powers and Russia vis-à-vis its Ottoman Armenian citizens. Consecutive sultans and their advisors viewed these moves suspiciously and understood their potentially destabilizing effect within the Empire. The Ottomans particularly mistrusted Russia, and understood Russian control of Transcaucasia and Echmiadzin as a means to an end: encouraging Armenian nationalism and irredentism with a focus on the eventual annexation of the provinces of eastern Anatolia, to include Van, Bitlis, Kars and Ardahan – all areas supporting rather large numbers of Armenians, albeit as a minority.[301]

Russian ambassador N. P. Ignat'ev wrote in 1874 that Armenian Catholics and Protestants, sympathetic to and helped by France and Britain, had done as much as they could to sever ties between Ottoman Armenians and the Catholicos in Echmiadzin. Ignat'ev was also concerned by

---

[300] See Selim Derengil. *The Well-Protected Domains: Ideology and the Legitimation of Power in the Ottoman Empire, 1876-1909* (London: 1998), chapter 5. See also Jeremy Salt. *Imperialism, Evangelism and the Ottoman Armenians, 1878-1896* (London: 1993).

[301] See Mustafa Aydın. "Securitization of History and Geography: Understanding of Security in Turkey." *Southeast European and Black Sea Studies* 3, no. 2 (2003): 169.

efforts on the part of some Ottoman Armenians to instill a sense of dissatisfaction with Russian rule in eastern Armenia. The Russian Viceroy of the Caucasus, Bariatinskii, stated in 1857, "Either the (Turkish) Armenians will throw themselves into our embrace or they will direct their desires and sympathy to some other power."[302]

Under provisions of the 1856 Ottoman reform decree referenced previously, Ottoman Armenians were able to gain a new constitution for the administration of their affairs in the Empire. This effectively ended clerical control over the Armenian *millet*, either from Echmiadzin or elsewhere. The changes wrought by the short-lived constitution also had the side effect of consolidating Ottoman Armenian power in the hands of an urban and educated elite based in Istanbul. From the mid-nineteenth century on, a Istanbul Armenian elite largely conducted affairs on behalf of the Armenians inhabiting the rest of the Empire, on account of their wealth, prestige and proximity to the centers of Ottoman power. Through unintended consequences brought about by the promulgation of the Ottoman constitution, a liberal, educated, largely westernized and decidedly more nationalist group of Armenian elites in Istanbul assumed the power formerly held by clerical rulers.[303]

In order to counteract European-inspired, urban, Ottoman Armenian influence and gain leverage over the rural Armenians of eastern Anatolia, Russia endeavored to include all Armenian dioceses in Russian, Ottoman and Persian territories in the election process of the Catholicos

---

[302] Werth, 213.

[303] For more on these changes in leadership, see Hagop Barsoumian. "The Eastern Question and the Tanzimat Era." In Richard Hovannisian (ed.), *The Armenian People: From Ancient to Modern Times; Vol. II*, (New York: St. Martin's Press, 1997): 175-202. See also Vartin Artinian. *The Armenian Constitutional System in the Ottoman Empire, 1839-1863* (Istanbul, 1988): 51-91. See also Louise Nalbandian. *The Armenian Revolutionary Movement: The Development of the Armenian Political Parties through the Nineteenth Century* (Berkeley, CA: University of California at Berkeley Press, 1963): 42-48.

at Echmiadzin. This move was strongly resisted and the power of the urban, Ottoman Armenian elite was such that they were able to consistently win the elections, thereby forcing Russian acceptance of an Ottoman Armenian citizen as Catholicos. This not only frustrated St. Petersburg, but antagonized the "obedient" clergy and laypeople of the Russian-controlled dioceses in Transcaucasia, according to a Russian interior ministry election observer.[304]

As a result, questions were raised in St. Petersburg about Russia's continued patronage of Echmiadzin for two reasons. First, while successive Catholicos, at the behest of Russia, attempted to consolidate their authority over Ottoman Armenians, they correspondingly neglected confessional affairs within Russian-controlled Armenia. This had led to schisms, vocal complaints and a semblance of chaos arising from a perceived vacuum of leadership on the part of the Catholicos. Thus, instead of consolidating and legitimizing Russian rule, the Catholicos of Echmiadzin, from St. Petersburg's perspective, served themselves and their Ottoman flock at the expense of Armenians residing in Transcaucasia.

Second, some Russian ministers argued that rather than the Catholicos serving as an instrument of Russian expansion and influence abroad, it was the other way around. That is, the Catholicos was being influenced from abroad and, "… had become a conduit for the transmission of dangerous ideas of Armenian independence *from* the Ottoman empire *into* Russia."[305]

The eventual Russian confrontation with the Armenian church resulted directly from its policy of currying favor with the Catholicos in order to gain influence over Ottoman Armenians as part of Russian efforts to destabilize the Ottoman Empire. As early as 1865, Viceroy Bariatinskii contended that while the merging of Armenians with Russians in the Russian Empire was a central goal,

---

[304] Werth, 217.
[305] Ibid, 217.

enhancing the power and political significance of Echmiadzin would only lead to greater separatism.[306]

The Russian battle against Armenian separatism eventually required "... drastic measures in order to purge the Armenian clergy of 'political' accretions."'[307] Accordingly, and in order to influence the Armenian clergy and the Catholicos, the Russian government closed Armenian schools and curtailed the activities of the Armenian Church. The Russian government fully confiscated Church lands in 1903, thus removing the Church's primary sources of revenue. Armenian nationalists, previously a fractious bunch and generally ambivalent in regards to the Catholicos and the Apostolic Church, briefly united and resisted Russian actions through armed skirmishes, sabotage and propaganda efforts. The czarist government eventually backed down.

Importantly, the lessons learned from this brief period of Armenian nationalist unity and the effects it achieved were lost neither on the Armenians themselves nor the Russians. These lessons would eventually be employed against the Ottoman Empire with the full support of St. Petersburg and with devastating consequences for both the Russian and Ottoman Empires and their Armenians inhabitants.

The Bulgarian Revolt and the Treaty of Berlin

When the Bulgarian provinces of the Ottoman Empire revolted in 1876 with the help and encouragement of Russia and the tacit support of other Great Powers, reports filtered into Europe and Russia about the brutality of Ottoman troops and irregulars in suppressing the rebellion. Though most of these reports were patently exaggerated and false and ignored the far more serious massacres and atrocities committed by Bulgarians against Muslim,[308] the reports further solidified the popular, racist and Orientalist image of the "terrible Turk" in Europe and Russia: swarthy,

[306] Ibid, 219.

[307] Ibid, 218.

[308] McCarthy. *Death and Exile*, 62-63, 71-81.

uncivilized, cruel and uncouth savages from Asia. This image also percolated into Armenian national consciousness. "Massacres, outrage and devastation have always been congenial to the Turks," argued one Armenian.[309] Another noted that through his actions, the Turk perpetually affirmed that "he is as cruel and brutal as he was when he first swooped down as the scourge of God in Asia Minor one thousand years ago."[310]

An international conference in Istanbul, demanded by the *Dreikaiserbund,* composed of Austria-Hungary, Germany and Russia, ostensibly attempted to address Ottoman reprisals and "Muslim fanaticism" in Bulgaria.[311] The conference completely ignored the atrocities perpetrated against Muslims in Bulgaria and instead rewarded these acts of ethnic cleansing by producing proposals for two autonomous Bulgarian regions centered at Sofia and Turnovo.

The Ottoman sultan, Abdülhamid, rejected the conference propositions outright. This provoked a public outcry in Russia that called for solidarity with their southern Slav brothers, the Bulgarians. Bolstered by Russian public opinion and using Sultan Abdülhamid's rejection of the proposals as a *fait accompli*, Russia unilaterally declared war on the Ottoman Empire. Russian troops promptly marched south and west into Bulgaria and toward Istanbul.

Portions of the Russian army, which included Armenian subjects of the czar, also marched into the Ottoman Empire in eastern Anatolia from Russian-controlled Transcaucasia. These troops marched under the command of a Russian Armenian, Mikayel Loris-Melikov (the Armenian form of his name was Melikian) and were helped by Ottoman Armenians who acted as guides.[312]

---

309 Lewy, 246.

310 Ibid.

311 Heinz A. Richter. "The Grand Game and Britain's Acquisition of Cyprus." *Çanakkale Araştırmaları Türk Yıllığı* 12, no. 17 (2014): 87.

312 Lewy, 7.

The ideas of nationalism, ethnicity and racism that had slowly trickled back and forth from Transcaucasia into eastern Anatolia turned into a torrent as Russian troops marched towards Erzurum in the Ottoman province of the same name. Pro-Russian sentiment spread among some Armenians of eastern Anatolia as Russian troops occupied ever larger swathes of the Ottoman Empire in the east and, in the west, encamped within miles of Istanbul. Massacres and rapes of Muslim inhabitants along with massive theft of properties occurred at the hands of local and Transcaucasian Armenians with an impunity encouraged by Russia's invasion.[313]

A hasty truce was brokered in 1878 with the signing of the Treaty of San Stefano. At the recommendation of the Armenian Patriarch, who would openly support the detachment of Armenia from the Ottoman Empire only one year later,[314] the treaty included a provision for the protection of Armenians in the Ottoman Empire. Protection was felt necessary for Armenians particularly from nomadic Muslim Kurds as well as Muslim Circassians (*Çerkes*) who had recently been resettled in eastern Anatolia, having fled Russia's expansion into the Caucasus with only their lives.[315] Furthermore, the Treaty stipulated that Russian troops remain in eastern Anatolia until reforms were implemented by the Ottoman government, guaranteeing the security of the Armenians.

Ultimately the Russian territorial gains in Anatolia and on the Black Sea coast awakened an age-old, British fear that the Ottoman Empire would crumble and Russia would take control of Istanbul and the Straits, thus shattering the fragile balance of power in the Mediterranean, which favored Britain. Accordingly, and in concert with other European powers - particularly that of Germany under the deft leadership of Count Otto von Bismarck - pressure was brought to bear on Russia and St. Petersburg signing the

---

[313] McCarthy. *Death and Exile*, 111-113.

[314] Ibid, 117.

[315] Ibid, 32-39.

Treaty of Berlin in July 1878. According to this treaty's stipulations, Bulgaria's independence as a vassal state of Russia was revoked and Bulgaria was placed back under Ottoman rule, albeit severely curtailed. Russian territorial gains in Anatolia and the Black Sea coast were also nullified. Russian troops were ordered to leave eastern Anatolia and the Treaty of Berlin, "... placed the responsibility for enforcing the Armenian reform provisions of the Treaty of San Stefano (article 61 of the new treaty) upon the entire Concert of Europe."[316] George Douglas Campbell, Duke of Argyll referring to the Armenian security reforms later wrote, "What was [once] everybody's business was [now] nobody's business."[317]

The Bulgarian revolt and subsequent treaties resulted in calls for separate and distinct Armenian security and political reforms. This correspondingly led to an increase in suspicion and animosity between Ottoman Muslims and Armenian Christians, on a general level. On a more localized level, when Russian troops withdrew from Ottoman territory in eastern Anatolia, Muslim Kurds and Circassians pillaged and looted Armenian homes, business and properties and many Armenians fled the violence to Russian-controlled Transcaucasia. While reprehensible, this was to be expected given previous Armenian massacres against the region's Muslim inhabitants at the behest of, or collusion with, Russian troops.[318] In essence, as incidences of conflict and outrage multiplied in eastern Anatolia, an eye for an eye mentality and practice ensued pitting the Empire's Muslims against Christians and vice-versa.

As the situation of both the Christian Armenians and Ottoman Muslims deteriorated in the eastern portions of the Ottoman Empire, where rule of law was tenuous in the best of times, ideas of nationalism and revolution spread

---

[316] Lewy, 8.

[317] George Douglas Campbell, Duke of Argyll. *Our Responsibilities for Turkey: Facts and Memories of Forty Years* (London: John Murray, 1896), 68.

[318] McCarthy. *Death and Exile*, 113.

and gained currency. The Concert of Europe dithered as to what to do regarding Ottoman security reforms and the protection of minorities within the Empire, including Armenians. However, the reforms were never implemented. Indeed, British and wider European insistence and objections regarding Ottoman treatment of the Armenians and other ethnic groups within the empire only managed to irritate Sultan Abdülhamid further and led to an almost personal suspicion on his part of the motives and loyalty of not just Armenians, but also Greeks, Jews and other non-Muslim Ottoman minorities. This resulted in what Lord James Bryce referred to as "…the storm of fire, famine and slaughter which descended upon them [the Armenians]…" Lord Bryce added, "Before the Treaty of Berlin the Sultan had no special enmity to the Armenians, nor had the Armenian nation any political aspirations. It was the stipulations then made for their protection that first marked them out for suspicion and hatred, and that first roused in them hopes of deliverance whose expression increased the hatred of their rulers."[319]

The unfolding massacres and recriminations of and against Muslim and Christian, Turk, Armenian, Kurd and Circassian can only be understood against the backdrop of religiously-defined, national revolts such as that in Bulgaria. These tragic events were predicated and informed by the general decline of the multi-ethnic, multi-confessional Ottoman Empire and the crises associated therewith. Indeed, as ideas of nationalism, self-determination and the example of homogeneous nation-states spread, they were accompanied by waves of forced migrations made by displaced Muslims from former Ottoman territories in the Balkans, Crimea, Transcaucasia and elsewhere.[320] These Muslim refugees fled to the shrinking Ottoman Empire. Many were not so lucky. From 1864 until 1912-13, several million Ottoman Muslims, mostly Turks, were massacred or died as victims of ethnic

---

[319] James Bryce. *Transcaucasia and Ararat: Being Notes of a Vacation Tour in the Autumn of 1876* (London: MacMillan, 1896), 523 as quoted in Lewy, 8-9.
[320] See McCarthy. *Death and Exile.*

cleansing in former Ottoman territories.[321] When the Ottomans lost Crete in 1897, much of the Muslim population, which is estimated to have constituted forty-five percent of the population, was forced to leave.[322]

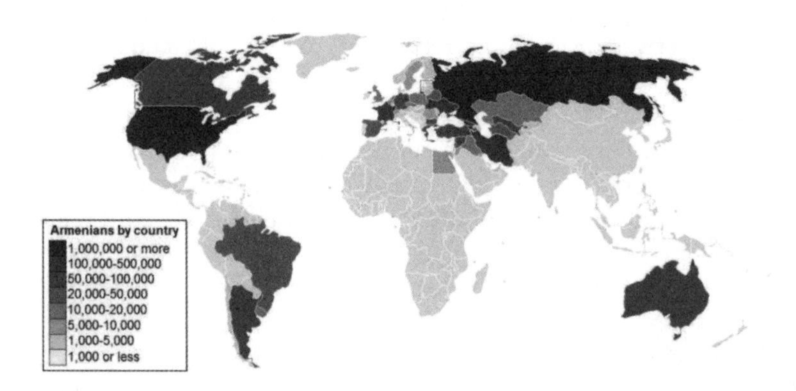

Armenian population by country[323]

Even after the departure of thousands of Muslims and despite the 'protected' legal status of the Muslims, as the Cretan state became increasingly oriented towards political union with the independent Greek state, political tension and renewed, violent inter-ethnic clashes led Muslims to gradually flee the island. Between the years 1900 and 1911, the Muslim population of the island decreased from 33,496

---

[321] See M. R. Khan. "The Ottoman Eastern Question and the Problematic Origins of Ethnic Cleansing, Genocide, and Humanitarian Interventionism in Modern Europe and the Middle East." In M. H. Yavuz and P. Sluglett (eds) *War and Diplomacy: The Russo-Turkish War of 1877–78 and the Treaty of Berlin* (Salt Lake City, UT: University of Utah Press, 2011), pp. 98–122.

[322] Hamit Bozarslan. "The General Ottoman and Turkish Contexts: from the Tanzimat (1838) to the Suppression of the Dersim Rebellion (1938)." *Online Encyclopedia of Mass Violence,* March 2008, http://www.massviolence.org/The-General-Ottoman-and-Turkish-Contexts-From-the-Tanzimat

[323]https://commons.wikimedia.org/wiki/File:ArmenianDiaspora.png

to 27,852.[324] Most were resettled in Anatolia, a place already desperately poor, crowded and awakening from the pre-modern era to the gray dawn of modernity with its accompanying and bitter breakfast of nationalism, ethnicity and territory. "It was the misfortune of Muslim communities in the Balkans, Anatolia, and the Caucasus that they lay in the path of the new [Christian] nationalisms. Their misfortune was compounded by the fact that the power upon which they depended, the Ottoman Empire, did not have the strength to defend them. Their sufferings were ironic, because, had the Turks in their days of power been nationalists of the Greek [or Bulgarian or Armenian] sort, it would have been the Christians who were driven out, leaving lands that were purely Muslim Turkish. Instead, the Ottomans suffered the Christians to remain. They had often treated the Christians well, often poorly, but they had allowed them to exist and to keep their languages, traditions, and religions. They were right to do so, but if fifteenth-century Turks had not been tolerant, nineteenth-century Turks might have survived in their homes [rather than being killed or expelled by Christian nationalists]."[325]

In addition to the events described above, two further developments within the Armenian community occurred at this time. These not only influenced events in the late Ottoman Empire, but continue to have an impact on inter-Armenian dialogue and relations as well as the political and social agendas espoused by various Armenian diaspora communities.

The Beginnings of an Armenian Exit

The exit of Armenians from the Ottoman Empire to France, South America, the United States and elsewhere began as a trickle in the late nineteenth century. Armenian emigrants constituted elements of the entire strata of

---

[324] Anna Kouvaraki. *Historical and Cultural Dimensions of the Muslim Cretans in Turkey*. PhD diss., İstanbul Bilgi Üniversitesi, 2014: 48.
[325] McCarthy. *Death and Exile*, 13.

Ottoman Armenians, from the poorest subsistence farmers of eastern Anatolia to the richest merchants of İzmir and Istanbul. Like most migrant groups, strong ties to family and to the Russian- and Ottoman-controlled motherland dissipated little over time. As such, diaspora Armenians sent news and remittances, encouraged and furthered the possibility of future emigration, and assisted in the education of multiple generations of Ottoman Armenians in European and, to a lesser extent, American schools.[326] While only one hundred Armenians are thought to have emigrated to the United States by the mid-nineteenth century, it is estimated that approximately 66,000 Armenian emigrants had arrived in the United States by 1914. This figure includes almost 52,000 Armenians who left the Ottoman Empire between the years 1899 and 1914.[327] Only 4,000 Armenians are estimated to have emigrated to France prior to 1914.[328] At least some of these Armenian emigrants were touched by the reprisals and violence engendered by the increasing Muslim/Christian tensions developing in the Ottoman Empire at the time. They were also fully aware of a nascent and increasingly violent Armenian nationalism. The memories of these early Armenian migrants were added to the catalogue of memories and experiences of those who emigrated after 1915. As such, they assisted in the genesis and development of a fecund and powerful diaspora Armenian identity.[329]

The reaction to Ottoman reprisals and the suppression of Armenian nationalism and acts of terrorism within its

---

[326] For theoretical work on immigrants and ties to the homeland, see David A. Gerber and Alan M. Kraut. ed., *American Immigration and Ethnicity: A Reader* (New York: Palgrave Macmillan, 2005).

[327] Robert Mirak,105-118.

[328] Maud Mandel. *In the Aftermath of Genocide: Armenians and Jews in Twentieth-Century France*. Duke University Press, 2003: 11.

[329] See Anny Bakalian. *Armenian-Americans: From Being to Feeling Armenian* (New Brunswick, NJ: Transaction Publishers, 1996). See also Knarik Avakian., *The History of the Armenian Community of the United States* of *America: From the Beginning to 1924* (Yerevan, Armenia: Gitutiun Publishing House, 2000).

borders, coupled with the unwillingness, for political and strategic reasons, of European powers and Russia to implement and enforce the reforms demanded by various treaties, led to various reactions and forms of resistance, most of it violent, by Armenians. Armenians nationalists in the Ottoman Empire were encouraged in their actions against the Ottoman state by Russia and further emboldened by the success of other nationalities, particularly the Greeks and Bulgarians, who had achieved their independence from Istanbul, in the process expelling tens of thousands of Muslims and creating the beginnings of homogenous nation-states. As such, and mirroring then-current developments in both Russia and Eastern Europe, Armenian nationalist societies, secret or openly political, were founded, mainly in eastern Anatolia beginning in the 1880s. These societies insisted on autonomy for Armenians at the very least, and, at most, their independence and the removal of all Muslims from what they considered to be "Armenian" territories.

Interestingly, Muslim Ottomans, particularly members of the Ottoman Turkish elite, were experiencing a similar national awakening, though it was a reactive rather than proactive awakening, thus differentiating it from its Armenian or Bulgarian counterparts. Often educated in Europe, these Muslim students pledged their "… allegiance to the ideas of social equality, liberty, and legal rights as well as to the abstract concept of the state. Personal allegiance to the sultan was therefore eclipsed by a patriotic allegiance to the Ottoman 'state.'"[330] Similar to the Armenians, Greeks and other minorities, Muslims began to form secret societies, the most well-known being the Young Ottomans and the Young Turks. The Ottoman state took a dim view of any national society, Turkish, Armenian or otherwise,

---

[330] Fatma Müge Göçek. "Ethnic Segmentation, Western Education, and Political Outcomes: Nineteenth-Century Ottoman Society." *Poetics Today* (1993): 530.

and their meetings were often broken up, their leaders arrested and then exiled.[331]

The Development of Armenian Political Factions

The two most influential Armenian national societies were the Hunchaks and the Dashnaks. They were similar to Greek and Bulgarian revolutionary organizations in their membership, tactics and aims. However, unlike their counterparts, Armenians formed a distinct minority in the lands they planned to seize.[332] Their emergence heralded the end of loosely organized Armenian pressure for evolutionary change in the Ottoman Empire. Not only were the Hunchaks and Dashnaks responding to changes within the Empire, they also attempted to stress the grievances of Armenians, real or perceived, as a means of intensifying support for reform, autonomy and independence. Their agenda was pushed via violent acts committed against Muslims and Christians, to include fellow Armenians, as demonstrated below.

"The parties certainly desired reform, but their version of reform was not just a desire for equality and security but for a very specific form of national status. Thus the parties were neither a particular 'provocation' of the state nor the only 'logical' expression of Armenian suffering, though they have been portrayed as the former in Turkish nationalist historiography and as the latter in much 'Armenian' scholarship. From the view of the [Ottoman] palace, the significant characteristic of the parties was the agenda they shared with the previously successful Bulgarian revolutionaries, and the geographical location of the community they sought to 'liberate.'"[333] As such, they were a threat to the Ottoman state and attempts were made to

---

[331] M. Şükrü Hanioğlu. *Osmanlı İttihad ve Terakki cemiyeti" ve" Jön Türklük": (1889-1902).* Vol. 1. İletişim Yayınları, 1985: 177.
[332] McCarthy. *Death and Exile*, 118.
[333] Bloxham, 50.

suppress the parties and the cause they espoused: an independent and religiously homogenous Armenia.

In 1887, a group of Armenian exiles in Geneva, Switzerland organized the Hunchakian Revolutionary Party (named after the newspaper *Hunchak* or *Hnchak*, meaning "bell"). The Hunchaks, as they were commonly known, advocated a socialist government for an independent Armenia that would include territory peopled by Armenians in Russia, Persia and the Ottoman Empire. Similar to other revolutionary movements of the time, particularly the Russian *Narodnaya Volya,* the Hunchaks advocated Armenian independence through armed struggle, political terror and the dissemination of oral and written propaganda. The Hunchak party's manifesto listed Article 6 as, "The time for the general revolution [in the Ottoman Empire] will be when a foreign power attacks Turkey externally. The party shall [then] revolt internally."[334]

In June 1890, Russian Armenians founded a second party in Tiflis (Tbilisi), in Russian Transcaucasia. The Armenian Revolutionary Federation (ARF) or "Dashnaks," as they were popularly known (*Dashnaktsuthiun* means "federation") argued for the political and economic emancipation of Turkish Armenia.[335] While most members were socialists like their Hunchak counterparts, many felt that an emphasis on socialism would occur at the expense of the Armenian nationalist cause. Dashnaks intended to achieve independence from the Ottoman Empire by revolutionary and violent means; arming Armenians, destroying government institutions, killing non-Armenians (Muslims) and using "… the weapon of terror on corrupt government officers, spies, traitors, grafters, and all sorts of oppressors."[336] The first Dashnak leaflet to circulate in the Empire declared the Dashnak's intention to fight "…until

---

[334] Sarkis Atamian. *The Armenian Community: The Historical Development of a Social and Ideological Conflict* (New York: Philosophical Library, 1955): 96, as quoted in Lewy, 12.
[335] Lewy, 12.
[336] Ibid.

its last drop of blood for the liberation of the fatherland."[337] Another Dashnak leaflet claimed Dashnak members "... would set for itself 'the exact hour of the common uprising in Turkish Armenia.' Similar statements emerged from the Hunchaks."[338]

Ottoman minorities such as the Armenians came to the realization that political independence was their overriding and ultimate goal, either through political activism or violent means via an intricate process. "They determined their course of social action by reinterpreting their relationship with the Western powers (including their Western-style education) and their changing relationship with the Ottoman state. Two important external factors led the minorities to gravitate toward political independence as a possible course of action: the nature of their interactions with the Western powers, and the impact of the notion of nationalism generated in the West. The Western powers, through their protection of Ottoman minorities, had fostered an ideology of separateness."[339] They also, often and blatantly, encouraged it. For example, it was Russian policy to destabilize and dismember the Ottoman Empire. One of the ways Russia implemented this policy was to not only allow, but encourage the Dashnaks and Hunchaks to organize and mobilize in order to foment armed attacks in the Ottoman Empire using both Russia and Russian-controlled Transcaucasia as a springboard. Russia did so while strenuously discouraging any whiff of Armenian separatism in its own territories. As historical and demographic records demonstrate as well as the statements and sentiments highlighted above, Armenians needed no encouragement from Russia and were itching for a fight.[340]

British reports from the time mention the murder of a number of Ottoman officials. Interestingly, these officials were not only ethnic Turks and Kurds but also included

---

[337] Bloxham, 50.

[338] Ibid.

[339] Göçek, 531.

[340] See McCarthy. *Death and Exile*, chapter 6.

Ottoman officials who were Armenians.[341] For example, in November 1892, an Armenian villager attempted to assassinate the governor of Van Province in eastern Anatolia. When arrested, the villager claimed to have acted under the guidance of several others, including his brother and the Armenian village priest. When asked why he had attempted to perpetrate the crime, he noted that the assassination would further the "Armenian national cause."[342] The *kaymakam,* or head district official, of the largely Armenian town of Gevash was assassinated as were numerous Armenian policemen, at least one Armenian Chief of Police and a number of Armenian advisors to the Ottoman government. In 1912, the Armenian and twice-elected mayor of Van, Bedros Kapamaciyan, was assassinated by Dashnaks. Kapmaciyan's crime was to eschew Armenian independence in favor of a more inclusive Ottoman state. "Kapamaciyan stood as a representative of the Armenians, particularly the Armenian merchant class, who were willing to cooperate with the Ottoman power structure and support gradual reform. His political stand was steadfastly Ottoman, supporting the governor and the central government."[343] On top of his position as an Ottoman official and his stance against Armenian revolutionary movements in the Ottoman Empire, Kapamaciyan also refused to sign a Dashnak-inspired petition calling for the removal of the Ottoman governor of Van. Not only did he refuse to affix his signature, but Kapamaciyan swayed other Armenian merchants in Van to disassociate themselves from the violent and revolutionary Armenian independence movement.[344]

---

[341] Lewy, 13.

[342] Ibid.

[343] Justin McCarthy, Esat Arslan, Cemalettin Taşkıran and Ömer Turan. *The Armenian Rebellion at Van* (Salt Lake City: University of Utah Press, 2006), 164.

[344] Ibid. See also Hasan Oktay. "On the Assassination of Mayor Kapamaciyan by the Tashnak Committee." *Review of Armenian Studies* I, no. 1 (2002): 79-89.

Politics and Actions of the Armenian Revolutionaries

Both the Hunchaks and Dashnaks advocated and carried out armed struggles, other forms of violence and assassinations to achieve their aims. However, they were split along theoretical lines regarding the actual form Armenian independence should take. The Hunchaks demanded a fully independent Armenia. Dashnaks opted for the vaguer notion of what they termed "free Armenia." This is important because these apparently minor divisions, as distilled over time, continued to inform, shape and galvanize Armenian diaspora identity. However, these ideological lines blurred when it came to confronting the Ottoman state. Members of both groups attacked Ottoman army units, posts, Kurdish villages and executed ethnic Armenians who cooperated with the Ottoman state. In these acts, the Dashnaks and Hunchaks often acted in concert with one another. According to the historian Louise Nalbandian, "there was no radical difference between the Dashnak Program… and the aims and activities of the Hunchaks."[345] For example, in 1890, a group of Armenians headed by a former student and Russian Armenian, Sarkis Gugunian, led an armed expedition into Ottoman Anatolia in the hopes of mobilizing support for an independent Armenia. The expedition was funded by wealthy Armenians living in Russian-controlled Baku and Tiflis and initially had the backing of the Dashnaks, though they later tried to dissuade Gugunian from his "unrealistic" expedition. After clashing with Ottoman troops, Gugunian and his party of 125 men ran low on food and supplies and crossed back into Russian territory where 43 members of the group were promptly arrested by Cossack irregulars. The Russians were not only embarrassed by the operation, they were also fearful of Gugunian's brand of revolutionary Armenian nationalism, fearing that it might topple not just the Ottoman state, but Russian rule in Transcaucasia as well. As

[345] Nalbandian, 172.

such, twenty-seven members of the Gugunian expedition were exiled to Siberia.

Though the Gungunian armed foray into eastern Anatolia appears to have gained some popularity among urbanites in eastern Armenia, it failed to gain the support and sympathy of the largely apolitical peasantry in eastern Anatolia. More importantly, the expedition and accompanying ideas of Armenian independence failed to gain as much currency among the prosperous, urban, Armenian inhabitants of the Ottoman Empire's great trading cities.[346] However, this would change by 1915, as the majority of Armenians in eastern Anatolia came to not only support but actively advance the cause, and therefore violence, of nationalist Armenians. They actively revolted against the Ottoman state and supported the invading Russian armies and Armenian troops.[347]

The Gugunian expedition again highlights the often-conflicting nature of cooperation between Russian officials and Armenian nationalists. While many in St. Petersburg were fearful of Armenian nationalism and what it might mean for the future of Russian rule in Transcaucasia, these same ministers of state were equally interested in dismembering the Ottoman Empire. Accordingly, they strongly encouraged Armenian acts of nationalism, propaganda and violence directed at the Ottoman Empire while discouraging any similar acts on Russian territory. Furthermore, while publicly insisting on reforms and protection for Ottoman minorities, Russia, along with France, actively dissuaded and obstructed the implementation of any reforms within the Ottoman Empire that may have improved the lot of minorities, to include the Armenians.[348] As long as the revolutionary Armenian nationalism espoused by Dashnaks, Hunchaks and others focused its energies, assassinations, massacres and propaganda successfully on the Ottoman Empire and

346 Lewy, 14.

347 McCarthy. *Death and Exile*, 185-187.

348 Suny, *Looking Toward* Ararat, 80.

Muslims, it was tolerated by the Russian Czarist government. However, when Russian-supported activities such as Gugunian's raids foundered, assassinations proved embarrassing or when the Armenian nationalism fostered on Russian soil shifted its focus to a free Armenia that necessarily included western *and* eastern Armenia, Russian authorities responded with arrests and exile. Yet even at the height anti-Armenian sentiment amongst Russian government circles in the 1880s and 1890s, when church lands were confiscated and Armenian nationalist activities and raids were discouraged, "…Armenian nationalists revolutionaries refused to concentrate on fighting the Russian autocracy and instead (continued to direct) their activities against the Ottoman Empire."[349]

Reactions by the Ottoman State

Just as Armenian Dashnak and Hunchak violence often did not differentiate between "innocent" Kurdish or Armenian villagers and "guilty" Ottoman soldiers, so the Ottoman government's reaction to Armenian demands for autonomy and independence was characterized by its lack of nuance. Large-scale arrests occurred in 1893, in Marsovan, after the appearance of placards inciting Armenians to revolt against Ottoman rule. In 1894, after a number of Armenians refused to pay nomadic Kurdish tribes customary tribute and Armenian revolutionary groups indiscriminately attacked and killed large numers of the Kurdish Bekhran and Zadian tribes, Ottoman troops were deployed. After bitter fighting, the Armenians negotiated a surrender. However, even after their surrender and given the atrocities committed by Armenian nationalists, the massacre of ethnic Armenian villagers that followed did not differentiate in regards to age or sex.[350]

Why was the Ottoman state so heavy-handed when it came to calls for autonomy, let alone independence? The

---

[349] Ibid, 23.

[350] McCarthy, et al., *The Armenian Rebellion at Van*, 56-61.

answer lies with previous calls for autonomy that had directly resulted in the independence of various states such as Bulgaria and Greece at the expense of the Ottoman Empire and accompanied by large-scale ethnic cleansing of Muslims. "According to the Ottoman state's collective memory, the only demand by minorities for any other type of autonomy was that initiated by the Ottoman Greeks. Although they had initially demanded communal autonomy, this soon became a demand for 'territorial' autonomy and ultimately led to the formation of an independent Greek state. Thus, the Ottoman state perceived all minority attempts to attain communal autonomy in this vein, that is, as demands for an actual territorial autonomy that would rapidly progress to political independence. This view of autonomy adopted by the Ottoman state became the most significant internal factor to polarize those Ottoman minorities whose political agendas did not already include territorial autonomy or political independence."[351] Armenian actions and increasingly vocal calls for outright independence were part of this rubric. Similarly, the often-violent reaction by the Ottoman state was informed by previous, traumatic experiences that involved the loss of territory, wealth and prestige. In essence, the Ottoman Empire was collapsing. The Ottoman state was under no illusion by the late nineteenth century that outright independence for the Empire's minorities would lead to the demise of the Empire itself. As such, it was literally fighting for its life.

By provoking the Ottoman state through violence, Armenian nationalists were implementing a strategy designed to gain the sympathy of the United States, Russia and the European powers and bring about Great Power intervention in the hopes that this would eventually result in a free Armenian state. Cyrus Hamlin, the American founder of Robert College in Istanbul, was told by an "an eloquent defender of the [Armenian] revolution" that the Armenian rebels would "... watch their opportunity to kill Turks and

[351] Göçek, 532.

Kurds, set fire to their villages, and then make their escape into the mountains. The enraged Moslems will then rise, and fall upon the defenseless Armenians and slaughter them with such barbarity that Russia will enter in the name of humanity and Christian civilization and take possession."[352]

The Hunchak platform actively encouraged the incitement of Armenians in the Ottoman Empire "…against their enemies and were to 'profit' from the retaliatory actions of these same enemies."[353] The American author and self-proclaimed friend of the Armenians, George Hepworth, as saying, "The [Armenian] revolutionists are doing what they can to make fresh outrages possible. That is their avowed purpose. They reason that if they can induce the Turks to kill more of the Armenians, themselves excepted, Europe will be forced to intervene."[354]

Incitement to Action: The Armenian Seizure of the Ottoman Bank

The tense situation in eastern Anatolia in the mid-1890s was a result of a number of factors: continued Armenian revolutionary violence and the often-violent Ottoman responses; the overall weakness of the Ottoman state; multiple refugee crises that resulted in the resettlement to eastern and southern Anatolia of uprooted, impoverished and traumatized Muslims from the Balkans, Crete and Transcaucasia; the raids and slaughter of Armenians by nomadic, Kurdish tribes in eastern and southern Anatolia; and the lack of overt European support – military or otherwise - for an independent Armenia. These tensions were further exacerbated when a group of Dashnak revolutionaries seized the Imperial Ottoman Bank in

---

[352] Letter by Cyrus Hamlin in the *Boston Congregationalist*, 23 December 1893, reprinted in United States Department of State, *Papers Relating to Foreign Relations of the United States, 1895*, 1416; as quoted in Lewy, 17-18.

[353] Nalbandian, 110.

[354] George H. Hepworth. *Through Armenian on Horseback* (London: Isbister, 1898), 341.

Istanbul on August 26, 1896. Armed with pistols, grenades, dynamite and hand-held bombs, the Dashnaks threatened to blow up the Bank if various demands were not met by the Ottoman government. "The demands [of the Dashnaks] included the appointment of a European high commissioner for the Armenian provinces and a general amnesty for Armenians convicted on political charges."[355]

While the Dashnaks were unable to bring about the wanted intervention of European powers or Russia, those who survived the initial efforts by Ottoman authorities to free the bank, did manage to negotiate their escape from the Ottoman Bank and get themselves safe passage to France. This was done via the assistance of European diplomats living in the city. Their actions, rather than achieving a degree of autonomy or protection for Armenians in the Empire, are said to have provoked the first recorded slaughter of Armenians in Istanbul.[356]

There is evidence that at least some in the Armenian community knew of the impending bank seizure.[357] Many wealthy Armenian families left Istanbul that morning. After the seizure, some Ottoman officials reportedly provided Muslims, including Kurds and Laz who held deep-seated grievances and prejudices from experiences in eastern Anatolia, with iron bars and cudgels, inciting them to violence against the Armenian "perpetrators" who also happened to be their neighbors and fellow Ottoman citizens.[358] The ensuing slaughter claimed an estimated five to six thousand Armenians, with most of the deaths occurring amongst the very poor.

As noted, the provocations, assassinations, murder of Ottoman Muslims and sabotage performed by Armenian revolutionaries were coldly calculated to provoke the reactive slaughter and murder of fellow Armenians for the consumption of Europeans and Russians via lurid press

---

[355] Ibid, 24.

[356] Bloxham, 55.

[357] Lewy, 25.

[358] William L. Langer. *The Diplomacy of Imperialism: 1890-1902* (New York: Alfred A. Knopf, 1935), vol. 1, 325 as quoted in Ibid.

articles informed by knee-jerk sympathies for Christians and racist views of Turks, in particular, and Muslims, in general. The Ottoman reaction was also cold and indiscriminate. Judging from numerous historical accounts, Ottoman responses to Armenian violence and demands for outright independence varied from province to province and town to town, but resulted in the killing of innocent people. These people may have had no connection to Armenian revolutionary movements, but they were marked because of their Christian, Armenian identity. Men, women and children who fled and survived these massacres often starved to death in the harsh winters or cruel summers of eastern Anatolia. The often severe Ottoman reaction to the violence provoked by Armenian nationalists received widespread coverage in Europe, the United States and Russia and continued to inform the racist image of the "terrible Turk," however erroneous.[359]

By underlining the highly complex and volatile situation that existed in the Ottoman Empire, but particularly in eastern and southern Anatolia, this book calls attention to the plight and horrific demise of many innocents, both Muslim and Christian. It also underscores the direct links between the often-violent actions of Armenian revolutionaries and the reactive, Ottoman massacres that ensued in the 1890s. These purposely provocative, often murderous Armenian actions and the reactions they provoked represent a startling prelude of what was to befall the Empire and many of its Armenian citizens in 1915. However, prior to those cataclysmic events, the Empire experienced a renaissance of sorts and, for a brief moment in time, a modicum of stability and cooperation between Muslims and non-Muslims ensued.

The Young Turk Period

Fighting and slaughter between Muslims and Armenians continued intermittently in eastern Anatolia until the

[359] See Yavuz. "Orientalism, the 'Terrible Turk' and Genocide."

overthrow of Sultan Abdülhamid II in 1909 by a group of liberal Ottoman officers from Selanik (Salonika) who belonged to a secret society. Members of this secret society, named the Committee of Union and Progress (CUP) or *Ittihad ve Terraki,* were committed to replacing Sultan Abdülhamid and restoring the 1876 constitution. The upstart officers who successfully carried out this *coup d'etat* were popularly known inside and outside of the Ottoman Empire as "Young Turks."

Beyond restoring the suspended 1878 constitution and deposing Abdülhamid II, the CUP called upon the European powers to fulfill their treaty obligations vis-à-vis the Ottoman Empire. This pleased many Ottoman Armenians who had hoped for the proper implementation of Article 61 of the 1878 Treaty of Berlin for years. As noted earlier, the Article placed the onus of ensuring Armenian safety and well-being on the entire Concert of Europe with predictably dismal results.

Representative of the general bonhomie and optimism that characterized the initial rule of the CUP, the Dashnak party worked openly with the Young Turk regime, electing six of 12 delegates to the new Ottoman parliament. The Dashnaks also became defenders of the new sultan, Mehmed Reşad V (Reşat Mehmet or Mehmed Reshad). At their fifth congress in 1909, the Dashnak organization publicly proclaimed their policy of cooperation with the sultan and the Young Turks and an end to their underground activities in support of Armenian independence and the accompanying destabilization of the Ottoman state.[360] However, in hindsight, this was only a bid for time.

Members affiliated with the Hunchak organization were less willing to embrace the new regime and believe its egalitarian promises than their Dashnak counterparts. The Hunchak stance was perhaps more indicative of the overall

---

[360] Hratch Dasnabendian. *History of the Armenian Revolutionary Federation Dashnaktsutiun 1890-1924.* Translated by Bryan Fleming and Vahe Habeshian (Milan: Oemme Edizioni, 1990), 87-92.

Armenian nationalist stance and its aims that were espoused by both Dashnaks and Hunchaks: the dissolution or dismemberment of the Ottoman Empire and the subsequent establishment of an independent Armenian state created by and for Armenians.

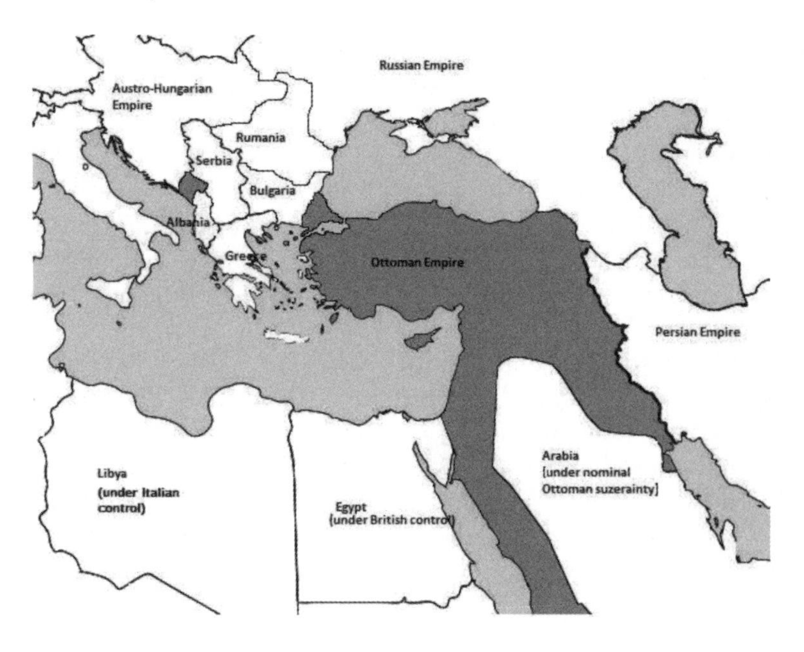

The Ottoman Empire in 1913

Though the Dashnak Committee and its members were broadly supportive of these ends and the means used to achieve it, they occasionally utilized rather more nuanced strategies and tactics than their Hunchak counterparts. In fact, the genesis of the Dashnak détente with the CUP regime dated back to the 1890s when Dashnak members were exiled in Europe and established an alliance with disgruntled Ottoman Muslims – some of whom eventually became CUP supporters and leaders - against a common enemy, the reactionary and authoritarian sultan,

Abdülhamid II.[361] The Dashnaks and the so-called Reformed Hunchak Committees even agreed to participate in a CUP-sponsored conference in Paris in 1902, but only if the CUP agreed to support their demands of Armenian autonomy.[362] Some in the CUP strongly disagreed with extending any degree autonomy to minorities within the Empire, Muslim and non-Muslim alike, be they Christian Armenians or Muslim Albanians. Many in the CUP, akin to Sultan Abdülhamid and his ministers, viewed autonomy as simply a step to outright independence. However, others in the CUP worked for a compromise with the Dashnaks, Hunchaks and other minority organizations, viewing a grand alliance of all the Empire's ethnic and religious groups as their only chance of deposing the sultan and preserving the Empire.[363]

Interestingly, some scholars view this alliance between Armenian revolutionary organizations and the CUP - both prior to and after the deposition of Abdülhamid II - as ultimately destructive to the Ottoman Empire. In particular, the historian Justin McCarthy posits that the ostensible "Revolutionary Brotherhood" between the various factions opposing the sultan blinded the Ottoman democrats and, to some extent, the Armenian nationalists, as to their essentially heterogeneous world views.[364] The Ottoman Muslim reformers were interested in just that: the political reformation and modernization of the Empire. Thus, there were some Young Turks who were willing to cede autonomy to minority groups who ostensibly shared their overarching aims, ideals and, ultimately, the longevity of the Empire. However, there is little indication that either the Hunchaks or, to a lesser degree, the Dashnaks were willing to compromise on the issue of independence for long.

---

[361] M. Şükrü Hanioğlu. *The Young Turks in Opposition* (Oxford: Oxford University Press, 1995), 87, 90, 116.
[362] Nalbandian, 128-131.
[363] See M. Şükrü Hanioğlu. *Preparation for a Revolution: The Young Turks, 1902-1908* (Oxford: Oxford University Press, 1995), 35-49. See also Dasnabedian, 56.
[364] McCarthy, et al. *The Armenian Rebellion at Van*, 39.

Indeed, the historical record indicates that both groups never viewed autonomy within the Empire as anything less than a stepping-stone on their road to an independent Armenia for Armenians.

The Young Turk revolution signaled a heady time period in the Empire, regardless of the volatile ethnic and religious fault lines, and, for a short while, it appeared that the multi-cultural, multi-confessional, polyglot Ottoman Empire would survive for many years to come. This was quickly shattered by the outbreak of the First Balkan War in 1912, which resulted in yet more Ottoman losses in the Balkans; territories considered integral to the survival and viability of the Empire.[365]

The defeats suffered during the brief reign of the CUP were shocking in their breadth and scope. When they were posited against the backdrop of previous losses of territory, populations and revenues, these military defeats and the feelings of impotence and humiliation experienced by the Ottoman elite, let alone the average Ottoman Muslim citizen, must have been profound. By 1912, for close to a century and beginning with the loss of Greece in the 1820s, the Ottoman Empire had lost 32.7 percent of its territory and twenty percent of its population – territory and populations the Empire had ruled for close to five hundred years.[366] And the losses steadily mounted. Egypt gained *de facto* independence in 1841; losses in the Crimea and Transcaucasia to an increasingly powerful Russian Empire continued throughout the nineteenth century; Romania was lost in 1877; Bulgaria, Bosnia-Herzogovina and Crete were all lost within days of each other in 1908; the Ottoman provinces that form the modern state of Libya were lost to Italy in 1911. By 1913, the Ottoman Empire had lost 83 percent of its territories in Europe, considered the most

---

[365] For an in-depth study the Balkan War and accompanying acts of ethnic cleansing, see Edward J. Erickson, *Defeat in Detail: The Ottoman Army in the Balkans, 1912-1913* (Westport, CT: Praeger Publishers, 2003).

[366] Lewy, 35.

important, integral and lucrative part of the Empire for the previous five hundred years.

The catastrophic loss of predominantly Muslim Albania in 1913 proved to be momentous as far as Young Turk ideology and rhetoric. It also resulted in a *coup d'etat* which replaced the more egalitarian and liberal members of the CUP with a more nationalistic and conservative triumvirate of leaders led by the capable, if megalomaniacal, Ismail Enver Beyefendi, commonly known as Enver Paşa (Enver Pasha).[367]

Many in Enver's cadre were deeply affected by a type of siege mentality on account of the almost constant hemorrhaging of Ottoman territory accompanied by acts of ethnic cleansing and forced migration of Muslim communities on a massive scale from the Caucasus to Aegean islands to the Balkans. As importantly, Ottoman Muslim feelings of resentment toward many states in Europe and, not surprisingly, Russia tended to color foreign and domestic actions and policies by Ottoman officials.

The losses suffered by the Ottomans from 1823 onward – the independence of Greece, Romania and others - were made possible with the significant support, armaments and sometimes outright annexation of various European states. The Europeans wanted the Ottomans out of Europe, in particular. The European powers and Russia also issued strenuous and incessant calls for better treatment, protection and greater autonomy for what were termed the Empire's Christian minorities. This was ostensibly done for the good of the minorities, but was also used to cloak efforts to support dismemberment of the Empire from within. Yet the calls for protection of an increasingly diverse set of minorities, from Armenian Protestant to Maronite Catholic to Bulgarian Orthodox, and reified by new and imported categorizations and classifications from Europe and Russia, were transmitted to the Empire and spread like a virus. This led to the facilitation and creation of spaces

---

[367] See Salahi R. Sonyel. "Mustafa Kemal and Enver in conflict, 1919–22." *Middle Eastern Studies* 25, no. 4 (1989): 506-515.

inhabited by the Self and its mutually constitutive Other: Christian Self versus Muslim Other; i.e. Christian Greek versus Muslim Turk and Christian Armenian versus Muslim Turk or, more generally, Ottoman Muslim. In turn, this provoked the ethnic cleansing of Muslims from newly-independent states in the Balkans and in the regions conquered by Russia in the Black Sea Region and the Caucasus.

It is important to understand that for European powers, Ottoman Muslim rule anywhere on the European continent was anathema and an affront to their constructed sense of moral, cultural and industrial superiority. Ottoman rule simply flew in the face of what had become, by the late nineteenth century, reason - as perceived by an increasingly bellicose and confident Europe. European powers became less tolerant of Ottoman Turkish rule in Europe not because of Christianity, *per se*, though this did dominate some of the discourse and rationale for European actions aimed at the Ottoman Empire. Rather, "it was in the 'liberal' and 'secular' era [of the late nineteenth century] that European leaders asked how was it possible that an Islamic entity could rule Christian populations in Europe's backyard? This question led them to marshal their resources to expel the Ottoman state from the European continent."[368] They did so by concluding that the Ottoman Turks should be expelled from Europe at all costs. Correspondingly, Russia, which had previously paid little or no attention to Balkan Christians, now encouraged them to rebel against their Muslim Turkish "oppressors," kill or forcibly remove their Muslim neighbors and declare their autonomy or outright independence while Great Britain and France looked on and offered their tacit support while decrying Ottoman reactions.[369] "This dialectic of a European 'self' and Turkish 'other' played a key role in the

[368] Yavuz. "Orientalism, the 'Terrible Turk' and Genocide," 114.
[369] McCarthy. *Death and Exile*, 65-81.

formation of public opinion to end the Ottoman presence in Europe regardless of the human cost."[370]

Given these well-understood European and Russian pressures, contingencies and their calculating use of the Empire's Christian minorities, some prominent members of Enver's cadre voiced a desire for a Muslim empire or, at the very least, a "Turkish" state. Correspondingly, Enver and clique increasingly viewed the Empire's Christians and, to a lesser extent, Jews suspiciously.[371] Indeed, CUP suspicions of the Empire's significant Christian minorities have been cited in order to demonstrate that at least some officials in the Young Turk regime were convinced of the need to get rid of not just Armenians, but all Christians, in order to achieve a Turkish empire.[372] Many in the CUP did eventually identify the Empire's salvation with that of a Muslim, and to a lesser extent, Turkish state. However, this ideological shift from Pan-Ottomanism to something more akin to Turkish nationalism or Pan-Islamism should be placed in context. In this, the CUP differed little from their Greek and Armenian nationalist counterparts. The only difference being that the CUP officials awoke to their Turkishness rather late.[373] Indeed, recent scholarship indicates that many Ottoman Turks never "awoke" at all.

---

[370] Yavuz, 114.

[371] The sense of distrust among some CUP members was largely directed at Ottoman Jews espousing Zionism. The CUP actually included many high-ranking, Ottoman Jewish officials. See Jacob M. Landau. "Ottoman Turkey." In Reeva S. Simon, Michael M. Laskier, and Sara Reguer. *The Jews of the Middle East and North Africa in Modern Times*. Columbia University Press, 2003: 288-289. See also Jacob M. Landau. *The" Young Turks" and Zionism: Some Comments*. Hebrew University of Jerusalem, Harry S. Truman Research Institute for the Advancement of Peace, 1983: 202-203.

[372] See Vahram Ayvazyan. "Genocide: Intent, Motivation and Types." *Suvremene teme* 5, no. 1 (2012): 26. See also Taner Akçam. *From Empire to Republic: Turkish Nationalism and the Armenian Genocide*. Zed Books, 2004, 146.

[373] Erol Ülker. "Assimilation of the Muslim communities in the first decade of the Turkish Republic (1923-1934)." *European Journal of Turkish Studies. Social Sciences on Contemporary Turkey* (2008): 9.

Even the disastrous Balkan Wars "… did not result in the construction of a dominant ideology but rather a cacophony of different strands of intellectual responses. It was not until the emergence of a Turkish nation-state after a successful war of independence that Turkism became a dominant ideology. Indeed, it was only at this point that, logically, Turkism could come into its own, for without a Turkish national state it remained only one of many competing ideological strands of thought."[374]

The examples set by European nation-states, the latest being the influential states of Italy and Germany, had demonstrated in tremendous detail the ostensible supremacy of nationalism as defined and espoused ideologically in European notions of what constituted the nation. First and foremost, the nation needed to be homogeneous, i.e. France for the French and Italy for the Italians. If French and Italians had not existed prior to the creation of the nation-state, they would soon be socially engineered thus.

The newly created nation-states in the Balkans that had broken away from the Ottoman Empire were patterned precisely on European notions of what constituted the nation-state. As such, the main goal for Bulgarian nationalists was the creation of a Bulgaria for Bulgarians. Because the concept of Bulgaria, similar the concept of Italy, was misunderstood or held no currency for many within its territories, the criteria for who was a Bulgarian quickly became associated with religion - just as it had in Greece. Christians, preferably Orthodox Christians, were Bulgarians. Muslims were categorically not.

As early as the 1820s in the case of Greece, ethnic Greek Muslims as well as Greek-speaking Muslims (ethnic Turks, for example) were an affront and an impediment to the creation of a homogenous Greek state. As such, these undesirables were all deemed as Turks – as they later were in Bulgaria and elsewhere in the Balkans - and were made

---

[374] Ebru Boyar. "The Impact of the Balkan Wars on Ottoman History Writing: Searching for a Soul." *Middle East Critique* 23, no. 2 (2014): 155.

unwelcome. This resulted in multiple, often overlapping waves of ethnic cleansing and the forced migration of Muslims from Greece and then the Balkans in the wake of "national" victories.[375] This firmly demonstrated the measures newly independent nation-states would take in order to create a Greece for Greeks and Bulgaria for Bulgarians. Referencing the Balkan Wars, Philipp Ther drily noted, "The nation-states involved were struggling for dominance over disputed areas by means of ethnic homogenization and pursued purposeful, large-scale resettlement policies to this end."[376]

In western European countries with smaller ethnic and regional minorities such as France, the nation-building process was accompanied with violence against perceived enemies of the state in the form of institutions or political order, such as the Roman Catholic Church, Jews, and, at times, the monarchy. In countries with larger and more distinct ethnic groups, particularly the patchwork quilt that made up the former Ottoman provinces of the Balkan Peninsula or eastern Anatolia, the nation-building process led to a sharp increase in violence. This was exacerbated by the power vacuum created with the withdrawal of the Ottoman state in former territories. It created an atmosphere in which to settle scores for remembered and real grievances alike.

Viewed in this light, it is actually surprising how little nationalist rhetoric emanated officially or unofficially from the Young Turks. Indeed, statements issued by the CUP indicated their overwhelming commitment to the preservation of the multi-ethnic Empire.[377] The Young

---

[375] For a detailed study of the ethnic cleansing, massacres and forced population exchanges of Greek Muslims in the wake of Greek independence, see McCarthy. *Death and Exile*, 10-13. For Bulgarian atrocities against Muslims, see Boyar, chapter 3.

[376] Philipp Ther. *The Dark Side of Nation-States: Ethnic Cleansing in Modern Europe*. Vol. 19. Berghahn Books, 2014: 11.

[377] See Taha Parla. *The Social and Political Thought of Ziya Gökalp: 1876-1924* (Leiden: E.J. Brill, 1985), 15. See also Niyazi Berkes. *The*

Turks' very prestige, prosperity and authority rested on their ability to remain in control of what was still a powerful, if slightly impoverished, empire. The building of a Muslim state, let alone a Turkish one, would have necessarily involved more costs than the CUP was willing to entertain. Further rubbishing claims that the CUP devised a plan to exterminate the Ottoman Empire's Armenians to create a Turkish or Muslim state, it should be noted that such a state would require the removal of hundreds of thousands people from various ethnic and religious backgrounds: not just Armenians, but Greeks, Jews, Bulgarians, Assyrians, Georgians and Poles. These were just a few of the non-Muslim minorities inhabiting an already truncated Ottoman state.

An Increasingly Strained Relationship

Raids by nomadic Kurds against Christians, to include Armenians, continued in eastern Anatolia during CUP rule, as did assassinations and sabotage on the part of Armenian nationalists.[378] By 1913, relations had become strained between the Dashnaks and the Young Turks – even though they had both agreed on a common platform to contest the parliamentary elections of 1912.

Russia also experienced frequent bouts of instability within its own borders. Fearful that an Armenian uprising in eastern Anatolia, funded and organized from Russian territory, would spread to its own territory, St. Petersburg called for an international conference to address the perennial Armenian Question. By doing so, Russia hoped to deflect Armenian pressure against Russia and gain further concessions from the Ottoman Empire, thereby offering

---

Development of Secularism in Turkey (Montreal: McGill University Press, 1964), 415-16.

[378] Nomadic Kurdish tribes, as distinct from their settled counterparts, constituted an almost constant and uncontrollable force in the Ottoman east. They regularly targeted Muslims and Christians, to include Ottoman government officials and troops. See McCarthy. *Death and Exile*, 40-47.

Armenians nationalists an expanded space in the Ottoman Empire in which to operate. By keeping the Armenians focused on the Ottoman Empire, it hoped to avoid an accompanying loss of stability in the Russian Transcaucasia. These Russian machinations confirmed to most Armenian nationalists that Christian Russia was their protector and they were correspondingly emboldened to act against the Ottoman state and Ottoman Muslims. Hunchak representatives at a conference in Romania hoped to signal a move from legal to illegal activities through assassination attempts on Ottoman officials, among them Mehmet Talat, or Talat Paşa, the CUP minister of the interior.[379]

Russia's international conference addressing the Armenian Question occurred during the summer of 1913 and was held in the Ottoman capital, Istanbul. It was attended by all the major European powers with the exception of the Ottoman Empire. By refusing to allow the Ottoman government to attend the conference and negotiate regarding its citizens and its future, Russia and the other powers humiliated the CUP.

Though a Russian and European agreement promulgated some minor reforms and called for European inspectors to be based in six eastern Ottoman provinces, the Young Turks refused to implement the agreement. Some Armenians also reacted skeptically, sensing yet another bluff by Russia and the European powers as well as intransigence from Istanbul.[380] The Geneva chapter of Dashnaks cautioned, "… before placing our trust in diplomatic reforms, the [Armenian] Nation must subject itself to basic renovations; it must extirpate the curse of cowardly passiveness; it must be inspired by the healthy and redeeming principle of self-assistance; it must arm and be prepared!"[381]

---

[379] Lewy, 36.

[380] Salahi R. Sonyel. *The Ottoman Armenians: Victims of Great Power Diplomacy*. London: K. Rustem and Brothers, 1987: 300.

[381] Dashnak official as quoted in Lewy, 38.

World War I and the Ottoman Empire on the Eastern Front

When Austria-Hungary declared war on Russia, with Germany following suit in late July of 1914, the Ottoman Empire remained neutral. However, it was reported that Enver Paşa, the most popular and strongest leader in the ruling CUP triumvirate, exhibited pro-German sympathies and the Ottoman Empire soon joined the war effort on the side of Germany.[382]

Many scholars have questioned the rationale behind the Ottoman Empire's decision to join its old enemy, Austria-Hungary, along with imperial Germany. Some CUP officials were reportedly pro-British and pro-French, though this has been questioned.[383] However, it would have been counterintuitive for the Ottomans to side with Great Britain and France, powers that had joined the war effort as allies of imperial Russia. If the Ottoman Empire had developed an eternal enemy, it was Russia. CUP officials believed that a Russian victory, whether they were allies or not, would, at best, result in the loss of more Ottoman territory and, at worst, the loss of Istanbul, the Straits and perhaps the dissolution of the entire Ottoman Empire.[384]

The CUP leadership as well as most Ottoman Muslims despised the role the Great Powers had played in the loss of Ottoman territory and their emphasis on the rights of Ottoman Christian minorities. Yet it was Russia's role that was most often singled out, blamed and despised. The 1914 reform agreement, "… seemed like a prelude to a Russian protectorate over eastern Anatolia…"[385] As such, many

---

[382] Gerard E. Silberstein. *The Troubled Alliance: German-Austrian Relations, 1914--1917*. University Press of Kentucky, 2015: 6.

[383] Hasan Ünal. "Young Turk assessments of international politics, 1906–9."*Middle Eastern Studies* 32, no. 2 (1996): 30-44.

[384] McCarthy, *The Ottoman Turks*, 356.

[385] Feroz Ahmad. "Unionist Relations with the Greek, Armenian and Jewish Communities of the Ottoman Empire, 1908-1914," in Benjamin Braude and Bernard Lewis, eds., *Christians and Jews in the*

Ottomans looked to an alliance with a powerful Germany as a way of potentially defeating Russia and removing the Russian threat to eastern Anatolia and Istanbul.

The Ottoman Empire declared war on the side of Germany and Austria-Hungary and against Russia in November 1914. The roles initially played by Armenians in the war effort, particularly in eastern Anatolia, were significant for both the Ottomans and Russians from a strategic standpoint: Armenians inhabited areas straddling both empires. When the Ottoman government issued a general call for mobilization in August 1914, the Armenian patriarch in Istanbul and Dashnak officials both affirmed their ostensible loyalty to the Ottoman Empire. Indeed, at least some Ottoman Armenians responded as loyal Ottoman citizens to the mobilization, even though a number of Greek Orthodox and Armenian religious leaders had previously insisted that soldiers from their communities serve in separate, ethnically and religiously uniform units.[386] Yet, historian Richard Hovannisian has argued that though most Ottoman Armenians maintained what he termed a "correct stance" vis-à-vis the Ottoman state, "It can be asserted with some substantiation that the manifestations of loyalty were insincere, for the sympathy of most Armenians throughout the world war was with the Entente [France, Great Britain and Russia], not with the Central Powers [Germany, Austria-Hungary, the Ottoman Empire and Italy]."[387]

While there were reports of draft dodging by many Ottoman Armenians, this activity was performed on many occasions by Ottoman Turks, as well.[388] Contrary to

---

Ottoman Empire: The Functioning of a Plural Society (New York: Holmes and Meier, 1982), 424.

386 Mehmet Beşikçi. *The Ottoman mobilization of manpower in the First World War: between voluntarism and resistance*. Brill, 2012: 98.

387 Richard Hovannisian. *Armenia on the Road to Independence, 1918* (Berkeley, CA: University of California Press, 1969), 42.

388 Mehmet Beşikçi. "When a Military Problem Became a Social Issue: Ottoman Desertions and Deserters in World War I." In *War*

Hovannisian's claims, there are reports of Armenian men enlisting to serve on the front line as late as 1915 and Ottoman Armenian soldiers were fighting in Palestine against the British as late as 1916.[389] Thus, not all Armenians were nationalists and violent revolutionaries. Nor were they all loyal and innocent citizens. This explains the Ottoman government's differing and equivocal policies towards its Armenian citizens after the outbreak of Armenian revolts and traitorous actions in support of Russia's invasion of the Empire. Furthermore, it demonstrates the lack of a genocidal blueprint on the part of the Ottoman government, a centerpiece of the Armenian campaign to recognize the events of 1915 as the Armenian Genocide.

In order to gain the further support of Ottoman Armenians and possibly foment an anti-Russian uprising in Transcaucasia, the CUP government sent a mission to the Dashnak-affiliated Armenian National Organization, which was holding its annual meeting in Erzurum in 1914. The Dashnaks reportedly pledged their support for the Ottoman war effort against Russia, but refused to support an Ottoman-initiated rebellion among Russian Armenians in Transcaucasia.[390] At the same time, CUP officials in Istanbul warned Armenian civic leaders and the patriarchate that should Armenian offensives in support of Russia or acts of sabotage continue within the Ottoman Empire, the entire Armenian community would be held responsible. The titular CUP leader, Enver Paşa, reportedly informed the United States ambassador to Istanbul, Henry Morgenthau, that he had repeatedly warned the Armenian Apostolic Patriarch that "if the Armenians make any attack on the Turks or rendered any assistance to the Russians while the war was

---

and Collapse: World War I and the Ottoman State. M. Hakan Yavuz and Feroz Ahmed, eds. (Salt Lake City: University of Utah Press, 2016).

[389] Ibid, 255. See also Erik Jan Zürcher. "Ottoman Labour Battalions in World War I." In Kieser, Hans-Lukas and Schaller, Dominik J. Schaller, eds. *Der Völkermord an den Armeniern und die Shoah*, (Zurich: Chronos, 2002): 192.

[390] Hovannisian. *Armenia on the Road to Independence, 1918*, 42.

pending, he [Enver Paşa and the Ottoman government] will be compelled to use extreme measures against them."[391]

In Russian-controlled Armenia, many Armenians were already serving in the regular army and more signed up to invade the Ottoman Empire as part of Russia's war efforts. Just prior to an outbreak of hostilities between Russia and the Ottoman Empire, Czar Nicholas II visited Transcaucasia in 1914 and held meetings with the Armenian Catholicos, Gevorg V. The Catholicos praised the Czar for the benevolence shown by the Russian people to the Armenians. The Catholicos requested assistance from the Czar and the Russian Empire in order to deliver Ottoman Armenians from "Turkish domination." The Czar responded that Armenia had a "brilliant future" ahead of it.[392]

Preceding the Czar's visit, Count Varantzoff Dashkof, the Russian viceroy of the Caucasus, met with Armenian civic and religious leaders who proposed the establishment of a volunteer force of Armenians who had fled from the Ottoman to the Russian Empire. Soon, four full regiments, comprising Armenian volunteers, were assembled in Tiflis (Tbilisi).[393]

After the outbreak of fighting and Russian incursions into eastern Anatolia, CUP officials quickly became aware of the open sympathy and outright support many Ottoman Armenians gave the Russian invaders. Instances of Armenian insurrection, rebellion and the massacre of Ottoman Muslims became commonplace. Given the emergency situation, CUP leaders explored extreme measures to address the problem, such as the displacement and removal of the Armenian population in the frontier regions of eastern Anatolia; i.e. the Russian/Ottoman front. It was hoped that this drastic measure would stave off the

---

[391] Lewy, 101.

[392] Ibid

[393] Christopher J. Walker. "World War I and the Armenian Genocide." In *Armenian People from Ancient to Modern Times, vol. II* Richard Hovannisian, ed. (New York: Palgrave Macmillan, 2004), 244.

loss of yet more Ottoman territory and ultimately save the Empire by depriving the invading Russian and Armenian forces of fifth column support. It was also to be the beginning of what some in the Ottoman government viewed as the meting out of justice for the high treason of Armenian nationalists that dated back almost thirty years.[394] After eleventh hour attempts in 1914 to effect some sort of compromise between Armenian nationalists and the CUP broke down, the die was cast.[395] What a minority of Ottoman Armenians had hoped to gain through incremental reform was the eventual and complete liberation from Ottoman Turkish rule. Yet, most Armenians in the east resorted to extreme violence and outright rebellion to achieve these aims. What the Armenians may not have realized is that "… the Turks would do anything in their power, no matter how ruthless, in order to prevent the loss of what they regarded as the heartland of Turkish Anatolia."[396]

As Russian troops already mobilized in Transcaucasia prior to the outbreak of hostilities, bolstered by Armenian units and irregulars, poured across the Ottoman border in late 1914 and early 1915, Ottoman troops attempted to repel their advance.[397] Enver Paşa, the CUP Minister of War, opted for an immediate offensive even though it was winter. He promptly ordered the march of 95,000 Ottoman troops over mountain passes as high as 6,500 feet where

---

[394] For more of Armenian and Russian offensive action and fears of an impending Armenian rebellion by Ottoman officials, see Edward J. Erickson. *Ordered to Die: A History of the Ottoman Army in the First World War* (Westport, CT: Greenwood Press, 2001).

[395] Ahmet Şeyhun. "A Last Attempt to Solve the Armenian Question: The Reform of 1914." In *War and Collapse: World War I and the Ottoman State*. M. Hakan Yavuz and Feroz Ahmed, eds. (Salt Lake City: University of Utah Press, 2016).

[396] Lewy, 39.

[397] Mustafa Tanrıverdi. "Russian Military Mobilization in the Caucasus before World War I." In *War and Collapse: World War I and the Ottoman State*. M. Hakan Yavuz and Feroz Ahmed, eds. (Salt Lake City: University of Utah Press, 2016).

winter snow drifts are often reported in excess of ten feet. Ottoman commanders resigned or were sacked when they refused to cooperate with Enver's audacious plan, but the Ottoman troops set out on December 22, 1914, anyway, with few winter uniforms or coats and no winter boots. Incredibly, over 70,000 troops survived the trek and Enver immediately ordered them to attack the well-entrenched Russian army of 65,000 at Sarıkamış. The Ottomans forces were decimated and only 20,000 soldiers survived. As the troops hastily retreated, leaving their weapons and artillery behind, they effectively opened the gates to Anatolia to the Russians and their Armenian allies.[398]

The terrible conditions and inadequacy of supplies the Ottoman army suffered during the war from its very beginning were perhaps a sad harbinger for what lay in store for the Empire's Armenians. "If the Turkish authorities were unable or unwilling to provide adequate clothing, decent hygienic conditions, and appropriate medical attention for their Muslim soldiers, why should one expect them to be concerned about the fate of the Armenian deportees, whom they regarded as a fifth column?"[399] The political scientist Guenter Lewy added, "A government as callous about the suffering of its own population as was the Young Turk regime could hardly be expected to be very concerned about the terrible human misery that would rise from deporting its Armenian population, rightly or wrongly suspected of treason."[400]

The sheer incompetence of the CUP regime should not exonerate the Ottoman state for their actions during World War I. Rather their actions, inaction and the results – illness contributed to nearly seven times the death rate as wounds from combat for Ottoman soldiers - should serve as a damning reminder of the CUP's overall lack of decency, competency and their callousness vis-à-vis the entire population of the Ottoman Empire during the war years,

---

[398] Justin McCarthy, *The Ottoman Turks*, 359.
[399] Bloxham, 57.
[400] Lewy, 61.

not just Ottoman Armenians.[401] The overall weakness of the Ottoman state simply prevented it from fulfilling the primary function of any state, the protection of its citizens, to include Armenian deportees. This is especially true when Ottoman officials were faced with a stark choice: either keeping Ottoman troops at the front to thwart a combined Russian/Armenian invasion or sending Ottoman troops to protect Armenians as they were removed from the frontlines from nomadic Kurds, venal Ottoman officials and local Muslims looking to settle scores.[402]

Characterizing and Politicizing History

What occurred beginning in 1915 has influenced Turkish-Armenian relations for over a century. It has resulted in fights over semantics, efforts to gain closure, compensation, dignity and the development of multiple meanings of history. Not only has the shared past of 1915 influenced events and relations on state, regional and community levels, it has shaped the very identity of Armenians the world over and, to a much lesser degree, it has informed the identity of modern Turkey. More than anything else, the events of 1915 are the pivotal disasters that have shaped and molded the strong identity of Armenians of the diaspora. It is also of utmost importance to underscore the shared nature of the events of 1915 and the common past of both Turks and Armenians. The memories of shared trauma may be less palpable and play a lesser role in the Turkish psyche and large group identity, but the scars and pain are there and inform Turkish reactions to the Armenian campaign.

From scholarly works to memoirs, what occurred in 1915 has been created, recreated and variously characterized in novels, films, educational curricula, legislation and textbooks. Depending on the source, the events may be shown from a "Turkish" or "Armenian" perspective. The

---

[401] Erik Jan Zürcher. "Between Death and Desertion: The Ottoman Army in World War I." *Turcica* 28 (1996): 245.
[402] McCarthy. *Death and Exile*, 193-196.

numbers of people deported, many of whom were killed or died of starvation in the process, are debated as are the terms used to characterize the events. What is not debated by most scholars and, importantly, what is not questioned in this book, is the fact that the vast majority of Ottoman Armenians were gone from Anatolia at the end of World War I in 1918 and the subsequent nationalist struggles that followed into 1922. Rather, it is the questions of how, when, how many and under what circumstances these vibrant, centuries-old Armenian communities disappeared - men, women and children - that are subject to such relentless and mordacious debates.

The historical record and archival sources demonstrate that a majority of Ottoman Armenians in eastern Anatolia revolted against Ottoman rule and actively supported the Russian-led invasion of the Ottoman Empire. Most Armenians were sympathetic; many were willing supporters.[403] Numerous revolts across eastern Anatolia, in Van, Muş, Reşadiye and elsewhere, all occurred prior to any Ottoman orders for deportation.[404] As a result of the reactive and extreme measures taken by the Ottoman government to put down the plague of Armenian insurrections, deportations were ordered for all Armenians living in areas abutting the Ottoman and Russian front lines. A combination of malnutrition brought on by famine-like conditions affecting the entire Empire, predatory raids by nomadic Kurdish tribes as well as the neglect, murder and outright ambivalence of Turkish officials led to an appalling death rate.[405] This is known. What remains the subject of debate is how many Armenians were killed. Armenian

---

[403] See Kamuran Gürün, *The Armenian File: The Myth of Innocence Exposed* (London: Rustem, 1985). See also Esat Uras. *Tarihte Ermeniler ve Ermeni Meselesi, 2. Baskı* (İstanbul: Belge Yayınları, 1987).
[404] McCarthy. *Death and Exile*, 185-187.
[405] See Kemal Çiçek. "Forced Migration of Ottoman Armenians during World War I: How Security Concerns Affected Decision Making." In *War and Collapse: World War I and the Ottoman State*. M. Hakan Yavuz and Feroz Ahmed, eds. (Salt Lake City: University of Utah Press, 2016). See also McCarthy. *Death and Exile*, 195-197.

publicists as well as Armenian representatives to the Paris Peace Conference in 1919 estimated that 600,000 to 800,000 Armenians had died during the war years.[406] This figure has been inflated by many scholars in more recent times to 1.5 million and, occasionally, as high as 2.5 million. Yet, as Justin McCarthy noted, "the method of finding the actual number of Armenian dead is deceptively simple–subtract the number of Armenians who survived the wars from those who were present at war's beginning. This does not strictly provide statistics of mortality, but rather "population loss", because an unknowable number of children were born in the wartime period and a number of adults and children would have died of natural causes under normal circumstances. The result, however, is a good surrogate for mortality."[407] Based on his study of Ottoman demographic statistics, McCarthy found that there were 1.465 million Armenians in Ottoman Anatolia in 1912, before the wars began. At the end of the wars in 1922, 881,000 Armenians were alive, showing the loss of 584,000 Ottoman Armenians; 41 percent of the pre-war total.[408] These are staggering numbers, but should be put in perspective. As will be discussed in further detail, most of those killed were victims of the intercommunal violence – in reality the war – fought between Christian Armenians and Muslims that resulted in the deportations and starvation of thousands of Ottoman Armenians. In comparison, Ottoman Muslims suffered equally staggering losses. For example, the Muslim population of Erzurum decreased by 31 percent, Bitlis by 42 percent and that of Van Province by 62 percent.[409] These are figures and events that are blatantly ignored by the Armenian campaign. This is understandable given the political nature of the campaign for Armenian Genocide recognition. What is not so easily understood is why so

---

[406] Justin McCarthy. *The Population of the Ottoman Armenians*. na, 2001, 76.

[407] Ibid, 76-77.

[408] Ibid, 78.

[409] Ibid.

many historians and so-called genocide scholars also ignore these precise and indisputable demographic facts. Indeed, their research and work continues to inform and support the "Armenian" version of events.

In simplistic terms, the "Armenian" version of events offers a narrative replete with Ottoman treachery against harmless and innocent Armenians, a treachery that was motivated by bigoted and bloodthirsty Turkish nationalism as well as Muslim fanaticism.[410] As noted, the Armenian version argues that, at the very least, one million Armenians were slaughtered as part of a concerted and well-planned effort by the CUP and other Ottoman officials throughout the Empire to successfully deal with the Armenians threat once and for all. In essence, this narrative argues that innocent Armenians were brutally murdered, regardless of age or sex, in order to bring about a primarily Muslim, if not Turkish empire or nation-state.[411] For example, in this narrative, the eastern city of Van was the scene of a defiant and heroic defense by Armenians who were vastly outnumbered by their Ottoman adversaries.[412] In reality, the city of Van experienced an Armenian rebellion in support of invading Russian and Armenian troops. The rebellion directly resulted in the slaughter of almost the entire Muslim population of the city. It was only after the Russian-supplied, Armenian troops fled or were overcome by Ottoman soldiers sent to retake city that the full scope of the atrocities came to light.[413]

---

[410] See Vahakhn N. Dadrian. *The Key Elements in the Turkish Denial of the Armenian Genocide: A Case Study of Distortion and Falsification* (Toronto: Zoryan Institute, 1999).

[411] See Vahakn N. Dadrian. *The History of the Armenian Genocide: Ethnic Conflict from the Balkans to Anatolia to the Caucasus* (New York, Oxford: Berghahn Books, 2003). See also Christopher J. Walker. *Armenia: The Survival of a Nation* (London: Croom Helm, 1980).

[412] Richard G. Hovannisian. *Armenian Van/Vaspurakan (UCLA Armenian History and Culture Series)* (Costa Mesa, CA: Mazda Publishers, 2000), particularly chapters 12, 13, 14.

[413] McCarthy, et al. *The Armenian Rebellion at Van,* particularly chapters 8-9.

Beyond the rhetoric and polemics of the debate on display above and, regardless of the opposing historical texts marshalled to bolster arguments, these accounts possess a common denominator: Ottoman Armenians were killed or forced from their homes in Anatolia. If this is the case, and regardless of the plausible reasons for the deportation of Armenians from the Ottoman eastern front, then the major issue at stake seems to be how one references the events that led to the Armenian deaths and removal. Did the events of 1915 constitute the Armenian Genocide? Or were they a series of massacres over five decades in the making that, in some instances, constituted ethnic cleansing?

The Issue of Intent

The ongoing emphasis on the semantics used to describe the events of 1915 necessarily dwarfs a more substantive examination of the historical method and the writing and teaching of history. In essence, should definitive evidence of an Ottoman blueprint to exterminate the Empire's Armenians be unearthed, recognition of the Armenian Genocide "... should be a by-product of the historian's work, not its ultimate aim or underpinning."[414] This is how some historians view the issue. Yet, for any instance of genocide to be fully recognized – given that it is a crime – this same historical evidence must be marshalled and withstand the scrutiny of a court of law. This will be explicated in a more fulsome manner in later chapters.

Connectedly, the real issue with genocide is the perpetrator's intent. Without intent there cannot be genocide. But therein lies the problem. Intent need not be clear-cut, nor is it a one-time materialization of events or deeds. Intent by its very nature may develop, whither or continue to nourish itself and events exponentially. "Pinpointing the precise time within that period of radicalization at which a state framework that is demonstrably permissive of murder and atrocity becomes

[414] Bloxham, 95.

explicitly genocidal is extremely difficult and unlikely ever to be achieved definitively."[415]

What have historians and other scholars found regarding the issue of Ottoman government intent? Not surprisingly, the record is mixed. For example, Donald Bloxham, went so far as to classify the events of 1915 as a genocide,[416] but with significant caveats. Bloxham stated that the very term "genocide" is contextually problematic, given that it is a post-World War II term and concept that is being applied as a "retrospective projection" upon historical events that occurred decades prior.[417] Ronald Grigor Suny adopted a similar view to Bloxham's, noting that the deportations of Armenians from Anatolia by the Ottoman government were equal to the mass murder of a people. But as an historian, Suny importantly views the massacres contextually, adding that it was part and parcel of the imminent collapse of the entire Ottoman Empire. He also remains skeptical of the claims such as those made by the sociologist and historian Vahakn Dadrian,[418] that these were part of a pre-1914,

---

[415] Ibid, 96.

[416] Bloxham concluded in Ibid that what happened to Ottoman Armenians in 1915 constituted genocide. However, he arrived at this conclusion despite stating in a previous article "that there was no *a priori* blueprint for genocide [in the Ottoman Empire], and that it emerged from a series of more limited regional measures in a process of cumulative policy radicalization." See Michael M. Gunter. "What Is Genocide? The Armenian Case." *Middle East Quarterly* (2013).

[417] Ibid.

[418] Dadrian was once considered the doyen of Armenian genocide scholarship. He taught for many years at multiple universities in the United States, all of from which he was reportedly removed for offences other than his fabricated histories. In his polemical and accusatory works – more suited to a lawyer trying to prove a case than an historian - Dadrian argues that the ingrained militarism of the Ottoman Turks, combined with the profound intolerance of Islam, set the stage for the Armenian Genocide. See M. Hakan Yavuz. "A Topography of Positions in the Turkish-Armenian Debate." In *War and Collapse: World War I and the Ottoman State*. M. Hakan Yavuz and Feroz Ahmed, eds. (Salt Lake City: University of Utah Press, 2016), 7-9. See also "Secret life of professor Vahakn Dadrian." *Academic Integrity*. (April 15, 2013)

premeditated Ottoman blueprint for genocide.[419] Suny's reading of the historical record found that the deportations became "... a vengeful and determined act of suppression that turned into an opportunistic policy to rid Anatolia of Armenians once and for all, eliminate the wedge that they provided for foreign intervention in the region, and open the way for the fantastic dream of a Turanian [Turkic] empire."[420]

The political scientist Guenther Lewy also found little substantive evidence of Ottoman premeditated mass homicide or genocide.[421] Lewy admits that evidence of this may be discovered in the future, but thus far remains unsubstantiated. This is possibly the fault of problematic archives or the fact that no such blueprint ever existed. Lewy is particularly critical of the state of affairs at the Ottoman Archives in Turkey. He notes that crucial archival documents have gone missing, have been destroyed or have not been made available to historians and other scholars by Turkish authorities.[422]

Hilmar Kaiser, a historian of German-Ottoman relations, echoes a position similar to those of Suny and Bloxham: that the events of 1915 may have constituted the genocide of Ottoman Armenians, but that proof is lacking.[423] On the other hand, Christian Gerlach, a historian and the Associate Editor of the *Journal of Genocide Research*, agrees with Lewy

---

http://academicintegrityresearch.blogspot.co.ke/2013/04/secret-life-of-professor-vahakn-dadrian.html

419 Suny. "Empire and Nation: Armenians, Turks and the End of the Ottoman Empire." In *Armenian Forum* I, no. 2 (Summer 1998), 17-51 as quoted in Lewy, 249.

420 Ibid.

421 Lewy, particularly 150-161.

422 Ibid, 131-133.

423 Hilmar Kaiser. "'A Scene from the Inferno:' The Armenians of Erzurum and the Genocide, 1915-1916." In *Der Völkermord an den Armeniern und die Shoah.* Hans-Lukas Kieser and Dominik J. Schaller, eds. (Zurich: Chronos, 2002), 172.

that the Ottoman deportations of Armenians did not constitute genocide.[424]

Justin McCarthy, through his exhaustive archival studies, particularly those relating to Ottoman population statistics, perhaps provides the most compelling evidence that what happened to the Ottoman Empire's Armenians in eastern Anatolia cannot have constituted the genocide of Ottoman Armenians.[425] McCarthy's nuanced and well-sourced documentation of the ethnic cleansing of Ottoman Muslims between the years 1821-1922 provide compelling evidence that eastern Anatolia's Armenians – guilty or innocent of rebellion and collusion with Russia – were caught up in a perfect storm of battles, massacres and counter-massacres pitting three groups against each other. First, settled Muslims, including Turks, Kurds and others. Second, Armenians, other Ottoman Christians and the invading Russians. Third, the tribal Kurds, an essentially neutral but malignant force that worked against the other two parties for their own benefit.[426] Indeed, the greatest threat and cause of mortality to Armenians came from the nomadic [mainly Kurdish] tribes who raided the unprotected Armenian convoys being deported from the Ottoman/Russian front lines.[427]

As noted previously, Ottoman officials were faced with a difficult decision. They could either remove the Armenians – most of whom were in active rebellion against the Ottoman state and in collusion with the invading Russians – in well-armed and protected convoys or keep their soldiers at the front fighting against Russian and Armenian troops. The Ottoman officials chose to protect Ottoman Muslims and save the state, thereby thwarting the creation of an

---

[424] Christian Gerlach. "Nationsbildung im Krieg: Wirtschaftliche Faktoren bei der Vernichtung der Armenier und beim Mord an den ungarischen Juden." In *Der Völkermord an den Armeniern und die Shoah,* 358-359.

[425] McCarthy. *Death and Exile.*

[426] Ibid, 187.

[427] Ibid, 195.

Armenian state.[428] "They [Ottoman officials] could have been under no illusion as to what would happen to Muslims if an Armenian state were created. The Balkan Wars had taught them what to expect. The fate of Muslim refugees from Russian-conquered territories also held an obvious lesson. The quickest way to ensure that the same happened in eastern Anatolia was to lose the war…"[429] Withdrawing Ottoman troops from the front to protect Armenian deportees would have resulted in exactly this outcome. In the end, the Ottomans neglected their Armenian citizens resulting the deaths of thousands. Yet, the harsh policy of removing the Armenian populations from the front lines in eastern Anatolia also had the desired effect: Armenian revolts, sabotage and the massacre of Ottoman Muslims ceased in areas still under Ottoman control.[430]

Given the research of McCarthy and others, and regardless of Lewy's very plausible assertions regarding the precarious nature of the Ottoman archives, another scholar utilized Ottoman military histories based on archival sources to further dispute some key accusations made by proponents of the Armenian thesis, thereby casting further doubts that the events of 1915 constituted the Armenian Genocide.

Questioning Selective Histories and the Making of Myths

To the military historian, Edward J. Erickson, in history, details matter. For Erickson, far too much of the time, "… historical debate upon which politicians pass judgment is tinged more by polemic than by fact. Nine decades after hundreds of thousands of Armenians—and millions of others—died during World War I, it is important to dig

---

[428] Çiçek.

[429] McCarthy. *Death and Exile*, 195.

[430] Ibid, 196.

down into the archives to show what the historical record really says."[431]

In his significant research on World War I and, particularly, the Ottoman Eastern Front, Erickson has come to question the role of a group that often forms the cornerstones of the Armenian Genocide recognition argument: that of the Special Organization or *Teşkilât-ı Mahsusa*, which some have claimed as the equivalent to Ottoman special forces.[432] In particular, Erickson critiques Vahakn Dadrian's assertions regarding the Special Organization and its relationship with a German artillery officer of Prussian extraction referred to in archival sources by only his last name, Stange. Dadrian wrote that Stange was the "highest-ranking German guerrilla commander operating in the Turko-Russian border," one of several "arch-accomplices in the implementation of the massacres," and a Special Organization commander.[433] Dadrian argued that the Ottoman government utilized the Special Organization in order to carry out deportations of Ottoman Armenians located in rear areas abutting the front lines. The Special Organization became the primary instigators and perpetrators of the Armenian massacres of 1915, according to Dadrian.[434]

Erickson argues that Dadrian based his claims on Stange and his role with the Special Organization on second-hand German reports of massacres in the areas of operation where Stange was reportedly located. Erickson also asserts that Dadrian utilized controversial and unsubstantiated

---

[431] Edward J. Erickson. "Armenian Massacres: New Records undercut Old Blame: Reexaming History." *Middle East Quarterly*, Summer 2006, 67.

[432] See Taner Akçam. *Der Völkermord an den Armeniern*. Hamburger Institut für Sozialforschung, 1995: 65.

[433] Vahakn Dadrian, "The Role of the Special Organization in the Armenian Genocide during the First World War." In *Minorities in Wartime: National and Racial Groupings in Europe, North America and Australia in Two World Wars*, Panikos Panayi, ed. (Oxford: Berg, 1993), 58-63.

[434] Ibid.

testimony from courts-martial proceedings carried out in 1919 in Istanbul, which was then occupied by French, British and other victorious allied troops. Erickson is equally alarmed by the fact that certain scholars and groups have simply taken Dadrian's assertions at face value.[435]

Erickson utilized the 27-volume Turkish Military History of World War I to form the basis of his critique of Dadrian's assertions about Stange and the actions of the Special Organization. Regarding the Turkish volumes of military history, Erickson noted, "Far from the politicized debate surrounding the massacres, these histories shed light on nitty-gritty details such as which officers and units were deployed where and when. Within the set, the Third Army histories help flesh out Stange's wartime record."[436]

Indeed, Erickson found that though early Special Organization operations were characterized by unconventional and guerrilla tactics, huge operations such as the ill-fated Sarıkamış expedition effectively meant that units of the Special Organization were kept on the front lines and were therefore unavailable for actions involving the deportation of Armenians.[437] Furthermore, Stange himself was uninvolved in the deportations and subsequent deaths and massacres of Ottoman Armenians. According to the records, Stange did technically command all Ottoman forces near Ardahan in 1914, but he had no control of Special Organization operations. After Stange gained full command in December 1914, he organized all units under his command, including Special Organization units, in the conventional defense of the Ottoman eastern front with Russia.

Guenther Lewy's research of German Foreign Ministry archives bolsters Erickson's findings. Lewy found that Stange was never in areas of eastern Anatolia where deportations and massacres of Armenians took place. Indeed, the "Stange Detachment" to which Dadrian

---

[435] Erickson, "Armenian Massacres," 67.
[436] Ibid, 69.
[437] Ibid, 73.

referred, also included Armenians. This assertion was made by a German officer who commended the Armenians for their fighting skills in fighting against many of their own people as well as the Russians. "The supreme irony of the situation is rather striking: here is an alleged unit of the [Special Organization], the organization that Dadrian calls the primary instrument in the implementation of the Armenian genocide, that included Armenians!"[438]

Erickson's conclusions regarding the *Teşkilât-ı Mahsusa* have been further supported by the recent work of Yücel Yiğit and Tetsuya Sahara.[439] By placing the Special Organization within the theoretical context of Ottoman state capacity, Yiğit's study demonstrates conclusively that it came into being due to weakening state capacity in the post-1878 period. As such, it should be viewed within a political and military context of insurgency and counter-insurgency, primarily in the Balkans.[440] The Special Organization should be considered as the "special forces" of the Ottoman Empire, acting as an extension of the CUP and performing actions against separatism and Western imperialist expansion. Indeed, the Special Organization was just one of the tools used in the Ottoman Empire's evolving and increasingly complex counterinsurgency struggle.[441] This would necessarily place them at odds with the widespread instances of Armenian revolts and insurrection. Yet, of the five Special Organization groups on the eastern front, there is no evidence of participation in the deportations of Armenians.[442] Rather, they, along with the rest the Ottoman

---

[438] Lewy, 84-5.

[439] Yücel Yiğit. "The Teşkilat-ı Mahsusa and World War I." *Middle East Critique*23, no. 2 (2014): 157-174. See also Tetsuya Sahara. "The Military Origins of the Teşkilat-ı Mahsusa: The IMRO and the Ottoman Special Force on the Eve of World War I." In *War and Collapse: World War I and the Ottoman State*. M. Hakan Yavuz and Feroz Ahmed, eds. (Salt Lake City: University of Utah Press, 2016).

[440] Ibid, 159-60.

[441] Edward J. Erickson. *Ottomans and Armenians: A Study in Counterinsurgency*. Palgrave Macmillan, 2013.

[442] Ibid, 170-71.

forces, were kept at the front fighting the invading Russian troops and their Armenian counterparts. The deportation of Armenians occurred against the backdrop of a major counterinsurgency campaign that was empire-wide in scope.[443] They were categorically not part of a policy, planned or otherwise, to exterminate the Ottoman Empire's Armenians, as the campaign for Armenian Genocide recognition claims. The deaths of large numbers of Armenians in eastern Anatolia and Cilica, many no doubt innocent of collusion with the enemies of the state, did not occur as part of some Ottoman Final Solution and cannot be termed genocidal in any sense of the word. If the Ottomans, to include the Special Organization and the CUP leadership, were guilty of a crime it was in their inability to provide adequate protection to their own citizens – the Armenian deportees - even though the records show that at least some efforts were made in this regard.[444] Rather than providing protection or, as Dadrian posits, massacring Armenians,[445] the Special Organization and the rest of the Ottoman soldiery were forced to fulfill their first obligation: protecting the state. By doing so, the weak Ottoman state did fail at least some of its citizenry, leaving the deported Armenians at the mercy of nomadic Kurdish tribes and Ottoman Muslims thirsty for revenge on account of previous Armenian revolts and the accompanying mass murder of Muslims.[446]

Armenian and Turkish Identity Development

In assembling a plausible narrative of identity development, it is useful to consult the history of the Armenian diaspora and its many communities, the Republic

---

443 Erickson. *Ottomans and Armenians*, 226-227.

444 Ibid, 227.

445 See Vahakn Dadrian, "The Role of the Special Organization in the Armenian Genocide during the First World War." Also see Vahakn N. Dadrian. *The History of the Armenian Genocide: Ethnic Conflict from the Balkans to Anatolia to the Caucasus*, 236-37.

446 McCarthy. *Death and Exile*, 194.

of Armenia and the Turkish Republic. It is common knowledge that history is written by the victors. In the case under discussion here, neither the Armenians nor the Ottoman Turks can in any way be considered victorious at the end of World War I and the subsequent nationalist, ethnic and sectarian struggles. Indeed, during the course of the wars, hundreds of thousands of Muslims and Christians in eastern and southern Anatolia experienced the penultimate loss: their lives and those of their loved ones. In the Armenian case, if they managed to keep their lives, they likely lost their homes, property, families, friends, ways of life and a centuries-old culture. By 1922, Armenians no longer inhabited Anatolia as they had done for thousands of years, prior to and after the arrival of the Ottoman Turks. Likewise, in some regions such as Van, Bitlis and in the Transcaucasia region, over fifty percent of the Muslim population vanished, most on account of massacres committed by Armenians.[447] By the early 1920s, in the aftermath of revolutions, civil wars and the establishment of colonial mandates, both Armenians and Turks - the Turks having suffered defeat and destruction at the hands of multiple enemies - saw the foundation of nation-states devoted, at least in name, to their respective peoples. However, the Armenians gained little of what they had yearned for, either in territory or sovereignty.[448]

Having both suffered multiple and severe traumas, Turks, almost entirely residing within the borders of the Republic of Turkey, and Armenians, the majority in diaspora communities, began the process of constructing historical accounts and narratives. These narratives covered not only the four years of 1914-1918, but also attempted to reconstruct what had occurred, or was imagined and

[447] McCarthy. *Death and Exile*, 211-218; 229-230.

[448] The nation-state of Armenia, centered around Yerevan in eastern Armenia, survived in little more than name only as the Armenian Soviet Socialist Republic (ASSR) from 1920 until the dissolution of the Soviet Union in 1991 when full independence of the Republic of Armenia was proclaimed.

reimagined to have occurred, for the preceding one thousand years.[449]

Identity Development in Turkey: Victory without Continuity

Turkey was born fighting for its life. Its birth as a nation-state was difficult and lengthy. European powers of the Triple Entente were intentionally destroying the Ottoman Empire and dividing the spoils, though Russia was no longer involved or interested on account of the 1917 Bolshevik Revolution and the ongoing Russian civil war.

The 1920 Treaty of Sèvres was signed between the victorious Allied powers and representatives of the government of the Ottoman Empire. It called for the abolishment of the Empire, an Ottoman renunciation of all holdings in North Africa and the Middle East, and the establishment of a truncated Ottoman Turkey that would occupy a sliver of territory centered around modern-day Ankara with only a small stretch of coastline on the Black Sea. Istanbul, İzmir, Antalya and Adana along with the entire Mediterranean and Aegean coast and their hinterland would now be under the thumb of either the French, Greeks, Italians or support an international contingent of troops. The Treaty of Sèvres also demanded the creation of an independent Armenia, centered in eastern Anatolia encompassing the region many Armenians still refer to as western Armenia.

Analytically, the Treaty of Sèvres should be viewed as the culmination of the numerous anti-Muslim and anti-Turkish treaties developed by the Great Powers, to include Russia,

---

[449] See Richard G. Hovannisian, ed. *The Armenian People from Ancient to Modern Time*, vol. 2 (New York: St. Martin's Press, 2004). While suspect on multiple levels, for the theoretical underpinnings of primordial nationalism of the Armenians, see Anthony D. Smith, particularly 64-65, 115-117. Regarding early Republican Turkish theories of the Hittites, see Taha Parla. *Türkiye'de Siyasal Kültürün Resmi Kaynakları* (İstanbul: İletişim Yayınları, 1991).

and informed by their outright prejudices since the independence of Greece in the 1820s. Where it departed from previous treaties such as those of San Stefano and Berlin that kept the Ottoman Empire in place if only the frustrate or bolster the strategic goals of one or another Great Power, was in its outright and unequivocal aim of destroying any vestiges of Muslim Turkish rule in the major population centers of the former Ottoman Empire as well as Aegean and Mediterranean Anatolia and eastern Anatolia.[450]

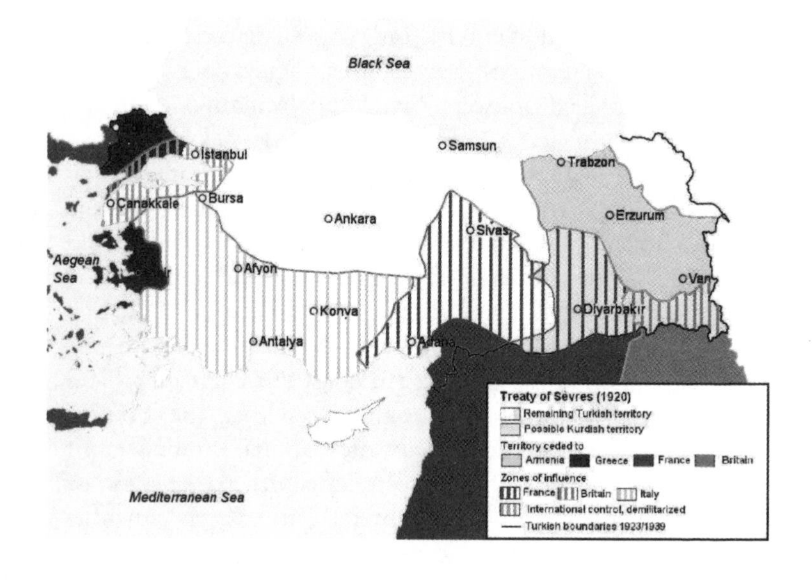

Treaty of Sèvres borders[451]

These were all areas with overwhelming Muslim, and therefore Turkish, populations. Yet, U.S. President Woodrow Wilson's and U.K. Prime Minister David Lloyd George's notoriously anti-Turkish and pro-Christian (Armenian and Greek) sympathies were made abundantly

---

[450] McCarthy. *Death and Exile*, 211-223 and 256-258;

[451]https://en.wikipedia.org/wiki/Treaty_of_S%C3%A8vres#/media/File:TreatyOfSevres_(corrected).PNG

clear in the spirit of the Treaty of Sèvres and the subsequent Paris Peace Conference in 1919 that attempted to carve the remnants of the Ottoman Empire like a cake.[452] Wilson's well-documented racism also likely informed his bellicose support for a Greek invasion of Anatolia and the creation of an independent Armenian state.[453] Yet, none of the treaty's articles was ever fully-implemented because remnants of the Ottoman army successfully prosecuted the Turkish War of Independence and founded the Republic of Turkey on October 29, 1923. As such, the Treaty of Sèvres was never ratified or came into effect.[454] However, its stated intent to dismember the Anatolian Turkish heartland remains, to this day, deeply embedded in Turkey's collective psyche with a corresponding, almost paranoid emphasis on Turkey's territorial integrity. "Although Sèvres is not remembered by many Europeans, Turks turned it into a major trauma and a living document to understand European policies toward Turkey. This preserved 'chosen trauma' is a powerful tool that has been used to delegitimize European criticism of Turkey…"[455]

As a result of its Ottoman past, difficult birth and repeated humiliation at the hands of multiple European states, Turkey was left on the defensive with what seems, at times,

[452] See Perin Gürel. "Turkey and the United States After World War I: National Memory, Local Categories, and Provincializing the Transnational." *American Quarterly* 67, no. 2 (2015): 353-376. See also Justin Fantauzzo. "Ending Ottoman Misrule: British Soldiers, Liberal Imperialism, and the First World War in Palestine." *The Journal of the Middle East and Africa* 6, no. 1 (2015): 17-32.

[453] See Jeffrey L. Lauck, "Lost Cause in the Oval Office: Woodrow Wilson's Racist Policies and White-Washed Memory of the Civil War." *The Gettysburg Compiler: On the Front Lines of History*. Paper 136 (2015). See also Eric Arnesen. "Racism in the Nation's Service: Government Workers and the Color Line in Woodrow Wilson's America." *The Journal of Southern History* 80, no. 4 (2014): 1006.

[454] For details regarding the abrogation of the Treaty of Sèvres and negotiations regarding the fate of Istanbul, the Straits and Turkey, see Sevtap Demirci. *Strategies and struggles: British rhetoric and Turkish response: the Lausanne Conference (1922-1923)*. Isis Press, 2005.

[455] Yavuz, *Islamic Political Identity in Turkey*, 45.

to be a correspondingly low self-esteem informed by a deep-seated insecurity. "The strong belief that internal elements collaborated with foreign powers in the dismantling of the Empire led to an entrenched belief in the threat of internal and external foes. The Sèvres syndrome, or the belief that the country is permanently under the threat of dissolution from internal and external enemies, is the result of this historical experience."[456] In order to counteract this insecurity, protect against foreign threats and establish a new nation-state, Turkey's founders attempted to homogenize diverse ethnic and religious textures in order to create Turkish citizens. This constructed and socially-engineered identity ignored the former Empire's cultural richness almost entirely. As such, when the Republic of Turkey eventually won its independence and sovereignty under the leadership of the Republic's principal founder, Mustafa Kemal Atatürk, the ensuing Kemalist reforms carried out to forge a new, Turkish nation-state, essentially and effectively severed modern Turkey from its Ottoman past.

Atatürk allegedly changed the centuries-old Ottoman alphabet from the Arabic to the Latin script in 1927 in order to combat illiteracy. This is very possible, as a full 89.4 percent of the population were thought to be illiterate when the first census was conducted the same year. However, many outsiders and Turks alike understood the reforms as an attempt to cut Turks off from their deep, historically and culturally significant Ottoman past.[457] For example, Halide Edip Adıvar, a famous author, feminist, Turkish nationalist and supporter of Mustafa Kemal throughout Turkey's War of Independence, was censorious of the alphabet reform policy. "The continuity of Turkish culture has been abruptly

---

[456] Şule Toktaş and Bülent Aras. "National Security Culture in Turkey: A Qualitative Study on Think Tanks." *Bilig* 61 (2012): 250.

[457] For more on the modern Turkish language and reform, see Agop Dilaçar. *Atatürk ve Türkçe, Atatürk ve Türk Dili*. (Ankara: Türk Dil Kurumu, 1963). For education reform in the early years of the Turkish Republic, see Mustafa Ergün. *Atatürk Devri Türk Eğitimi*. (Ankara Üniversitesi, Dil ve Tarih-Coğrafya Fakültesi, 1982).

broken. The younger people will read and write, but will not be at home with any culture half a century old. Without a past, without a [collective] memory of the accumulated beauty in the national consciousness, there will be a certain crudeness, a lowering of aesthetic standards."[458] Turkish authors such as Ahmet Hamdi Tanpınar (1901-1962) whose lives straddled both the Ottoman Empire and Republican Turkey also wrote of the jarring sense of dislocation and lost identities that accompanied the birth of modern Turkey.[459]

This rupture with the past may have been precisely what Atatürk and his cadre desired in order to purge the new, essentially Muslim nation-state of its Ottoman Islamic and imperial past; a past replete with its poly-ethnic, religiously diverse and multi-lingual cultural milieu. The new Republic became a largely Turkish and Muslim state after the disappearance of the majority of Anatolia's Christian populations - Greeks, Armenians, Assyrians and others - through forced migration, massacres or population exchanges.

Atatürk and the Kemalist, Republican elite surrounding him were obsessed with creating a "new Turk." In order to do so, they created, recreated and fabricated historical documentation in an effort to prove that the Turks were the original settlers of Anatolia; they were the descendants of the ancient Hittites and Sumerians.[460] The Kemalist thought

---

[458] Halide Edip Adıvar, *Turkey Faces West: A Turkish View of Recent Changes and Their Origins* (New Haven: Yale University Press, 1930), 235.

[459] Ahmet Hamdi Tanpınar. *Huzur*. Vol. 97. Dergâh Yayınları, 2009.

[460] The theory allegedly bandied about by Mustafa Kemal and some of his associates argued vaguely that the Turks were a white, Aryan people originating in Central Asia. They had progressively moved westward because of land desiccation, eventually settling in Anatolia. Thus, the Turks had inhabited Anatolia since antiquity. This mix of truths and half-truths was proclaimed official doctrine and researchers endeavored to "prove" the thesis. However, these theories never gained wide traction and were soon discarded. See

process followed that if all civilizations, particularly European civilizations, emanated from the "original Turks" of Anatolia, then the new Turks were not only Europeans, but the founding race of Europe.

Atatürk's and his cadre's usage of the Hittites was shrewd from a political and symbolic standpoint: it allowed themselves as well as other Turks the possibility of circumventing uncomfortable facts regarding the recent history of European domination, defeat, humiliation, and the trauma associated with the Treaty of Sèvres. That is, the Hittite theory provided an overarching narrative - false though it was - of Turks as not only Europeans, but the forebears of today's Europeans. No longer could they be racially construed as the "terrible Turk," the swarthy offspring of a degenerate and bloodthirsty Asiatic race.[461] The new Turks, according to Kemalist propaganda, not only possessed an ancient and glorious history centered in the cradle of civilization, the Fertile Crescent, they correspondingly had a firm stake in Europe's past, present and future.

Eric Hobsbawm, in analyzing the efforts of nation-states to create pseudoscientific theories, has argued that historical writings are very significant in what he termed the "invention of traditions." These contribute, "to the creation, dismantling and restructuring of images of the past which belong not only to the world of specialist investigation but to the public sphere of man as a political being."[462] These texts and images necessarily become more real than the reality of unwritten memory. "The element of invention is particularly clear here, since the history which became part of the fund of knowledge or the ideology of the nation-state or movement is not what has actually been preserved in popular memory, but what has been selected, written,

---

Bernard Lewis. *The Emergence of Modern Turkey*, 2nd ed. (Oxford: Oxford University Press, 1968), 359.

[461] See Yavuz. "Orientalism, the 'Terrible Turk' and Genocide," 114.

[462] Eric Hobsbawm and T. Ranger, eds., *The Invention of Tradition* (Cambridge: Cambridge University Press, 1983), 13.

pictured, popularized and institutionalized by those whose function it is to do so."[463]

While it can be argued that Kemalist attempts at nation building and social engineering were largely successful in divorcing Turks and Turkey from their Ottoman past, this engineered identity was, and continues to be, built on an unsteady foundation. Beyond the death and disappearance of the vast majority of the Ottoman Empire's Armenians, there were massive population exchanges involving Christians and Muslims, regardless of their actual ethnicity, between Turkey and Greece that occurred in 1923, following the conclusion of the Turkish War of Independence.[464] This was only the last in a series of forced population exchanges, most involving Muslims from former Ottoman lands and accompanied by ethnic cleansing and other atrocities, stretching back to 1821.[465]

Further rupturing its ties with the Ottoman Empire, the Kemalist elite also instituted a process of de-Islamization while at the same time centralizing political power in the new nation-state from its central Anatolian capital of Ankara. These actions had the effect of antagonizing non-ethnic Turks, mainly Kurds, and Islamists alike.[466]

---

[463] Ibid.

[464] Significantly the population exchanges were based on religion rather than ethnicity. Thus, all Greek Orthodox Christians (Greek- or Turkish-speaking) of Asia Minor, including a Turkish-speaking Greek Orthodox population from middle Anatolia (the Karamanlides), the Ionia region (Izmir, Ayvalık), the Pontus region (Trabzon, Samsun), Bursa and the wider Marmara region, East Thrace, and other regions were either expelled or formally denaturalized from Turkish territory, numbering up to 1.2 million people. Over half a million people were expelled from Greece, predominantly Turks, but also other Muslims, such as Pomaks, Cham Albanians, Megleno-Romanians and Muslim Roma. See Stanford J. Shaw and Ezel Kural Shaw, *History of the Ottoman Empire and Modern Turkey* (Cambridge: Cambridge University Press, 1976), 239-241. See also Bruce Clark. *Twice a Stranger: How Mass Expulsion forged Modern Greece and Turkey*. Granta, 2007.

[465] See McCarthy. *Death and Exile.*

[466] For information on opposition to Kemalist reforms and the accompanying Menemen Rebellion, see Kemal Üstün. *Menemen Olayı*

Ethnoreligious rebellions promptly broke out and continued into the late 1930s, representing a failure of the state and its modernizing policies to penetrate the periphery.[467] Yet by the 1940s, the Turkish, Kemalist elite had learned to use these rebellions to their advantage and frame the events in terms of a new, Kemalist version of the Turkish Self at odds with the backward, tradition-bound, overly-religious and not necessarily Turkish Other. "These rebellions against the young and inexperienced [Turkish] Republic created a cumulative image of the people of rural Anatolia as socially tribal, religiously fanatical, economically backward, and most important, a threat to the national integrity of the Republic of Turkey. For example, in the way the state framed the Kurdish resistance it sought to legitimize its own claims and justify its domination. In other words, the Kemalist state discourse on the Kurdish issue evolved as a result of these rebellions, with the state becoming more sensitive about its policies of creating a secular Turkish nation. Thus one needs to take these rebellions into account to explain the securitization of Kurdish and Islamic identity claims by the state."[468]

Unlike Ukrainians, Uzbeks, Georgians and the many other nationalities that experienced the high level of social engineering in the Soviet system first-hand and then rejected it outright, many Turks still cling to the Kemalist identity and system inherited from the days of Atatürk. "Nationalist taboos on questioning official history are held in place as much by society as by Turkey's controlling state… Legal complaints (against historians, authors and others who question Turkey's "official" historiography)… emerge from the most insecure part of society: a nationalist, sometimes violent fringe, whose political backers are the staunchly

ve Kubilay Olayı.(İstanbul: Çağdaş Yayınları, 1990). See also Tarık Zafer Tunaya. *İslamcılık Akımı.* (İstanbul: Simavi Yayınları, 1991), 174.

[467] For information on the ethnoreligious Kurdish rebellions of the 1920s, see Metin Toker. *Şeyh Sait ve isyanı.* Akis Yayınları, 1968.

[468] Yavuz. *Islamic Political Identity in Turkey*, 53-54.

secular old guard."[469] For over three quarters of a century, the old guard, known in Turkish as the *derin devlet* or deep state, possessed immense power coupled with limited accountability, making them resemble senior Soviet apparatchiks rather than the guardians of what is often billed as a modern and secular nation. This cadre was composed of largely urban, educated Turks with ties to or positions in the military and, to a lesser extent, the judiciary. This made any attempts at reform, let alone revisions to Turkey's official history, difficult. Indeed, the Kemalist elite that professed secularism and represented Western values was and often remains deeply suspicious of the very freedoms these concepts, if implemented, would bring.

Against these significant odds, a number of Turkish intellectuals and writers attempted to publicly question their past and called for openness and dialogue on a wide range of issues, including the events of 1915, which a few explicitly refer to as "genocide".[470] When the power of the old guard began to crumble in the late 1990s and with the election of the Justice and Development Party (Turkish: *Adalet ve Kalkınma Partisi* or AKP) in 2002, under the charismatic leadership of Recep Tayyip Erdoğan, major economic, social and political change occurred. These included initial reforms carried out by the AKP government as part of a wider effort to gain entry into the European Union.[471] A number of conferences regarding the "Armenian Question" were also held in Turkey and the AKP government of then-Prime Minister Erdoğan called

---

[469] Sabrina Tavernise. "Turkey to Alter Speech Law." *New York Times*, January 25, 2008.
http://www.nytimes.com/2008/01/25/world/europe/25turkey.html

[470] See Kemal H. Karpat. *Ottoman Past and Today's Turkey* (Leiden: Brill, 2000), 160. See also Taner Akçam. *A Shameful Act: The Armenian Genocide and the Question of Turkish Responsibility* (New York: Macmillan, 2006).

[471] See Fırat Cengiz and Lars Hoffmann. "Rethinking conditionality: Turkey's European Union accession and the Kurdish question." *JCMS: Journal of Common Market Studies* 51, no. 3 (2013): 416-432.

for a joint international commission to review the events, including better access to the Turkish and Ottoman archives. Yet the openness exhibited by the Turkish government soon closed. Charges of insulting Turkishness were brought against various scholars and journalists, to include the son of the slain, Turkish-Armenian activist Hrant Dink. The charges stemmed from his publication of his late father's comments on the events of 1915.[472] Academics have also been arrested for various offences, including criticizing the Turkish military, criticizing the AKP and advocating a peaceful solution to the unrest in the southeast of the country.

The official sanction in Turkey to substantively address and debate what happened to Ottoman Armenians in eastern Anatolia in 1915 may have passed. Indeed, some view the increasing authoritarianism of Presidnet Erdoğan and his party as part of the wider inability of Turkish society to come to terms with its traumatic past. The political scientist, Onur Bakıner, sees the possibility that the discredited Kemalist narrative will be discarded for what he terms the AKP's *majoritarian conservatism*. This represents, "… a new government-sanctioned shared memory that promotes uncritical and conservative-nationalist interpretations of the past that have popular appeal, while enforcing silence on critical historiographies that challenge this hegemonic memory and identity project."[473]

Narratives Divorced from the Past: Identity Development in Soviet Armenia and the Diaspora Awakening

A few months after the Russian Bolsheviks seized power in 1917, effectively signaling the end of the imperial Russian Empire, Armenian Dashnaks proclaimed the independent

[472] Mutlu Koser. "301'den 1 Yıl Hapis." *Hürriyet*, October 12, 2007. http://www.hurriyet.com.tr/301-den-1-yil-hapis-7470839
[473] Onur Bakıner. "Is Turkey Coming to Terms with Its Past? Politics of Memory and Majoritarian Conservatism." *Nationalities Papers* 41, no. 5 (2013): 698-700.

state of Armenia in May 1918. Armenia then fought short and unsuccessful wars against both Georgia and Azerbaijan – newly independent states themselves - in an attempt to secure what they viewed as predominantly Armenian-inhabited territories in the Caucasus, particularly the region of Nagorno-Karabakh in Azerbaijan. The new Armenian nation-state encompassed most of the territory inhabited predominantly by Armenians in the now defunct Russian Empire. However, it contained only one-sixth of the territory of historic Armenia, thus severing the new state from territories that had been part of the Ottoman Empire.

The 1920 Treaty of Sèvres stipulated the official partition of the Ottoman Empire and recognized Armenian independence.[474] The Ottoman regime under the new sultan, Mehmed VI, accepted the treaty provisions under duress and proceeded to implement the provisions in a piecemeal fashion. Armenian independence in Transcaucasia seemed secure and it appeared, for a time, that it might expand its territories to include much of western Armenia. This was not to be. The Treaty of Sèvres was never implemented because a nascent and rebellious Turkish government in eastern Anatolia rejected the treaty despite the Ottoman government's acceptance of the terms. As noted previously, a struggle for Turkish independence from Greek, French, British and Italian control ensued during which time Turkish troops, under the command of Mustafa Kemal, re-established control over what is today the Republic of Turkey. Eastern Anatolia and much of the newly independent state of Armenia was occupied by returning Turkish troops. The new leaders of Russia, the Bolsheviks, reacted immediately and sent the Red Army to invade Armenia in order to re-establish Russian control over Transcaucasia and prevent a Turkish takeover.

---

[474] For more information on the demise of the Ottoman Empire, the Treaty of Sèvres and its profound effect on the Turkish psyche, see Seha L. Meray and Osman Olcay. *Osmanlı İmparatorluğu Çöküş Belgeleri (Mondros Bırakışması, Sèvres Andlaşması ve İlgili Belgeler),* Ankara: SBF Yayınları, 1977.

The Russian Bolsheviks and the new Turkish Grand National Assembly first signed the Treaty of Moscow in 1921, followed by the Treaty of Kars in 1922, which established the borders of Turkey and the Soviet Union and thus, by proxy, the borders of Armenia. These treaties effectively led to another Russian occupation, in the guise of the Soviet Union, and ended Armenia's brief experiment with independence for another seventy years.

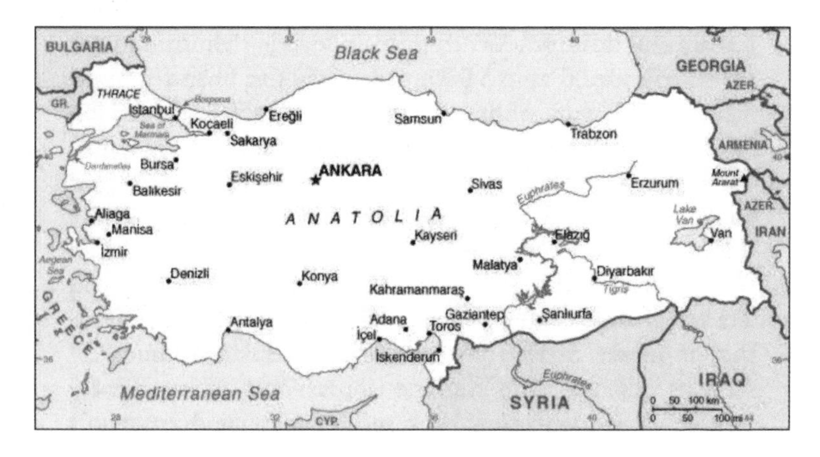

The Republic of Turkey[475]

The 1920s and 1930s were dark days for Armenia and Armenians, replete as they were with Soviet social-engineering experiments, Stalinist purges, policies of forced collectivization, state-sponsored atheism and the suppression of religion. The Soviet regime strenuously attempted to destroy or, at the very least, neutralize nationalist sentiment and religious observance in Armenia. After the Dashnak party was outlawed in 1923, the Communist Party became the only legal, political party allowed to operate in Soviet Armenia. Churches were closed, property confiscated and church leaders – regardless of affiliation – were persecuted. The Soviet regime also

[475]https://en.wikipedia.org/wiki/Energy_in_Turkey#/media/File:Map_of_Turkey_(2007).gif

banned much of the literature written by nineteenth century Armenian authors. Late in the 1920s, numerous Armenian nationalists and others opposed to the Soviet regime were executed or deported to labor camps in Siberia. The purges and execution intensified in the 1930s under the paranoid reign of Josef Stalin, though Stalin did grant autonomy to the Armenian minority in Nagorno-Karabakh in July 1923 thus sowing the seeds for territorial disputes across the former Soviet Union that continue to fester.[476]

Though Soviet authorities relaxed their grip on the cultural sphere briefly during World War II and again after the death of Stalin in 1953, the importance of Armenian nationalism, the church, language and culture declined precipitously, but did not disappear, throughout the seventy years of the Soviet Union's existence. Over time, the semi-autonomous Armenian Soviet Socialist Republic (ASSR), home to many of the world's Armenians, became the most homogeneous of all the Soviet republics. The capital, Yerevan, was touted as the cultural center of Armenian national identity, and Soviet Armenia claimed to be the voice of the authentic Armenian homeland. These proclamations struck a dissonant chord with many diaspora Armenians.[477] Those affiliated with the Dashnak organization, in particular, rejected Soviet Armenia as a viable Armenian homeland. However, records show that many members of the Armenian diaspora bourgeoisie chose to cooperate on a communal level with the USSR.[478]

In time, diaspora activists realized that both Soviet Armenia and diaspora life were long-term facts and the activists, "...shifted to an emphasis on identity retention (focusing primarily on the memory of the genocide) 'over here' (in the diaspora) at the expense of national aspirations

---

[476] Aytan Gahramanova. "Paradigms of Political Mythologies and Perspectives of Reconciliation in the Case of the Nagorno-Karabakh Conflict." *International Negotiation* 15, no. 1 (2010): 143.

[477] Razmik Panossian. "Between Ambivalence and Intrusion: Politics and Identity in Armenia-Diaspora Relations." *Diaspora: A Journal of Transnational Studies* 7, no. 2 (1998): 155.

[478] Ibid, 156-157.

'over there' (in the ASSR)."[479] Most diaspora Armenians, particularly those informed by their Dashnak affiliation, maintained cultural and political distance from their cousins in Soviet Armenia. This distance was characterized by acute feelings of embarrassment on account of Armenia being under Soviet domination.[480] With the exception of a few communist sympathizers and those who returned after being resettled or exiled during Stalin's rule, very few diaspora Armenians chose to lead life under Soviet rule. What Ronald Grigor Suny terms "Armenian Zionism," or the return of diaspora Armenians to the state of Armenia, remained and continues to remain a minority movement.[481]

An Armenian national awakening, of sorts, became possible when Soviet authorities, in 1965, acceded to the demands of Armenian demonstrations in Yerevan to recognize the events of 1915 as the Armenian Genocide.The demonstrators also demanded, importantly, for the return of "Armenian lands" in Turkey and Soviet Azerbaijan.[482]

Many diaspora Armenians affiliated with the Dashnaks understood this move as a détente, of sorts, with the Soviet Union. Soviet authorities were now willing to officially allow commemorations. They were also willing to officially refer to the events of 1915 as not just a series of massacres, but as the Armenian Genocide. This was in line with Dashnak and wider diaspora efforts to gain acceptance of this particular nomenclature.

Added to the opening of political space in Soviet Armenia and the fusion of diaspora and Soviet Armenian commemoration and recognition efforts, a newer and more radicalized Armenian diaspora generation aimed to achieve genocide recognition through greater militancy and violence. In their campaign, they sought to perform violently what

---

[479] Yossi Shain and Aharon Barth, 468.
[480] Suny, 221-229.
[481] Suny, *Looking toward Ararat*, 216.
[482] Maike Lehmann. "Apricot Socialism: The National Past, the Soviet Project, and the Imagining of Community in Late Soviet Armenia." *Slavic Review* 74, no. 1 (2015): 9, 16-18.

others were doing at conference tables, diplomatic meetings and legislative offices: enhance Armenian identity through their participation in a "genocide struggle." As discussed briefly in a previous chapter, Armenian terrorism, aimed mostly at Turkey and Turkish targets, was driven by the inordinate amount of attention given to terrorism from the international community and an internationalized Marxist-Leninist ideology. Begun by diaspora Armenians in Lebanon, the Armenian Secret Army for the Liberation of Armenia (ASALA) targeted and killed Turkish diplomats and bombed Turkish government and commercial targets in disparate geographic locales. These included a 1982 attack on Esenboğa International Airport in Ankara in which nine individuals perished and 82 were injured, and a 1983 attack at a Turkish Airlines counter at Orly Airport, near Paris, in which eight people were killed.[483]

Not to be outdone, a number of diaspora Armenians, some with Dashnak affiliation, felt that ASALA's high level of visibility posed a threat to their own existence and popularity. They responded in like fashion, establishing their own terrorist organization, aptly named the Justice Commando for the Armenian Genocide (JDAG).[484] The violence committed by ASALA and JDAG provoked condemnation from certain individuals in the diaspora, though some have questioned the timing and sincerity of the condemnations.[485] It also achieved the international attention desired by the terrorist groups and, perhaps perversely, acted as a catalyst in rallying the full support of the Armenian diaspora in their efforts to have the events of 1915 recognized as the Armenian Genocide.

Khachig Tölölyan, a scholar who has written extensively on the Armenian diaspora, has argued that the Armenian

---

[483] Michael M. Gunter *"Pursuing the Just Cause of Their People": A Study of Contemporary Armenian Terrorism*. New York: Greenwood Press, 1986.

[484] Anat Kurz and Ariel Marari. *ASALA: Irrational Terror or Political Tool?* (Boulder, CO: Westview Press, 1985).

[485] Maxime Gauin. "Remembering the Orly Attack." *Uluslararası Hukuk ve Politika*. 7, no. 27 (2011): 121.

terrorist attacks were aimed not at Turkey and its NATO allies, but at the Armenian diaspora in a symbolic sense. The acts were perpetrated with the hope that they would reenergize the Armenian diaspora, "... whose fraying culture is constituted to a remarkable degree by old stories."[486] Echoing this sentiment, in part, an Armenian survivor of the 1915 massacres and deportations stated, "Until the recent assassinations, [the cause of genocide commemoration] was dormant. Everything was quiet because people were after their own living and family. It was almost like it was forgotten... All this commotion may not be doing any good to the young people, but it sure is awakening us."[487] Thus, the acts of Armenian terrorism - the killings perpetrated by the Self against the Other; i.e. the Turks - politicized and reified Armenian large group memories and the reconstructed narratives of 1915.

Throughout the 1980s, diaspora Armenian activists and interest groups attempted to keep the memories of 1915 alive and renewed their campaigns to gain international recognition for the events as the Armenian Genocide. "Because 80 percent of diasporic Armenians were descendants of genocide survivors, the memory of this atrocity became the most important vehicle with which to trigger a national identity dynamic."[488] The campaigns were further strengthened by the refusal of successive Turkish governments to recognize the events of 1915 as genocide.

Fin de Siècle and Armenian Dreams

The cataclysm that was World War I had been in the making for over half a century. The war's disastrous results and tragic changes adversely affected millions of people. Polyglot, heterogeneous and multi-confessional empires – Ottoman, Russian and Austro-Hungarian - were destroyed and buried along with a correspondingly large number of

---

[486] Khachig Tölölyan. "Cultural Narrative and the Motivation of the Terrorist." *Journal of Strategic Studies* 10, no. 4 (1987): 232.
[487] Miller and Miller, 29.
[488] Yossi Shain and Aharon Barth, 468.

their populations. These empires were replaced with smaller, often forcibly homogenized (ethnically and religiously) and monoglot nation-states. These rump states and the treaties penned from 1919-1923 that brought them into existence may have brought an end to outright hostilities, but they did nothing to end national aspirations and irredentism. Former empires were carved into states that left Austrians under Italian rule, Italians under Yugoslav rule, Hungarians under Romanian and Czechoslovak rule and Ukrainians, Tatars, Armenians, Georgians, Uzbeks and countless other groups under a repackaged form of Russian rule, the Soviet Union.

For Ottoman Armenians, the massacres and deportations of 1915 resulted in their disappearance from eastern Anatolia, a land they had inhabited for millennia. Those who managed to survive the forcible deportations across inhospitable terrain, disease, starvation, predation, rapes and massacres, emigrated to the four corners of the earth. Once again, their hopes, dreams and the promise of an Armenian state for Armenians were dashed by a combination of Great Power perfidy, betrayal and the harshness of the Ottoman response to the reality of Armenian aggression, collaboration with an invading Russia and agitation for independence.

The demarcation of the borders of the Republic of Turkey in 1923 by the Treaty of Lausanne as well as separate treaties between Turkey and the Soviet Union represented the final nail in the coffin of a greater Armenian state, encompassing the eastern provinces of Anatolia and Cilicia and what had been the historic Kingdom of Armenia. Yet memories and dreams were kept alive and an awakening of sorts occurred in the 1960s and 1970s regarding what was now referred to as the Armenian Genocide of 1915. History, particularly oral histories and transmitted memories, were increasingly utilized as political tools in order to popularize, vocalize and commemorate Ottoman massacres and atrocities, the injustices and suffering of the Armenian nation. These also downplayed the acts of outright rebellion against the Ottoman state, the massacres of Muslims and vanguard action of Armenians in support of

Russia's invasion. The diaspora, in particular, latched onto the chosen trauma of 1915 and their identity as Armenians increasingly became informed, and then dominated by 1915. As the narratives of the Armenian diaspora became increasingly homogeneous, two thousand years of brilliant history, languages, culture and kingdoms were sidelined for an identity of victimhood.

Though an Armenian state continued to exist, it was under Soviet and Russian domination, comprising territories of little consequence to most diaspora Armenians whose ancestors hailed from former Ottoman territories. Their dreams, however, were recurrent and refused to die. Their campaign for recognition of the events of 1915 as genocide, bolstered by acts of Armenian terrorism and the killing of Turks, remains informed by and, in turn, shapes Armenian large group identity.

CHAPTER 4

ARMENIAN DIASPORA POLITICAL ACTIVISM

Certain factors set the diaspora Armenian ethnic lobby apart from other ethic lobbies in the United States, France, Australia and elsewhere. This chapter will attempt to describe and deconstruct Armenian diaspora political activism and how it relates to, and is mutually reinforced by, Armenian diaspora large group identity and chosen trauma. A theoretical discussion of lobbying efforts, organization and strategy is included to provide a framework with which to better understand Armenian lobbying efforts and political divisions. As importantly, this chapter will demonstrate how these political divisions are overcome, or at least muzzled, by the centrality of the year 1915 to diaspora Armenian identity. The politicization, indeed the hypermobilization of the Armenian diaspora, as discussed in a previous chapter, will also be revisited and discussed in greater detail.

A number of factors make the Armenian diaspora and their related lobbying and civil society groups distinct, especially when compared to other diaspora groups and lobbies. First, diaspora Armenians and their interest groups are involved to an inordinate degree and maintain an almost single-minded focus on one issue: recognition of the events of 1915 as the Armenian Genocide. This focus on a single issue sets them apart from other diaspora or ethnic lobbying groups, regardless of location. Second, the issue at stake for diaspora Armenians, while having major present-day implications, occurred over one century ago. Simply put, most lobbies do not spend the majority of their time focused on the successful passage legislation dealing with events in the recent past, let alone events that occurred at the beginning of the previous century. Third, the power, sustained interest and longevity of Armenian diaspora lobbying efforts, stretching back over fifty years, separates it from a host of other diaspora lobbying and legislative efforts. Fourth, the diaspora Armenian lobby is characterized by the relative wealth of its members and supporters and the impressive organization of its efforts internationally. Armenian lobbies, civil society groups and interest groups have an almost global reach, working simultaneously on local, national and international stages. Via the politicization of Armenian diaspora large-group identity and the chosen trauma of 1915 which enhances that identity, Armenian interest groups compete for material and political support amongst the diaspora's highly charged and divided political, religious and social groups. Fifth, the Armenian diaspora experiences a hypermobilization of resources. To clarify, and as described in a previous chapter, despite their deep political, linguistic and religious divisions, diaspora Armenians across the board largely agree with and strongly support efforts to gain local, national and international recognition for what is the cornerstone of Armenian identity, the Armenian Genocide. What separates individual diaspora Armenians is how to best accomplish this recognition.

Whether a lobbying or interest group is more closely allied with one political movement or another, for example Dashnak or Hunchak, generally informs decisions regarding which group to fund. Differences over relations with the Republic of Armenia or another state such as Russia as well as the future of Nagorno-Karabakh are of importance, but of secondary concern in the decision-making process. These issues pale in comparison to the penultimate goal of

Armenian Genocide recognition. It is this identity-based issue that best explains the power, wealth expended, longevity and influence of the Armenian diaspora campaign, especially given its relatively small population size regardless of geographic location.

Finally, because of the centrality of the events of 1915 to Armenian diaspora large group identity, active support for the prolonged campaign is equally impressive and unparalleled. From volunteer drives to fund-raisers to workshops to clubs and social activities, the Armenian diaspora's ability to organize, educate and ensure legislation passes is remarkable. One has simply to broach the subject of being an ethnic Armenian with a member of the diaspora, regardless of age or sex, to understand how the events of 1915 are of utmost, indeed urgent importance to that individual's identity, worldview and politics. This identity has galvanized prolonged support and mobilization amongst the diaspora for their campaign to gain recognition of the events of 1915 as the Armenian Genocide. However, it has also had the corollary effect of complicating the diaspora's relations with the Republic of Armenia as well as Turkey.

Armenian diaspora interest and lobbying groups display remarkable differences with other ethnic and diaspora lobbying groups, but they also display similarities, such as focusing, at times, on one issue to the detriment of other, important issues. In the Armenian diaspora case, research for this book indicates that their initial lobbying efforts to gain recognition of the events of 1915 as the Armenian Genocide displayed a corresponding decrease in the amount of success these same lobbying groups achieved for another pet lobbying project, that of gaining funding and the provision of materiel for the Republic of Armenia from countries such as the United States and France.

This does not suggest a zero sum game; rather the research seems to point to what could be termed a steep learning curve for Armenian lobby groups. In the case of Armenian diaspora lobbies operating in the United States, the single-minded emphasis of one issue, the Armenian

Genocide, opened up opportunity spaces for other diaspora interest and lobbying groups in which to act. That is, newer lobbying organizations were established that practiced different tactics than their older counterparts.[489] This occurred because, to paraphrase one diaspora Armenian interviewee and lobbyist, certain Armenian-American lobbying groups concerned themselves exclusively with the issue of Armenian Genocide recognition.[490] These groups broadcast the issue of genocide recognition all the time and then broadcast it again. This had the effect of scaring away some lawmakers, who studiously avoid the Armenian Genocide lobbyists because of the international implications that genocide recognition carries. Explicitly, official United States recognition of the Armenian Genocide would have a chilling effect on important geo-strategic ties with Turkey. The interviewee wondered aloud how an Armenian-American lobbying organizations could be so tone deaf when pushing genocide recognition legislation that could possibly contradict and damage the strategic goals and interests of the United States. It was further opined that Armenian-American lobbying groups should avoid the non-stop proselytization of what has arguably become the "religion" of Armenian Genocide recognition.[491]

Does this mean that Armenian diaspora lobbying groups will eschew engagement with U.S. lawmakers when it comes to their identity-driven campaign for genocide recognition? Definitely not. Rather, it demonstrates a change of tactics and arguments on the part of at least one organization.

A theoretical assumption of this study is that individuals working to further the aims of ethnic or diaspora lobbying groups are highly mobilized and motivated individuals. Lobbying groups, in general, work to further an agenda or agendas and work within a highly politicized arena that

---

[489] See Michael M. Gunter. *Armenian History and the Question of Genocide*. Palgrave Macmillan US, 2011: 94.

[490] Excerpts from an interview with a representative of an Armenian-American lobbying organization, conducted in Washington, D.C. on 08 June 2007.

[491] Garbis.

requires constant attention; an experience that is largely foreign to the average voter or grassroots activist.

John de Figueredo and Charles Cameron, using the Potters-van Winden-Grossman-Helpman (PWGH) model, note that special interest and lobby groups operate according to the model by increasing lobbying expenditures when the legislative branch of government is controlled by "enemies" rather than "friends." Correspondingly, they increasingly exit the lobbying process as lobbying costs rise.[492] Yet, the Armenian-American lobbying groups, in particular, exhibit neither of the behaviors outlined by the PWGH model. That is, neither Democrats nor Republicans in the U.S. are viewed as particularly friendly or antagonistic when it comes to passing legislation supporting recognition of the events of 1915 as the Armenian Genocide. Both parties largely support the existence and survival of the Republic of Armenia through aid, financial assistance and arms to the tune of billions of dollars.[493] Both parties broadly agree, through public statements, that the events of 1915 constituted the Armenian Genocide. For example, a bipartisan resolution calling for the United States to formally recognize the Armenian Genocide was introduced to Congress on March 18, 2015. The Congressional press release issued at the time made an urgent call for America to finally use the word "genocide" when referencing the events of 1915.[494] Yet regardless of threats to do so, neither Republicans nor Democrats have brought this volatile issue to the floor of the House of Representative for a vote, generally kowtowing to pressure from the White House,

---

[492] John M. De Figueiredo and Charles M. Cameron. "Endogenous cost lobbying: Theory and evidence." In *CELS 2009 4th Annual Conference on Empirical Legal Studies Paper*. 2009: 3-4.

[493] Gunter, *Armenian History and the Question of Genocide*: 95-96.

[494] Anna R. Vetter. "Press Release: Valadao, Forty House Members Introduce Bipartisan Resolution to Recognize the Armenian Genocide." *Congressman David G. Valadao*, March 18, 2015, http://www.valadao.house.gov/news/documentsingle.aspx?DocumentID=398000#sthash.aFeP3ISh.dpuf

whether the administration is Democratic or Republican.[495] This has occurred against the backdrop of increasing costs for lobbying groups that are largely blamed on congressional gridlock and an emphasis on soft lobbying. This begs the question as to what motivates Armenian diaspora lobbying groups, particularly in the U.S., to not only continue lobbying, but to exhibit increases in numbers of supporters and supporting organizations?

The Genocide Recognition Campaign and Money

A cynical view indicates that the many activities surrounding Armenian Genocide recognition, to include lobbying, represent a steady money-maker. Examples include the large number of novels, semi-scholarly histories, artwork and poems that have been written regarding the tragedy.[496] Musicians and bands, such as the Armenian-American heavy metal band System of a Down, have recorded and released songs about the events of 1915, carving out an arguably lucrative career in the process.[497] Paintings, sculptures and other works of art both attempt to capture and capitalize on the reimagined tragedies that befell Ottoman Armenians in 1915 as well as the memories and the identity they promote. As early as 1919, the first film about the massacres and deportations of Ottoman Armenians appeared. This Hollywood film, entitled "Ravished Armenia," and produced for the American Committee for Armenian and Syrian Relief was reportedly based on the narrative account of a young Ottoman Armenian woman, Aurora Mardiganian. Replete with stock images of lily white, Armenian maidens suffering at the hands of swarthy Turks, the film largely agreed with and

---

[495] H.A. Goodman. "Lemkin's Words and Formally Recognize the Armenian Genocide." *Huffington Post*, June 13, 2015. http://www.huffingtonpost.com/h-a-goodman/the-united-states-should-_2_b_7053052.html

[496] Garbis.

[497] See Paul A. Aitken. "Attack/Affect: System of a Down and Genocide Activism." *MUSICultures* 38 (2013).

confirmed the Triple Entente's and its allies' World War I propaganda that depicted the citizens of the Central Powers, to include Ottoman Turks, as subhuman butchers and rapists.[498]

Atom Egoyan's 2002 film "Ararat" depicted the events of 1915 from the perspective of a fictional filmmaker named Edward Saroyan, thereby demonstrating the alleged monstrosities of Turks yesterday and today.[499] Another film, Carla Garapedian's "Screamers," focused on the aforementioned band System of a Down. Garapedian's film attempted to demonstrate just how the refusal of countries such as the United States, the United Kingdom and Turkey to acknowledge the events of 1915 as the Armenian Genocide has given other countries the "courage" and wherewithal to perpetrate acts of ethnic cleansing or genocide.[500]

In 2007, there were rumors that the actor Sylvester Stallone would produce and direct a film representation of Austrian writer Franz Werfel's 1933 novel "40 Days at Musa Dagh," a fictional account of the 1915 fighting, expulsions and massacres of Armenians in south-eastern Anatolia. Stallone was reportedly convinced not to pursue the film project on account of the historical controversy surrounding the events and an email campaign by a Turkish foundation.[501]

---

498 See a newly restored, 24-minute segment of "Ravished Armenia," as produced by the Armenian Genocide Resource Center of Northern California for a screening held on April 28, 2009 at the San Francisco Public Library:
https://archive.org/details/RavishedArmenia1919

499 Murray Whyte. "Film: Facing the Pain of a Past Long Hidden," *New York Times*, November 17, 2002,
http://query.nytimes.com/gst/fullpage.html?res=9803E3D71131F934A25752C1A9649C8B63&scp=1&sq=egoyan&st=nyt

500 Jeannette Catsoulis. "Film in Review: Screamers," *New York Times*, January 26, 2007,
http://query.nytimes.com/gst/fullpage.html?res=9B03E4DD173FF935A15752C0A9619C8B63&scp=6&sq=egoyan&st=nyt

501 James Reidel. "The Epic of Genocide." *The New York Review of Books*, April 24, 2015,

There is no doubt that the interest group and lobbying industry is big business, particularly in the United States. Prodigious amounts of money are made, raised and spent, and the Armenian diaspora lobbies are no different than their counterparts in this respect. "It perhaps cannot be gauged whether it is ethical to earn a salary from promoting a crime against humanity. Surely the fact that the [Armenian] Genocide is being propagated… is not something that should be scorned. Yet the fact remains that profit is being made at the expense of 1.5 million dead to the enthusiasm of the masses. The boundary between the sacred and the renown has worn thin."[502]

Niche Theory and Resource Dependence Theory

While Armenian diaspora political identity resulting in highly motivated individuals as well as money may explain much of what mobilizes the diaspora community and their lobbying representatives, a more general exploration as to why organized interests lobby is in order. Indeed, the simple question of why organized interests lobby is a surprisingly difficult one to answer. This is because most political science studies begin with the simple assumption that interest groups are motivated actors whose main goal and purpose is to influence public policy. According to the professor of public administration, David Lowery, "This assumption is incorrect. Rather, interest organizations are motivated by actors whose primary purpose is to survive."[503] Using this assumption, Lowery employs *niche theory* and *resource dependence theory* to detail how a more complete and satisfying theory of interest representation can be constructed. These concepts will then be employed to

---

http://www.nybooks.com/daily/2015/04/24/epic-armenian-genocide/

[502] Garbis.

[503] David Lowery. "Why Do Organized Interest Lobby? A Multi-Goal, Multi-Context Theory of Lobbying." *Polity* 39, no. 1 (January 2007), 29.

explain the survival of lobbying groups and interests and how their functions are inextricably conflated.

Niche theory and analysis looks at the relationship between a population or organism and variables in the environment that influence survival. Scholars have separately applied this theory to the study of organized interests.[504] In niche analysis, each necessary environmental resource is conceptualized as an array. "In this way an n-dimensional hypervolume is defined, every point of which corresponds to a state in the environment which would permit the species [S.sub.1] to exist indefinitely."[505] When a space is constituted, as such, it defines the space in which a species might survive. Given competition with similar species or similar organizations over space on shared resource arrays, the realized niche of most species is simply a part of each resource array defining its fundamental niche.

When applied to organized interests, niche theory requires scholars to specify the resources that might enable a lobbying organization and/or lobbying function within an organization to survive. These could be defined as members, if the organization is a membership group, or patrons, if the organization is an institution. Furthermore, survival may depend on other variables: financial resources, access to decision-makers, and issues around which lobbying is performed. "Given competition over these resources with other organized interests, an organization's core task is to construct a viable realized niche comprised of some portion of each of the resource arrays constituting its fundamental niche. Should its space on any one resource

[504] See Virginia Gray and David Lowery. "A niche theory of interest representation." *The Journal of Politics* 58, no. 01 (1996): 91-111. See also James Q. Wilson. *Political Organizations* (New York: Basic Books, 1973). See also William P. Browne. "Organized Interests and Their Issue Niches: A Search for Pluralism in a Policy Domain." *Journal of Politics* 52 (1990): 477-509.

[505] G. Evelyn Hutchinson. "Concluding Remarks." *Population Studies: Animal Ecology and Demography, Cold Spring Harbor Symposia on Quantitative Biology* 22 (1957): 416.

array shrink below the level sufficient to sustain the organization, it will cease to exist."[506]

Niche theory is important for two reasons. First, the many resource arrays of the fundamental niche may be viewed as defining the multiple goals that the organization may pursue when lobbying. For example, retaining members and/or soliciting the membership of newcomers, securing financial support from a patron or patrons, the maintenance of or attempt to regulate a favorable public opinion climate, or securing a final policy outcome. Second, niche theory posits that the determination of goals that necessarily dominate the selection of lobbying targets and tactics depends critically on which of several resource arrays the organization gains sustenance. Thus, a membership-based organization that loses members may need to move from lobbying on narrow but potentially achievable policy goals to lobbying on divisive or politically charged issues that stimulate interest and membership. This would occur even if achievement of advocated goals is unlikely.

An organization with weak public opinion support might shift from direct or inside lobbying on issues about which members care deeply to, "fuzzier outside lobbying in order to create a more favorable public opinion environment."[507] Furthermore, a membership organization with a strong membership base but weak finances may have to group its lobbying activities around issues that better reflect the preferences of a few wealthy patrons for survival. "If the existence of an organization… is in fact fundamentally threatened by a proposed change in policy, it will have no choice but to lobby in pursuit of final policy outcomes irrespective of the odds going into the fight. In this sense, purely instrumental lobbying can be accounted for as merely one of a broader range of lobbying modes, each determined by the search for a viable realized niche."[508]

---

[506] Lowery, "Why Do Organized Interests Lobby?", 40.
[507] Ibid, 41.
[508] Ibid.

In conclusion, the nature of the competition for any of the several resource arrays will necessarily determine which of multiple lobbying goals actually channels the decision to lobby, the selection of lobby targets and the selection among available influence tools. Accordingly, this exploration of niche theory, by linking lobbying goals and resource arrays, can perform much of the work in transforming *ad hoc* suspicions and ideas that posit lobbying is conducted for multiple purposes into a useful tool able to extract testable hypotheses. This should make it possible to shed further light on the lobbying efforts by the multiple organizations, including those of the Armenian diaspora. Yet a caveat is in order. This is because niche theory can be rather static while political environments are highly dynamic. Furthermore, niche theory is fundamentally about competition among similar organizations. This is an important corrective to most of the literature, which often frames competition solely in terms of final policy opponents – such as environmentalists versus manufacturers. Significantly, the most serious threat to an environmental organization is the existence of another environmental group. However, "there are other actors involved in lobbying – the public, political elites, policy opponents and so on – who may well influence the structure of the resource arrays comprising an organized interest's fundamental niche and, thereby, the level of competition it faces from similar organizations in constructing a viable realized niche."[509]

Rivalry at Home and Rivalry Abroad: Contextualizing Diaspora Political Efforts

One century ago, many Armenians, both inside and outside the Ottoman Empire, whether Protestant, Catholic or Orthodox, generally allied themselves with one of two competing, nationalist parties or organizations, the Armenian Revolutionary Force (ARF), or Dashnaks, and

---

[509] Ibid, 41-42.

the Hunchaks, who would later join the Armenian Ramgavar Party to oppose Dashnaks political aspirations and platforms. This political and ideological split resulted in the construction of parallel organizations by the diaspora in the form of schools, social clubs, lobbying organizations and charities.[510] This rift, characterized rather simplistically as those Armenians who were either pro-Dashnak or anti-Dashnak, dates back to the 1890s and widened significantly when eastern Armenia achieved independence briefly from Russia in 1918.[511] The ARF, or Dashnaks, controlled the government of an independent Armenia until the Soviet takeover in December 1920. Those Armenians who were pro-ARF were generally anti-Bolshevik, anti-communist and fully supported an independent Armenia. The anti-ARF Armenians, at least passively, supported the Soviet occupation of Armenia, if only to prevent further attacks or outright conquest by Turkey, Georgia and Azerbaijan.[512]

Even before Armenia's post-World War I independence, ideological and political differences over the future of an Armenian nation-state impacted diaspora Armenians as far away as the United States. For example, Protestant Armenians who opposed revolutionary and violent nationalism founded their own separate church in Worcester, Massachusetts, in 1891. Differences also had an impact on charities. For example, the anti-ARF Armenian General Benevolent Union (AGBU) was created to neutrally assist diaspora Armenians with education, medical access, development and assistance, but remains to this day largely partisan in constitution.[513] Pro-ARF individuals promptly

---

[510] In the case of Lebanon, the rivalry has been particularly stark with interesting results. See Ohannes Geukjian. "From Positive Neutrality to Partisanship: How and Why the Armenian Political Parties Took Sides in Lebanese Politics in the Post-Taif Period (1989–Present)." *Middle Eastern Studies* 45, no. 5 (2009): 739-767.

[511] Bakalian, 95.

[512] Jenny Phillips. *Symbols, Myth, and Rhetoric: The Politics of Culture in an Armenian-American Population* (New York: AMS Press, 1989), 119.

[513] Gregg, 6-7.

founded the Armenian Relief Society (ARS) as an answer to the AGBU.[514]

These divisions had profound effects on the development and, ultimately, the effectiveness of Armenian diaspora lobbies. The ARF founded their first lobbying group in 1918. This group evolved into the Armenian National Committee (ANC) and, in the United States, the Armenian National Committee of America (ANCA).[515] Decades later, influential members of the anti-ARF community founded the Armenian Assembly of America, most often referred to as The Assembly, in 1972, with the hope of, "… securing increasingly more effective collaboration among Armenian-American organizations and to establish results-oriented working relationships with non-partisan advocacy entities and relevant individuals worldwide."[516]

These two lobby groups, often pursuing the same strategy to achieve differing goals, continue to function independently. Indeed, the ANCA's and the Armenian Assembly's differing goals and structure mirror the strong ideological split of the Armenian-American diaspora community.[517]

Diaspora Lobbies

While both the ANC, which includes the ANCA, and the Assembly maintain their headquarters in Washington, D.C., the ANC's structure can be characterized as the more diffuse and international. The ANC maintains offices in France, the United Kingdom, Italy and a European Union office in Brussels. It also has offices in Yerevan and Stepanakert, the capital of the disputed Nagorno-Karabakh

---

[514] Ibid, 7.

[515] Ibid, 9.

[516] AAINC. "Our Mission: To Lead." *Armenian Assembly of America.* http://www.aaainc.org/assembly/mission.php

[517] See Rachel Anderson Paul. "Grassroots Mobilization and Diaspora Politics: Armenian Interest Groups and the Role of Collective Memory." *Nationalism and Ethnic Politics*, 6, (1), (Spring 2000), 24-47.

region. In the United States, the ANCA has well over 50 offices. The Communications Director at the Washington, D.C. offices of the ANC stated that power equals people for the ANC, hence the large number of offices and an international presence. These ANC activists are generally politically active, committed to causes such as recognition of the Armenian Genocide, and depend on the ANC to provide them with sources of information and strategies that inform their actions.[518]

In contrast, the Armenian Assembly maintains its national headquarters in Washington, D.C. and one regional office in Beverly Hills, California. Besides these offices, which handle lobbying efforts, policy issues, relations with the Armenian government and membership, the Assembly has an office in New York City that liaises with the United Nations.

In the U.S. context, both the ANCA and the Assembly are committed to the longevity and deep support of ties between the Republic of Armenia as well as the disputed region of Nagorno-Karabakh and the United States. The ANC outwardly maintains cordial relations with the Assembly and other Armenian diaspora interest groups and they do share at least two overarching goals: the longevity and survival of the Republic of Armenia and, most importantly, gaining recognition that the events of 1915 constituted the Armenian Genocide. Both the ANCA and the Assembly call for "increasing US aid levels to Armenia to promote economic and democratic development… ensuring the appropriate commemoration of the Armenian Genocide; and encouraging Turkey and Azerbaijan to lift their blockades and adhere to the international standards for human rights and humanitarian practices."[519]

---

[518] Author's interview with Elizabeth Chouldjian, ANCA Communications Director, April 4, 2007, Washington, D.C.
[519]ANCA. "About the ANCA." *Armenian National Committee of America* http://www.anca.org/ancaprofile.php

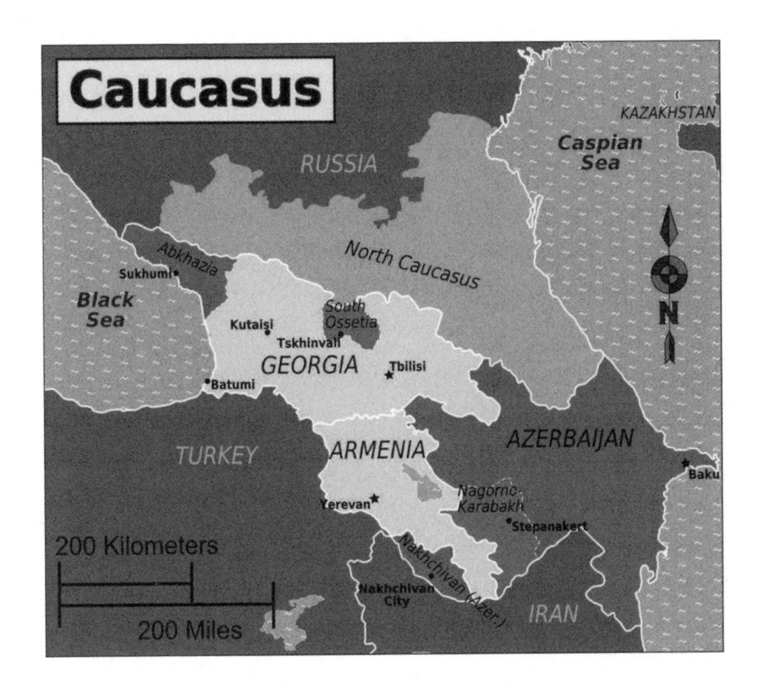

The Caucasus Region[520]

The list of legislative achievements by the ANCA in the United States, in concert with other Armenian-American interest groups, is impressive if not yet entirely successful. This includes regular attempts to introduce bills that reference the Armenian Genocide and attempts at further recognition.[521] This dovetails with its three stated goals: the increase of public awareness in support of an independent Armenia, the influence and guidance of United States policy vis-à-vis matters of interest to the Armenian-American community, and to serve as a liaison between the Armenian-American community and their elected officials in

---

[520]https://commons.wikimedia.org/wiki/File:Caucasus_regions_map 2.png

[521] ANCA. "Key Legislation." *Armenian National Committee of America.* https://anca.org/key-legislation/

representing collective viewpoints held by the community in regards to public policy.[522]

Similar to the ANC, the Armenian Assembly lists as one of its main goals the expansion of "the organization's pioneering research, education and advocacy campaign for universal affirmation of the Armenian Genocide and to secure diaspora-wide consensus for the government of the Republic of Armenia to deal with the consequences of this crime against humanity."[523]

Membership and Mobilization Strategies

In the United States, the two lobbies differ in their approaches to membership and mobilization. The ANCA, perhaps indicative of its longer history, claims to be a grass-roots organization with 50 chapters in across the United States – each reportedly striving to ensure that the Armenian American community's voice is heard at all levels of government, federal, state and local. The Assembly seems to attract Armenian academics and the business elite who support the lobby group financially. This is perhaps indicative of its late founding by influential diaspora Armenians.

The ANCA and the Assembly have established similar, but separate, alliances with other organizations, states and interest groups. These alliances are part of a wider effort to block military and economic aid to Turkey and, more importantly, gain international recognition for the Armenian Genocide. The international ANC and the ANCA in the United States both boast strong ties with Greek and Greek Cypriot national and diaspora communities as well as Kurdish diaspora communities.[524]

---

[522] Ibid.

[523] AAINC, "Our Mission: To Lead." *Armenian Assembly of America.* http://www.aaainc.org/assembly/mission.php

[524] See ANCA. "ANCA joins Greek-Americans in Opposing Free Transfer of Guided Missile Frigates to Turkey." *Armenian National Committee of America.* December 31, 2012. https://anca.org/press-

The Assembly maintains that it has "the highest non-governmental organization status of any Armenian organization" at the United Nations, has special consultative status at the United Nations Economic and Social Council and works closely with the staff at the US Holocaust Memorial Museum to raise awareness of the Armenian genocide.[525]

Social Networking and Political Activism

Indicative of the ANCA's grass roots support are sub-organizations such as the Armenian National Committee Professional Network (ANC-PN) or the Armenian National Committee of Central California. These local organizations are affiliated with ANCA at the very local level and enlist support for Armenian causes not only from local diaspora Armenians, but also from local political leaders. They also educate both diaspora Armenians and non-Armenians about the Armenian Genocide, the status of Nagorno-Karabakh and the importance of a viable Republic of Armenia. By building bridges to the local community, by politicizing each generation of Armenian-Americans and by utilizing these politically involved interest groups at the local level, the ANCA has brought the issue of the Armenian Genocide and its recognition to a mainstream and widespread audience of non-Armenians. The support the ANCA provides is mutually beneficial and it also engenders a continuous, high level of support for the ANCA and its activities.

In a fashion similar to the ANC-PN, the Armenian Network of America is dedicated to providing a forum for the advancement of Armenian-Americans, promoting the interests of the Armenian-American community via a forum that is "ecumenical, non-partisan, global and broad-minded

---

release/anca-joins-greek-americans-in-opposing-free-transfer-of-guided-missile-frigates-to-turkey/

[525] Gregg, 13.

in practice and in opinions."[526] It also hopes to address issues which face Armenians worldwide.

Alliances and Lobbying Efforts

Despite their differences in history, constituencies and tactics, the Assembly and the ANCA present a united front in Washington, D.C. The forum they utilize is the bipartisan Congressional Caucus on Armenian Issues. The Caucus works with members of the House of Representatives to encourage awareness of Armenian issues and initiatives on behalf of the Republic of Armenia. Besides the Armenian Caucus in Congress, both the ANCA and the Assembly lend their support to the Armenian-American Democratic Leadership Council (AADLC) and members as well as Armenian-American supporters of both groups belong to the National Organization of Republican Armenians (NORA).

The Armenian-American lobbies are certainly considered influential and powerful though their actual influence and successes have been questioned.[527] Before Armenia achieved independence from the Soviet Union, both the ANCA and the Assembly focused largely on obtaining recognition of the Armenian Genocide. Following Armenia's independence, genocide recognition remains the main issue, but thwarting military and economic aid to Turkey and Azerbaijan and encouraging a boycott of Transcaucasian oil and gas pipelines as well as other infrastructure projects and links that bypass Armenia have been added.

One of the Assembly's annual reports noted that "Capitol Hill legislators and their staffs look to the Assembly as a trusted source of information on issues related to the continued vibrancy of Armenia and [the disputed territory

---

526 "About Us." *Armenian Network of America Inc.* http://www.armnet.org/about_us

527 See Julien Zarifian. "The Armenian-American lobby and its impact on US foreign policy." *Society* 51, no. 5 (2014): 503-512.

of Nagorno-Karabakh]."[528] The policy demands of both the Assembly and ANCA include, but are not limited to, US government recognition of the events of 1915 as the Armenian Genocide, US government recognition of Nagorno-Karabakh's independence, continued aid to both Armenia and Nagorno-Karabakh, blocking arms sales to Turkey and Azerbaijan and blocking all aid to Azerbaijan.

Both the ANCA and the Assembly support legislation that would lessen Turkey's and Azerbaijan's isolation of Armenia. The Assembly specifically notes Turkey's and Azerbaijan's efforts to build the Kars–Tbilisi–Baku railway that will bypass Armenia completely by crossing Georgia. The Assembly and the ANCA were successful in blocking any US assistance or development for, "… rail connections that traverse or connect Azerbaijan, Georgia and Turkey and that specifically exclude Armenia."[529] Yet this has had little impact on the building of the Kars–Tbilisi–Baku railway, which will still bypass Armenia completely when operational.

Similarly, efforts by Armenian diaspora lobbies in the United States, France and elsewhere to oppose the building of a crude oil pipeline came to naught. The Baku–Tbilisi–Ceyhan (BTC) pipeline is a 1768 kilometer-long crude oil pipeline connecting Baku, the capital of Azerbaijan and Ceyhan, a port on the south-eastern Mediterranean coast of Turkey, via Tbilisi, the capital of Georgia. It was completed in 2006 and bypasses Armenia.

These lobbying failures, if indeed they can be termed as such, are not necessarily a sign of Armenian diaspora ineffectiveness and lack of influence in Washington, D.C. or Paris. Rather, these large-scale infrastructure projects were funded and completed largely as a result of the world's

---

[528] AAAINC, "2005 Annual Report," *Armenian American Assembly of America.* http://www.aaainc.org/fileadmin/aaainc/pdf/Annual_Reports/AAA_Annual_Report_2005.pdf

[529] Ibid.

interest in gaining access to Azerbaijan's massive oil and gas reserves.

The ANCA and the Assembly have been rather more successful in their primary policy objective: gaining recognition of the Armenian Genocide. Currently over forty US states have been persuaded in one form or another to recognize the events of 1915 as the Armenian Genocide and cities such as Boston commemorate April 24th as a Day of Remembrance for Armenian victims of the massacres and deportations of 1915.[530] ANC offices worldwide have also pressured governments, with considerable success, to recognize the Armenian Genocide. Indeed, the ANC-France lobby was the driving force behind the French Senate's recognition of the events of 1915 as genocide in 2000 and of the French National Assembly's criminalization of the "denial of the Armenian Genocide" in 2006.[531] The Italian parliament, pressured by the Italian ANC chapter, adopted a resolution in 2000 that overwhelmingly supported recognizing the massacres of 1915 as the Armenian Genocide, calling on Turkey to do the same. "The success of this effort, in the face of intense pressure from the Turkish government, represents a real tribute to the devotion of the Italian government and people to fairness, human rights, and justice," explained ANC of Italy representative Alecco Bezikian.[532]

As of 2015, although the Armenian lobby had succeeded in persuading more than twenty-nine countries to recognize

---

[530] Zarifian, 509.

[531] See ANCA. "French Senate approves Armenian Genoçide Recognition," *Armenian National Committee of America*, 08 November 2000. https://anca.org/press-release/french-senate-approves-armenian-genocide-resolution/. See also Thomas Crampton. "French Pass Bill that Punishes Denial of Armenian Genocide," *The New York Times*, 12 October 2006, http://www.nytimes.com/2006/10/13/world/europe/13turkey.htm l

[532] ANCA. "Italian Parliament Calls on Turkey to End Armenian Genocide Denial," *Armenian National Committee of America*, November 17, 2000. https://anca.org/press-release/italian-parliament-calls-on-turkeyto-end-armenian-genocide-denial/

the Armenian Genocide, success in the United States, at least at the federal government level remains elusive. The U.S. Congress has come close to recognizing the Armenian Genocide several times since the early 1990s but has generally deferred to the Executive Branch and the State Department, both of which fear angering Turkey.[533]

The Communications Director at the ANCA laid the blame for failure to gain recognition for the Armenian Genocide at the door of the White House, regardless of which party controls the Executive Branch. The approaches of successive administrations to the issue were characterized as flawed and ultimately doomed to failure, given that the administrations were swimming against the tide of American public opinion.[534]

The largely symbolic resolutions put forward by the ANC and the Assembly internationally demand that states - the United States, France, Brazil, Egypt, Japan etc. - officially acknowledge that the Ottoman Empire and, by proxy, Turkey committed genocide against the Armenian people in the early twentieth century. As such, an exploration of what is behind Armenian diaspora efforts to achieve the passage of *ad hoc* and symbolic legislation is in order. Specifically, what does genocide recognition entail and what does this mean for Armenians, Turks and others?

---

[533] Zarifian, 509.

[534] Author's interview with Elizabeth Chouldjian, ANCA Communications Director, April 4, 2007, Washington, D.C.

CHAPTER 5

THE GENOCIDE RECOGNITION CAMPAIGN: REASONING AND RATIONALE

According to an Issue Brief published by the Armenian Assembly, US recognition of the events of 1915 as a genocide requires that the President of the United States properly acknowledge and use the term "the Armenian Genocide" in his/her annual April 24th commemorative address.[535] Furthermore, the recognition of the US and other states of the Armenian Genocide by the Ottoman Empire is instrumental in ensuring that the legacy of the genocide is remembered in order to allow for the cessation of other, future crimes against humanity.[536] "Despite the international recognition and affirmation of the Armenian Genocide, the failure of the domestic and

[535] US Presidents annually issue statements regarding the events of 1915 on April 24th. They are generally disappointing to the Armenian diaspora because the issued statements avoid employing the term "genocide." See "Statement of President Barack Obama on Armenian Remembrance Day," *The White House, Office of the Press Secretary*, April 24, 2009, April 24, 2010, April 24, 2011, April 24, 2012, April 24, 2013, April 24,2014, April 24, 2015.

[536] AAINC, "Issue Brief: Armenian Genocide Affirmation," *Armenian Assembly of America*, http://www.aaainc.org/index.php?id=114

international authorities to punish those responsible for the Armenian Genocide is a reason why similar genocides have recurred and may recur in the future, and that a just resolution will help prevent future genocides."[537]

This is a powerful, normative argument that outlines ostensibly direct repercussions. That is, the failure of states such as the US and Turkey, to recognize the events of 1915 as the Armenian Genocide has led directly to other cases of genocide. If this same logic is applied, then the symbolic act of recognizing the events of 1915 as genocide, through legislation and official statements, would lead to direct action on the part of the world's states in curbing cases of genocide, or those that appear as such. While the sentiment is perhaps profound, is there any causal proof that such is the case?

Definitions of Genocide

A discussion of efforts to gain genocide recognition necessarily leads to an exploration of what constitutes and defines genocide. As with so much else, the definition of genocide often varies from scholar to scholar or legislative body to state official. For example, Chalk and Jonassohn define genocide as "… a form of one-sided mass killing in which a state or other authority intends to destroy a group, as that group and membership in it are defined by the perpetrator."[538] Israel Charny notes that "Genocide in the generic sense is the mass killing of substantial numbers of human beings, when not in the course of military forces of an avowed enemy, under conditions of the essential defenselessness and helplessness of the victims."[539] Steven

---

[537] "Affirmation of the United States Record on the Armenian Genocide." *US House Resolution 106*. (110th Congress, 1st Session). http://www.thomas.gov/cgi-bin/query/z?c110:H.RES.106

[538] Frank Chalk and Kurt Jonassohn. *The History and Sociology of Genocide* (New Haven, CT: Yale University Press, 1990).

[539] Israel W. Charny. "Toward a Generic Definition of Genocide." In *Genocide: Conceptual and Historical Dimensions* ed. George J.

Katz disagrees with Charny, writing that "the concept of genocide applies *only* when there is an actualized intent, however successfully carried out, to physically destroy an *entire* group (as such a group is defined by the perpetrators)."[540] Numerous scholars, to include Horowitz, Dadrian and Drost, have all proposed alternatively broad or narrow definitions of genocide.[541]

On the contrary, and to the chagrin of many scholars and humanitarian groups, genocide is strictly defined by the Convention on the Prevention and Punishment of the Crime of Genocide adopted by resolution 260 (III) A of the United Nations General Assembly on December 9, 1948. According to Article II of the Convention, "Genocide means any of the following acts committed with intent to destroy, in whole or in part, a national, ethnical, racial or religious group, as such:

(a) Killing members of the group;
(b) Causing serious bodily or mental harm to members of the group;
(c) Deliberately inflicting on the group conditions of life calculated to bring about its physical destruction in whole or in part;
(d) Imposing measures intended to prevent births within the group;
(e) Forcibly transferring children of the group to another group.

Article III: the following acts shall be punishable:

(a) Genocide;
(b) Conspiracy to commit genocide;

Andreopoulos (Philadelphia, PA: University of Pennsylvania Press, 1994).

[540] Steven T. Katz. *The Holocaust in Historical Context, Volume 1: The Holocaust and Mass Death Before the Modern Age*. (1994).

[541] See Irving Louis Horowitz. *Taking Lives: Genocide and State Power* (New Brunswick, NJ: Transaction Publishers, 1980). See also Vahakn N. Dadrian. "A Typology of Genocide." *International Review of Modern Sociology*, 5 (Fall 1975), 123. See also Pieter Drost. *The Crime of State, vol. 2* (Leyden: A.W. Sythoff, 1959).

(c) Direct and public incitement to commit genocide;
(d) Attempt to commit genocide;
(e) Complicity in genocide."[542]

Article IV adds that any persons committing genocide will be punished, whether they are "constitutionally responsible rulers, public officials or private individuals."[543]

According to the Convention, if the events of 1915 constituted the Armenian Genocide, officials of the Ottoman Empire, as private individuals, would be eligible for punishment – even though the Convention was passed and the word "genocide" was coined over 30 years after the events transpired. Complicating the issue further, the Convention does not recognize retroactive claims. That is, it does not recognize events that occurred prior to its adoption in 1948. Even if the retroactivity clause were to be changed, the Convention does not explicate the punishments and penalties to be meted out, though it does present a road map for addressing grievances in Article IX. "Disputes between the Contracting Parties relating to the interpretation, application or fulfillment of the present Convention, including those relating to the responsibility of a State for genocide or for any of the other acts enumerated in Article III, shall be submitted to the International Court of Justice (ICJ) at the request of any of the parties to the dispute."[544]

Gündüz Aktan, a diplomat, member of the Turkish-Armenian Reconciliation Committee (TARC) and columnist for *Radikal*, a Turkish daily newspaper noted, "According to the Genocide Convention only a competent court would be able to decide whether that [the events of 1915] had been a case of genocide. No such court decision existed. And there was no way for the Armenian side to have a convention (that took force in 1951) implemented retroactively. However, to overcome that obstacle, Turkey could accept

---

542 "Convention on the Prevention and Punishment of the Crime of Genocide," adopted by resolution 260 (III) A of the U.N. General Assembly; December 9, 1948.
543 Ibid.
544 Ibid.

retroactive application of the convention and Turkey and Armenia could, together, take this issue to an international tribunal for adjudication or seek arbitration."[545] According to Aktan, Armenians and particularly the Armenian diaspora have never requested this because "...they knew the law was not on their side."[546]

While the veracity of Aktan's claims may be suspect, research on the subject unearthed nothing to indicate that either the Republic of Armenia or the Armenian diaspora communities have requested this from Turkey, though certain members of the Armenian diaspora community applaud such a move as will be discussed in greater detail.[547] Thus, neither the nation-state of Armenia nor the Armenian diaspora communities have ever sought to submit their list of grievances, which occurred at the beginning of the twentieth century to the ICJ.[548]

Turkey has been accused of being unwilling to attend the ICJ and face the matter in court.[549] However, Yücel Güçlü, author of *The Holocaust and the Armenian Case in Comparative*

---

[545] Gündüz Aktan. "How Shameful (1) (On Armenian Issue)." *The Journal of Turkish Weekly*, April 2, 2005.
http://www.turkishweekly.net/2005/04/02/op-ed/how-shameful-1-on-armenian-issue/

[546] Ibid.

[547] Harut Sassounian. "Armenians Demand Justice, not Recognition." *The California Courier,* 06 December 2007.
http://www.armeniapedia.org/wiki/Armenians_Demand_Justice,_Not_Recognition
George Jerjian. *The Truth will set Us Free: Armenians and Turks Reconciled* (London: GJ Communications, 2003)

[548] Ara Papian. "Recognition of the Armenian Genocide and territorial claims are two different fights." *Repair*. September 24, 2015. http://www.repairfuture.net/index.php/en/armenian-genocide-recognition-and-reparations-standpoint-of-armenia/recognition-of-the-armenian-genocide-and-territorial-claims-are-two-different-fights

[549] Harut Sassounian. "Sassounian: Leading Expert's Final Words on Turkey's Legal Responsibility for the Genocide." The Armenian Weekly. September 16, 2013. http://armenianweekly.com/2013/09/16/sassounian-leading-experts-final-words-on-turkeys-legal-responsibility-for-the-genocide/

Perspective, argues that Turkey is not the aggrieved party in this case. He noted that there are many in Turkey who believe that Turkey should take this case to the ICJ to clear Turkey's name or establish its guilt in regards to the events of 1915. However, he offered no details and no such move has been made by either party, though some are now demanding precisely this.[550]

The fact remains that any Ottoman officials involved in the tragic events of 1915 are long dead. Most Armenian survivors have also died. Indeed, the Ottoman Empire itself was killed off soon after the events in question. What then, beyond purely symbolic and commemorative acts, do Armenians, particularly those of the diaspora, hope to achieve by the passage of *ad hoc* legislative resolutions designating the events of 1915 as the Armenian Genocide? Furthermore, what general steps can be taken to address historical atrocities?

Recognition of the Armenian Genocide and What It Entails

Ad hoc resolutions, as passed by various cities, local assemblies and states, would lead to the formal recognition, of sorts, that Ottoman Armenians who suffered the massacres and deportations of 1915 – necessarily termed the Armenian Genocide in the resolution - would be recognized and commemorated as the victims and survivors of the world's first genocide or, at very least, the first genocide of the twentieth century.[551] The importance of commemoration is underscored repeatedly in various legislative acts. The goal of this, according to the former

---

[550] Author's interviews with Yücel Güçlü, First Counselor to the Ambassador of the Republic of Turkey, March 30 and November 15, 2007. Washington, D.C.

[551] ANCA. "10th Annual ANCA Armenian Genocide Observance on Capitol Hill Draws 40 Members of Congress." *Armenian National Committee of America.* May 5, 2004. https://anca.org/press-release/10th-annual-anca-armenian-genocide-observance-on-capitol-hill-draws-40-members-of-congress/

Foreign Minister of the Republic of Armenia, Vartan Oksanian, is memorialization and commemoration on a global scale. Of note and echoing what House Resolution 106 says, Okasanian opined that "These commemorations are very critical in the face of the growing threat of genocide in the world today from Bosnia to Rwanda to Darfur. Commemoration is a way of countering the distortion of history, countering the subversion of truth by power. Commemoration is the victory of truth over expediency. Commemoration is a condemnation of the violence. Commemoration is a call to responsibility, and therefore to prevention. Commemoration is an acknowledgement of the past, and even the present, but not an obstacle to the future."[552]

As noted previously and explicit in Oksanian's statement and others by the ANC and the Assembly, for example, is the view that through the specific act of recognition of the Armenian Genocide via *ad hoc* legislation, future genocides will be prevented. Mirroring this, the International Relations Committee of the United States House of Representatives stated in a discussion of the Armenian case that, "What we are saying is that this time in history [1915] needs to be remembered because what has passed is often prologue, and failure to remember, failure to recognize, sweeping under the carpet of history is a mistake that ultimately we are doomed to repeat time and time again... If we believe that unrecognized genocide contributes to future genocides, don't we have an obligation to assure that our diplomatic staff and those who advise our leaders learn about this history, learn about [the Armenian] genocide?"[553]

---

[552] "Minister Oksanian Speaks on Genocide Remembrance in Brussels." *Ministry of Foreign Affairs of Armenia*. (Brussels: 25 April 2007). http://www.mfa.am/en/speeches/item/2007/04/25/vo-genocide-brussels/

[553] Markups before the Committee on International Relations, House of Representatives, 106th Congress, 2nd session, 28 September and 3 October, 2000; as quoted in Bertil Dunér. "What can be done about Historical Atrocities? The Armenian Case," *International Journal of Human Rights*, vol. 8, No. 2, Summer 2004; 219.

While the sentiments encapsulated in these lofty statements is understandable, the fact remains that that they have no basis in fact. Commemoration is a purely symbolic act, no matter how powerful it may be as tool for mobilization vis-à-vis people and their identities. Neither justice, bread, jobs, natural resources, land nor money are to be issued to the few survivors of the events of 1915. Commemoration will not give any of these to the aggrieved survivors of the genocide in Rwanda or elsewhere.

Relatedly, and implicit or explicit in any of the arguments categorizing the events of 1915 as the Armenian Genocide is that the lack of such an acknowledgement by the Turkish government and many scholars constitutes a twofold denial. It denies the Armenians of their proper place in history. It also constitutes a denial of what they feel was their overwhelming suffering and loss, while ignoring that of their Muslim counterparts in eastern Anatolia and the Caucasus.

"The Turkish-American governmental act of smothering the facts has a profound impact of how the American mass media, motion pictures, television networks, local broadcast stations and newspapers will handle or not handle, this established historical fact, and Armenian attempts to establish a just recognition. The denial by the Turks and silence in Washington could be merely bizarre, like refusing to acknowledge the plague. But it has deeper consequences. It suggests to any evil group that it is possible to commit crimes against humanity and get away with it. It denies to Armenians the dignity and catharsis of their suffering. Ironically, it limits Turkey itself. Like an unacknowledged crime in an individual, repressed guilt will distort Turkey's ability to deal rationally with itself."[554]

According to this argument, recognition would lead to closure, dignity and catharsis for Armenians, though it is unclear how or what this entails or whether this would be on an individual or communal level, or both. This is

---

[554] "The Armenian Genocide: Simplified." *ArmenianGenocide1915.* http://www.genocide1915.info/research/view.asp?ID=30

certainly the assumption the Armenian campaign rests on: that by the sheer accretion of countries and cities recognizing the events of 1915 as the Armenian Genocide the combined weight will force some sort of recognition from Turkey. Yet, if each resolution was taken on a case-by-case basis, one is still left wondering what has actually been achieved? For example, the European Parliament adopted a resolution in April 2015 entitled "European Parliament Resolution on the Armenian Genocide 100th Anniversary." The resolution was passed by 351 to 269 votes and 22 abstentions. Via the resolution the European Parliament recognized "the tragic events that took place in 1915-1917 against the Armenians in the territory of the Ottoman Empire" as "genocide as defined in the Convention on the Prevention and Punishment of the Crime of Genocide of 1948."[555] It added that it came to this less-than-unanimous decision based, in part, through reliance on the "increasing number of [EU] Member States and national parliaments" that recognize the 'Armenian [G]enocide'"[556] Importantly, Article 2 of the 2015 resolution referred to a 1987 European Parliament resolution that labeled the events of 1915 as the Armenian Genocide. This 1987 was resolution was used by Marseille-based *Euro-Arménie ASBL* and two French-Armenians in 1999 to apply to the Court of First Instance of the European Communities (which became the General Court as a constituent court of the Court of Justice of the European Union after 2009). This application to the court was done immediately after Turkey had achieved candidate status for EU membership and asked for "compensation for the harm caused to them by, inter allia, recognition of Turkey's status as a candidate for accession to the European Union, although that State [Turkey] has refused to acknowledge the genocide perpetrated in 1915 against the Armenians living in Turkey."[557]

---

[555] Tuncel, 5-6.

[556] Tuncel, 6.

[557] Ibid, 6-7.

It is through the actions of French-Armenians that one can begin to gain an understanding of what is at stake. To wit, *ad hoc* resolutions are political, but their passage can be used for legal leverage. Unfortunately for the plaintiffs, the Court ruled in Turkey's favor by judging that no causal relationship existed between European Council's acceptance of Turkey's candidacy to the EU membership and the allegedly harmed dignity of the Armenians. As importantly, the Court stated "It suffices to point out that the 1987 [European Parliament] Resolution is a document containing declarations of a purely political nature, which may be amended by the Parliament at any time. It cannot therefore have binding legal consequences for its author nor, *a fortiori*, for the other defendant institutions."[558]

From a legal standpoint, an accusation of a crime leveled by an individual or party – even the European Parliament - against another individual or party does not constitute proof of guilt. Indeed, laws in many countries consider continuous and unsubstantiated accusations as character assassination and the accusatory party may be tried for slander or libel, amongst other things. Yet this is precisely what has occurred via the passage of *ad hoc* legislation in Paris, Moscow, Athens and Bern. The legislation formally, though not legally, accuses an entire large group, the Turks, and a nation-state, Turkey, of the most serious crime known to humanity. Indeed, this legislation, resting as it does on questionable history and being informed by geopolitical and highly politicized considerations, recognizes that Turkey, as the successor state to the Ottoman Empire, committed the crime of genocide in 1915. Thus, in the case of the events of 1915, it is unclear how reconciliation, dignity and closure will be achieved when the dignity of one large group is enhanced only through the denigration of its Other. Yet this is one of the plausible outcomes of the extra-legal campaign for recognition of the Armenian Genocide. It is equally unclear what effects eventual recognition by Turkey, the United States and other states would have on overall

---

[558] Ibid, 7.

Armenian and particularly Armenian diaspora identity. This is because Armenian identity is largely constructed and informed by the refusal of the Republic of Turkey to formally accept a highly politicized version of historical events that many scholars of Ottoman and Turkish history consider to be a patently biased misrepresentation.

There are other concerns as well that encompass territorial claims and restitution that are inherent in any claim of genocide. The historian, Donald Bloxham queried, "How would Armenian historians and politicians exploit the situation; to what uses would the history of the genocide be put? As the case of the Holocaust has shown, history can be appropriated for a host of political ends that have nothing but an emotive connection with the historical record."[559] These are important and prescient questions. They should not effect a genocide-perpetrating country or large group from accepting responsibility – should that be proved in an independent and relevant court of law – yet issues of reparations and claims by diaspora Armenians are absent from the current discourse surrounding attempts to gain *ad hoc* legislation that recognizes the Armenian Genocide.

An official at the ANCA provided a partial, if informal answer, stating that if and when Turkey recognized the events of 1915 as the Armenian Genocide, an "appropriate" international commission would be constituted that would necessarily include Armenian diaspora representatives. This commission would be charged with handling territorial, land, housing and reparation claims.[560]

Each time a country in the world approves legislation labeling the events of 1915 as the Armenian Genocide, there are calls for celebration amongst the Armenian diaspora communities. *Ad hoc* legislation or official commemorative speeches or events equal success because it means that one more government entity or association has recognized the events of 1915 as the Armenian Genocide.

---

[559] Bloxham, 229.

[560] Author's interview with Elizabeth Chouldjian, ANCA Communications Director, April 4, 2007, Washington, D.C.

According to one author, these international commemorations and *ad hoc* legislation, "… give faith and hope that justice is somehow being served, but exactly how no one can really pinpoint. It is sacrilege to question what the end result will be for the ultimate recognition – that by Turkey. No one dares to make any kind of prediction."[561] An exploration is therefore in order as to what is desired by the Armenian diaspora and the Republic of Armenia and what will actually be gained, or possibly be gained, vis-à-vis formal recognition by the Republic of Turkey that the Armenian Genocide occurred in 1915. The court cases in Europe based on parliamentary resolutions, as outlined previously, give an idea that more is at stake than the healing of deep wounds via recognition.

The Many Facets of Armenian Genocide Recognition

George Jerjian, author, marketing analyst, diaspora Armenian and British citizen authored an instructive book regarding the possibility of truth and reconciliation between Armenians and Turks[562]. Jerjian's tone is hopeful and maintains a disarming and conciliatory tone throughout. Everything is easy in Jerjian's opinion. Turks simply have to face the truth regarding the actions of their Ottoman ancestors. To this end and not surprisingly, Jerjian is unequivocal in his call for Turkish recognition of the events of 1915 as the Armenian Genocide. To support his claims, he cites much of the vast compendium supporting the so-called Armenian thesis of events, focusing particularly on claims and works by Vahakn Dadrian and Taner Akçam.[563]

---

[561] Garbis.

[562] George Jerjian. *The Truth will set Us Free: Armenians and Turks Reconciled.* London: GJ Communications, 2003.

[563] Taner Akçam, a Turkish sociologist, spectacularly broke with Turkey's official narrative and concluded that the "Ottoman authorities' genocidal intent becomes clear." See Taner Akçam, *A Shameful Act* p. 187. However, like Dadrian's own works, Akçam's conclusions were roundly criticized and challenged, notably by Turkish researcher Erman Şahin who accused Akçam of

He also poses interesting and instructive questions such as why would scholars and politicians denigrate Turkey's reputation and insult its people as genocide perpetrators if the Armenian Genocide never occurred? "Why would all these people cast aspersions against the Turks? Is it because they hate Turkey and want to harm it? Are they liars and cheats? Do they have nothing better to do?"[564] Instead of answering these questions, Jerjian poses further questions that are apparently more germane and fundamental in nature:

- Why is Turkey failing in silencing its enemies, who accuse it of such horrific crimes?
- Why is Turkey afraid to go to an International Court or Tribunal?
- Why were the Turks not told about this?
- Why is this information hidden from them?
- Who is being protected?
- How can we find the whole truth and resolve this issue?
- Do we really want to know the truth?

His answer is simplistic, perhaps to a fault. "If the average Turk had the courage to face the truth, if they really wanted

---

"dishonesty—which manifests itself in the form of numerous deliberate alterations and distortions, misleading quotations and doctoring of data—casts doubt on the accuracy of his claims as well as his conclusions." Şahin also critiqued Akçam's subsequent works, concluding: "These are substantive matters that raise serious concerns as to the author's theses, which appear to be based on a selective and distorted presentation of Ottoman archival materials and other sources. … Such errors seriously undermine the author's and the book's credibility." See Erman Şahin, "Review Essay: A Scrutiny of Akçam's Version of History and the Armenian Genocide," *Journal of Muslim Minority Affairs*, Aug. 2008, p. 316. See also Erman Şahin, "Review Essay: The Armenian Question," *Middle East Policy*, Spring 2010, p. 157. See also See Michael M. Gunter. "What Is Genocide? The Armenian Case."

[564] Jerjian, 51.

to know the truth, they would come to the same conclusions as Dr. Taner Akçam, a courageous and honorable Turk."[565]

In a partial answer to Jerjian's assertions and the questions he and others in the diaspora have posed, it should be noted that the Republic of Turkey has previously and openly called for a joint commission of historians to study the events of 1915.[566] It has also promised, but has yet to prove, that it will allow easy access to all parties to the Ottoman Archives in Istanbul.[567] However, Yerevan has rejected Turkey's offer, on the table since 2005, for a joint commission.[568] In 2015, Armenia's president, Serzh Sargsyan, stated that it was obvious that the Turkish proposal of establishing a commission of historians had only one goal: delaying the process of Armenian Genocide recognition, and divert the attention of international community from that crime. According to Sargsyan, "That is not only our view but also the view of the international community that goes on recognizing and condemning the Armenian Genocide."[569]

---

[565] Ibid, 51-52.

[566] The idea of the establishment of a joint commission composed of historians from Turkey and Armenia, which would examine both countries' national archives and disclose the findings of their research to the international public was approved by the Turkish Grand National Assembly. See "Declaration by the Turkish Grand National Assembly, supporting the Turkish proposal to form a joint historical commission with Armenia." *Republic of Turkey Ministry of Foreign Affairs*, April 13, 2005. http://www.mfa.gov.tr/declaration-by-the-turkish-grand-national-assembly_-supporting-the-turkish-proposal-to-form-a-joint-historical-commission-with.en.mfa

[567] "Sealed Turkish archives could support genocide claims." *Times Higher Education*, April 27, 2001. https://www.timeshighereducation.com/news/sealed-turkish-archives-could-support-genocide-claims/159455.article.

[568] "Armenia makes Centenary call for Turkey to recognise 1915 killings as genocide." *Centenary News*. February 9, 2015. http://www.centenarynews.com/article/armenia-makes-centenary-call-for-turkey-to-recognise-1915-killings-as-genocide

[569] Cansu Çamlıbel. "Armenia ready for normalization of ties, President Sargsyan says." *Hürriyet Daily*, April 24, 2015.

Turkey's position vis-à-vis an international court hearing or tribunal is changing too, with many politicians and citizens openly calling for just such an act; believing that the diaspora's claims and proof of genocide in 1915 are so weak and unsubstantiated that they would never hold up to the scrutiny of a formal legal body. Şükrü Elekdağ, formerly Turkey's Ambassador to the United States, broached the possibility of Turkey and France visiting the ICJ in The Hague in order to ascertain the legality of France's 2001 legislation recognizing the events of 1915 as the Armenian Genocide. By doing so, Elekdağ hoped that the larger question of whether those events constituted genocide would be decided in a court of law. Elekdağ and others in Turkey have pointed out that France's many genocide resolutions, as outlined in a previous chapter, have no legal basis as they were never based on a ruling by a French court of law. Rather, they are similar to the other *ad hoc* legislation passed at the behest of the Armenian diaspora elsewhere. Elekdağ stated, "There is no international court ruling on the Armenian so-called genocide allegations. Is the French parliament a court? France is thus in the position of having disregarded the 1948 UN Convention."[570]

Relatedly, in 2008, the government of then-Prime Minister Recep Tayyip Erdoğan proposed that Turkey and Armenia each name three judges who would then name a chairman. Composed thus, the proposed panel would then review not only the Ottoman Archives, but also the archives of the Armenian Patriarchate in Istanbul. The panel would also review foreign legation archives and documents dating to the late Ottoman Empire, some of which may have been purposely mislaid or buried.[571] Importantly, the proposal

---

http://www.hurriyetdailynews.com/armenia-ready-for-normalization-of-ties-president-sargsyan-says.aspx?pageID=238&nID=81490&NewsCatID=510

[570] John C. K. Daly. "Turkey plans to combat Armenian Genocide Issue at The Hague," *Eurasia Daily Monitor* 5, no. 23 (2008).

[571] McCarthy argues persuasively that the Niles and Sutherland report of the situation in eastern Anatolia documenting Armenian atrocities against Muslims was purposely buried and not included among the

called for a review of the Dashnak Party archives housed in Boston, Massachusetts, in the United States. Ankara also proposed that an exhaustive forensic survey follow, taking particular note of possible contributory factors such as demographics and disease, ending with testimony from relevant parties.[572] Turkey's proposal was never taken seriously, either by the Republic of Armenia or the Armenian diaspora. This is possibly because their campaign for genocide recognition through *ad hoc* legislation and changes to educational curricula have been largely successful. "Erdoğan's offer to open Ottoman archives to a panel of international scholars to determine the truth of what happened is superfluous in light of scholarship [affirming the Armenian Genocide] there for all to see."[573] Mirroring this uncompromising stance, Harut Sassounian, the publisher of the *California Courier* newspaper and a leading voice in the Armenian diaspora, noted, "Any group, no matter who they are, that denies any genocide or holocaust, I cannot with a clear conscience call them a respectable group."[574]

Undeterred by all these possibilities, Jerjian confidently offers a roadmap that would ostensibly lead Turks away from the dark path they have walked since sweeping into Anatolia from Central Asia over one thousand years ago. This path to redemption is offered in the example of Vahakn Dadrian's former student and ethnic Turk, Taner Akçam. In doing so, Jerjian's description of Turks parrots that of the "terrible Turk," a racist depiction that continues to inform Armenian large group identity. This illustrative depiction also leaves Turks strangely lacking in agency and entirely at the mercy of a predatory and disingenuous state.

---

wider Harbord and King-Crane Commission reports. See Justin McCarthy. "The Report of Niles and Sutherland." See also McCarthy. *Death and Exile*, 252, footnote 215.

[572] Daly.

[573] David Gardiner. "Armenia's genocide: death and denial." *Financial Times*, April 17, 2015. http://www.ft.com/cms/s/2/56d61e36-e28d-11e4-aa1d-00144feab7de.html

[574] Gunter, *Armenian History and the Question of Genocide*: 123.

Turks can only achieve redemption, personal and national, by following the path of Akçam and accepting unequivocally that the events of 1915 constituted the Armenian Genocide. By doing so, Turks can be honored by wearing the mantle of honorary Armenians like Akçam. No longer an accessory to murder via his Turkish ethnicity and large group identity, Akçam and his works can be paraded and touted, much as Jerjian has done, as the road to redemption for Turks and the any others who dare to question the veracity of the Armenian campaign for genocide recognition.

Recognition, Reparations and Return

It is Jerjian's brief, final chapter that is most instructive and illustrative vis-à-vis genocide recognition and what it may entail for Armenia, Turkey and diaspora Armenians, namely recognition, reparations and the return of territory. In Jerjian's fanciful scenario, Turkey eventually chooses, in 2015, to recognize the events of 1915 as the Armenian Genocide on account of international pressure and isolation. By doing so, Turkey "...opened the much feared debate on land and reparations. Much debate raged everywhere. These ranged from extremist Turks not wanting to cede any lands to extremist Armenians wanted [sic] all six provinces returned."[575] According to Jerjian, a compromise was reached with representatives of the Republics of Turkey and Armenia, the Armenian diaspora and the enclave of Nagorno-Karabakh. This compromise saw Turkey ceding back to Armenia a "sliver" of land that included the territories of Kars, Ardahan, Ani, Artvin and territory that gave Armenia access to the Black Sea. In essence, a truncated version of the "Wilsonian Armenia" that never came into being at the end of World War I. In this scenario, Turkey also established a Genocide Reparations Council, which agreed to pay "sensible reparations" to unnamed non-state actors from the

[575] Ibid, 72.

Armenian diaspora in the sum of US$X million for the next 100 years. This symbolic sum paid out over one century would represent one year of payment for each year of Turkey's denial.[576]

While Jerjian's scenario and plans are fanciful, they are extremely instructive of what many members of the Armenian diaspora communities desire most from Turkey: recognition, reparations and territory. They desire formal recognition and acceptance that the events of 1915 constituted the Armenian Genocide, the world's first genocide or, alternately, the first genocide of the twentieth century. They also desire unidentified reparations, but similar and commensurate to those paid by Germany to Israel to compensate for the Nazi Holocaust. Lastly, implicit in the Armenian campaign for genocide recognition is a claim for the return of territory to the descendants of Ottoman Armenians, territory that has been an integral part of the Republic of Turkey since its difficult birth in 1923.

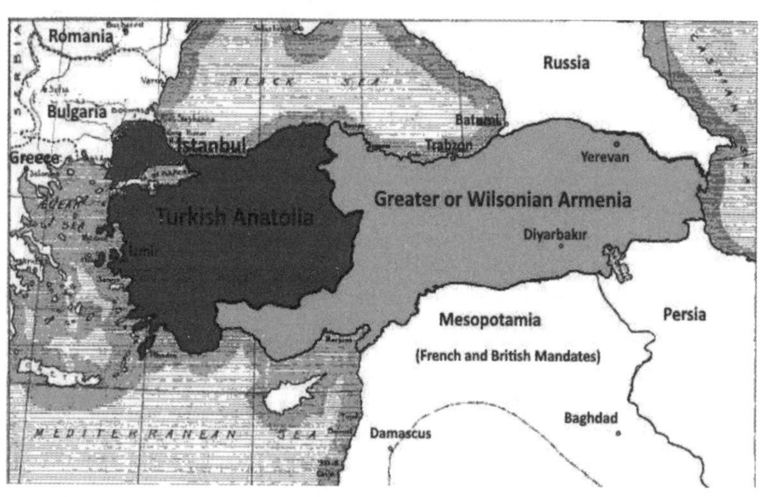

Wilsonian or Greater Armenia

Echoing Jerjian's scenario, Grigor Pltian, a French-Armenian writer, noted that the real problems diaspora

---

[576] Ibid, 72-74.

Armenians have with Turkey and the Turks will actually begin *after* Turkey's recognition of the events of 1915 as the Armenian Genocide. "The question starts now: I am not ready at all to leave the seized property of my [Armenian] grandparents – houses, lands, shops – to Turks, you see, why should I?"[577]

A letter written by Kenneth V. Hachikian, Chairman of the ANCA since 2000 to the ANCA Foreign Affairs Legislative Assistant, is perhaps more indicative of the official attitudes and aims of the Armenian diaspora.[578] Hachikian's 2005 letter responded to the independent study performed by the International Center for Transitional Justice (ICTJ) as requested by the Turkish Armenian Reconciliation Commission (TARC).[579] The ICTJ study of concern to Hachikian had concluded in 2003 that the events of 1915 in the Ottoman Empire met the internationally accepted definition of genocide. Not surprisingly, Turks were dissatisfied with the ICTJ report's findings. However, so were many Armenians. According to Hachikian's letter, the ICTJ ruling was deemed insufficient by some in the Armenian diaspora. This was largely because the ICTJ did not author the study, thereby depriving it of considerable legal and formal weight. Hachikian charged the ICTJ with assisting the TARC to procure an anonymous author or authors to document the findings of the independent study.

---

[577] Vahan Ishkhanyan "Prospective: A Different Viewpoint on Recognition," *ArmeniaNow.com*, Issue 44 (254), November 2, 2007. http://www.armenianow.com/?action=viewArticle&AID=2578&CID=2560&IID=1158&lng=eng.

[578] Kennth Hachikian. "Letter from Kenneth V. Hachikian to ANCA: Concern over Flawed TARC/ICTJ Findings on the Armenian Genocide." Armenian National Committee of America. March 24, 2005.

[579] TARC was formed in Geneva in 2001 with the purpose to improve relations between Turkey and Armenia and between Turks and Armenians. It was composed of scholars, historians, and public figures from both Turkish and Armenian backgrounds. For more information on TARC and the findings of ICTJ. See "Turkish Armenian Reconciliation Commission." *American University*, 2003-2004. http://www1.american.edu/cgp/TARC/.

Furthermore, "Despite the report's confirmation of the obvious, namely that the planned annihilation of 1.5 million Armenians constituted the legal definition of "genocide," its true significance lies in its deeply flawed conclusion that the U.N. Genocide Convention does *not* apply to the Armenian Genocide. The Armenian American community rejects this legally unsound and highly misleading TARC/ICTJ finding on the matter of accountability, and is deeply concerned that statements favorably citing this document could add a measure of undeserved credibility to a conclusion that is deeply prejudicial to the rights of Americans of Armenian descent and, worst [sic] yet, may be misinterpreted as support for denying a just resolution to the Armenian Genocide."[580] Given what Hachikian considers the report's highly flawed and misleading conclusions, he counseled the ANCA against creating this type of impression and urged them to consider carefully any reference or citation they may make to the TARC/ICTJ study in ANC or ANCA public or written statements.[581]

In some respects, Hachikian's rancor is difficult to understand. After all, the findings by the TARC-sponsored ICTJ study were profound. They categorized the events of 1915 as genocide – even if they cannot technically be considered as such because the UN Convention cannot be retroactively applied. Thus, the Armenian diaspora communities and interest groups achieved what they had hoped and worked for: a condemnation by a legal body in the form of a non-binding study labeling the events of 1915 as genocide. However, as Hachikian's letter confirms, the Armenian diaspora, particularly in the form of its lobbying and special interest groups, are not only intent on achieving recognition. They are also very invested in achieving the tangible elements of territory and reparations from Turkey that would necessarily follow its formal recognition of the events of 1915 as the Armenian Genocide. Indeed, some Armenians have voiced their displeasure at any efforts to

---

[580] Hachikian.

[581] Ibid.

establish commissions or even the need for court rulings when it comes to what they consider as the Armenian Genocide. "I'm not the one who needs fact-finding... I don't need to find out what happened. I know what happened [in 1915]."[582]

An ANCA representative voiced the organization's mistrust of TARC and noted that the ANCA had expressed its concern soon after the group was established.[583] Specifically, members of the ANCA were deeply concerned that some members of the TARC did not acknowledge nor did they explicitly refer to the events of 1915 as the Armenian Genocide. Yet even with these fundamental flaws in the eyes of some in Armenian diaspora communities, both the ANCA and the Assembly continue to tout the findings of the ICTJ as yet further proof that the massacres of 1915 constituted genocide.[584]

TARC was formally disbanded in 2004. However, according to some in the Armenian diaspora, the organization continued to keep the sources of its funding, its activities, expenditures, discussions and decisions a secret. This led to further suspicion and some continued to profess a belief in the TARC's existence and "sinister work" even after it was disbanded.[585]

Jerjian's and Hachikian's views on and demands of territorial claims and reparation are all part of what Harut Sassounian openly referred to as the Armenian campaign of the three R's.[586] The three R's are *Recognition* by the world, but most importantly Turkey, of the Armenian Genocide; *Reparations* for losses suffered at that time; and *Return* of

---

[582] Gunter, *Armenian History and the Question of Genocide*: 123.
[583] Author's interview with Elizabeth Chouldjian, ANCA Communications Director, April 4, 2007, Washington, D.C.
[584] AAINC. "Issue Brief: Armenian Genocide Affirmation." *Armenian Assembly of America*, http://www.aaainc.org/index.php?id=114&type=98.
[585] Harut Sassounian "TARC." *California Courier*, no date. http://www.armeniapedia.org/index.php?title=Turkish_Armenian_Reconciliation_Commission.
[586] Harut Sassounian. "Armenians Demand Justice, not Recognition."

territories in Anatolia that many diaspora Armenians claim held a majority Armenian population for thousands of years until 1915.[587] Sassounian noted that these three R's have been demanded by Armenians for decades and that a constructive platform must be built around these obvious demands.[588] Writing in 2007, Sassounian stated, "More than 20 countries, the European Parliament, a UN human rights panel and many genocide and Holocaust scholars have acknowledged the Armenian genocide. Therefore, continuing attempts to seek genocide recognition from the international community is no longer necessary and distracts from the pursuit of more significant Armenian political objectives."[589] Sassounian declared that he is more interested in justice than recognition. Irrespective of his final goal, he believes that whether genocide recognition has already been accomplished or not (depending on how recognition is gauged), Armenians the world over must take legal action against Turkey. "There is no prerequisite that the Turks—or the United States or anybody else, for that matter—first acknowledge the genocide before Armenians can take legal action. Armenians should present their demands to appropriate national and international courts, regardless of whether the Turks recognize the genocide."[590]

Sassounian argued that judicial action and justice required that the Turks be punished, reparations be paid, and that rights to territory and property be returned. However,

---

[587] Ottoman Armenian population figures are contested. See Justin McCarthy. *The Population of the Ottoman Armenians*. na, 2001. See also Adam Jones. "Case Study: The Armenian Genocide, 1915-17." *Gendercide Watch*, 2002.
http://www.anca.org/assets/pdf/armenian_genocide_reference/Case%20Study%20-%20The%20Armenian%20Genocide.pdf

[588] The demand for Turkish territory was internationally registered in 1975 with a memorandum to the UN submitted by the three main Armenian diaspora parties calling for "the return of Turkish-held Armenian territories to the Armenian people" and "moral, financial and territorial reparations." See Nigar Göksel. "Turkey and Armenia Post-Protocols: Back to Square One?." *Istanbul: TESEV* (2012); 12.

[589] Sassounian. "Armenians Demand Justice, not Recognition."

[590] Ibid.

Sassounian acknowledged that the issue of the three R's is contentious and divisive. It also requires constant vigilance.[591]

If nothing else, Harut Sassounian is bold and refreshingly honest. It is rare for Armenians in the diaspora and even less so for Armenians in Armenia to emphasize the three R's in public because of the damage it could do to their campaign that emphasizes closure and commemoration for victims rather than revenge. "No one publicly mentions post-Turkish acceptance, in other words monetary reparations or land transfers. The reasons for this are not exactly clear, but the best explanation would be to promote an unconditional recognition, without the necessary expectation of retribution, in proving to the world that there are no strings attached. In other words, the mere admission of wrongdoing on behalf of the Turkish government seems to be the end-all solution."[592] The Armenian diaspora faces a conundrum. As much as individuals like Sassounian or groups like the ANCA wish to take Turkey to court, they cannot do so. Nor can they, as diaspora Armenians make claims to what they consider Armenian land in Turkey. This is because they do not hold nation-state status and therefore cannot press their large group claims in a court of law.

The Republic of Armenia has officially made no claims on Turkish territory and has insisted repeatedly on the opening of the Turkish-Armenian border without preconditions. Turkey reacted strongly to a statement by the Armenian prosecutor general, Aghvan Hovsepyan, who stated that Armenian should regain unspecified territory from Turkey in 2015 on the one hundredth anniversary of the events of 1915.[593] In fact, Armenians themselves are divided on the

---

[591] Harut Sassounian. "Those Who Want Reconciliation Versus Those Who Seek Justice." *Western Diocese of the Armenian Church*, December 11, 2007.
http://www.armenianchurchwd.com/news/Those-Who-Want-Reconciliation-Versus-Those-Who-Seek-Justice/.

[592] Garbis.

[593] Nikolaus Schrodt. *Modern Turkey and the Armenian Genocide: An Argument About the Meaning of the Past*. Springer, 2014: 86.

issue of the three R's, as admitted by Sassounian.[594] The "religion" of genocide recognition that binds Armenian diaspora communities together may ultimately prove their undoing through their implicit and, occasionally, explicit calls for recognition, reparations and return. This is because there is no entity under current international law and the international system, beyond the Republic of Armenia, that can speak on behalf diaspora Armenians regarding the three R's. Furthermore, the current security paradigm and vested interests of many countries vis-à-vis Turkey make the changing of current borders and the return of land and property highly unrealistic.

There are concrete implications for the Armenian diaspora in their continued attempts to gain *ad hoc* legislation with the end goal of applying pressure on Turkey and thereby eventually gaining official Turkish recognition that the events of 1915 constituted the Armenian Genocide. Donald Bloxham, for example, does not argue against continued lobbying of American and European politicians or against the diaspora public education and awareness campaigns. Rather, he argues against the idealism of the diaspora's campaign. He does so in the sense that the campaign as currently constituted is "exaggerating [Armenian] hopes and expectations by implanting our desires in the minds of others. This is a historian's contention, drawn from the sorry history of the manipulated aspirations of supplicant peoples by the Great Powers."[595] Yet, how idealistic is this highly politicized, polemical and emotive campaign?

Explicitly, the Armenian diaspora campaign for genocide recognition is about dignity through recognition. This would entail a "proper" understanding of what occurred and the requisite usage of the term genocide to describe the events of 1915. It is claimed this would offer the victims and their progeny the cathartic peace and dignity denied to them through the opposite of recognition, denial. Yet, as

---

[594] Sassounian. "Those Who Want Reconciliation Versus Those Who Seek Justice."
[595] Bloxham, 225.

demonstrated, the Armenian diaspora campaign is Janus-faced when it comes to specifics of what recognition entails. Either through publications, public and private statements or online postings, many diaspora Armenians make it clear that Turkish recognition of the Armenian Genocide clearly involves the three R's. Some diaspora Armenians openly call for justice, meaning the three R's, rather than recognition. However, they represent the minority - at least in public. Most Armenian large group organizations, for example the ANC or the Assembly, remain rather silent on the issues of reparation and rights to territory. Instead, the discourse that informs *ad hoc* legislative efforts emphasizes the ostensible healing and dignity that genocide recognition and commemoration would confer on the victims of 1915 and their ancestors. Yet there also appears to be an element of subtle subterfuge at work. Perhaps this is because irredentism, property claims and monetary compensation may color or stunt the success of the public relations and legislative engine constructed and harnessed by the Armenian diaspora. They certainly complicate the issue.

In essence, current Armenian diaspora lobbying efforts emphasize the very real pain, suffering and loss of Ottoman Armenians while entirely ignoring the very real atrocities, revolts and ethnic cleansing committed against Ottoman Muslims by Ottoman Armenians. This one-sided story leads the public, their elected (or unelected) representatives, civil society groups and many scholars to question the reasons as to why anyone would *not* wish to commemorate and recognize the Armenian Genocide. Why would anyone willingly dishonor the suffering and pain of innocents? Packaged as such, the question necessarily becomes one of why legislation, *ad hoc* or otherwise, should not be passed to remember the dead of what has been cast as the twentieth century's first genocide; the precursor to, indeed the blueprint for, the Nazi Holocaust of the Jews? Furthermore, what would commemorative legislation really result in besides the hurt feelings of another large group regarding long-past events? This would correspondingly be offset by the restored dignity and honor of another large group. But the devil, as always, is in the details.

According to the current campaign, *ad hoc*, politically-motivated legislation is desired as a means to an end: recognition that the events of 1915 constituted the Armenian Genocide. Recognition by various bodies in Sweden, Russia or Argentina are deemed to be a victory thereby ending the "denial of accepted, historical truths" in these countries, municipalities or cities. Yet, if one takes a closer look at the previously-mentioned 2015 European Parliament resolution or any other non-unanimous resolution, certain uncomfortable questions are raised. The 2015 European Parliament Resolution was adopted by the votes of 351 MPs out of a total of 642. This number only equals 54.7 percent of the total votes. This means the resolution was passed neither with a substantial majority nor anything approaching unanimity. As the sociologist and political scientist, Turgut Kerem Tuncel presciently noted, "Besides the question on whether it is legitimate and correct to make decisions on controversial historical events with a small margin and if politicians are licensed to make judgments on the character of such complex set of events, the question remains whether 45.3 [percent] of the MPs in the European Parliament… are remorseless and unethical 'deniers' who have not internalized "European values." If one or more of these is true, the legitimacy of the entire European Parliament and many of the European country parliaments [that have passed Armenian Genocide resolutions] should be questioned."[596]

Tuncel also highlighted that an answer must be found to the following question. "If the 'Armenian genocide' is such an established fact, how can 45.3 [percent] of the MPs in the European Parliament vote against the resolution?" Further calling into the question the "established historical truth" that the events of 1915 amounted to the Armenian Genocide, the verdict of the Second Chamber of the European Court of Human Rights on Perinçek v.

[596] Tuncel, 12.

Switzerland case noted, "It is even doubtful that there could be a 'general consensus,' in particular a scientific one, on events such as those that are in question here, given that historical research is by definition open to debate and discussion and hardly lends itself to definitive conclusions or objective and absolute truths."[597]

For many diaspora Armenians, yearly commemorations and legislative recognition that the events of 1915 constituted the Armenian Genocide, regardless of the politicization of history and attempts to legislate reality, offer a victory of sorts. Yet, as is obvious more is wanted. Beyond the glaring inconsistencies of the current legislative campaigns being waged by Armenian diaspora interest groups, which includes the perpetuation of one large-group's version of events that many scholars find suspect as well as the loss of dignity and character assassination of another large-group, there are the inescapable demands that recognition entails: reparation and return.

The reactions by successive Turkish governments to veiled or overt claims that involve reparations and territory can be characterized as vehement, even paranoid. This is in large part because of Turkey's own traumatic relationship with the events of 1915, the Treaty of Sèvres, and the corresponding, deep-seated fear of territorial loss the Treaty spawned. Indeed, the Turkish government's stance vis-à-vis the campaign for Armenian Genocide recognition and that of Turkish public opinion mirror the development of their own large group identity in relation to the Ottoman Empire and the massive trauma that accompanied its demise.

---

[597] "Case of Perinçek v. Switzerland (Application no. 27510/08): Judgement." *European Court of Human Rights*, 17 December 2013. http://hudoc.echr.coe.int/eng?i=001-139724

CHAPTER 6

MASSACRES, NOT GENOCIDE: TURKISH PUBLIC OPINION AND THE OFFICIAL STANCE OF THE TURKISH REPUBLIC

The official stance of multiple Turkish governments characterize the events of 1915 as "mutual massacres" that affected both Ottoman Christians and Muslims. These massacres resulted in the relocation of a rebellious, Ottoman Armenian population in eastern and southern Anatolia. This relocation was unplanned, reactive and occurred as a direct result of wider World War I hostilities and the Russian invasion of the Empire, in particular.[598]

The Turkish government strenuously denies Armenian and Armenian diaspora claims that the 1915 massacres were akin to the Nazi Holocaust. Government officials and many scholars characterize these allegations as spurious and without historical merit, highlighting a history of violent Armenian nationalist separatism, revolts and efforts by many Ottoman Armenians to organize and arm themselves with the express purpose of overthrowing of the Ottoman

[598] Author's interviews with Yücel Güçlü, First Counselor to the Ambassador of the Republic of Turkey, March 30 and November 15, 2007. Washington, D.C.

state.[599] To this end, many Armenians cooperated with occupying troops, mainly Russian, and attempted to partition the Ottoman Empire in order to create an independent Armenia or one under Russian suzerainty.[600]

Turkish officials and many scholars argue that no evidence exists that Nazi leaders in Germany utilized the forced relocation of many Ottoman Armenians as the blueprint for Hitler's Final Solution, regardless of how much this story has been bandied about by the Armenian campaign and so-called genocide scholars.[601] As highlighted in a previous chapter, there are no factors common to the events of 1915 and the Nazi Holocaust. According to Yücel Güçlü, the events of 1915 should be considered on their own terms.[602] As evidence, Güçlü highlighted that the Nazi perpetrators of the Holocaust were tried and found guilty of genocide at the Nuremberg trials. In contrast, the victors of World War I in the form of Great Britain, France, the United States and Italy exonerated all 144 detained Ottoman statesmen and officials held in Malta of charges of "maladministration of the Armenian relocation policies."[603]

Beyond Güçlü's verbal claims and as this book demonstrates, Turkey has cogent, forceful and understandable reasons to dispute the historical record as utilized by the Armenian diaspora and its campaign for genocide recognition. The Turkish government's characterization that the events of 1915 constituted "mutual massacres" is valid and based on sound, non-political records, particularly demographic records as well as eyewitness reports dating from the years just after the cessation of World War I hostilities – when eastern Anatolia had become a graveyard for most of the former citizens of

---

599 McCarthy. *Death and Exile*, 185.

600 Gürün.

601 See Türkkaya Ataöv. "The 'Armenian Question': Conflict, Trauma and Objectivity." *Ministry of Foreign Affairs, Center for Strategic Research, Republic of Turkey, SAM Papers*, no. 3 / 97 (1999). See also Lewy, 265.

602 Yücel Güçlü. *The Holocaust and the Armenian case in comparative perspective*. University Press of America, 2012: 1.

603 Ibid.

the Ottoman Empire: Armenians, Turks, Kurds, Circassians, Laz, Greeks and others. Yet, the Armenian campaign for genocide recognition in its current form willfully ignores the fact that Ottoman Armenians were themselves guilty of numerous atrocities. While there were certainly very few Armenians left in eastern Anatolia after 1922, on account of the deportations, migration and flight from advancing Turkish forces, there were also far fewer Muslims in a vast area in which they had always constituted an absolute majority. The disappearance of Armenians needs to be studied and explained. It needs to be memorialized and perhaps commemorated as a testament to the inhuman acts of which human beings are capable. However, the very real suffering of Ottoman Muslims committed at the hands of Ottoman Armenians should also form more than a historical footnote. It should definitely not be ignored or "denied," as it is now, any more than that of the plight of many Ottoman Armenians.

This leads to an interesting conundrum. What difference would it really make if the entire world recognized Ottoman relocation policies and the massacres of 1915 as actions that constituted the Armenian Genocide? When this question was posed to Güçlü, then acting as First Counselor to the Ambassador of the Republic of Turkey to the United States, he stated that this would be the equivalent of a great crime, blacklisting Turks and Turkey for crimes they did not commit. According to Güçlü and the Turkish government, recognition by any party, through legislation or otherwise, would not reflect the complicated truth of what actually happened in 1915. Moreover, it would be construed as character assassination, a violation of Turkish dignity and would enhance an already potent Sèvres Syndrome.[604] Furthermore, a genocidal country is a justifiably shamed country. Yet Turkey should not be subject to this shame because the claims made by Armenians are considered

---

[604] Author's interviews with Yücel Güçlü, First Counselor to the Ambassador of the Republic of Turkey, March 30 and November 15, 2007. Washington, D.C.

patently false by the Turkish government, a position backed up major scholarly works utilizing demographic and archival records.[605] When it was suggested that whatever happened in the court of world opinion vis-à-vis, these allegations could not and should not affect the present-day Turkish Republic as the events of 1915 occurred under Ottoman Empire, Güçlü retorted that the assertion and acceptance of genocide would still shame the entire Turkish people.[606]

Successive Turkish governments can be construed as intransigent when it comes to their refusal to recognize the events of 1915 as the Armenian Genocide. In this, they mirror their Armenian counterparts who are equally intransigent in demanding precisely the opposite. However, Güçlü did highlight another conundrum inherent in the current Armenian campaign for genocide recognition. The penultimate goal of the campaign is official Turkish acceptance of the Armenian Genocide. Though the UN Convention on Genocide is neither retroactive nor does it apply to states, the Armenian diaspora campaign casts the Republic of Turkey as the successor state to the Ottoman Empire and thus its inhabitants – some of them ancestors of Ottoman officials – are necessarily implicated as criminals. Because genocide is a crime, it requires a court verdict to uphold any accusation of such a crime. However, should the Republic of Turkey unilaterally declare its recognition of the Armenian Genocide - even without a court verdict - it would likely open the door for the reparations and rights inherent in the diaspora campaign and vocally desired by some in the diaspora. It would also fly in the face of the historical record that clearly demonstrates that the events of 1915 cannot be construed as constituting a genocide. Regardless, given Turkey's paranoia vis-à-vis its territorial integrity on account of its

---

[605] For example, see M. Hakan Yavuz and Feroz Ahmed, eds. *War and Collapse: World War I and the Ottoman State.* (Salt Lake City: University of Utah Press, 2016). See also McCarthy. *Death and Exile.*
[606] Author's interviews with Yücel Güçlü, First Counselor to the Ambassador of the Republic of Turkey, March 30 and November 15, 2007. Washington, D.C.

Sèvres Syndrome, it is clear that any mention of territorial claims will be met with derision and outright opposition.[607]

Turkish Lobbying Efforts in the United States

Turkish lobbying efforts in the United States and elsewhere can be characterized as reactive and responsive to local conditions. There are numerous variables at play that influence this behavior. First, with the possible exception of Germany, Turks maintain a relatively small presence in most countries outside Turkey. Second, Turks possess relatively little wealth compared to other diaspora communities in Europe and North America. Third, most Turks began emigrating in large numbers only in the 1950s and 1960s. Because of these mitigating factors, Turkey generally deals with lobbying issues on a state-to-state level. If possible, business groups and intellectuals have been utilized and employed to further Turkish aims in a given country.[608] For example, in the United States, the Turkish Coalition USA Political Action Committee (TC-USA-PAC) was founded in 2007. It bills itself as an organization committed to:

- Identify candidates and incumbents that support a strong US-Turkish relationship,
- Identifying candidates and incumbents who advocate balanced positions on the global and regional issues that impact Turkey and US-Turkish relations,
- Identify and support Turkish-Americans and friends of Turkey to serve in local or national political offices.

---

[607] See Mehmet Arısan. "Eternal Sunshine of an Obscure Mind": World War I, the Imperial Collapse, and Trauma Management in the New Turkish Republic." In *War and Collapse: World War I and the Ottoman State*. M. Hakan Yavuz and Feroz Ahmed, eds. (Salt Lake City: University of Utah Press, 2016).

[608] See Alyssa Voorwald. *The influence of Turkish ethnic interest groups on Dutch domestic policy towards the Turkish community in The Netherlands: A powerful lobby?* M.A Thesis: University of Leiden (2015).

TC-USA-PAC also runs the tenthousandturks.org campaign, reportedly dedicated to reaching out to over 10,000 Turkish-Americans and friends of Turkey willing to take a stand to support candidates who understand "the value of positive US-Turkish relations."[609] TC-USA-PAC is not the only lobbying organization, nor is it the most powerful one. Rather, Turkey reportedly relies heavily on the lobbying services of former US government officials, with former Congressman Richard A. Gephardt and former Representative Robert L. Livingston being the most visible.[610] In doing so, Turkey spends a lot of money on lobbying efforts. For example, in 2007, when the US House Committee on Foreign Affairs approved a resolution labeling the events of 1915 as the Armenian Genocide, Turkey reportedly spent anywhere from $1.7 to $3.5 million and Turkey's lobbyists made contact with the Executive Branch an estimated one hundred times in order pressure US congressional leaders to quash the resolution. Turkey also reportedly had the most congressional contacts of any country lobbying in the US at 2,268.[611]

Turkish Recognition of Armenia and Armenian Economic Migrants in Turkey

Turkey was one of the first countries to recognize the Republic of Armenia's independence from the Soviet Union

---

[609] "About Us." *Turkish Coalition USA Political Action Committee.* http://www.tenthousandturks.org/index.php?option=com_content&view=article&id=23&Itemid=3

[610] Marilyn Thompson. "An Ex-Leader in Congress Is Now Turkey's Man in the Lobbies of Capitol Hill." *New York Times* (October 17, 2007). http://www.nytimes.com/2007/10/17/washington/17lobby.html?_r=0

[611] See Eric Lichtblau. "Arab Unrest Puts Their Lobbyists in Uneasy Spot." *New York Times*, March 1, 2011. http://www.nytimes.com/2011/03/02/world/middleeast/02lobby.html?scp=1&sq=arab%20lobby&st=cse. See also Anupama Narayanswamy, Luke Rosiak, and Jennifer LaFleur. "Opening the Window on Foreign Lobbying." *Pro Publica* (August 8, 2009).

on September 23, 1991. However, diplomatic relations remain non-existent. Though Armenia has voiced support for the establishment of diplomatic relations, Turkey has balked at such a prospect, arguing that Armenia does not recognize the present-day borders of the Turkish Republic. As noted, these were established by a series of treaties with the Soviet Union dating to the 1920s. Turkey also disagrees with Armenia's official position on the Armenian Genocide, which is enshrined in both its declaration of independence and its constitution. For Turkey, official treaties demarcating borders remain non-negotiable. Turkish government officials argue that Armenia must abide by international treaties in the same way and acknowledge the current borders.[612] This is an emotional issue on both sides of the border, as well as for the Armenian diaspora. Indeed, the issue of borders rather than the Armenian claims of genocide are perhaps the biggest obstacle in the normalization of ties between Turkey and Armenia.

Though diplomatic relations remain frozen, Turkey represents a key destination for Armenian economic migrants. In 2011, Armenia reported an official unemployment rate of 6.6 percent, but unofficial estimates put that figure in the double digits. Its economy has also suffered, particularly after the 2008 financial crisis, posting a mere 2.6 percent increase in 2010. Contrasting this with Turkey's economic expansion of 8.9 percent in 2010, it is understandable why as many as 100,000 Armenian economic migrants, most of them illegal, have come to Turkey.[613]

---

[612] Author's interviews with Yücel Güçlü, First Counselor to the Ambassador of the Republic of Turkey, March 30 and November 15, 2007. Washington, D.C.

[613] See Marianna Grigoryan and Anahit Hayrapetyan. "Turkey: Armenian Illegal Migrants Put National Grievances Aside for Work." *Eurasianet*, September 2, 2011. http://www.eurasianet.org/node/64116. See also Umut Uras. "Armenian immigrants look for a better life in Turkey." *Al-Jazeera*, April 20, 2015. http://www.aljazeera.com/news/2015/04/armenian-immigrants-life-turkey-150420070803126.html

Political Judgement and History: Turkish Public Opinion and the Armenian Campaign

A nationwide survey carried out in early 2007 provides perhaps the best snapshot of Turkish public opinion in relation to Armenian Genocide resolutions, particularly in relation to the annual resolutions submitted to the US House and Senate. The poll was carried out by the Turkey-based ARI Movement and the US-based ARI Foundation along with the Terror Free Tomorrow organization that describes itself as a non-partisan, not-for-profit organization that researches attitudes toward extremism worldwide.[614] The results of the surveys were reportedly based on face-to-face interviews among a representative nationwide random sample of the adult population and conducted in Turkish in all fifteen provinces of Turkey between January 27, 2007 and February 8, 2007.[615] The survey aimed to uncover whether the passage of resolutions related to designating the events of 1915 as the Armenian Genocide would actually set back the cause it purports to achieve: Turkey's recognition of its own past and reconciliation with Armenia today.[616]

According to the results of the survey, 78 percent of respondents opposed any United States Congressional resolution on the issue. Furthermore, and indicative of the important strategic relation the United States shares with Turkey, almost four-fifths of Turks favored action on the part of the Turkish government if a resolution regarding the events of 1915 were to pass in the U.S. Congress, to include suspension of diplomatic ties and a boycott of U.S. goods. Furthermore, the survey's results highlighted the reasons behind Turkish opinions on the matter. Interestingly, they have less to do with history and what actually occurred in

---

614 "About Us." *Terror Free Tomorrow.*
http://www.terrorfreetomorrow.org/template.php?section=AU
615 "New Public Opinion Survey of Turkey." *Terror Free Tomorrow*, 2007.
http://www.terrorfreetomorrow.org/template.php?section=PL
616 Ibid.

1915 than with what they consider to be an outsider's judgment of history based on politics.[617] That is, three-quarters of respondents indicated that they would accept the findings based on the studies and scholarship of "independent historians" regarding what occurred in 1915. As importantly, a full seven percent of respondents surveyed favored the passage of a US Congressional resolution, primarily because they believe that Turkey must recognize its past wrongs: the genocide against Ottoman Armenians.[618] This means that approximately five million Turks are ready and willing to recognize the Armenian Genocide in some form or another, a fact readily pointed out by some in the Armenian diaspora.[619]

Given the results of the opinion pool, it appears that one of the problems confronting Armenians in their quest to see Turks recognize the events of 1915 as the Armenian Genocide is actually their campaign for *ad hoc* resolutions and official commemoration. The resolutions looked at by the U.S. Congress, or passed by the French Parliament or the Russian Duma are problematic for reasons discussed previously,[620] though this is not the real problem according to the Turks polled. Rather, it is the fact that most Turks do not consider the members of these bodies, elected or unelected, either neutral or well-informed judges on the issue. The Turks who were surveyed viewed these resolutions as reflective of internal domestic politics and informed by historical bias against Turkey and general anti-Muslim feelings, which are, in part, viewed as being driven by the Armenian diaspora campaign. The survey showed these sentiments held firm regardless of age, education level, income or views of the United States, in general. Furthermore, if one of the main goals of a U.S.

---

617 Ibid.

618 Ibid.

619 Harut Sassounian. "First Nationwide Turkish Survey Reveals Millions of Turks Support Genocide Bill." *Huffington Post*, May 25, 2011. http://www.huffingtonpost.com/harut-sassounian/first-nationwide-turkish-_b_74141.html

620 Tuncel.

Congressional resolution is to promote reconciliation between Turkey and Armenia - as the resolution purports to do - 73 percent of Turks think a resolution will have the opposite effect and actually worsen relations between Turkey and Armenia."[621]

The majority of Turks believe that the events of 1915 should continue to be studied by historians and other scholars and that one version of history or another should not be accepted as a *fait accompli.* Of course, the Turkish governmental would no doubt prefer the issue disappear altogether or, barring that remote eventuality, see the "Turkish thesis" of events, as backed by a significant body of research, accepted as fact – with or without further study. Yet, as the results of the survey demonstrate, the Armenian diaspora campaign for genocide recognition does nothing to improve relations between Armenia and Turkey and, as importantly, between Armenians and Turks. Rather, the effects of the campaign are direct, adverse and counterproductive to many of its stated aims. As will be demonstrated, this has important and long-term implications and illustrates some of the dissonance and cross-purposes of the Armenian campaign for recognition of the Armenian Genocide.

---

[621] "New Public Opinion Survey of Turkey." *Terror Free Tomorrow*, 2007.
http://www.terrorfreetomorrow.org/template.php?section=PL

CHAPTER 7

WHOSE GENOCIDE AND WHEN? ARMENIAN AND ARMENIAN DIASPORA VISIONS OF THE PAST, PRESENT AND FUTURE

The campaign for recognition of the events of 1915 as the Armenian Genocide is largely an Armenian diaspora creation, driven by diaspora lobbies, interest groups and their supporters. That is, though Armenians in the country of Armenia consider the events of 1915 as the Armenian Genocide and item 11 of the Republic of Armenia's 1991 Declaration of Independence supports efforts to recognize the events as such, some outside Armenian government circles have neither the proclivity, the financial resources nor interest in furthering this highly symbolic issue. Simply put, the diaspora Armenian identity as victim and survivor of the events of 1915 is not shared on the same substantive and identity-based level with their cousins in Armenia. Important as this distinction may be, it by no means indicates that the events of 1915 are inconsequential to Armenians in Armenia.[622] Yet the often-sharp differences between Armenians and diaspora Armenians actually stem directly from the events of 1915.

[622] "Armenian National Study." *International Republican Institute*, January 13-20, 2008.

The century-old events led to a physical and psychological gap between Ottoman or Western Armenians and Eastern Armenians or those in Russian Transcaucasia in an area that was, for centuries, considered geographically and, less often, politically uniform.[623] "Although the Genocide was a pan-Armenian wound, it physically affected on [sic] the Western Armenians. Eastern Armenians, in the Russian Empire, did not experience it first hand, nor did they lose their land, although hundreds of thousands of refugees from the Ottoman Empire did escape to Russian… Armenia."[624]

As previously demonstrated, the events of 1915 supersede those of the Armenian churches and language and provide the glue that bonds the diaspora communities, "… for they are comprised mainly of families whose extended members have suffered during the tragedy as well as its aftermath (with the exception of people whose roots were based in Eastern, or Russian, Armenia)."[625] For many diaspora Armenians, questions of regional politics in the Caucasus, to include the Republic of Armenia and the disputed territory of Nagorno-Karabakh – though important - pale in comparison to what they consider *the* paramount issue: recognition of the Armenian Genocide. "The genocide is part of Armenian diaspora identity today, not necessarily for political reasons. Nor is it because of anti-Turkish feelings, *per se.* Primarily it's there because it's part of family history… I would say that for the 'silent majority' of Armenians, the moral issue comes first… They want an acknowledgment that their grandparents and their relatives were murdered…"[626]

What happened in 1915 did seep into Eastern Armenian identity and has become increasingly important since

---

[623] McCarthy. *Death and Exile*, 23-29.

[624] Panossian. "The Impact of the Genocide on Armenian National Identity."

[625] Garbis

[626] Jonathan Gorvett. "Thaw in Turkey-Armenian Relations." *Al-Jazeera*, December 21, 2003. http://www.aljazeera.com/archive/2003/12/200841011541297627 3.html

Armenia's independence.[627] However, the events have yet to develop into the core identity of Armenians in Armenia in the way they have for those in the diaspora. "The [Armenian] Genocide entered Soviet Armenian consciousness as a learnt injustice rather than an experienced reality. The idea of being victims of the Turks did [already] exist, and was further nurtured by Soviet-inspired historiography. After 1965, Eastern Armenians, too, had the 1915 Genocide at the core of their identity, albeit not as prevalently as their Western, diasporacized brethren."[628]

The notion of victimhood still permeates both Eastern and Western Armenian lives, but the issue of who perpetrated the crimes and when is muddier and less succinct in the "Eastern" nation-state of Armenia. This is precisely because their history and continued suffering at the hands of successive Soviet governments after 1915 differs so greatly from their diaspora counterparts. The scattered Armenian diaspora was transformed by the events of 1915 and achieved a new identity: genocide victim and survivor. The diaspora was also transformed by the political and economic opportunity spaces that often existed in their diaspora homelands. The freedoms, economic climate, mobility and stability afforded to many Armenian diaspora communities, particularly in the West, not only allowed, but often encouraged these same communities to remember, publish, preach, campaign and disseminate their memories

---

[627] Influential members of the Armenian diaspora have taken an increasingly visible role in "genocide awareness" events in Armenia. For example, in April 2015, Kim and Khloe Kardashian, along with Kim's husband, rapper Kanye West visited Armenia in order to raise awareness about the Armenian Genocide on the one hundredth anniversary of the events of 1915. See Vana Derohanessian. "Seeking the Next Saroyan: Cultural Representations of Armenian Americans of Los Angeles." *Rediscovering LA* California State University, Northridge (2015): 319.

[628] Panossian, "The Impact of the Genocide on Armenian National Identity."

of 1915. In a mutually-constitutive process, their diaspora identity was developed and nourished.

Learning versus Experiencing History

Eastern Armenians *learned* about the history of 1915, at least officially, only after 1965. Many of their ancestors did not experience these events, though demographic records and historical accounts indicate that, after the withdrawal of Russian troops in 1917, thousands of Ottoman Armenians escaped into Armenia after massacring thousands of Ottoman Muslims and destroying much of eastern Anatolia.[629] In contrast, Western Armenians *experienced* their history and, decades after 1915, those events are the core attribute of modern Armenian diaspora identity and what arguably should be Armenian large group identity. But this is not the case. "The trauma [of 1915] which has been detrimental in the making of diasporan identity seems not to be focal in the minds of the citizens of the state [of Armenia]. This does not mean that Armenians in Armenia have no interest to pursue Genocide recognition… What it can be a result of is the experience of statehood – as Soviet Armenia was considered a form of a state – that helped the population to transcend the victim mentality and look at non-traumatic events to shape their identity."[630]

This duality between diaspora Armenians and Armenians has developed into what Asbed Kotchikian terms, "a juxtaposition of a state's interest and a nation's interest."[631] Often, these two interests do not overlap and continue to be a contested arena. "The difference of strategy between the two is that while in the case of diasporan Armenians, Genocide recognition is pursued *without any other considerations*, in the case of Armenia, the state has to have other considerations as well… What it means is that the

---

[629] McCarthy. *Death and Exile*, 208-228.

[630] Asbed Kotchikian. "From Vertical to Diagonal Interactions" *The Armenian Weekly: Armenian Genocide Insert*, Vol. 73, No. 16, 21 April 2007.

[631] Ibid.

issue of Genocide recognition will end up being a part and parcel of a larger policy that the [Armenian] state would implement in its relations with Turkey."[632]

A poll conducted by the International Republican Institute in the Republic of Armenia showed that only two percent of respondents in Armenia said that recognition of the Armenian Genocide was their top priority. Only three percent of those polled listed the factor of genocide recognition at all. Most were concerned about jobs and their livelihood. The same poll also showed that 48 percent of Armenians agreed that the Republic of Armenia should open its border with Turkey, regardless of whether Turkey recognized the events of 1915 as the Armenian Genocide or not. This number was up from a low of 39 percent in August 2006.[633]

Clearly some Armenians in the Republic of Armenia feel other issues are more important than Armenian Genocide recognition. Indeed, some argue that the term "genocide" means something different for non-diaspora Armenians.[634] Hrag Varjabedian, an Armenian-American ethnographer, performed comparative research in Armenia and discovered that diaspora Armenians use the word "genocide" only when referring to the events of 1915. Those in the Republic of Armenia, however, use the concept, if not necessarily the word, to refer to various tragedies and troubles.[635] Indeed, intellectuals in Soviet times referred to Stalin's purges and massacres as genocide and later characterized the Russification of the Soviet Union as "white genocide."[636]

Armenians in Armenia are distinctly aware of how life and the stories they have heard are different from those of their diaspora cousins. "Diaspora Armenians, especially those who grew up in the West, have had a comfortable life and

---

[632] Ibid. My emphasis.
[633] IRI.
[634] Ishkhanyan.
[635] Hrag Varjabedian. *The Poetics of History and Memory: The Multiple Instrumentalities of Armenian Genocide Narratives.* PhD diss., University of Wisconsin-Madison, 2009.
[636] Ishkhanyan.

their attention has not diverted [sic] from 1915 and there have been no tragedies to darken the Genocide in their memory."[637] This does not mean that there is not an implicit understanding of the dreams, frustrations and desires of diaspora Armenians when it comes to Armenian Genocide legislation and resolutions, but questions remain as to what it will actually provide Armenia and Armenians there.

As discussed in previous chapters, many diaspora Armenians demand not only recognition that the events of 1915 constituted a crime - the Armenian Genocide - but the reparations and rights of return that come from such demands. This diaspora Armenian attitude toward, and overwhelming emphasis on, the events of 1915 and Armenian Genocide recognition, is perhaps where the acute identity differences between Armenians and diaspora Armenians are on display. One Armenian writer queried from whom he should demand compensation for all the losses he and his relatives had suffered over the centuries. Should it be from the Turks or the Russians, the Soviets or the government of the Republic of Armenia, the same government that seized his ancestor's property on account of its sudden rise in value?[638] This author, unlike his diaspora cousins, has no like-minded supporters to raise the issue of his and his family's multiple "genocides" in the U.S. Congress or any other forum and wonders if *ad hoc* Armenian Genocide recognition by the United States Congress or any other body would result in the return of his family's properties or bring back the dead from Stalin's purges.

Voices of disapproval have been raised when Armenian diaspora-driven laws have been passed in various countries, recognizing the Armenian Genocide and criminalizing the denial thereof. As highlighted in a previous chapter, when France passed a law making it a criminal act to deny the "historical fact" of the Armenian Genocide, Turkish-

---

[637] Ibid.

[638] Ibid.

Armenian journalist and critic Hrant Dink noted, "When this bill appeared first, we were fast to declare as a group that it would lead to bad results......As you know, I have been tried [under Article 301] in Turkey for saying the Armenian genocide exists, and I have talked about how wrong this is. But at the same time, I cannot accept that in France you could possibly now be tried for denying the Armenian genocide… I really think that France, if it makes this bill law, will be hurting not only the E.U., but Armenians across the world. It will also damage the normalizing of relations between Armenia and Turkey. What the peoples of these two countries need is dialogue, and all these laws do is harm such dialogue"[639]

The Turkish author, Elif Shafak, was also charged under Turkey's Article 301 for her portrayal of Armenian survivors of the events of 1915 in her novel *The Bastard of Istanbul.* Regarding the bill passed in France and other laws in Europe, she noted, "If we are pro-freedom of expression in Turkey, we cannot have double standards. Being pro-freedom of expression requires defending this fundamental principle in all countries. What is happening in Holland [where Turkish candidates have been expelled from their parties because of their refusal to acknowledge an Armenian genocide] and France is highly problematical not only in terms of curbing freedom of expression but also in terms of undermining any potential bonds of empathy and amity between Armenians and Turks. This move will only create a nationalist backlash in Turkey. It will harm all attempts to build dialogue."[640]

Many diaspora Armenians admit that the quest for Armenian Genocide recognition is a diaspora affair, not that of Armenians in the Republic of Armenia or Armenians in Turkey. Yet the campaign for recognition of Armenian

---

639 "France: Parliament decides to Criminalize Denials of the Armenian Genocide," *English Pen.* October 23, 2006. https://www.englishpen.org/campaigns/france-parliament-decides-to-criminalise-denials-of-the-armenian-genocide/

640 Ibid.

massacres and deportations in 1915 as the Armenian Genocide continues unaltered. It is as if no other options are worthy of consideration. For diaspora Armenians, Armenia is more of an idea rather than a country full of living, breathing people.[641]

This is not to imply that diaspora Armenians do not care deeply about Armenians and the Republic of Armenia, to include the disputed territory of Nagorno-Karabakh. However, the near-century of Armenia's isolation under Soviet rule as well as time and space have led to a diaspora construction of what the Republic of Armenia and its inhabitants should be, rather than what or who they really are. The disparate identities that emerged between diaspora communities and their counterparts in Eastern Armenia have, in some cases, led to confusion and an emphasis on very different goals. Indeed, the diaspora's attempts to influence events based on its "imagined" Armenia have had interesting consequences for the Republic of Armenia, its inhabitants and its future.

---

641 Ishkhanyan.

CHAPTER 8

THE COST OF GENOCIDE RECOGNITION: DIASPORA DESIRES AND ARMENIA'S SURVIVAL

Since its independence in 1991, the Republic of Armenia, largely through diaspora lobbying efforts, has received large amounts of foreign aid and direct investment from the United States, the European Union and Russia. Sixteen years after independence, it was estimated that the United States alone had poured more than $1.7 billion into the country.[642] At the end of 2007, the US House approved the Fiscal Year 2008 Omnibus Spending Bill that earmarked $58.5 million in assistance to Armenia. This was $23.5 million above and beyond what the Administration had requested, but far short of the $75 million approved for Armenia in the Fiscal Year 2007. In addition, the final measure provides continued funding through the Millennium Challenge Account (MCA) program to the tune of $1.5 billion. The Armenian Assembly of America and other Armenian-American lobbying groups consistently advocate for the highest level of assistance to

[642] Maria Danilova. "Armenian PM Sarkisian Wins Presidency" *Washington Post*, February 20, 2008.

both Armenia and the disputed territories of Nagorno-Karabakh and have been largely successful.[643]

The United States and the European Union reportedly share three main priorities in the Caucasus region, to include Armenia. First, the building and strengthening of democracy with market principles; second, enhancing regional stability and security; and third, the exploitation of rich oil and gas resources in the region.[644] These goals are not necessarily mutually constitutive, and demands by United States and European multinationals for access to the Azerbaijan's oil and gas reserves have largely outpaced calls for democracy in the region, to include Armenia, and a peaceful settlement to the Nagorno-Karabakh dispute. It is precisely this exploitation of Azerbaijan's vast mineral wealth by the extractives industry that most worries Yerevan and the Armenian diaspora. This is because Armenia possesses few natural resources of its own and has generated relatively little interest in international finance and investment capitals. Compare this to Azerbaijan, where Western oil and gas companies have rushed to sign billions of dollars in contracts with the government in Baku. Armenia justifiably worries that the proceeds from Azerbaijan's oil and gas wealth will be used to supply, arm and embolden its neighbor and isolate Armenia to an ever-greater degree. They are correct. Over the course of President Ilham Aliyev's rule (2003-present), Azerbaijan has increased its annual military spending almost thirty times, with a projected total of $3.6 billion in 2015. This amount is more than Armenia's entire state budget.[645] In comparison, the

---

[643] Ibid.

[644] Aram Harutyunyan. "Armenia as a Factor of Balance in the Southern Caucasus Region." *Security Sector Governance in Southern Caucasus –Challenges and Visions.* (Vienna: National Defence Academy and Bureau for Security Policy, in cooperation with PfP Consortium of Defence Academies and Security Studies Institutes, 2004): 166.

[645] Emil Danielyan. "Why Armenia's Military Alliance with Russia Is Not at Risk." *REFRL.* November 7, 2015.
http://www.rferl.org/content/caucasus-report-armenian-russia-military-alliance/27351046.html

Republic of Armenia's 2015 defense budget was reportedly only $500 million.[646]

The Azerbaijani army has been refitted with new weapons, reportedly including $4 billion worth of Russian tanks, combat helicopters, air-defense systems and other military hardware since 2010. President Aliyev has also become more forceful in his statements regarding Azerbaijan's desire to retake the disputed territory of Nagorno-Karabakh from Armenia.[647]

Though Armenia may be unable to spend in the same amounts as Azerbaijan, it still spends a huge amount on its military as a percentage of GDP. In the years 2001-2015, Armenia spent from 3.6 to 4.0 percent of its GDP on military expenditures. In comparison, Azerbaijan spent 4.7 to 4.8 percent during the same period.[648] Armenia has also been able to maintain military parity with its wealthier neighbor, Azerbaijan, reportedly through bilateral defense agreements with Russia and membership in the Russian-led collective treaties that allow it to procure Russian weapons at free of charge or at bargain prices. This military aid from Russia remains largely opaque and unpublicized.[649]

Largely because of the threat of Azerbaijan's increasing military strength based on its vast extractives-derived wealth, many in the Armenian diaspora, particularly in the United States, have endeavored to cast Armenia as a dependable ally in the Caucasus region. According to this picture, Armenia represents a shining beacon of democracy surrounded by authoritarian neighbors. According to the diaspora, Armenia is the Israel of the Caucasus, democratic and militarily strong, though dependent on foreign aid to maintain a razor-thin parity with its neighbors.[650] The truth is rather more complicated.

---

[646] Ibid.

[647] Ibid.

[648] "Military expenditure (% of GDP)." *The World Bank*. 2015. http://data.worldbank.org/indicator/MS.MIL.XPND.GD.ZS

[649] Emil Danielyan. "Why Armenia's Military Alliance with Russia Is Not at Risk."

[650] Gunter, *Armenian History and the Question of Genocide*, 93.

A 2014 democracy index, which ranked states according to their levels of political freedoms and civil liberties, listed Armenia as number 113, right behind Mauritania and Iraq and just above Burkina Faso and Niger.[651] In contrast, Israel was listed as a "flawed democracy," but ranked number 36.[652] Armenia also scored consistently low on such democracy indicators as government functioning, political participation and political culture. In relation to its neighbors, relatively democratic Georgia ranked number 81 and Armenia beat its arch-enemy Azerbaijan, which ranked further down the list at 148.[653]

Armenia's deficit of democracy is perhaps to be expected for a country that suffered for over seventy years under the repressive policies and stultification of political and economic life in the Soviet Union. However, Armenia's dismal ranking for the past two decades unequivocally refutes the diaspora's broad claims and demonstrates the falsehood of Armenia's reported status as the "Israel of the Caucasus" and a democratic powerhouse in the region. Correspondingly, Armenia's continued occupation of the territories of the Nagorno-Karabakh enclave and the diaspora lobbies' insistence that Armenia retain these disputed territories may have led to a lack of transparency in Armenia's electoral processes and thereby hampered the development of democracy. Because of the importance of the Caucasus as an energy conduit, the United States and the European Union are arguably interested, albeit fitfully, in a negotiated settlement of the Nagorno-Karabakh dispute. When former President Robert Kocharian of Armenia and President Ilham Aliyev of Azerbaijan were both elected in 2003, under less than transparent conditions, both strategically voiced an interest in discussing a settlement to the Nagorno-Karabakh crisis. Some voices in both the Armenian and Azerbaijani opposition allege that Washington and Brussels were held hostage to both

---

[651] "The Economist Intelligence Unit's Index of Democracy 2014." *The Economist*. 2014.

[652] Ibid.

[653] Ibid.

Kocharian's and Aliyev's "false promises" in the hopes that another conflict between the two states would not affect the lucrative workings of the Baku–Tbilisi–Ceyhan (BTC) oil pipeline.[654]

Though parliamentary elections in 2007 were heralded as an improvement over past elections, there was a widely held belief in Armenia that vote rigging, particularly egregious in 2005 and 1998, comes from the highest echelons of government.[655]In the 2008 election, Serzh Sargsyan, in a tight race against former president, Levon Ter-Petrossian, won the presidency amidst allegations of ballot box-stuffing and fraud by the opposition accompanied by large protests that quickly turned violent.[656] Eight protestors lost their lives. Ter-Petrossian was put under house arrest for a time and 74 opposition demonstrators remained in jail in late 2008. Sargsyan published an appeal for calm, noting that, "violence has no place in democracy" and asking those, "promoting instability" to engage in political dialogue.[657] Yet, Sargsyan also claimed there were no political prisoners in Armenia.[658]

In 2015, the overall situation had not improved and Armenians still had to contend with serious irregularities in elections and referendums. Indeed, the referendum to boost the role of Armenia's prime minister while correspondingly reducing the role of president to the merely ceremonial was

---

[654] Emil Danielyan. "West Unlikely to Sanction Armenia Following Another Troubled Vote," *Eurasianet.* December 11, 2005.
http://www.eurasianet.org/departments/insight/articles/eav121205.shtml

[655] Ibid.

[656] "Armenia clamps down after Post-Election Violence," *New York Times.* March 2, 2008.
http://www.nytimes.com/2008/03/02/world/europe/02iht-armenia.4.10626008.html?_r=0

[657] Serzh Sargsyan and Arthur Baghdasaryan, "Moving Forward in Armenia." *The Washington Post.* March 17, 2008.

[658] "After the War." *The Economist*, October 18, 2008: 38.

assessed to be a vehicle for Sargsyan's political ambitions.[659] Having served two terms as president, Sargsyan hopes to be re-elected as prime minister in 2018 with the same powers he held as president.

Regardless of the transparency or lack thereof of in its politics, Armenia did receive huge amounts of aid from foreign donors, particularly the United States, for the first decade and a half of its independent existence. Armenia ranked number 22 on a list of the largest recipients of bilateral and multilateral aid, receiving $66 per head, per year in 2008.[660] This largesse assisted Armenia in showing the third highest growth in industrial output in the world, at 16.8 percent from 2000-2005.[661] Armenia also ranked high on the list of countries with the highest economic growth for the years 1995-2005; ranking sixth with an average annual percentage increase in real GDP of 8.6 percent.[662] Unfortunately, the rapid growth that characterized the years 1995-2005 had little impact on poverty reduction in Armenia. This was, in part, due to a continuing lack of improvement in the business environment. Indeed, Armenia is consistently rated as being business unfriendly. Furthermore, structural weaknesses in the rule of law and fair competition have arguably blunted incentives for private sector development.[663] Lastly, corruption is reportedly endemic, and Armenia scores accordingly, dropping from 79th place in 2003 to 94th place in 2014 on Transparency International's Corruption Perceptions Index.[664]

---

[659] "Armenia fraud claims mar referendum on constitution." *BBC.* December 17, 2015. http://www.bbc.com/news/world-europe-35025853

[660] "Pocket World in Figures, 2008 Edition." *The Economist* (London: Profile Books, 2007), 44.

[661] Ibid, 46.

[662] Ibid, 32.

[663] "Armenia Country Brief, 2007." *World Bank Group: Europe and Central Asia.* 2007.

[664] See "Corruption Perception Index 2003-2007." *Transparency International.* 2007. See also "Corruption Perception Index 2014." *Transparency International.* 2014.

Diaspora Investment in Armenia

The Armenian diaspora is viewed by many Armenians as an exceptional asset for the national economy in generating Foreign Direct Investment (FDI) and private monetary transfers. The diaspora also assists Armenia to gain critical political support in the West and is a strong advocate of Armenian culture abroad. Largely because of Armenian diaspora lobbying and the aid it generates, but also on account of direct investments in Armenia by the diaspora, Armenia experienced one of the fastest economic growth rates in the world in the decade stretching from 1995 to 2005. As noted previously, this growth rate has slowed precipitously in recent years, on account of the global economic recession that began in 2008, and poverty is widespread. A November 2013 report by the Armenian National Statistical Service claimed that nearly one-third of Armenian citizens lived in poverty in 2012, with 13.5 percent classified as "very poor" and 2.8 percent "extremely poor."[665] The economy has also taken a hit on account of "systemic vulnerabilities," particularly in the construction sector and has yet to recover.[666] Armenia's GDP grew an impressive 7.5 percent in the first quarter of 2013, but slowed to just 0.6 percent in the second quarter and 1.4 percent in the third.[667] Compounding Armenia's woes, foreign aid, particularly from the United States, has dropped despite the sustained efforts of Armenian diaspora lobbying groups. In 2015, the administration of U.S. President Barrack Obama requested a record low amount of aid for Armenia. However, this request still totaled $18.36 million,

---

[665] "Poverty Rate in Armenia Nearly Doubles." *Asbarez*. November 23, 2013. http://asbarez.com/116670/poverty-rate-in-armenia-nearly-doubles/

[666] "Freedom House: Nations in Transit 2014 – Armenia." *Freedom House*. June 12, 2014. http://www.ecoi.net/local_link/280851/411130_de.html

[667] Ibid.

down $2 million from the previous year.[668] In contrast, Azerbaijan was due to receive only $7.9 million. Military aid to both Armenian and Azerbaijan maintained parity at $1.7 million each.[669]

Though the diaspora has played an important role in attracting FDI and foreign aid and therefore contributing positively to Armenia's record of economic growth, its own level of involvement in Armenia is often less than what conventional wisdom would dictate. Approximately 69 percent of all foreigners who invested directly in the Armenian economy were diaspora-connected investors.[670] According to one estimate, diaspora investors invested $275 million from 1998 to 2004, which was approximately 25 percent of total FDI in Armenia. But the same study found that approximately 2,200 individuals or entities from the diaspora or possessing connections to the diaspora entered the Armenian market as investors from 1994 to 2004. "This analysis provides the evidence that although the diaspora's role in economic development of Armenia was extremely important, mainly charity and humanitarian aid, advocacy and political support, information and knowledge transfer and provision of market access were significant."[671] The scholars noted that Armenia does not yet possess a significant place in the hierarchy of investment alternatives for the Armenian diaspora largely because it suffers from a lack of competitive business appeal.[672]

Despite the overall paucity of diaspora investment, it remains a vital resource for Armenia from an investment capital perspective. Diaspora investors may invest relatively little in Armenia on account of the stifling business climate

---

[668] "Obama Budget Calls for Record Low Level of Aid to Armenia." *Asbarez*. February 3, 2015. http://asbarez.com/131444/obama-budget-calls-for-record-low-level-of-aid-to-armenia/

[669] Ibid.

[670] Manuk Hergnyan and Anna Makaryan. "The Role of the Diaspora in Generating Foreign Direct Investments in Armenia." *Armenian Journal of Public Policy* 2, no. 2 (January 2007), 7.

[671] Ibid, 18.

[672] Ibid.

and pervasiveness of corruption. "Many [Armenian] diasporics have become disillusioned with Armenia's progress and believe that diaspora funds are being misused or misappropriated by certain officials. This has engendered donor fatigue in virtually all the diaspora communities."[673]

Russia: The Perception of an Eternal Ally

The picture painted of Armenia by the Armenian diaspora as a partner possessing shared values – a part of Europe in the Caucasus - is further complicated by Armenia's ongoing relationship with its former colonizer and ruler, Russia. Russia is arguably Armenia's closest ally, militarily, politically and economically. Indeed, Armenia's relationship with Russia is so close that the Armenian-American historian, Gerard Libaridian, has characterized the relationship as unnatural.[674] He noted that Armenia's foreign policy since independence in 1991 has largely been based on security, the preservation of its independence and the integration of Armenia into regional and wider international organizations. To this end, Yerevan's immediate fear was that Russia would develop a post-Soviet Union, neo-imperial appetite for lost lands and swallow Armenia up in a new version of the Russian Empire. That fear initially, and incredibly, led Armenia to look to both Iran and Turkey as potential strategic partners.[675] However, the demands of the relatively rich and powerful Armenian diaspora that Armenia emphasize the importance of Armenian Genocide recognition and Armenia's occupation of Nagorno-Karabakh led to Turkey's correspondingly reactive blockade of Armenia. This led many Armenian politicians to agree with their diaspora cousins and conclude that Turkey was their eternal enemy. However, this particularly narrow view has had serious repercussions for Armenia. "If Turkey is the eternal enemy, then Russia is the eternally necessary friend.

---

[673] Ishkanian, 131.
[674] Libaridian.
[675] Ibid.

And this then creates pressures on [Armenia's] policy of independence."[676]

Russia has anywhere from 5,000 to 7,000 troops stationed in Armenia, 3,000 at the Russian 102nd Military Base close to Gyumri. Armenia is viewed inside and outside Russia as one of the Kremlin's most loyal, ex-Soviet allies. "The military alliance with Moscow has been the bedrock of Armenian foreign policy since the Soviet collapse in 1991. Successive governments in Yerevan have viewed the presence of Russian troops in Armenia as a national security necessity."[677] Russian troops patrol Armenia's borders with Turkey and Iran and were deployed *en masse* to the Turkish border after Turkey shot down a Russian aircraft that had reportedly violated Turkish airspace in late 2015.[678] Though Armenia has cooperated militarily with the U.S. and NATO, to include deploying Armenian troops to Afghanistan, Armenia's relationship with Russia is viewed as indispensable in guaranteeing Armenia's territorial integrity, to include control over the disputed territory of Nagorno-Karabakh. Though Russia has not voiced its support for Nagorno-Karabakh's independence, in 2013, the chief commander of the Russian base at Gyumri issued a warning that Russian forces may be obliged to come to Armenia's defense on account of collective security treaties, should Azerbaijan attempt to alter the status quo vis-à-vis Nagorno-Karabakh.[679] The security guarantees between Russia and Armenia directly contradict those between Turkey and Azerbaijan. The possibility of a regional war

---

[676] Libaridian.

[677] Emil Danielyan, "Armenia Signals Further Drift to the West." *Eurasia Insight.* October 18, 2005.

[678] "Why Will Russia Station 7,000 Soldiers on the Armenia-Turkey Border?" *Australia Network.* December 15, 2015. http://www.australianetworknews.com/will-russia-station-7000-soldiers-armenia-turkey-border/

[679] Joshua Kucera. "Russian Officer: We Would Intervene in Karabakh Against Azerbaijan." *Eurasianet.* November 1, 2013. http://www.eurasianet.org/node/67712

over Nagorno-Karabakh is therefore not only ever-present but increasingly likely.

Armenia's close military relationship with Russia further complicates already strained relationships with its neighbor Georgia, which views Russian aims in the region with deep misgivings and understandable suspicion. Georgia previously threatened to put a halt to troop movements across Georgian territory to reinforce Russian soldiers based in Armenia.[680] Yet Georgia's warnings do little to frustrate Russia's tantamount concern: maintaining effective control over Russia's "near abroad." This was illustrated in August 2008, as Russian troops poured into Georgia, defeating it militarily and swiftly annexing the formerly Georgian provinces of Abkhazia and South Ossetia.

Russia's harsh response to Georgia and the excesses of Russian troops in Gyumri, to include the murder of an entire Armenian family, have led some in Armenia to reassess their overreliance on Russia.[681] Other Armenians have voiced concerns over the Russification of Armenia in the years following Armenia's independence. Indeed, some economists posit that Russia owns fully 80 percent of energy sources and systems in Armenia, which has led to a form of energy colonization.[682] As early as 2006, when Russia significantly increased its prices for gas for Armenia, Georgia and Azerbaijan, Armenia agreed to relinquish various energy assets to Russian firms as payment for the increased price of gas.[683] As a result, Russian energy giant

---

[680] Peter Finn. "Russian Troops to Leave Georgia," *The Washington Post*, May 31, 2005, http://www.washingtonpost.com/wp-dyn/content/article/2005/05/30/AR2005053000397.html

[681] Richard Giragosian. "Armenia can't count on Russia anymore." *Al-Jazeera*, January 20, 2015. http://www.aljazeera.com/indepth/opinion/2015/01/armenia-can-count-russia-any-mo-201511852934497678.html

[682] Gayane Abrahamyan. "Debating Big Brother's Presence: Concerns linger of Armenia as 'Outpost.'" *Armenia Now*, Issue 44 (254).

[683] Jim Nichol. "Armenian, Azerbaijan and Georgia: Political Developments and Implications for United States Interests. *CRS*

Gazprom was able to secure a 45 percent stake in ArmRosGazProm.[684] ArmRosGazProm was a joint Russian-Armenian natural gas pipeline project that was also Russian oil and gas giant, Gazprom's subsidiary in Armenia. Gazprom was able to pay for its 45 percent acquisition in the equivalent of $148 million in gas rather than cash.[685] By 2013, Gazprom had gained full ownership of ArmRosGazProm, renaming it Gazprom Armenia, through the acquisition of Armenian government shares that were sold gradually. This was done in order for Armenia to gain temporary price freezes as well as delayed implementation of other, general pricing hikes by Gazprom in Russia.[686]

The last significant Armenian energy system, the fifth bloc of the Hrazdan Thermo-Electric Station, was ceded to Russia in 2006, with the other four blocs already belonging to a Russian company.[687] Russian companies also control a nuclear power plant at Metsamor, near Yerevan.[688]

Armenia's former President, Robert Kocharian, has been criticized in Armenia, with reports highlighting that Kocharian and his ministers accumulated vast sums of money for themselves by selling off Armenia's assets to Russian companies, thereby weakening Armenia's long-term viability and sovereignty.[689] Russia controls so much of Armenia that a Russian Duma chairman, Boris Gryzlov,

---

Report for Congress, July 31, 2007: 15.
http://www.au.af.mil/au/awc/awcgate/crs/rl33453.pdf

[684] Kateryna Boguslavska, Ingerid Maria Opdahl, Elena Kropatcheva, and Andrei V. Belyi. "Gazprom: Challenges at Home and Abroad." *Center for Security Studies*, October 26, 2015.

[685] Ibid.

[686] Ibid.

[687] Bertil Nygren. *The rebuilding of Greater Russia: Putin's foreign policy towards the CIS countries*. Vol. 4. Routledge, 2007; 116.

[688] Ibid.

[689] Kieran Cooke. "Armenia's Controversial Gold Rush." *BBC,* January 9, 2008; http://news.bbc.co.uk/2/hi/business/7153794.stm

referred to Armenia as nothing more than a "Russian outpost."[690]

One Armenian opposition newspaper agreed with Gryzlov, noting that Russia controlled not only the economic backbone of Armenia but also virtually all of Armenia's strategic resources.[691] As a case in point, in 2008, the BBC reported that Madneuli Resources purchased one of Armenia's largest mining concerns, the Ararat Gold Recovery Company (AGRC), in a little-publicized and complex deal. Madneuli was based in Georgia, but reports indicated that it is actually controlled by Industrial Investors, an influential group of Russian financiers headed by Sergei Generalov, a former Russian energy minister turned business oligarch.[692] In being held hostage to Armenian diaspora campaigns and meddling as well as Russian troops and business interests, questions are automatically raised as to the actual levels of sovereignty and independence in Armenia.

The Effects of Closed Borders on Armenia and the Region

The blockade of Armenia by Turkey and Azerbaijan has its roots in the complicated struggle for and subsequent Armenian occupation of the Nagorno-Karabakh region of the Caucasus.[693] This occurred soon after both Armenia and Azerbaijan gained their independence from the Soviet Union in 1991. The blockade of Armenia can also be said to be a tangible result and reaction by Turkey to the Armenian diaspora's influence in Yerevan and its insistence that Turkey recognize the events of 1915 as the Armenian Genocide.[694] Though Armenia insists that it sets no

690 Vladimir Socor. "The End of 'Complementarity' in Armenia's Foreign Policy." *Eurasia Daily Monitor* Volume: 10 Issue: 165, September 18, 2013.
691 Kieran Cooke. "Armenia's Controversial Gold Rush."
692 Ibid.
693 Cornell, "Turkey and the Conflict in Nagorno Karabakh." 61-62.
694 Ibid: 65-66.

preconditions to talks with Turkey, since independence, successive Armenian regimes have voiced support for the campaign of their diaspora cousins to recognize the Armenian Genocide, even though recognition of the events of 1915 as genocide by Turkey is a moral as well as a legal issue and cannot be accomplished through legislation and *ad hoc* resolutions.

The Declaration of Independence of the Republic of Armenia states: "The Republic of Armenia stands in support of the task of achieving international recognition of the 1915 Genocide in Ottoman Turkey and Western Armenia."[695] As noted previously, references to Western Armenia are construed in Ankara as a threat to Turkish territorial integrity and smacking of Armenian irredentism. Indeed, even prior to independence, Soviet Armenia declared that its non-recognition of the Turkey's and Armenia's existing borders, laid down in the Russo-Turkish treaties of 1921, thus blocking the establishment of future diplomatic relations.[696] Thus, unresolved national security issues in Turkey as well as deeply felt considerations that raise legal and moral questions inform Turkey's decision to continue its blockade of Armenia. "The removal of the blockade [of Armenia] will, almost surely, necessitate difficult compromises in all these regards. This is particularly true for Armenians (including those of Nagorno-Karabakh and the diaspora), as they are the ones holding lands most likely to be demanded in a settlement…"[697]

A study of the effects of Turkey's and Azerbaijan's blockade of Armenia argued, "Public opinion continues to overestimate the actual costs of blockade for Armenia… Because… Armenia has been losing much more from the

---

[695] "Armenian Declaration of Independence." *The Government of the Republic of Armenia*. http://www.gov.am/en/independence/

[696] Cornell, "Turkey and the Conflict in Nagorno Karabakh." 66.

[697] Richard Beilock. "Raining on the Parade: A Critique of Armenia's Trade Performance in 1995–2002 and the Effect of Closed Borders: A Cross-Country Perspective." *Armenian International Journal of Public Policy*, 2(1): 113.

deficiencies in the business environment than from the blockade, the top priority of government policy should be aimed at those elements of the investment climate, which in contrast to the blockade do not require complicated international negotiations but are entirely under the government control."[698] The study also noted that the costs of the blockade have steadily declined as Armenia has shifted to exports that are less susceptible to the blockade, such as jewelry.[699]

A subsequent study refuted these assertions on three levels.[700] "(1) Despite acknowledging the preeminence of indirect over direct costs associated with the blockade, [the authors of the study cited above] based their assessments of the size and trends in blockade-related costs solely on direct costs; (2) [They] Failed to note two important aspects of indirect costs, namely the blockade's impact on out-migration and that international crises are conducive to authoritarianism and opaqueness in government and, hence, to poor business environments; and (3) [They] Employed two approaches for estimating lost exports and selected the one indicating relatively low losses despite its serious problems. Rather than correcting the commonly held exaggerated view of the blockade's cost on the Armenian economy, as was their intent, [the authors'] work worsens the commonly held underestimation of those costs. The unpleasant reality is that the blockade's effects pervade the economy and are profoundly negative. Moreover, there is always the risk of heightened tensions or even renewed conflicts which could unravel Armenia's progress to date."[701]

This study highlighted that adjustments in exports made by Armenia in order to counter the blockade would make

---

698 Lev Freinkman, Evgeny Polyakov, and Caroline Revenco. "Armenia's Trade Performance in 1995-2002 and the Effect of Closed Borders: A Cross-Country Perspective." *Armenian International Policy Research Group Working Paper* 04/04 (2004): 2-3.

699 Ibid, 9.

700 Beilock.

701 Ibid., 118-119.

sense if Turkey's and Azerbaijan's blockade was permanent. But if it is not, the process of export adjustment becomes a double-edged sword. "The more that physical and human capital is committed to (diverted from) activities made more (less) attractive by the blockade, the lower the cost to Armenia of existing under the blockade, but the higher and more prolonged the adjustment costs when the blockade is removed. In general, the better Armenia adapts to living with the blockade, the worse its position if the blockade is removed. The cost of post-blockade readjustments, albeit deferred, is a cost of the blockade."[702] Given the above, it can be stated conclusively that not only has the blockade severely curtailed Armenia's economic prospects, but it has brought about other unwanted and serious consequences. Namely, Armenia's isolation and the accompanying loss of revenue by the state and per capita.

Armenia Bypassed: Pipelines, Railways and other Regional Projects

Armenian diaspora lobbying groups, particularly in the United States and the European Union, continue to support legislation that would ostensibly ease Armenia's isolation. However, their efforts, handicapped by overriding concerns of the campaign for Armenian Genocide recognition, have met with little success, as major infrastructure projects and initiatives in the region continue to bypass Armenia. As noted previously, the Armenian Assembly of America was briefly successful in blocking US assistance in support of Turkey's, Georgia's and Azerbaijan's efforts to build the Kars-Akhalkalaki-Tbilisi-Baku railway.[703] Yet this has had little impact on the building of the railway, which, when completed, will still bypass Armenia completely.

Efforts by Armenian diaspora lobbies to oppose the building of the Baku–Tbilisi–Ceyhan (BTC) pipeline were

---

[702] Ibid, 115.

[703] AAINC. "2005 Annual Report." *Armenian Assembly of America.* http://www.aaainc.org/fileadmin/aaainc/pdf/Annual_Reports/AAA_Annual_Report_2005.pdf

also frustrated. Though it would have made sense both economically and geographically, in terms of distance, to build the pipeline directly from Baku through Armenia and thence to Turkey, Armenia was purposely and scrupulously avoided. [704] The pipeline became operational in 2006. This was a harsh disappointment for Armenia and the Armenian diaspora, as serious thought had been given, at least in Washington, D.C., to advocate building the export pipeline through Armenia in the mid-1990s.

Armenia was bypassed for four key reasons. First, the unresolved military conflict between Azerbaijan and Armenia over Nagorno-Karabakh; second, the subsequent blockade of Armenia by both Turkey and Azerbaijan dissuaded negotiation, let alone cooperation on the project; third, Azerbaijan saw the revenues from the pipeline as a way of attaining not only military parity with Armenia, but as a way of eventually surpassing Armenia vis-a-vis military strength. Lastly, the Turkish government saw no value in attempting to reach an understanding with Armenia while it still occupied Nagorno-Karabakh. This rationale was further supported by the Armenian government's push – prodded and cajoled by the Armenian diaspora - for recognition of the events of 1915 as the Armenian Genocide.

The inability of Armenia to effectively broadcast its foreign policy, either because it was unwilling or unable to do so on account of diaspora and Russian pressure, has meant the loss of vast economic and political benefits. In the first half of 2007 alone, one year after the completion and launch of the Baku-Tbilisi-Ceyhan Pipeline, Azerbaijan's real GDP growth topped 35 percent.[705] Georgia expected to see transit fees of $62.5 million per

---

[704] It has been estimated that that a trans-Armenia route would have saved approximately $600 million compared to the current route from Baku, Azerbaijan to Tbilisi, Georgia to Ceyhan, Turkey. Harunyunyan, 176.

[705] "Republic of Azerbaijan – Concluding Statement of the IMF Mission, 30 August – 06 September 2007." *International Monetary Fund*, 2007. http://www.imf.org/external/np/ms/2007/092607.htm

year.[706] And Turkey expected to receive approximately $200 million per year in transit fees increasing to $290 million per year beginning in year 17 of operation.[707] Turkey's decision to build the pipeline through eastern Anatolia was also made for strategic and economic reasons.[708] It hopes to see an increase in economic activity in what has been an economically depressed, marginalized and restive region. Turkey also would like to further solidify its hold on precisely the area many diaspora Armenians and Armenia's Declaration of Independence refer to as "Western Armenia."

In 2011, the governments of Turkey and Azerbaijan signed a memorandum of understanding to establish a consortium to build and operate a new gas pipeline system named the Trans Anatolian Natural Gas Pipeline Project (*Trans-Anadolu Doğalgaz Boru Hattı*, or TANAP). The pipeline, when completed, will transport gas from Azerbaijan through Georgia and Turkey to Europe. It will be a central part of the Southern Gas Corridor, which will connect the giant Shah Deniz gas field in Azerbaijan to Europe through the South Caucasus Pipeline (SCP), TANAP and the Trans Adriatic Pipeline (TAP).[709] In March of 2015, Presidents Erdoğan and Aliyev met with Georgian President Giorgi Margvelashvili in the city of Kars, in eastern Turkey, to begin work on the pipeline by formally laying its foundations. Similar to the Baku-Tbilisi-Ceyhan oil pipeline, both Georgia and Turkey expect to receive millions of dollars in transit fees per year. The extraction and transport of gas will also further fill Azerbaijan's

---

706 Vladimir Papava. "The Baku-Tbilisi-Ceyhan Pipeline: Implications for Georgia." *The Baku-Tbilisi-Ceyhan Pipeline: Oil Window to the West* (2005): 87.

707 Jonathan Elkind. "Economic Implications of the Baku-Tbilisi-Ceyhan Pipeline." *Baku-Tbilisi-Ceyhan Pipeline: Oil Window to the West* (2005): 49.

708 Mert Bilgin. "Turkey's Energy Strategy: Synchronizing Geopolitics and Foreign Policy with Energy Security." *Insight Turkey* 17, no. 2 (2015): 78.

709 Ibid, 77-78.

coffers. The pipeline is expected to eventually receive shipments of Kazakh and Turkmen gas.[710]

There is little doubt as to the deleterious effects of the blockade of Armenia and human capital has noticeably deteriorated, in large part through emigration to the United States, Russia and, as noted previously, Turkey. Indeed, Armenia has one of the highest net emigration rates in the world. In the decade stretching from 2001 to 2011, the resident population of Armenia fell from 3.2 to 3.0 million persons.[711] "There can be little doubt that the blockade is an impetus for out migration [from Armenia] through its real and perceived negative impacts on the economy, dangers of renewed hostilities, sense of isolation, and the military draft."[712]

An ANCA position paper, citing 2007 World Bank figures, noted that the blockade of Armenia by Turkey and Azerbaijan cost Armenia between 30 and 38 percent of its GDP and blocks up to 50 percent of Armenia's potential exports.[713] According to other World Bank figures, the blockade costs Armenia between $570 to $722 million annually. Armenia's dependence on outside supplies of energy and most raw materials compounds the effects of the blockade as all land routes through Azerbaijan and Turkey are closed.[714]

Scholars have noted that Armenia must improve its business environment through the removal of administrative burdens, for example.[715] Yet there are also arguments that these reforms and the benefits accrued therefrom would be as great or greater than the removal of

---

[710] Ibid.

[711] "Armenia: The Demographic-Economic Framework of Migration, the Legal Framework of Migration, the Socio-Political Framework of Migration." *MPC – MIGRATION POLICY CENTRE*, (June 2013).

[712] Beilock, 116.

[713] "Position Papers: US Aid to Armenia." *Armenian National Committee of America*. https://anca.org/press-release/anca-publishes-position-papers-on-key-armenian-american-concerns/

[714] Ibid.

[715] Freinkman, et al., 5.

Turkey's and Azerbaijan's blockade.[716] Others have argued persuasively that this assertion remains unsubstantiated and without supporting evidence.[717] Indeed, it is difficult to separate the effects of the blockade and the fact that governments, such as Armenia's, tend to become more authoritarian when there are serious international security threats. And Armenia feels surrounded and threatened by both Azerbaijan and Turkey.[718]

[716] Ibid., 19.
[717] Beilock.
[718] Ibid, 125.

CHAPTER 9

VERTICAL, HORIZONTAL AND DIAGONAL PRESSURE

The Armenian diaspora's campaign for genocide recognition relies largely on what can be termed "vertical pressure."[719] The diaspora calculates that as the number of states, municipalities and international actors recognizing the events of 1915 as the Armenian Genocide multiply, irresistible pressure is applied on Turkey to do the same. In contradistinction, and as a reaction to the diaspora's application of vertical pressure, Turkey has employed what can be termed "horizontal pressure," emphasizing state-state (Armenia-Turkey) relations and nation-nation (Armenian-Turkish) relations in an effort to sideline the Armenian diaspora.[720] An exploration of these approaches may prove useful in outlining potential resolution strategies, at least on a theoretical level.

To begin with, there are two major flaws with the pressure applied by both parties, whether vertical or horizontal. First, interaction or negotiations would likely be more constructive than pressure. Even changing the semantic choice of the word "pressure" would likely be positive, given the negative connotations of the word. As a partial

[719] Kotchikian.

[720] Ibid.

prescriptive, an emphasis on the starting of negotiation and dialogue processes rather than the lobbying pressures as currently fomented by Turkey and the Armenian diaspora would possibly open the door to an interaction beyond the miniscule and remote. What currently exists is pressure and a combative interaction that rests solely, on the one hand, on forcing Turkey to recognize the events of 1915 as the Armenian Genocide and, on the other, the insistence by Turkey that Armenia and diaspora Armenians drop their demands for recognition of the events of 1915 as something more than "mutual massacres."[721] Such an attitude, if commonly shared, may lead to the beginnings of a partial solution to this emotive and painful issue. Employment of different tactics and semantics, though justifiably fraught with difficulty, could change the currently shrill tenor of the Armenian diaspora campaign to a more measured debate and interaction between Armenians and Turks, historians, other scholars, and even governments.

The second flaw in the diaspora's application of vertical pressure is the theory that this will eventually coerce Turkey to recognize the Armenian Genocide. "The fallacy of this argument lies in the reality of modern international relations and the fact that the prestige of any state – as emotional as it seems – is one of the very few things that a government is not willing to sacrifice."[722] History is replete with examples of states (or leaders of states) who have been issued ultimatums to comply with the demands of other, often more powerful states, only to have these demands rejected because they were felt to undermine the state's sovereignty; the pride and viability of the state. Serbia at the outbreak of World War I, Iraq in 1991 and 2003, and Georgia in 2008, are but a few examples. Yet, this argument cuts both ways, and Turkey's overt pressure on Armenia as manifest in its political and economic blockade, is also unlikely to lead to any positive resolution.

---

[721] Ibid.
[722] Ibid.

As demonstrated in previous chapters, Turkey has very legitimate reasons to dispute the Armenian diaspora's politicized account of the events of 1915. Yet, possibly because its attempts to encourage a dialogue amongst historians were viewed as disingenuous by the diaspora and therefore ignored, pressure remains the easiest option, one that satisfies the emotive nature of both the Turkish government stance and the obtuse and uncompromising diaspora campaign. Dialogue and interaction, on the contrary, remain tantalizingly out of reach precisely because of the black and white portrayals - lacking nuance and depth - of Armenian and Turkish historiographies.

Encumbered by the historical straightjacket it has created for itself, Armenian diaspora identity brooks no opposition in its quest for Armenian Genocide recognition. The diaspora has proverbially painted itself into a corner from which it cannot escape. Negotiations, let alone the utilization of another descriptive term beyond "genocide" are construed as an admission of defeat.

Theorizing Resolution Strategies

The Republic of Turkey and the Republic of Armenia, to a lesser extent, suffer from no such impediment. Turkey already describes the events as massacres, albeit mutual, and acknowledges the deaths and deportations of hundreds of thousands, rather than millions, of Ottoman Armenians. Furthermore, Turkey's identity is not built upon the foundation of a Self/Other relationship that involves Armenians or other minorities such as Greeks in the Ottoman Empire. Thus, Turkish identity is unencumbered by a re-imagined trauma on the scale or import of Armenian diaspora identity. This is extremely important and potentially gives Turks and their government more latitude to deal with the issue, the campaign and the exploration of resolution strategies. In a similar fashion, though Armenia officially describes the events of 1915 as the Armenian Genocide and Yerevan prominently hosts the *Tsitsernakaberd*, a genocide memorial built by the government of the Armenian SSR, official statements and actions vis-à-vis Turkey, in general, have been tempered by a pragmatism not witnessed in those of the diaspora.

Horizontal pressure, particularly from Turkey, has been used to sideline the Armenian diaspora. That is, though Turkey deals very little in strict state-state relations with Armenia, there is an increasingly high degree of nation-nation (Turkish-Armenian) relations occurring, largely and simply because of the two states' contiguity with each other. Direct flights between the two countries, business trips and vacations by Armenians to Turkey and vice versa as well as cultural exchanges, limited as they may be, have had arguably positive effects within Turkey and Armenia.[723] Personal and business relationships as developed by Armenians with Turks, discourage and discredit the recurrent and racist image of the "terrible Turk" as genocidal murderers used by the diaspora campaign. Similarly, many Turks, particularly in eastern Anatolia, favor the suspension of the Turkish blockade of Armenia to allow for further economic interaction.

For true resolution of the issue – should that prove possible – the campaign conducted by the Armenian diaspora must be properly addressed. As such, a thorough analysis of the campaign against the backdrop of global human rights regimes and legal mechanisms is in order.

---

[723] Out of 1162 [Armenian] respondents, 13 percent have had interactions with Turks and 6 percent have been in Turkey. The main purpose of these respondents' visits to Turkey was tourism (leisure) by 47 percent, while the second purpose (25 percent) was trade. The vast majority of Armenians, 80 percent, use Turkish products. *Towards a Shared Vision of Normalization of Armenian-Turkish Relations: Draft Report.* Caucasus Research Resource Center – Armenia: Yerevan, April 2015, 20.

CHAPTER 10

DEALING WITH HISTORICAL ATROCITIES

The attempts and efforts by the Armenian diaspora, successive Armenian governments and other interest groups and politicians to achieve a semblance of official recognition that the events of 1915 constituted the Armenian Genocide are problematic on a number of levels. The building blocks of the campaign for genocide recognition and the very political acts that have followed are informed by a loose reading of extremely complicated historical circumstances characterized by an overt and purposeful lack of nuance. Furthermore, while Armenian diaspora lobbies and interest groups justifiably highlight their efforts aimed at the awareness of human rights and the prevention of ethnic cleansing or genocide in Darfur, Bosnia and Rwanda, it is startling how little the concept of human rights has appeared in their campaign for genocide recognition.[724] An analysis of the campaign indicates that the issue of human rights and the legalities and mechanisms surrounding accountability and enforcement of norms are missing because the foundations of the campaign rest on

[724] See "ANC of South Florida Will Take Part in Genocide Prevention Project." *Pan Armenian,* March 27, 2009. http://www.armeniandiaspora.com/showthread.php?163981-ANC-Of-South-Florida-Will-Take-Part-In-Genocide-Prevention-Project

definitional elasticity and *ad hoc* resolutions rather than the accepted space designated for judgement on issues of purported genocide: the courts.

There has been a global human rights regime in existence for over six decades. Its importance is frequently hailed and referred to by various state and civil representatives. Indeed, the concept of inalienable and universal human rights is often noted as the idea and practice that separates "us" from our predecessors and the acts they perpetrated prior to 1945. In addition, the Convention on the Prevention and Punishment of the Crime of Genocide (CPPCG) was adopted by the United Nations General Assembly in late 1948 as General Assembly Resolution 260. The Convention defines genocide in legal terms and all participating states are required to prevent and punish actions of genocide, regardless of whether they occurred during war or in peacetime.

Human Rights, Human Rights Regimes and the Diaspora Campaign for Genocide Recognition

Should the Armenian question be debated and discussed against the backdrop of the current human rights regime and, correspondingly, in terms of human rights, a number of useful questions would automatically be raised. According to Bertil Dunér, a Senior Researcher on human rights at the Swedish Institute of International Affairs, these questions would necessarily afford all parties involved in the debates and campaigns for and against recognition of the Armenian Genocide the opportunity to view the issue from novel vantage points.[725] For example, do the campaign and efforts for recognition of the massacres and forced deportations of Ottoman Armenians as the Armenian Genocide fit with the tenets of the global human rights regime? Is it simply a deviation from the regime because it addresses events that took place some thirty years before the convention was signed? Or does this quest represent a

---

[725] Dunér, 218.

possible change in the scope of the convention, which could and should be carried out? Finally, are there inconsistencies with the campaign to recognize the events of 1915 as the Armenian Genocide and the model built around the UN Genocide Convention?[726]

There is little doubt that recognition of the events of 1915 as the Armenian Genocide is perceived as a goal in and of itself for the Armenian diaspora and the campaign's many supporters. According to the campaign, *ad hoc* legislation or statements – formal or informal, official or unofficial - issued on behalf or in support of the campaign simply recognize a historical truth. Indeed, the passage of the 2006 French parliamentary bill on the subject criminalized the act of "denying the Armenian genocide," stating that the massacres that occurred in 1915 constituted a simple historical fact: genocide.[727] Recognition of the Armenian genocide is popularly perceived as fulfilling an instrumental function, as well. A statement quoted in full in chapter five and issued during debates regarding the Armenian Genocide recognition bill in the United States House of Representatives in 2000 is instructive and raises numerous questions.[728] The final sentence, while parroting often-quoted language used in support of recognizing the Armenian Genocide, is problematic on a number of levels and necessarily raises further questions. For example, how does recognition of one genocide *per se* put a halt to another? Of, how does non-recognition necessitate or encourage further genocides? What is the causal link? In this particular case, how does non-recognition of the events of 1915, events which have never been proved by a court of law to constitute genocide, possibly lead to the belief that

---

[726] Ibid.

[727] Crampton. "French Pass Bill that Punishes Denial of Armenian Genocide."

[728] Quotations by Representatives Menendez and Rothman, respectively. Made at Markups before the Committee on International Relations, House of Representatives, 106th Congress, 2nd Session, 28 September and 3 October 2000, as quoted in Dunér, 219.

genocides will not only occur but be encouraged? Though these questions may appear pedantic, even this level of scrutiny has rarely, if ever, been applied to the campaign for recognition of the events of 1915 as the Armenian Genocide.

Definitional Elasticity and Genocide Recognition in the Age of Genocide

Though the United States has yet to pass a binding resolution regarding this emotive issue, over half of US states as well as multiple provincial, urban and community recognitions from across the globe in the forms of petitions, laws and/or declarations have been promulgated from Bolivia to the Vatican City to Austria.[729] It is precisely these pell-mell resolutions, declarations, legislation and laws that are deemed as a marker of the Armenian Genocide campaign's success. On one level this is correct. These *ad hoc* resolutions and statements, accompanied by media reports, have led to the campaign's notoriety and popularity. As importantly, it has led to a knee-jerk, tacit and popular acceptance that the events of 1915 indeed constituted the Armenian Genocide. This was not just one genocide in many, but the world's first genocide; a soundbite that has now been amended to the first genocide of the twentieth century.

This is problematic on its own account. However, the very nature of the campaign for *ad hoc* resolutions and legislation has led to a situation where many of the states and other legislative bodies unequivocally make reference to the UN Convention on Genocide even though this cannot apply to the events of 1915. For example, the Russian Duma (1995) and the European Parliament (1987) both state that their separate resolutions of recognition, on one level or another, are in accordance with the Convention. However, others

---

[729] "Recognition: States: Resolutions, Laws, and Declarations." *The Armenian Genocide Museum-Institute, National Academy of Sciences of the Republic of Armenia.* http://www.genocide-museum.am/eng/states.php

resolutions, such as that passed by the Belgian Senate (1998), make only indirect references to the Convention. Others simply create their own definition of genocide.[730]

According to Dunér, what can be termed as the "definitional frivolity" or what this book terms the "definitional elasticity" of the Armenian diaspora-driven campaign and the resultant resolutions and legislation described above, has led directly to the creation of an untenable situation. This situation is one in which, "… an accusation is made about actions which are frequently called the worst of all crimes, and yet the meaning of the crime [genocide] is not clarified."[731] Indeed, the situation is untenable precisely because it demands recognition of a crime not through the courts – the only prescribed avenue - but through extra-judicial means and modalities.

The 1948 UN Convention on Genocide is specific and unequivocal. The signatory states confirmed that the crime of genocide is a crime under international law, whether committed during war or peace. These same signatories also agreed to thwart and punish any perpetrators of genocide. Regardless of the veracity and virility of the Convention in preventing ethnic cleansing and genocide since 1948, the Convention does make it clear that no prosecutions may occur - as informed by the Convention - in cases of crimes alleged to have been perpetrated prior to 1948. This necessarily excludes the events of 1915 being brought before a court of law. Or does it? Furthermore, does it matter in regards to the Armenian Genocide campaign as currently constituted?

Currently, the Armenian campaign aims to gain recognition of the Armenian Genocide via pressure applied to Turkey from the court of world opinion, *not* from an actual court ruling using the specific terms unequivocally listed in the UN Convention. By creating a campaign that relies on definitional elasticity and *ad hoc* legislation, tribunals and courts can be circumvented and conveniently avoided.

---

730 Dunér, 220.

731 Ibid, 221.

This is essential, given that no court has ruled in accordance with the campaign, to date. Nor is the prospect bright that courts will do so in the future.[732] This is because, as pointed out, genocide is a legal term, not something that can be designated by legislation from the Russian Duma or the Bolivian Plurinational Legislative Assembly. In order to conclude whether genocide occurred, the actual physical killing of members of an ethnic, religious, racial and national group as well as the intention to destroy, in whole or in part, such a group, must be established *in a court of law*. It is up to a recognized court of international stature to determine whether the Ottoman government possessed intent to destroy Armenians. Or, as the case may be, "… whether the loss of life, regardless of how great the number, was an unanticipated result of the government's aim to remove a perceived security threat or to create more homogenous country."[733]

Given these contingencies, the Armenian campaign, by avoiding courts most of the time and relying on *ad hoc* legislation that is informed by politicized history and definitional elasticity, can largely avoid the scrutiny that would accompany historical and legal investigations. By branding their opponents as heartless genocide deniers, the campaign and its perpetrators can also avoid actual conversations regarding what occurred before, during and after the events of 1915. Put simply, the historical must be separated from the political. Yet, the campaign conflates the two or, most egregiously, simply ignores historical records that fail to conform to and reify their identity-driven campaign.

It is important to remember that on the few occasions Armenians have attempted to gain a court ruling in favor of *ad hoc* resolutions and legislation they have failed. The European Court of Human Rights, ruling on Perinçek v. Switzerland, explicitly stated that public and scholarly

---

[732] Diler. See also Tuncel, 6-10.

[733] M. Hakan Yavuz. "Contours of Scholarship on Armenian-Turkish Relations." *Middle East Critique* 20, no. 3 (2011): 233.

debates regarding the events of 1915 are "a matter of public interest." The ruling added that, at least in the democratic countries of the EU, there is no need to subject minority views "to a criminal penalty in order to protect the rights of the Armenian community." As Tuncel noted, "This is an important evaluation, which nullifies the attempts [by the Armenian campaign] to silence views that fall out of the ordinary."[734]

The definitional elasticity employed by the Armenian campaign matters deeply. This is because it makes a difference regarding the strict or loose application of the terms of the UN Convention. This is particularly the case if one considers the impact this definitional elasticity may have on future genocide prosecutions and prevention measures, issues in which diaspora Armenians and lobbying organizations claim to be heavily involved. For example, in resolutions like that of the Belgian Senate where definitions of genocide are applied to exclude political acts and instead explicitly mention the existence of the intent to destroy a group, they inevitably will be much less restrictive than those offered up in the original UN Convention of 1948. There is perhaps a reason for doing so as, "… the number of potential situations that would merit the label 'genocide' will be considerably increased, and the mater of verification becomes much less complicated."[735] Yet, this is precisely what has occurred with the politicized legislation born out of the Armenian diaspora-driven campaign to label the massacres of 1915 as the Armenian Genocide. If it cannot be firmly defined, determined or established whether a certain group, such as the Ottoman Armenians, were deliberately killed because of their ethnic makeup or political views, a real dilemma exists vis-a-vis the terms of the UN Genocide Convention. However, in terms of the Belgian Senate's loose definitional resolution, this is no longer a problem. Simply put, the events of 1915 are now considered the Armenian Genocide under Belgian law

[734] Tuncel, 14.

[735] Dunér, 220.

because of definitional elasticity. Yet, these same events are not considered as such - even if they were subject to juridical purview - under the 1948 UN Convention.

Belgium is not the only problem. Many state, municipal and provincial resolutions fail to mention or reference the UN Convention at all. The resolutions passed by the Chilean Senate (2007), the Swedish Parliament (2000) and the Slovakian National Assembly (2004), to name a few, fail to make any mention of the UN Convention. Indeed, they fail to mention any definition of genocide at all and simply call on Turkey to recognize the crimes for which it is accused. Dunér assumes that the lack of any definition at all in these resolutions means "... either the actors for all practical purposes do not have a definition or that they have one (probably different from that contained in the [UN] convention) which for some reason they are not willing to disclose. In either case, silence on this point seems difficult to defend..."[736] And, "The fact that a convention on genocide was adopted and, moreover, gained wide acceptance by the world's states makes problematical the neglect of the definition it provides. It seems strange, in fact arbitrary, to use other definitions or none at all."[737]

Ad hoc, politicized resolutions based on the definitional elasticity of crucial terms lead to another quandary. The major impetus behind many of the resolutions passed by various political bodies is *not* a relative appeal to evidence and truth. Rather, they are but simple references to previous, politicized legislative positions and the accompanying *ad hoc* resolutions passed by other governmental bodies. For example, both Chile's (2007) and Sweden's (2000) Armenian Genocide resolutions make reference to the United Nation's Sub-Commission meeting in 1985 that "... established the fact that the Ottoman Empire had committed genocide against the Armenian people at the beginning of this century."[738] This reference to

---

[736] Ibid, 221.

[737] Ibid.

[738] See "Sweden Parliament Report." *The Armenian Genocide Museum-Institute, National Academy of Sciences of the Republic of Armenia*, March 29,

the UN is helpful, at least, and lends some legitimacy to Chile's and Sweden's resolutions. This is because UN Sub-Commissions are not purely political bodies, especially when compared to entities such as the European Parliament, whose members are political appointees and whose resolutions – composed by less than reliable authorities - are often cited in resolutions recognizing the events of 1915 as the Armenian Genocide. However, Chile's and Sweden's citation of the 1985 UN Sub-Commission's finding is problematic for another reason. This is because both resolutions misconstrue the UN Sub-Commission's findings as UN recognition of the Armenian Genocide. This is at odds with the truth and *not* what the Sub-Commission concluded.[739] In fact, the special rapporteur, as a member of the UN Sub-Commission, submitted a report in 1985 that was then subject to debate. The special rapporteur's report and subsequent debate produced no recognition of any kind to the many human calamities referred to therein. Rather, the Sub-Commission simply "took note" of the rapporteur's study stating, "It should be emphasized that neither was there any recommendation to the superior Commission on Human Rights to adopt a resolution."[740]

According to Dunér, the rapporteur's report lacked authority for another important reason. The report did not adhere to the definition of genocide as defined by the 1948 Convention. Instead, the report referred to a number of "genocides" that occurred in the twentieth century – including the Armenians massacres of 1915 – but relativistically concluded, "It could seem pedantic to argue that some terrible mass-killings are legalistically not genocide, but on the other hand it could be counter-

---

2000. http://www.genocide-museum.am/eng/Sweden_Parliament_Report.php. See also "Text of the Chile Senate Resolution." *The Armenian Genocide Museum-Institute, National Academy of Sciences of the Republic of Armenia*, (June 5, 2007). http://www.genocide-museum.am/eng/Chile_Senate_Resolution.php

[739] Dunér, 222.

[740] Ibid.

productive to devalue genocide through over-diluting its definition."[741] The result of this definitional elasticity leads to an inevitable conclusion in which no one knows or understands which of the examples would be considered genocide within the meaning of the UN genocide convention.[742]

All this begets yet a further quandary. Does one label all massacres as genocide, whether they constitute the legal definition or not and thus dilute the definition? Or does one not label anything genocide that cannot be legalistically proven to be otherwise? This is problematic for the Armenian diaspora's position and their campaign. That is, recognition of the events of 1915 as the Armenian Genocide for the Armenian diaspora represents, at the very least, two things. One, it was the world's first genocide and two, it was therefore the blueprint for the Nazi Holocaust. In this particularistic and exclusive worldview, massacres preceding 1915 should either not be considered genocide or, if accepted as such, do not carry the same heft as the Armenian Genocide. As an advocate for expanding genocide recognition, in general, to include the Armenian Genocide, Donald Bloxham has warned against precisely such a scenario. "It would be regrettable if the campaign for recognition, if ultimately satisfied, transformed itself into the sort of memorial exclusivism that we have sometimes seen in the Holocaust case. Might we find the Armenian genocide ring-fenced in a sort of select club of "classic" genocides, along with the Holocaust and few others that have passed the politically determined criteria for admission and thereby gained entry into an internationally approved memorial pantheon?"[743]

Writing in 2005, Bloxham noted that the claims in the Armenian genocide campaign to be the world's "first" genocide had already sidelined such horrific events as the early twentieth century massacres of the Herero and Nama

---

[741] Ibid.

[742] Ibid.

[743] Bloxham, 230.

in present-day Namibia, which Bloxham considers examples of genocide.[744] Furthermore, genocide resolutions passed by Russia (1994), New South Wales, Australia (1997) and a Canadian Senate Resolution (2002) referred to the events of 1915 as the "first" genocide. The concept of first genocide was widely used in the Armenian Genocide campaign and often found in scholarly works, "... illustrating the tunnel vision often accompanying the pursuit of one cause in isolation from the others."[745]

Definitional elasticity, as employed as a strategic tactic, furthers the primary goal of the campaign to gain recognition through official statements and legislative acts. However, it becomes admittedly difficult to defend this tactic of definitional elasticity or, in some cases, the utter lack of any definition when the campaign necessarily accuses Turkey and its inhabitants, in perpetuity, of the worst crime known to humankind. This is not simply a case of a few, deceased Ottoman officials being accused of committing genocide in 1915. Rather the *ad hoc* resolutions that are the desired outcome of the Armenian Genocide campaign necessarily implicate all Turks in the same crime. This directly opposes the UN Convention on Genocide, which specifically states that crimes of genocide may not be linked to states and state offices, only individuals are held responsible. The so-called Nuremberg Principles firmly established the principle of individual criminal responsibility by stating, "... any person who commits an act which constitutes a crime under international law is responsible therefore and liable to punishment."[746] Yet Ottoman officials from the era of Armenian massacres and deportations, even if guilty of the crimes for which they are accused, are long dead and the question of the identity of

---

[744] Ibid.

[745] Ibid.

[746] "United Nations Principles for the Nuremberg Tribunal, 1946." *United Nations*, December 11, 1946. https://www.icrc.org/applic/ihl/ihl.nsf/Treaty.xsp?documentId=53D11A6719F4627BC12563CD002D6ACA&action=openDocument

individuals responsible for the crimes they are accused of has been entirely ignored by the Armenian Genocide campaign. Furthermore, these Ottoman officials are not being implicated in this crime, it is their offspring. And not just their offspring, but all Turks today are implicated in a crime they could not have possibly perpetrated. Adding to the injustice and farce, they are implicated not in a court of law, but by *ad hoc* resolutions passed by members of parliament or municipal councils, most of whom, it can be safely assumed, possess very little legal knowledge regarding the crime of genocide. It is safer to assume they possess even less substantive knowledge regarding the complicated history surrounding the events of 1915.[747]

As damning, Turkey's future and that of its citizens is directly affected by these resolutions. For example, when European Union membership negotiations were opened with Turkey in 2005, a European Parliamentary resolution was passed that specifically stated, "The European Parliament calls on Turkey to recognize the Armenian genocide [and] considers this recognition to be a prerequisite for accession to the European Union."[748] As noted in a previous chapter, this was preceded, in 1999, when *Euro-Arménie ASBL* and two French-Armenians applied to an EU Court for "compensation for the harm caused to them by, inter alia, recognition of Turkey's status as a candidate for accession to the European Union, although that State has refused to acknowledge the genocide perpetrated in 1915 against the Armenians living in Turkey."[749]

---

[747] See Şükrü M. Elekdağ. "An Assessment of Armenian Claims from the Perspective of International Law." In *War and Collapse: World War I and the Ottoman State.* M. Hakan Yavuz and Feroz Ahmed, eds. (Salt Lake City: University of Utah Press, 2016).

[748] "European Parliament Resolution on the Opening of Negotiations with Turkey." *The Armenian Genocide Museum-Institute, National Academy of Sciences of the Republic of Armenia.* http://www.genocide-museum.am/eng/European_Parliament_Resolution.php

[749] Tuncel, 7.

A crucial but suspect claim of the current campaign states that the Armenian Genocide must be recognized universally, particularly by Turkey, in order to protect others from a similar fate. There is an unequivocal and inherent understanding in the Armenian diaspora that genocide must not be allowed to occur again, to anyone. As such, Armenian diaspora lobbies and interest groups, to include grassroots civil society groups, work to prevent atrocities that may or may not constitute the crime of genocide, regardless of location or form.

As noble as the efforts of the Armenian diaspora and their lobbies may have been in the prevention of genocides or other atrocities, it is difficult to demonstrate the logical connection between Turkish recognition of the Armenian Genocide and preventing future genocides. For example, how would the acceptance of responsibility by the Turkish government for the events of 1915 have acted as a brake on the calculations of Serbians or Rwandan Hutus? No studies have conclusively answered this type of question, though Thomas Cushman highlighted, by utilizing examples of positivism and the philosophy of Auguste Comte, the ever-present "… problem of how to get from knowing to the point of exerting power over human imperfection and evil through the act of prevention."[750]

Taken a step further, it can be theoretically argued, based on the evidence, that the Armenian campaign for genocide recognition and the accompanying *ad hoc* resolutions with their definitional elasticity have undermined the sanctity, validity and importance of both the UN Convention for the Prevention of Genocide and the very term "genocide." This is no doubt an unintentional and unexpected consequence and should in no way impugn or denigrate the valiant, humane and important work that has been accomplished by the Armenian diaspora and their lobbies in promoting the idea of humanitarian intervention by states to prevent the slaughter of innocents. Nonetheless, it is an extremely

---

[750] Thomas Cushman. "Is genocide preventable? Some theoretical considerations." *Journal of Genocide Research* 5, no. 4 (2003): 528.

important consequence with major, indeed damning, implications.

CONCLUSION

Deep linguistic, geographic, religious and political differences all conspire to divide rather than unite Armenians. The campaign for recognition of the Armenian Genocide represents the glue that bonds Armenians together. It alone has the power to mobilize heterogeneous Armenians, particularly those of the diaspora. In order to gain an understanding of the campaign for Armenian Genocide recognition, an understanding of Armenian identity is critical. Accordingly, this book has attempted to explore how Armenian and Armenian diaspora identities have developed in relation to the events of 1915. By doing so, the absolute significance of the massacres and deportations of Ottoman Armenians becomes relevant as it relates to the Armenian Genocide campaign, informed by both the victim and survivor identities of today's Armenian diaspora. Indeed, based on the data, this identity and the identity-driven campaign are assessed to be mutually constitutive, reinforcing one another. This is the key reason that a cessation of the campaign by the diaspora remains next to impossible. In addition, and as highlighted throughout this book, Armenian diaspora identity in relation to the events of 1915 is crucial for understanding the Armenian diaspora's mixed relationship with the Republic of Armenia, its citizens and vice versa.

Problematic as it may be, the campaign for Armenian Genocide recognition has been relatively successful - at least in terms of convincing the overall court of public opinion that the events of 1915 constituted the Armenian Genocide. Regardless of the campaign's positive, spin-off contributions, such as calling attention to the seemingly genocidal events in Darfur and elsewhere, its successes are those that come from the propagation of a politicized history and corresponding attempts to legislate reality. Simply put, the campaign for Armenian Genocide recognition is historically inaccurate because it is based on ideological representations of events that occurred over one century ago. These ideological representations are then packaged in a highly politicized manner for political purposes.

The campaign, as currently constituted, is also flawed in that it actively undermines the strict legal definition and, therefore, legitimacy of the UN Convention on the Prevention and Punishment of the Crime of Genocide of 1948. It does so, first and foremost, through the wanton application of the term "genocide;" not only in relation to the events of 1915, but to other instances of atrocities, thus challenging established definitions and legal norms. Additionally, by doing so, the campaign not only allows, but encourages the rather elastic and, indeed, frivolous usage of the term genocide for largely political purposes. This is not only short-sighted, but has the consequence of further undermining the UN Convention. It may also complicate the ability of various international courts to punish actual genocide perpetrators.

An understanding of the campaign for Armenian Genocide recognition is important on account of its potentially massive geopolitical and economic ramifications. Indeed, the campaign as fought in the legislative halls of Washington, D.C., London and Paris, has direct effects on the Republic of Armenia, particularly vis-à-vis its relations with its neighbors. This has major implications for Armenia and Armenians, presently and in the uncertain future that is dawning in the South Caucasus. The campaign also deeply affects the Republic of Turkey's current relations with its allies, enemies and neighbors. Turkey's future and that of its inhabitants - Turks, Kurds, Circassians, Jews and Armenians - is also deeply affected, adversely in the case of Turkey's potential European Union membership. Regardless of Turkey's current desire or lack thereof to become a member of this "Christian club," the campaign's unequivocal demands that Turkey recognize the events of 1915 as the Armenian Genocide have impacted accession talks. Many EU member states, to include powerful members such as France, have parroted verbatim the Armenian campaign's demand that Turkey recognize the Armenian Genocide.

Turkey and its citizens are, accordingly, held hostage on socio-economic and political fronts by the Armenian campaign.

Viewed in this light, it is the firm assessment of this book that the campaign has been largely successful in one key area: branding Turkey, at least in the eyes of Western public opinion, as a genocidal nation. Yet, this too has been done by a flawed and highly politicized process. The campaign eschews, by both design and necessity, the legal pathways and norms established in the 1948 UN Convention. Rather, the campaign has managed to blacklist Turkey through *ad hoc* legislative or other acts, acts informed by Armenian large group identity (Armenian Self versus Turkish Other). These official statements or acts are passed by politicians who remain largely uninformed regarding this extremely complex and emotive issue. As such, they are passed, like most legislation, for purely political motivations and purposes.

In the foreseeable future, is there a possible resolution to this deeply disturbing, disputed history and the campaign and polemics it has spawned? This appears to be in the realm of the almost impossible. Yet, perhaps measures taken by parties other than the Armenian diaspora should be considered. For example, the historical record remains a bone of contention. Depending on the results of their research, multiple scholars have found themselves aligned, willingly or unwillingly, in either the "Armenian" or "Turkish" camp. Lack of access to archives on multiple continents has exacerbated the acrimony.

Current restrictions on access to the Ottoman Archives in Istanbul, those of the Turkish General Staff and others need to be lifted. This should not be done simply to dissipate some of the damage done by the Armenian diaspora campaign's rhetoric, but because it is the right thing to do. If history is simply to be left to historians, as multiple governments in Ankara have repeatedly stated, these same historians - regardless of nationality, ethnicity or bias - should be allowed free and easy access to all relevant archival holdings in Turkey. For example, the political scientist, Guenther Lewy, noted with concern that when the

Turkish Foreign Ministry announced the opening of the Ottoman Archives in 1989, a scant nine percent of the documents had been cataloged.[751] Access to the archives appear to be restricted, as well. According to accusations by both Vahakn Dadrian and Ara Sarafian, scholars who are sympathetic to the "Turkish thesis" of the events of 1915 such as Stanford Shaw, Justin McCarthy and Kemal Karpat, have been allowed unfettered access to the archives. Others, to include Armenians such as themselves, are harassed and allowed only limited access.[752] The military historian, Edward J. Erickson, among others, complained about the sorry state of affairs at the extensive archives of the Turkish General Staff. "Only a fraction of the massive Turkish archival holdings is available to researchers, and these are carefully controlled by the Turkish authorities."[753] Ottoman historian, Erik Jan Zürcher complained that the archives were largely closed to foreigners as well as most Turkish scholars.[754] In this case, "It is not the Armenian diaspora that is hampering the future of Turkish-Armenian relations. Rather, it is the sad fact that historians are being harassed by illiberal prosecutors, denied entry to Turkish archives and targeted by zealous nationalist activists."[755]

Clearly, free and easy access to the Turkish archives for all scholars, regardless of what is found or not found, is necessary not only as a major confidence-building measure but also to support the Turkish government's stance that history really should be left to historians. This process is two-pronged: the archives need to be thoroughly cataloged *and* access granted to all scholars – as it should be in any

---

[751] Lewy, 132.

[752] See Vahakn N. Dadrian. "Ottoman Archives and Denial of the Armenian Genocide." In *The Armenian Genocide: History, Politics, Ethics.* Hovannisian, Richard G., ed. (New York: St. Martin's Press, 1992): 303. See also Ara Sarafian. "The Issue of Access to Ottoman Archives." *Zeitschrift für Türkeistudien*, (1993), 98.

[753]. Lewy, 133.

[754] Ibid.

[755] Kerem Öktem. "A response to Norman Stone." *The Economist*, June 21-27, 2008, 24.

setting where free and unfettered access to information is considered a right - regardless of their biases and what they hope to prove. As in any research project, information may be found that may be unpalatable or disprove previously held hypotheses. This could represent the closest approximation of a definitive end to the dispute regarding history, semantics and identity. Yet, even assuming that full archival access is granted, not only Istanbul, but in Berlin, Moscow, Boston and elsewhere, it is difficult to see how scholarship could sway one side or the other to abandon their cherished positions. This is particularly true vis-a-vis the Armenian campaign as it mutually reinforces Armenian diaspora large group identity.

In the end, however, "History is not about the reification of events, but about processes, causation, integrating events in what came before and what followed. If using legal concepts [such as genocide] to define crimes become the only valid language with which to discuss the past, we not only deny ourselves historical understanding but, moreover, make any reciprocal debate impossible by creating a huge and partially legitimate sense of injustice."[756] In short, the historical must be separated from the political. "This requires independent and high quality historical scholarship. It is apparent that those who… have not [even] taken a look at the map of Anatolia once and yet dare to write a book on the 'Armenian genocide,' and certain international associations of 'genocide scholars' composed of researchers who have built their carriers to prove what they believe to be the truth, cannot contribute to this cause."[757]

Continued non-recognition - or denial, in the campaign's preferred parlance - of the events of 1915 as the Armenian Genocide by Turkey appears a *sine qua non*. There will be no breakthrough on this front. This is because Turkey has understandable and highly valid reasons to dispute the historical record as utilized by the Armenian diaspora and its campaign. Turkey's characterization, no matter how

---

[756] Lagrou, 285.
[757] Tuncel, 13.

obtuse and how often parroted, that the events of 1915 constituted "mutual massacres," is valid and based on sound, non-political records, particularly demographic records. The irony, if there is one, with the Armenian campaign for genocide recognition is that Ottoman Armenians are guilty of crimes against Ottoman Muslims equal to or surpassing those of the crimes committed against Armenians by Muslims during the years 1914-1918. The Armenians who avoided deportation by operating behind enemy lines in active rebellion against the Ottoman state and under the protection of Russian troops, left eastern Anatolia a graveyard when they finally fled advancing Ottoman troops at the end of the war. As noted in chapter two, Captain Emory Niles and Mr. Arthur Sunderland, during the course of their investigation of eastern Anatolia on behalf of the United States government and to inform relief efforts of the American Committee for Near East Relief (ACNRE), provided one of the few eyewitness and unbiased accounts of the reality of the situation. "At first we were most incredulous of the stories told us, but the unanimity of the testimony of all the witnesses, the apparent eagerness with which they told of wrongs done them, their evident hatred of Armenians, and, strongest of all, the material evidence on the ground itself, have convinced us of the general truth of the facts, first, that Armenians massacred Musulmans [Muslims] on a large scale with many refinements of cruelty, and second that that Armenians are responsible for most of the destruction done to towns and villages [in eastern Anatolia]... In 1917 the Russian Army disbanded and left the Armenians alone in control. At this period bands of Armenian irregulars roamed the country pillaging and murdering the Musulman civilian population. When the Turkish army advanced... the Armenian broke down and all of the soldiers, regular and irregular, turned themselves to destroying Musulman property and committing atrocities upon Musulman inhabitants. The result is a country completely ruined, containing about one-fourth of its former population and one-eighth of its former buildings, and a most bitter hatred of Musulmans and Armenians which makes it impossible for the two races to live together at the present time... This view is shared by Turkish officers, British officers, and Americans whom we have met."[758]

Given the traumas suffered by Ottoman Muslims throughout the century preceding the birth of the Republic of Turkey at the hands of Armenians, Greeks and foreign powers, any prospect of Turkey's territorial dismemberment, through recognition or other means – no matter how remote – remains anathema. As such, and given the historical and demographic record that validates in the extreme the reality of "mutual massacres," Turkey will not recognize the events of 1915 as the Armenian Genocide. Nor should it.

The suspension of the Armenian diaspora's campaign appears equally unlikely. The campaign is identity-driven and represents the cohesive bond that undergirds a sense of diaspora Armenian and, indeed, Armenian unity. Regardless of the veracity of the narrative, Armenian diaspora identity rests firmly on ideological representations of the events of 1915 as perpetrated by Ottoman Turks. To Armenians of the diaspora, the Turks of today are simply an extension of yesteryear's Ottoman Turks; a monolithic population of genocide perpetrators. Turkey's continued "denial" of the Armenian Genocide, maddening as it may be for the campaign's supporters, is actually required because Turkey's denial mutually reinforces Armenian diaspora identity and drums up support for the campaign.

In parrying the campaign's advances, Turkey has often acted as its own worst enemy. The Turkish government's unwillingness to accept Armenian diaspora claims *prima facie* is one element that may be forgiven on account of the outright politicization of history, definitional elasticity and *ad hoc* legislation that are the fodder of the Armenian Genocide campaign. However, needlessly simplistic and obtuse "official" historiography, harmful rhetoric and

---

[758] Niles and Sutherland Report, as quoted in McCarthy. *Death and Exile*, 228.

accompanying violence (to include murder) perpetrated by Turkish nationalists, and the Turkish government's overall reluctance to simply discuss the issue, all reinforce the stereotype the image of the "terrible Turk" in Armenian diaspora identity and memory. It should be noted that the behavior also reinforces long-held stereotypes, no matter how erroneous, outdated and racist, of the "terrible Turk" in the West and in Russia.

The highly political Turkish blockade of Armenia, though only partially connected to the issue of the Armenian Genocide campaign, is bandied about by the diaspora and the Republic of Armenia in equally political terms, and as further proof of Turkey's desire to extinguish Armenian civilization. In essence, the blockades of Turkey and its Turkic cousins in Azerbaijan are viewed as extensions of the massacres and deportations that occurred in 1915.

This dim view is reciprocated by Turks, many of whom have formed their own, arguably nuanced, albeit distrustful opinion of Armenians. Turks generally view the Armenian diaspora in a particularly bad light, based on its actions to sanction and isolate Turkey. Constant pressure by the Armenian diaspora to gain *ad hoc* resolutions labeling contested historical events as the Armenian Genocide also strongly rankles the government of Turkey and its citizens. Reactions to various French, Swiss and EU resolutions criminalizing the denial of what it has termed the Armenian Genocide have been particularly vociferous and negative.

For all the damage the diaspora's campaign has done to Turkish-Armenian relations, there have arguably been some positive outcomes. For example, references in Turkish textbooks to the massacres, deportations and the subsequent death and disappearance of the vast majority of Ottoman Armenians in 1915 remain glossed over and explained away. Yet, Turks are increasingly aware of the atrocities committed over a century ago – and many are prepared to acknowledge them and attempt to make amends, albeit in a different manner than that demanded by the diaspora. There is a direct, causal link between the Armenian diaspora campaign and *ad hoc* resolutions it has spawned and the fact that so many Turks are now conscious of the events of 1915. This is a favorable development in that it has led to further discussion in Turkey on issues that range from access to the Ottoman Archives to arguments over what degree of responsibility Turkey bears for the atrocities committed against Ottoman Armenians even as the discussion necessarily references the atrocities committed by Armenians against Ottoman Muslims – a historical fact that the Armenian campaign patently ignores. These conversations and debates also touch on issues of fundamental freedoms and human rights in Turkey and the region. The ways in which Turkey and its population deal with such prescient and weighty issues are a direct reflection of its democratic credentials or, alternatively, its authoritarian tendencies.

Given the Armenian diaspora's unyielding, identity-driven campaign and Turkish intransigence, might a state-to-state solution be possible? Unfortunately, the overall lack of a breakthrough in Armenia-Turkey relations is complicated by various geopolitical considerations, notably Nagorno-Karabakh and the presence of Russian troops in Armenia. There is also a state-state (Republic of Armenia – Republic of Turkey) and a nation - nation (Armenian - Turkish) component that further complicates the issue. Indeed, the Republic of Turkey has experienced close to one century of statehood and state-building while the Republic of Armenia has only begun dealing with the significant challenges of state-building over the past two decades. On the one hand, Turkey can be characterized as a state – nation, "… where the state (as exemplified by the rules of governance and priorities set by those rules) is the basis for the common culture it creates."[759] On the other hand, Armenia can be categorized as a nation – state; that is, a state peopled by a homogeneous or largely homogeneous ethnic group.[760]

[759] Juan Linz, Alfred Stepan, and Yogendra Yadav. "'Nation State' Or 'State Nation'? India in Comparative Perspective." *Democracy and diversity: India and the American experience* (2007): 53-54.
[760] Ibid.

However, Armenia is unlike the average nation-state, particularly in its efforts to create a common culture. This is because the state is every bit as important as the Armenian nation, writ large, in this effort. There is the Armenian state, a legal entity recognized by international law and treaties; an entity largely accountable for its actions on the world stage. Yet, there is also the Armenian nation, which includes the three million inhabitants of the Republic of Armenia as well as the approximately eight million diaspora Armenians. Given its relative wealth and larger population, the diaspora represents a trans-state entity that is not legally recognized by other states, yet invested with multiple nodes of power, money and influence. Given these complications, the challenge of policy-making for the Republic of Armenia and its residents is complicated and fraught. In addition, the Republic of Armenia's policy objectives as a state and those of the Armenian nation, particularly the diaspora, often differ. This may be just as much a result of physical space (distance) as differing large group histories (Armenian versus Armenian diaspora), which have produced identities and perceived realities that manifest themselves, on occasion, in opposition to one another. In this peculiar situation, the centrality of the Armenian Genocide narrative and corresponding campaign to Armenian diaspora identity is neither reciprocated in every instance nor in the same fashion by the Armenian state. This necessarily leads to conflicting state-state, nation-state and nation-nation interactions. Thus, the realities of the Armenian state and the choices it faces vis-à-vis its foreign relations, domestic policy and future may very much be at odds with that of the Armenian nation, writ large, in the form of the Armenian diaspora.

Paths of Engagement

The Armenian diaspora's campaign for genocide recognition relies largely on what can be termed vertical pressure, while Turkey has employed what can be termed horizontal pressure, emphasizing state-state (Armenia-

Turkey) relations and nation-nation (Armenian-Turkish) relations in an effort to sideline the Armenian diaspora. As demonstrated in chapter nine, both approaches are flawed as interaction or negotiation would likely be more constructive than either vertical or horizontal pressure. Furthermore, the diaspora's application of vertical pressure is theoretically and methodologically flawed in the assumption that overwhelming pressure from *ad hoc* announcements and legislative acts will eventually coerce Turkey to recognize the Armenian Genocide.

There is another option. Assuming horizontal interactions between Turkey and Armenia increase or, at least, stabilize, a "diagonal" or multilateral set of interactions is also possible. "The basic premise of diagonal relations is confidence building measures by both states to attract people on the opposite side of the 'divide.'"[761] The hope held out by diagonal interactions is that they would somehow create a positive atmosphere through confidence-building measures, thus bringing Armenians and Turks together in a form of constructive dialogue. Whether members of the Armenian diaspora would take part, at least at the beginning stages of such a dialogue, remains to be seen. However, as mentioned above, there are promising signs - along with the usual blustering from both Yerevan and Ankara - that the issue of genocide recognition, far from being "solved," can take a back seat in the context of Armenian-Turkish relations.

Polling performed in Armenia in 2015 reflects a firm desire for change – unlike their diaspora counterparts - vis-à-vis relations with Turkey.[762] Though Turkey's recognition of the Armenian Genocide was rated very important by a majority of the Armenians polled, it rated on the same level as improved ties with Turkey.[763] Furthermore, Armenians

---

[761] Kotchikian.
[762] *Towards a Shared Vision of Normalization of Armenian-Turkish Relations: Draft Report.* Caucasus Research Resource Center – Armenia: Yerevan, April 2015.
[763] Ibid, 24-25.

gave priority to cultural and economic ties rather than overt political or diplomatic ties.[764] This is potentially promising, in that economic and cultural ties could be developed between Armenia and Turkey prior to the establishment of full diplomatic relations. As the report noted, "Generally speaking, the potential agenda for Armenian-Turkish relations is not only rich, but also has embedded factors that are contentious, complicating the normalization process. Security issues and Genocide keep [Armenian] respondents away from approving normalization [with Turkey], while economic factors push them towards approval."[765]

There are significant obstacles to the betterment and normalization of relations from the Turkish side. Turkey refuses to establish formal ties with the Republic of Armenia, insisting that Armenia first take confidence-building measures such as striking out claims to Turkish territory in the Armenian constitution. As discussed previously, these claims are problematic, given that Turkey's recognition of the events of 1915 as the Armenian Genocide opens up the possibility of reparations and return of property and lands. It would also contradict an ever-increasing body of international scholarship that categorically refutes claims that the events of 1915 constituted an Armenian Genocide. Yet, the claims made in the Armenian Constitution are exacerbated in that diaspora Armenians and Armenians are interested in precisely these possibilities. A full 28 percent of Armenians polled in 2015 supported the restoration of territorial rights (returning land) at the expense of Turkey. Another nine percent supported some sort of financial compensation. Only six percent wished to see Turkey formally apologize for its role in the massacres and deportations of 1915.[766]

This is obviously a major impediment to the normalization of Armenia-Turkey ties, let alone some sort of resolution to the emotive issue at hand. Indeed, Armenians understood

---

[764] Ibid.

[765] Ibid, 27.

[766] Ibid, 23.

that the possibility of Turkey's recognition of the Armenian Genocide, and hence reparations and return, was slim at best. When asked whether they believed Turkey would recognize the Armenian Genocide in the next five to ten years, 65 percent of Armenian respondents found this either absolutely or rather impossible.[767] Furthermore, only seven percent assessed that an intensification of international events aimed at recognition of the Armenian Genocide by both Armenia and the Armenian diaspora would result in Turkey's recognition.[768] A paltry five percent of Armenian respondents saw any efficacy with the diaspora lobbying campaign vis-à-vis possible Turkish recognition.[769]

Turkish politicians and, indeed, the overwhelmingly majority of Turkey's public, continue to show solidarity with Azerbaijan and insist that Armenia and Azerbaijan solve the Nagorno-Karabakh issue first. Furthermore, the Turkish public still exhibits an overwhelmingly negative attitude (85 percent) towards Armenia.[770] Unfortunately, and despite the glimmers of hope for possible reconciliation discussed above, this mirrors the attitude of Armenians towards Turkey, where a full 70 percent of respondents "completely agreed" that Turkey could not be trusted.[771]

What of the Armenian diaspora? Consumed with their campaign of Armenian Genocide recognition, the diaspora eschews and discourages any dialogue with Turkey and Turks on the issue. In reality, this is the crux of the matter. Armenian diaspora identity, such as it is, necessarily demonizes Turks and Turkey as a genocide-perpetrators. Because of this intransigence, the diaspora is both benefactor and bane for the Republic of Armenia. Armenian politicians rely on powerful diaspora Armenian

---

[767] Ibid, 24.

[768] Ibid.

[769] Ibid.

[770] *Turkish Perceptions Survey 2015.* The German Marshall Fund of the United States, 2015: 5.
http://www.gmfus.org/listings/research/type/publication

[771] *Towards a Shared Vision of Normalization of Armenian-Turkish Relations: Draft Report*, 21.

lobbies and interest groups to persuade Western governments of the importance of Armenia strategically and politically. Aid, loans and military hardware procured from the West through constant Armenian diaspora lobbying efforts all support Armenia's quest to remain a viable, independent and sovereign nation state. But Armenia, by geographic and historic fate, is Turkey's neighbor. Both countries and people share a history, often forgotten, that predates 1915 and the simplistic relationship of oppressor and oppressed. The unalloyed truth is that Armenia needs Turkey much more than Turkey will ever need Armenia. Armenia requires Turkish goods, trade, open borders, and regional cooperation. The viability of the Republic of Armenia is possible without a rapprochement with Turkey, but a long-term, stable and sovereign Armenia is much more desirable. Turkey holds at least one of the keys to regional peace or, at very least, non-aggression between Armenian and Azerbaijan. Certain politicians and much of the Armenian population are aware of this. But reliance on the Armenian diaspora, with their constant emphasis on genocide recognition and abiding dislike and mistrust of Turkey, for aid, arms, and leverage in the West has led to a far larger stumbling block than the unresolved issue of Nagorno-Karabakh in Armenia-Turkey relations. Only through positive confidence-building measures emanating from both Ankara and Yerevan will the myths and stereotypes built up by the ideological representations of memory, history and politics leading to decades of non-interaction be broken. "Humiliating one state internationally and intentionally does not help dissipate the effects of propaganda, and prevents from building a strong foundation on which multilateral relations could develop."[772]

Conferences, free and easy access to archives, tourism, academic and cultural exchanges and a strengthening of economic ties, in effect making Turkey and Armenia indispensable to one another, could all be considered

[772] Kotchikian.

confidence-building measures with a chance, albeit small, of overcoming decades of mistrust, mutual humiliation and non-interaction. The development of social capital and perhaps the formation of significant and lasting bonds between individuals and groups in both countries holds out the potential of making it increasingly difficult for the Self, Armenian or Turkish, to objectify and dehumanize the Other. Of course, all this will take bold men and women, both Turks and Armenians, to happen. Armenian society, especially in the wake of the controversial occupation of Nagorno-Karabakh, the accompanying cold war with Azerbaijan and the Turkish embargo, has banded together against "the Turk." Threatened, the group has defined itself narrowly and sharply, distinguishing itself from its perceived enemies.[773] Attempts to mend the fissures and disagreements within Armenian society and improve national unity were accomplished with diaspora support for politicians who refused to make concessions with Azerbaijan on Nagorno-Karabakh. At the same time, popular images of Azeris and Turks increasingly coincide simply as "Turks," and are tied to the diaspora's systematic and politicized exploitation of the events of 1915. The diaspora's campaign of genocide recognition is recognized as the one link that unites, or is supposed to unite, Armenians worldwide. With the events of 1915 "…being central to Armenian [diaspora] nationalism, it is also believed to slow the assimilation of the young generations of diaspora Armenians and improve their attachment to the Armenian homeland."[774]

In conclusion, it appears that the solution or list of solutions rests firmly with two states: Armenia and Turkey - not with the Armenian diaspora. Issues such as Turkey's blockade of Armenia, diplomatic relations, trade and cultural issues, and the Nagorno-Karabakh issue as an

---

[773] Mack, 124.

[774] Emil Souleimanov. "The Politics of France's Criminalization of Genocide Denial." *Central Asia-Caucasus Institute*, October 18, 2006. http://old.cacianalyst.org/?q=node/4253

Armenian-Azeri issue rather than a Turkey/Armenia/Azerbaijan issue can all be handled on a state-to-state level. However, in the case of the campaign for Armenian Genocide recognition, the Armenian diaspora remains unequivocal and unmovable. Therefore, any attempt at dialogue, which does not address this issue - the fundamental cornerstone of diaspora identity - will fail to enlist the support of the large, vocal, and influential Armenian diaspora. The Armenian diaspora has insisted on nothing short of recognition by Turkey that the events of 1915 constituted the Armenian Genocide - with all the legal and moral ramifications that recognition entails. Because their identity demands precisely this, compromise with Turkey and the Turks is viewed as failure, looked on with opprobrium and remains decidedly uncountenanced.

In the end, the diaspora campaign - much to Turkey's chagrin - has been successful in that the fruits of their significant labor, the *ad hoc*, often official or semi-official and very public proclamations, legislation, speeches and commemorations all categorically define the events of 1915 as the Armenian Genocide. As highlighted, this makes Turkey, in much of the world's public opinion, a genocide-perpetrating nation. Thus, in return for a semblance of closure and dignity for Armenians, more than a semblance of Turkish dignity is lost as it joins the ranks of genocide-perpetrating peoples and nations without the benefit of a criminal case and ruling. The accusation of a crime leveled by an individual or party against another does not constitute proof of guilt, however. Yet, contradicting a solid body of scholarship based on archival sources, this is precisely what the campaign for Armenian Genocide recognition has accomplished, bypassing legal hurdles and grasping at legislation and statements based on a highly politicized and polemical history as passed in Paris, Moscow, Athens, and Bern. The legislation, formally though not legally, accuses an entire large group, the Turks, and a nation-state, Turkey, of the most serious crime known to humanity.

It is unclear how reconciliation, dignity, and closure will be achieved when the dignity of one large group's Self is enhanced only through the denigration of its Other. Yet this is the outcome of the extra-legal campaign for recognition of the Armenian Genocide, a campaign that attempts to legislate reality and politicize history. The possibility of reconciliation and resolution appears very slim indeed.

BIBLIOGRAPHY

A.A. "Fransız markaları boykot edilecek." *Hürriyet*, October 12, 2006. http://www.hurriyet.com.tr/fransiz-markalari-boykot-edilecek-5246217

AAINC. "2005 Annual Report." *Armenian Assembly of America.* http://www.aaainc.org/fileadmin/aaainc/pdf/Annual_Reports/AAA_Annual_Report_2005.pdf

AAINC. "Armenian Genocide Affirmation." *Armenian Assembly of America.* http://www.aaainc.org/index.php?id=114

AAINC. "Issue Brief: Armenian Genocide Affirmation." *Armenian Assembly of America.* http://www.aaainc.org/index.php?id=114&type=98

AAINC, "Our Mission: To Lead." *Armenian Assembly of America.* http://www.aaainc.org/assembly/mission.php (accessed March 2, 2016).

"About Us," *Armenian Network of America Inc.* http://www.armnet.org/about_us

"About Us." *Terror Free Tomorrow.* http://www.terrorfreetomorrow.org/template.php?section=AU

"About Us." *Turkish Coalition USA Political Action Committee.* http://www.tenthousandturks.org/index.php?option=com_content&view=article&id=23&Itemid=3

Abrahamyan, Gayane. "Debating Big Brother's Presence: Concerns linger of Armenia as 'Outpost.'" *ArmeniaNow.com* 44, no. 254. (2007)

http://www.armenianow.com/?action=viewArticle&AID=2579

Adanır, Fikret. "Armenian Deportations and Massacres in 1915." *Ethnopolitical Warfare: Causes, Consequences, and Possible Solutions*. Washington, D.C: American Psychological Association, 2001.

Adanır, Fikret. "Nicht-muslimische Eliten im Osmanischen Reich." *Eliten in Südosteuropa: Rolle, Kontinuitäten, Brüche in Geschichte und Gegenwart*. Munich: Südosteuropa-Gesellschaft, 1998.

Adıvar, Halide Edip. *Turkey Faces West: A Turkish View of Recent Changes and Their Origins*. New Haven: Yale University Press, 1930.

Affirmation of the United States Record on the Armenian Genocide." *US House Resolution 106*. (110th Congress, 1st Session). http://www.thomas.gov/cgi-bin/query/z?c110:H.RES.106

"After the War." *The Economist*, October 18, 2008.

Ahmad, Feroz. "Unionist Relations with the Greek, Armenian and Jewish Communities of the Ottoman Empire, 1908-1914." *Christians and Jews in the Ottoman Empire: The Functioning of a Plural Society*. New York: Holmes and Meier, 1982.

Aitken, Paul A. "Attack/Affect: System of a Down and Genocide Activism." *MUSICultures* 38 (2013).

Akçam, Taner. *A Shameful Act: The Armenian Genocide and the Question of Turkish Responsibility*. New York: Macmillan, 2006.

Akçam, Taner. *Der Völkermord an den Armeniern*. Hamburger Institut für Sozialforschung, 1995.

Akçam, Taner. *From Empire to Republic: Turkish Nationalism and the Armenian Genocide.* Zed Books, 2004.

Akgönül, Samim. "The Armenian Community of France and Turkey: Propaganda and Lobbyism," *Review of Armenian Studies*, Vol. 1, No. 3, 2003.

Akopian, Tigran. *Political Violence in Armenia (Sources, Public Perception, Ways to Overcome the Problem).* Central Asia and the Caucasus Press. No. 5 (17), 2002.

Aktan, Gündüz. "How Shameful (1) (On Armenian Issue)." *The Journal of Turkish Weekly*, April 2, 2005. http://www.turkishweekly.net/2005/04/02/op-ed/how-shameful-1-on-armenian-issue/

Akyol, Taha. "The 'genocide decision' of France's Constitutional Council." *Hürriyet*, January 12, 2016. http://www.hurriyetdailynews.com/the-genocide-decision-of-frances-constitutional-council-.aspx?PageID=238&NID=93720&NewsCatID=458

Alayarian, Aida. *Consequences of Denial: The Armenian Genocide.* Karnac Books, 2008.

Alexander, Benjamin F. *Armenian and American: The Changing Face of Ethnic Identity and Diasporic Nationalism, 1915-1955.* Ph.D. diss., The City University of New York, 2005.

Alexander, Jeffrey C. (ed.) *Cultural Trauma and Collective Identity.* Berkeley, CA: University of California Press, 2004.

Alexander, Jeffrey C. "On the Social Construction of Moral Universals: The Holocaust from War Crime to Trauma Drama." In *Cultural Trauma and Collective Identity.* Berkeley, CA: University of California Press, 2004.

Alexander, Jeffrey C. "Towards a Theory of Cultural Trauma." In *Cultural Trauma and Collective Identity*. Berkeley, CA: University of California Press, 2004.

Alexander, June Granatir. *Ethnic Pride, American Patriotism: Slovaks and Other New Immigrants in the Interwar Era.* Philadelphia, PA: Temple University Press, 2004.

Alonso, Ana Maria. "The Politics of Space, Time and Substance: State Formation, Nationalism, and Ethnicity." *Annual Review of Anthropology* 23, 1994: 388.

"ANC of South Florida Will Take Part in Genocide Prevention Project." *Pan Armenian*, March 27, 2009. http://www.armeniandiaspora.com/showthread.php?163981-ANC-Of-South-Florida-Will-Take-Part-In-Genocide-Prevention-Project

ANCA. "10th Annual ANCA Armenian Genocide Observance on Capitol Hill Draws 40 Members of Congress." *Armenian National Committee of America.* May 5, 2004. https://anca.org/press-release/10th-annual-anca-armenian-genocide-observance-on-capitol-hill-draws-40-members-of-congress/

ANCA. "About the ANCA." *Armenian National Committee of America* http://www.anca.org/ancaprofile.php

ANCA. "French Senate approves Armenian Genocide Recognition," *Armenian National Committee of America*, 08 November 2000. https://anca.org/press-release/french-senate-approves-armenian-genocide-resolution/

ANCA, "Italian Parliament Calls on Turkey to End Armenian Genocide Denial," *Armenian National Committee of America*, November 17, 2000. https://anca.org/press-release/italian-parliament-calls-on-turkeyto-end-armenian-genocide-denial/

ANCA. "Key Legislation." *Armenian National Committee of America.* https://anca.org/key-legislation/

ANCA. "Position Papers: US Aid to Armenia." *Armenian National Committee of America.* https://anca.org/press-release/anca-publishes-position-papers-on-key-armenian-american-concerns/

Anderson, Benedict. *Imagined Communities.* London: Verso, 1983.

"Anti-Armenian Aspirations of Turkey toppled in France." *Armenpress,* January 8, 2016. http://armenpress.am/eng/news/831385/anti-armenian-aspirations-of-turkey-toppled-in-france.html

Arısan, Mehmet. "Eternal Sunshine of an Obscure Mind": World War I, the Imperial Collapse, and Trauma Management in the New Turkish Republic." In *War and Collapse: World War I and the Ottoman State.* M. Hakan Yavuz and Feroz Ahmed, eds. (Salt Lake City: University of Utah Press, 2016).

"Armenia clamps down after Post-Election Violence," *New York Times.* March 2, 2008. http://www.nytimes.com/2008/03/02/world/europe/02iht-armenia.4.10626008.html?_r=0

"Armenia Country Brief, 2007." *World Bank Group: Europe and Central Asia.* 2007.

"Armenia fraud claims mar referendum on constitution." *BBC.* December 17, 2015. http://www.bbc.com/news/world-europe-35025853

"Armenia makes Centenary call for Turkey to recognise 1915 killings as genocide." *Centenary News.* February 9, 2015. http://www.centenarynews.com/article/armenia-makes-centenary-call-for-turkey-to-recognise-1915-killings-as-genocide

"Armenia: The Demographic-Economic Framework of Migration, the Legal Framework of Migration, the Socio-Political Framework of Migration." *MPC – MIGRATION POLICY CENTRE*, (June 2013).

"Armenian Declaration of Independence." *The Government of the Republic of Armenia.* http://www.gov.am/en/independence/

"Armenian National Study." *International Republican Institute*, January 13-20, 2008.

Arnesen, Eric. "Racism in the Nation's Service: Government Workers and the Color Line in Woodrow Wilson's America." *The Journal of Southern History* 80, no. 4 (2014): 1006.

Artinian, Vartin. *The Armenian Constitutional System in the Ottoman Empire, 1839*
1863. Istanbul, 1988.

Ash, Timothy Garton. "A Blanket Ban on Holocaust Denial would be a serious Mistake." *The Guardian,* January 18, 2007. http://www.theguardian.com/commentisfree/2007/jan/18/comment.secondworldwar

Atamian, Sarkis. *The Armenian Community: The Historical Development of a Social and Ideological Conflict.* New York: Philosophical Library, 1955.

Ataöv, Türkkaya, "The 'Armenian Question': Conflict, Trauma and Objectivity," *Ministry of Foreign Affairs, Center for Strategic Research, Republic of Turkey, SAM Papers*, no. 3 / 97 (1999).

Attallah, Maral N. *Choosing silence: The United States, Turkey, and The Armenian Genocide.* PhD diss., Humboldt State University, 2007.

Avakian, Knarik. *The History of the Armenian Community of the United States* of *America: From the Beginning to 1924*. Yerevan, Armenia: Gitutiun Publishing House, 2000.

Aydın, Mustafa. "Securitization of history and geography: understanding of security in Turkey." *Southeast European and Black Sea Studies* 3, no. 2 (2003): 163-184.

Ayvazyan, Vahram. "Genocide: Intent, Motivation and Types." *Suvremene Teme* 5, no. 1 (2012): 21-36.

Bagramyan, Kristina. *Diaspora –Enforced Identity: Construction of the Victim Identity in the Film "Ararat."* PhD diss., Central European University, 2006.

Bakalian, Anny. *Armenian-Americans: From Being to Feeling Armenian.* New Brunswick, NJ: Transaction Publishers, 1996.

Bakıner, Onur. "Is Turkey Coming to Terms with Its Past? Politics of Memory and Majoritarian Conservatism." *Nationalities Papers* 41, no. 5 (2013): 691-708.

Balakian, Peter. *The Burning Tigris: The Armenian Genocide and America's Response.* New York: HarperCollins, 2003.

Baliozian, Ara. "As I see It." *ARA Home Page.* March 19, 2008. http://baliozian.blogspot.com/

Baliozian, Ara. "Resurrection." *ARA Home Page.* March 23, 2008 http://baliozian.blogspot.com/

Bamberger, Joan. "Family and Kinship in an Armenian-American Community." *Journal of Armenian Studies*, Winter 1986-1987: 77-86.

Barsoumian, Hagop. "The Eastern Question and the Tanzimat Era." *The Armenian People: From Ancient to Modern Times; Vol. II.* New York: St. Martin's Press, 1997.

Barth, Fredrik. *Ethnic groups and boundaries: The social organization of culture difference.* Waveland Press, 1998.

Bar-Tal, Daniel. "Collective memory of physical violence: Its contribution to the culture of violence." *The Role of Memory in Ethnic Conflict.* (Houndmills, England: Palgrave Macmillan, 2003): 77-93.

Baser, Bahar, and Swain, Ashok. "Diaspora design versus homeland realities: case study of Armenian diaspora." *International Journal on World Peace* 25 (2008): 7-28.

Baumann, Timothy. "Defining ethnicity." *The SAA archaeological record* 4, no. 4 (2004): 12-14.

Beilock, Richard. "Raining on the Parade: A Critique of 'Armenia's Trade Performance in 1995-2002 and the Effect of Closed Borders: A Cross-Country Perspective." *Armenian Journal of Public Policy* 2, no. 1 (2005); 113-199.

Bell, Duncan. *Memory, Trauma and World Politics. Reflections on the Relationship between Past and Present*, London: Palgrave Macmillan (2006).

Berkes, Niyazi. *The Development of Secularism in Turkey.* Montreal: McGill University Press, 1964.

Berkowitz, Lenka, and Mügge, Liza M. "Transnational Diaspora Lobbying: Europeanization and the Kurdish Question." *Journal of Intercultural Studies* 35, no. 1 (2014): 74-90.

Beşikçi, Mehmet. *The Ottoman mobilization of manpower in the First World War: between voluntarism and resistance.* Brill, 2012.

Beşikçi, Mehmet. "When a Military Problem Became a Social Issue: Ottoman Desertions and Deserters in World War I." In *War and Collapse: World War I and the Ottoman State*. M. Hakan Yavuz and Feroz Ahmed, eds. (Salt Lake City: University of Utah Press, 2016).

Bilgin, Mert. "Turkey's Energy Strategy: Synchronizing Geopolitics and Foreign Policy with Energy Security." *Insight Turkey* 17, no. 2 (2015): 67-81.

Blaive, Muriel, and Gerbel, Christian. *Clashes in European Memory: The Case of Communist Repression and the Holocaust*. Studienverlag, 2011.

Bloxham, Donald. *The Great Game of Genocide: Imperialism, Nationalism and the Destruction of the Ottoman Armenians*. Oxford: Oxford University Press, 2005.

Boguslavska, Kateryna; Opdahl, Ingerid Maria; Kropatcheva, Elena, and Belyi, Andrei V. "Gazprom: Challenges at Home and Abroad." *Center for Security Studies*, October 26, 2015.

Boldişor, Adrian. "Human Rights in Orthodoxy and Islam: A Comparative Approach." *Review of Ecumenical Studies Sibiu* 7, no. 1 (2015): 116-133.

Boose, Lynda E. "Crossing the River Drina: Bosnian rape camps, Turkish impalement, and Serb cultural memory." *Signs* 28, no. 1 (2002): 71-96.

Bourke, Joanna. "When Torture Becomes Humdrum." *Times Higher Educational Supplement*. February 10, 2006.

Boyar, Ebru. "The Impact of the Balkan Wars on Ottoman History Writing: Searching for a Soul." *Middle East Critique* 23, no. 2 (2014): 147-156.

Bozarslan, Hamit. "The General Ottoman and Turkish Contexts: from the Tanzimat (1838) to the Suppression of the Dersim Rebellion (1938)," *Online Encyclopedia of Mass Violence.* http://www.massviolence.org/The-General-Ottoman-and-Turkish-Contexts-From-the-Tanzimat

Bozic-Roberson, Agneza. "Words before the war: Milosevic's use of mass media band rhetoric to provoke ethnopolitical conflict in former Yugoslavia (1)." *East European Quarterly* 38, no. 4 (2004): 395-409

Braude, Benjamin & Lewis, Bernard. *Christians and Jews in the Ottoman Empire: The Functioning of a Plural Society.* New York and London: Holmer & Meyer Publishers, Inc., 1982.

Browne, William P. "Organized Interests and Their Issue Niches: A Search for Pluralism in a Policy Domain." *Journal of Politics* 52 (1990): 477-509.

Bryce, James. *Transcaucasia and Ararat: Being Notes of a Vacation Tour in the Autumn of 1876.* London: MacMillan, 1896.

Bulbulian, Berge. *The Fresno Armenians: History of a Diaspora Community.* Fresno,CA: The Press at California State University, Fresno, 2000.

Buruma, Ian. "The Joys and Perils of Victimhood." *New York Review of Books* 46 (1999): 4-8.

Cairns E., and Roe, M.D. (eds.). *The Role of Memory in Ethnic Conflict.* (Houndmills, England: Palgrave Macmillan, 2003).

Çamlıbel, Cansu. "Armenia ready for normalization of ties, President Sargsyan says." *Hürriyet Daily*, April 24, 2015. http://www.hurriyetdailynews.com/armenia-ready-for-normalization-of-ties-president-sargsyan-says.aspx?pageID=238&nID=81490&NewsCatID=510

Campbell, George Douglas. *Our Responsibilities for Turkey: Facts and Memories of Forty Years.* London: John Murray, 1896.

Caruth, Cathy. "Introduction: Trauma and Experience." *Trauma: Explorations in Memory.* Baltimore, MD: Johns Hopkins University Press, 1995.

Caruth, Cathy. *Unclaimed Experience: Trauma, Narrative, and History.* London: Johns Hopkins University Press, 1996.

"Case of Perinçek v. Switzerland (Application no. 27510/08): Judgement." *European Court of Human Rights*, 17 December 2013. http://hudoc.echr.coe.int/eng?i=001-139724

Catsoulis, Jeannette. "Film in Review: Screamers," *New York Times*, January 26, 2007, http://query.nytimes.com/gst/fullpage.html?res=9B03E4DD173FF935A15752C0A9619C8B63&scp=6&sq=egoyan&st=nyt

Cengiz, Fırat, and Hoffmann, Lars. "Rethinking conditionality: Turkey's European Union accession and the Kurdish question." *JCMS: Journal of Common Market Studies* 51, no. 3 (2013): 416-432.

Chaliand, Gerard, and Ternon, Yves. *The Armenians, from Genocide to Resistance.* Zed Press, 1983.

Chalk, Frank & Jonassohn, Kurt. *The History and Sociology of Genocide.* New Haven, CT: Yale University Press, 1990.

Charny, Israel W. "Toward a Generic Definition of Genocide." *Genocide: Conceptual and Historical Dimensions.* Philadelphia, PA: University of Pennsylvania Press, 1994.

Chirot, Daniel, and Seligman, Martin E. P., eds. *Ethnopolitical Warfare: Causes, Consequences, and Possible Solutions*

(Washington, D.C: American Psychological Association, 2001)

Chrisafis, Angelique. "Turkey Warns France over Armenian Genocide Bill." *The Guardian*, October 11, 2006. http://www.theguardian.com/world/2006/oct/11/turkey.eu

Çiçek, Kemal. "Forced Migration of Ottoman Armenians during World War I: How Security Concerns Affected Decision Making." In *War and Collapse: World War I and the Ottoman State*. M. Hakan Yavuz and Feroz Ahmed, eds. (Salt Lake City: University of Utah Press, 2016).

Clark, Bruce. *Twice a Stranger: How Mass Expulsion forged Modern Greece and Turkey*. Granta, 2007.

Cohen, Michael J. "When Did They Know and What Could They Have Done? More on the Allies' Response to the Holocaust." *Israel Journal of Foreign Affairs* 7, no. 1 (2013): 127-133.

Cohen, Robin. *Global diasporas: An Introduction*. Routledge, 2008.

Cohen, Roger. "To His Death in Jail, Milosevic Exalted Image of Serb Suffering." *New York Times*. March 12, 2006 http://www.nytimes.com/2006/03/12/international/europe/12assess.html?pagewanted=1

Collier, Paul, and Hoeffler, Anke. *Greed and Grievances in Civil War*. Policy Working Paper 2344. Washington, D.C: World Bank, 2000.

"Convention on the Prevention and Punishment of the Crime of Genocide." *U.N General Assembly*, December 9, 1948.

Cooke, Kieran. "Armenia's Controversial Gold Rush," *BBC,* January 9, 2008; http://news.bbc.co.uk/2/hi/business/7153794.stm

Cornell, Svante E. *The Nagorno-Karabakh Conflict.* Inst. für Osteuropastudien, 1999.

Cornell, Svante E. "Turkey and the Conflict in Nagorno Karabakh: A Delicate Balance." *Middle Eastern Studies* 34, no. 1 (1998): 51-72.

"Corruption Perception Index 2003-2007." *Transparency International.* 2007.

"Corruption Perception Index 2014." *Transparency International.* 2014.

"Countries that Recognize the Armenian Genocide." *Armenian National Institute.* http://www.armenian-genocide.org/recognition_countries.html

"Court Decree," *2nd Penal Court of First Instance for the District of Şişli,* File Number: 2006/1208, Decree Number: 2007/1106, Prosecution No.: 2006/8617.

Crampton, Thomas, "French Pass Bill that Punishes Denial of Armenian Genocide," *The New York Times,* 12 October 2006.
http://www.nytimes.com/2006/10/13/world/europe/13turkey.html

Cruz, Consuelo. "Identity and Persuasion: How Nations remember their Pasts and Make their Futures." *World Politics,* no. 52 (2000): 310.

Cullingford, C. *Prejudice: From Individual Identity to Nationalism in Young People.* London: Kogan Page, 2000.

Cushman, Thomas. "Is genocide preventable? Some theoretical considerations." *Journal of Genocide Research* 5, no. 4 (2003): 523-542.

Dadoyan, Seta B. *The Armenians in the Medieval Islamic World, Volume Three: Medieval Cosmopolitanism and Images of Islam. Vol. 3*. Transaction Publishers, 2013

Dadrian, Vahakn N. "A Typology of Genocide." *International Review of Modern Sociology*, 5 (1975), 123.

Dadrian, Vahakn N. "Ottoman Archives and Denial of the Armenian Genocide." *The Armenian Genocide: History, Politics, Ethics*. New York: St. Martin's Press, 1992.

Dadrian, Vahakn N. *The History of the Armenian Genocide: Ethnic Conflict from the Balkans to Anatolia to the Caucasus*. New York, Oxford: Berghahn Books, 2003.

Dadrian, Vahakhn N. *The Key Elements in the Turkish Denial of the Armenian Genocide: A Case Study of Distortion and Falsification*. Toronto: Zoryan Institute, 1999.

Dadrian, Vahakn. "The Role of the Special Organization in the Armenian Genocide during the First World War." *Minorities in Wartime: National and Racial Groupings in Europe, North America and Australia in Two World Wars*. Oxford: Berg, 1993.

Dadrian, Vahakn N. *Warrant for Genocide: Key elements of Turko-Armenian Conflict*. Transaction Publishers, 1999.

Daly, John C. K. "Turkey plans to combat Armenian Genocide Issue at The Hague." *Eurasia Daily Monitor* 5, no. 23 (2008).

Danielyan, Eduard L. *Armenian Statehood and Governance through Millennia: History and Modernity*. 21st Century 1 (17) (2015).

Danielyan, Emil. "Why Armenia's Military Alliance with Russia Is Not at Risk." *REFRL*, November 7, 2015. http://www.rferl.org/content/caucasus-report-armenian-russia-military-alliance/27351046.html

Danielyan, Emil. "Armenia Signals Further Drift to the West." *Eurasia Insight*. October 17, 2005. http://www.eurasianet.org/departments/insight/articles/eav101805.shtml

Danielyan, Emil. "Putin Visit Highlights Russian Interest in Armenia." *Eurasia Daily Monitor* 2, no. 62 (2007).

Danielyan, Emil. "West Unlikely to Sanction Armenia Following Another Troubled Vote," *Eurasia Net*. December 11, 2005. http://www.eurasianet.org/departments/insight/articles/eav121205.shtml

Danilova, Maria. "Armenian PM Sarkisian Wins Presidency." *Washington Post*, February 20, 2008. http://www.washingtonpost.com/wp-dyn/content/article/2008/02/20/AR2008022000708.html

Darieva, Tsypylma. ""The Road to Golgotha": Representing Loss in Postsocialist Armenia." *Focaal* 2008, no. 52 (2008): 92-108.

Dasnabendian, Hratch. *History of the Armenian Revolutionary Federation Dashnaktsutiun 1890-1924*. Milan: Oemme Edizioni, 1990.

Daughtry, J. Martin. "Russia's new anthem and the negotiation of national identity." *Ethnomusicology* 47, no. 1 (2003): 42-67.

"Declaration by the Turkish Grand National Assembly, supporting the Turkish proposal to form a joint historical commission with Armenia." *Republic of Turkey Ministry of Foreign Affairs*, April 13, 2005. http://www.mfa.gov.tr/declaration-by-the-turkish-grand-national-assembly -supporting-the-turkish-proposal-to-form-a-joint-historical-commission-with.en.mfa

De Figueiredo, John M., and Charles M. Cameron. "Endogenous cost lobbying: Theory and evidence." In *CELS 2009 4th Annual Conference on Empirical Legal Studies Paper.* 2009.

De los Angeles Torres, Maria. "Encuentros y Encontronazos: Homeland in the Politics and Identity of the Cuban Diaspora." *Diaspora* 4, no. 2.

Demirci, Sevtap. *Strategies and struggles: British rhetoric and Turkish response: the Lausanne Conference (1922-1923).* Isis Press, 2005.

Deringil, Selim. *Conversion and apostasy in the late Ottoman Empire.* Cambridge University Press, 2012.

Deringil, Selim. *The Well-Protected Domains: Ideology and the Legitimation of Power in the Ottoman Empire, 1876-1909.* London: 1998.

Derohanessian, Vana. "Seeking the Next Saroyan: Cultural Representations of Armenian Americans of Los Angeles." *Rediscovering LA.* California State University, Northridge (2015): 301-323.

Devine-Wright, Patrick. "A Theoretical Overview of Memory and Conflict." *The Role of Memory in Ethnic Conflict.* (New York: Palgrave, 2003), 243.

De Waal, Thomas. *Great Catastrophe: Armenians and Turks in the Shadow of Genocide.* Oxford University Press, 2015

Dilaçar, Agop, *Atatürk ve Türkçe, Atatürk ve Türk Dili.* (Ankara: Türk Dil Kurumu, 1963).

Diler, Fatih Gökhan. "What does French court's 'genocide decision' mean? *Agos*, January 13, 2016. http://www.agos.com.tr/en/article/14004/what-does-french-court-s-genocide-decision-mean

Dressler, Markus. "Historical Trajectories and Ambivalences of Turkish Minority Discourse." *New Diversities* (2015): 9-26.

Drost, Pieter. *The Crime of State.* Leyden: A.W. Sythoff, 1959.

Dunér, Bertil. "What can be done about Historical Atrocities? The Armenian Case." *International Journal of Human Rights* 8, no. 2 (2004): 217-233.

Egan, Timothy. "True Irish." *New York Times.* March 12, 2008.

Elekdağ, Şükrü M. "An Assessment of Armenian Claims from the Perspective of International Law." In *War and Collapse: World War I and the Ottoman State.* M. Hakan Yavuz and Feroz Ahmed, eds. (Salt Lake City: University of Utah Press, 2016).

Elkind, Jonathan. "Economic Implications of the Baku-Tbilisi-Ceyhan Pipeline." *Baku-Tbilisi-Ceyhan Pipeline: Oil Window to the West* (2005): 39-60.

Emmert, Thomas. "The Kosovo Legacy." *Serbian Studies* 5, no. 2 (1989): 5-32.

Ergün, Mustafa. *Atatürk Devri Türk Eğitimi.* (Ankara Üniversitesi, Dil ve Tarih-Coğrafya Fakültesi, 1982).

Erickson, Edward J. "Armenian Massacres: New Records undercut Old Blame: Reexamining History" *Middle East Quarterly*, 2006: 67.

Erickson, Edward J. *Defeat in Detail: The Ottoman Army in the Balkans, 1912-1913.* Westport, CT: Praeger Publishers, 2003.

Erickson, Edward J. *Ordered to Die: A History of the Ottoman Army in the First World War.* Westport, CT: Greenwood Press, 2001.

Erickson, Edward J. *Ottomans and Armenians: A Study in Counterinsurgency.* Palgrave Macmillan, 2013.

"European Parliament Resolution on the Opening of Negotiations with Turkey." *The Armenian Genocide Museum-Institute, National Academy of Sciences of the Republic of Armenia.* http://www.genocide-museum.am/eng/European_Parliament_Resolution.php

Evans, R. J. "History, Memory, and the Law: The Historian as Expert Witness." *History and Theory*, 41 (2002), 342.

Fantauzzo, Justin. "Ending Ottoman Misrule: British Soldiers, Liberal Imperialism, and the First World War in Palestine." *The Journal of the Middle East and Africa* 6, no. 1 (2015): 17-32.

Fein, Helen. "A Formula for Genocide: Comparison of the Turkish Genocide (1915) and the German Holocaust (1939-1945)." *Comparative Studies in Sociology* 1 (1978): 271-294.

Fierke, K.M. "Bewitched by the Past: Social Memory, Trauma, and International Relations." In *Memory, Trauma and World Politics.* Duncan Bell, ed. London: Palgrave Macmillan (2006)

Finkelstein, Norman G. *The Holocaust Industry: Reflections on the Exploitation of Jewish Suffering.* London: Verso, 2000.

Finn, Peter. "Russian Troops to Leave Georgia," *The Washington Post*, May 31, 2005, http://www.washingtonpost.com/wp-dyn/content/article/2005/05/30/AR2005053000397.html

Finnemore, Martha, and Sikkink, Kathryn. "International norm dynamics and political change." *International Organization* 52, no. 04 (1998): 887-917.

"France: Parliament decides to Criminalize Denials of the Armenian Genocide," *English Pen.* October 23, 2006. https://www.englishpen.org/campaigns/france-parliament-decides-to-criminalise-denials-of-the-armenian-genocide/

"Freedom House: Nations in Transit 2014 – Armenia." *Freedom House.* June 12, 2014. http://www.ecoi.net/local_link/280851/411130_de.html

Freinkman, Lev, Evgeny Polyakov, and Caroline Revenco. "Armenia's Trade Performance in 1995-2002 and the Effect of Closed Borders: A Cross-Country Perspective." *Armenian International Policy Research Group Working Paper* 04/04 (2004).

Freinkman, Lev. "Role of the Diasporas in Transition Economies: Lessons from Armenia." *Cuba in Transition-ASCE* (2001).

Fullilove, Michael. "Chinese Diaspora carries Torch for Old Country." *Financial Times* http://www.brookings.edu/opinions/2008/0519_china_fullilove.aspx?rssid=china

Furman, Robert A. "The Pilgrims: Myth and Reality." *Mind and Human Interaction* 9 (1998), 5-17.

Gahramanova, Aytan. "Paradigms of Political Mythologies and Perspectives of Reconciliation in the Case of the Nagorno-Karabakh Conflict." *International Negotiation* 15, no. 1 (2010): 133-152.

Gans, Herbert J. "Symbolic Ethnicity: The Future of Ethnic

Groups and Cultures in America." *Ethnic and Racial Studies* 2, 1 (1979).

Garbis, Christian. "The 'Religion' of Genocide: A Uniting Force Stronger than the Armenian Church and Language." *The Armenian Weekly: Armenian Genocide Insert* 73, no. 16, 2007.

Gardiner, David. "Armenia's Genocide: Death and Denial." *Financial Times*, April 17, 2015. http://www.ft.com/cms/s/2/56d61e36-e28d-11e4-aa1d-00144feab7de.html

Gauin, Maxime. "Remembering the Orly Attack." *Uluslararası Hukuk ve Politika* 7, no. 27 (2011): 113-139.

Gellner, Ernest. *Nations and Nationalisms.* Ithaca, NY: Cornell University Press, 1983.

Gerber, David A. & Kraut, Alan M. *American Immigration and Ethnicity: A Reader.* New York: Palgrave, 2005.

Gerlach, Christian. "Nationsbildung im Krieg: Wirtschaftliche Faktoren bei der Vernichtung der Armenier und beim Mord an den ungarischen Juden." In *Der Völkermord an den Armeniern und die Shoah.* Kieser, Hans-Lukas and Schaller, Dominik J. Schaller, eds. (Zurich: Chronos, 2002).

Geukjian, Ohannes. "From Positive Neutrality to Partisanship: How and Why the Armenian Political Parties Took Sides in Lebanese Politics in the Post-Taif Period (1989–Present)." *Middle Eastern Studies* 45, no. 5 (2009): 739-767.

Gillis, John R. (ed.). *Commemorations: The Politics of National Identity* (Princeton: Princeton University Press, 1994).

Giragosian, Richard. "Armenia can't count on Russia anymore." *Al-Jazeera*, January 20, 2015. http://www.aljazeera.com/indepth/opinion/2015/01/armenia-can-count-russia-any-mo-201511852934497678.html

Glazer, Nathan, and Moynihan, Daniel Patrick. *Ethnicity: Theory and Experience*. No. 109. Harvard University Press, 1975.

Göçek, Fatma Müge. "Ethnic Segmentation, Western Education, and Political Outcomes: Nineteenth-Century Ottoman Society." *Poetics Today* (1993): 507-538.

Goffman, Daniel. *The Ottoman Empire and Early Modern Europe*. Cambridge: Cambridge University Press, 2002.

Göksel, Nigar. "Turkey and Armenia Post-Protocols: Back to Square One?." *Istanbul: TESEV* (2012): 1-22.

Goodman, H.A. "Lemkin's Words and Formally Recognize the Armenian Genocide." *Huffington Post*, June 13, 2015. http://www.huffingtonpost.com/h-a-goodman/the-united-states-should-_2_b_7053052.html

Gorvett, Jonathan. "Thaw in Turkey-Armenian Relations." *Al-Jazeera*, December 21, 2003. http://www.aljazeera.com/archive/2003/12/2008410115412976273.html

Gottlieb, Benjamin. "101-year-old Armenian genocide survivor tells her story." *PRI*. April 27, 2015. http://www.pri.org/stories/2015-04-27/101-year-old-armenian-genocide-survivor-tells-her-story

Gottschlich, Jürgen. "Dispute over Mass Killings of Armenians: French Law Outrages Turks." *Der Spiegel*, October 13, 2006. http://www.spiegel.de/international/dispute-over-mass-killings-of-armenians-french-law-outrages-turks-a-442422.html

Gráda, Cormac Ó. *Black '47 and Beyond: The Great Irish Famine in History, Economy, and Memory*. Princeton University Press, 2000.

Gray, Virginia and Lowery, David. "A niche theory of interest representation." *The Journal of Politics* 58, no. 01 (1996): 91-111.

Gregg, Heather S. *Divided They Conquer: The Success of Armenian Ethnic Lobbies in the US*. Precis, 2001.

Greene, Victor. *For God and Country: The Rise of Polish and Lithuanian Ethnic Consciousness in America, 1860-1910.* Madison, WI: The State Historical Society of Wisconsin, 1975.

Grigoryan, Marianna and Hayrapetyan, Anahit. "Turkey: Armenian Illegal Migrants Put National Grievances Aside for Work." *EurasiaNet,* September 2, 2011. http://www.eurasianet.org/node/64116

Güçlü, Yücel. *The Holocaust and the Armenian case in comparative perspective.* University Press of America, 2012.

Güçlü, Yücel. "Will untapped Ottoman archives reshape the Armenian debate?." *Middle East Quarterly* (2009).

Guibernau, Montserrat. "Anthony D. Smith on nations and national identity: a critical assessment." *Nations and Nationalism* 10, no. 1- 2 (2004): 125-141.

Gunter, Michael M. *Armenian History and the Question of Genocide.* Palgrave Macmillan US, 2011.

Gunter, Michael M. "Politicizing History." In *Armenian History and the Question of Genocide.* Palgrave Macmillan US, 2011.

Gunter, Michael M. *"Pursuing the Just Cause of Their People": A Study of Contemporary Armenian Terrorism.* New York: Greenwood Press, 1986.

Gunter, Michael M. "The Historical Origins of the Turkish-Armenian Animosity." In *Armenian History and the Question of Genocide*, pp. 1-26. Palgrave Macmillan US, 2011.

Gunter, Michael M. "What Is Genocide? The Armenian Case." *Middle East Quarterly* (2013).

Gürel, Perin. "Turkey and the United States After World War I: National Memory, Local Categories, and Provincializing the Transnational." *American Quarterly* 67, no. 2 (2015): 353-376.

Gürün, Kamuran. *The Armenian File: The Myth of Innocence Exposed.* London: K. Rustem, 1985.

Gust, Wolfgang. "Die Verdrängung des Völkermords an den Armeniern-Ein Signal für die Shoah." *Der Völkermord an den Armeniern und die Shoah.* In Kieser, Hans-Lukas and Schaller, Dominik J. Schaller, eds. (Zurich: Chronos, 2002).

Hachikian, Kenneth. "Letter from Kenneth V. Hachikian to ANCA: Concern over Flawed TARC/ICTJ Findings on the Armenian Genocide." *Armenian National Committee of America.* March 24, 2005.

Halter, Marilyn. *Shopping for Identity: The Marketing of Ethnicity.* New York: Schocken Books, 2000.

Hanioğlu, M. Şükrü. *Osmanlı İttihad ve Terakki cemiyeti" ve" Jön Türklük": (1889-1902).* Vol. 1. İletişim Yayınları, 1985.

Hanioğlu, M. Şükrü. *Preparation for a Revolution: The Young Turks, 1902-1908*. Oxford: Oxford University Press, 1995.

Hanioğlu, M. Şükrü. *The Young Turks in Opposition*. Oxford: Oxford University Press, 1995.

Harris, Jason. *Stumbling blocks: Geopolitics, the Armenian Genocide, and the American Jewish community*. Brandeis University: PhD diss., 2008

Harutyunyan, Aram. "Armenia as a Factor of Balance in the Southern Caucasus Region." *Security Sector Governance in Southern Caucasus –Challenges and Visions*. Vienna: National Defence Academy and Bureau for Security Policy, in cooperation with PfP Consortium of Defence Academies and Security Studies Institutes, 2004.

Hatcher, R. & Troyna, B. "Racialization and Children." *Race, Identity and Representation in Education*. New York: Routledge, 1993.

Henderson, Jane. "Rapports: Russia: Signs and Portents." *European public law* 8, no. 3 (2002): 321-332.

Hergnyan, Manuk, and Makaryan, Anna. "The Role of the Diaspora in Generating Foreign Direct Investments in Armenia." *Armenian Journal of Public Policy* 2, no. 2 (2007): 276.

Hepworth, George H. *Through Armenian on Horseback*. London: Isbister, 1898.

Hess, Monika, and Korf, Benedikt. "Tamil diaspora and the political spaces of second- generation activism in Switzerland." *Global Networks* 14, no. 4 (2014): 419-437

Hobsbawm, Eric & Ranger, T. *The Invention of Tradition*. Cambridge: Cambridge University Press, 1983.

Hofmann, Tessa. *Armenians in Turkey today: A critical assessment of the situation of the Armenian minority in the Turkish Republic.* Forum of Armenian Associations of Europe, 2003.

Horowitz, Donald L. "Ethnic Identity." *Ethnicity: Theory and Experience.* No. 109. Harvard University Press, 1975.

Horowitz, Irving Louis. *Taking Lives: Genocide and State Power.* New Brunswick, NJ: Transaction Publishers, 1980.

Hovannisian, Richard. *Armenia on the Road to Independence, 1918.* Berkeley, CA: University of California Press, 1969.

Hovannisian, Richard G. *Armenian Van/Vaspurakan (UCLA Armenian History and Culture Series).* Costa Mesa, CA: Mazda Publishers, 2000.

Hovannisian, Richard G. "Caucasian Armenia Between Imperial and Soviet Rule: The Interlude of Independence." *Transcaucasia, Nationalism and Social Change: Essays in the History of Armenia, Azerbaijan and Georgia.* Ann Arbor, MI: University of Michigan Press, 1999.

Hovannisian, Richard G. "Denial of the Armenian Genocide 100 Years Later: The New Practitioners and Their Trade." *Genocide Studies International* 9, no. 2 (2015): 228-247

Hovannisian, Richard G. "Denial of the Armenian Genocide in Comparison with Holocaust Denial." *Remembrance and Denial: The Case of the Armenian Genocide* (1999): 201-236.

Hovannisian, Richard G. *The Armenian genocide: history, politics, ethics.* New York: St. Martin's Press, 1992.

Hovannisian, Richard G. *The Armenian Genocide in Perspective.* New Brunswick, NJ: Transaction Books, 1986, 29.

Hovannisian, Richard G. *The Armenian People: From Ancient to Modern Times, Volume II.* New York: St. Martin's Press.

Hutchby, I. & Moran-Ellis, J. *Children and Social Competence: Arenas of Action.* London: Falmer Press, 1998.

Hutchinson, G. Evelyn. "Concluding Remarks." *Population Studies: Animal Ecology and Demography, Cold Spring Harbor Symposia on Quantitative Biology* 22 (1957): 416.

Hyland, Francis P. *Armenian Terrorism: The Past, The Present, The Prospects.* Boulder, CO: Westview Press, 1991.

Inalcik, Halil. *Osmanlı Toplumu.* İstanbul: Eren, 1993.

"International Affirmation of the Armenian Genocide." *Armenian National Institute.* http://www.armenian-genocide.org/current_category.11/affirmation_list.html

"Irony of Genocide Museum: A Sore Point for Armenians, Bliss for Turks." *The Armenian Mirror-Spectator.* http://www.mirrorspectator.com/?s=cafesjian

Ishkanian, Armine. "Diaspora and Global Civil Society: The Impact of Transnational Diasporic Activism on Armenia's Post-Soviet Transition." *Central Asia and the Caucasus: Transnationalism and Diaspora.* (New York: Routledge, 2005), 120.

Ishkhanyan, Vahan. "Prospective: A different Viewpoint on Recognition," *Armenia Now.* November 2, 2007. http://www.armenianow.com/features/7800/prospective_a_different_viewpoint

Jacobson, Matthew Frye. *Special Sorrows: The Diasporic Imagination of Irish, Polish and Jewish Immigrants in the United States.* Berkeley, CA: University of California Press, 2002.

James, Allison. *Childhood Identities: Self and Social Relationships in the Experience of the Child* (Edinburgh: Edinburgh University Press, 1993).

Jerjian, George. *The Truth will set Us Free: Armenians and Turks Reconciled.* London: GJ Communications, 2003.

Jones, Adam. "Case Study: The Armenian Genocide, 1915-17." *Gendercide Watch*, 2002. http://www.anca.org/assets/pdf/armenian_genocide_reference/Case%20Study%20-%20The%20Armenian%20Genocide.pdf

Kaiser, Hilmar. "'A Scene from the Inferno:' The Armenians of Erzurum and the Genocide, 1915-1916." *Der Völkermord an den Armeniern und die Shoah.* Kieser, Hans-Lukas and Schaller, Dominik J. Schaller, eds. (Zurich: Chronos, 2002).

Karpat, Kemal H. *Ottoman Past and Today's Turkey.* Leiden: Brill, 2000.

Katz, Steven T. *The Holocaust in Historical Context, Volume 1: The Holocaust and Mass Death Before the Modern Age.* (New York: Oxford University Press, 1994).

Kayalı, Hasan. "Elections and the Electoral Process in the Ottoman Empire, 1876–1919." *International Journal of Middle East Studies* 27, no. 03 (1995): 265-286.

Khan, M.R. "The Ottoman Eastern Question and the Problematic Origins of Ethnic Cleansing, Genocide, and Humanitarian Interventionism in Modern Europe and the Middle East." In *War and Diplomacy: The Russo-Turkish War of 1877–78 and the Treaty of Berlin* Yavuz, M. H. and Sluglett, P. eds., (Salt Lake City, UT: University of Utah Press), pp. 98–122.

Kieser, Hans-Lukas and Schaller, Dominik J. Schaller, eds. *Der Völkermord an den Armeniern und die Shoah*, (Zurich: Chronos, 2002).

Kılınçoğlu, Deniz T. *Economics and Capitalism in the Ottoman Empire*. Vol. 174. Routledge, 2015.

King, Charles, and Melvin, Neil J. "Diaspora Politics: Ethnic Linkages, Foreign Policy and Security in Eurasia." *International Security* 24, no. 3 (1999/2000): 108-38.

Koester, D. "Childhood in National Consciousness and National Consciousness in Childhood." *Childhood* 4: 125-142.

Koser, Mutlu. "301'den 1 Yıl Hapis." Hürriyet, October 12, 2007. http://www.hurriyet.com.tr/301-den-1-yil-hapis-7470839

Kotchikian, Asbed. "From Vertical to Diagonal Interactions." *The Armenian Weekly: Armenian Genocide Insert* 73, no. 16.

Kouvaraki, Anna. *Historical and Cultural Dimensions of the Muslim Cretans in Turkey*. PhD diss., İstanbul Bilgi Üniversitesi, 2014.

Kucera, Joshua. "Russian Officer: We Would Intervene in Karabakh Against Azerbaijan." *Eurasianet*. November 1, 2013. http://www.eurasianet.org/node/67712

Kuran, Timur. "Diffusion of Ethnic Dissimilation." In *The International Spread of Ethnic Conflict: Fear, Diffusion, and Escalation*. David A. Lake and Donald Rothchild, eds., (Princeton, NJ: Princeton University Press, 1998), 35-60.

Kurz, Anat, and Marari, Ariel. *ASALA: Irrational Terror or Political Tool?* Boulder, CO: Westview Press, 1985.

"La loi contre la négation du génocide arménien est censure." *Liberation*, February 28, 2012. http://www.liberation.fr/planete/2012/02/28/la-loi-contre-la-negation-du-genocide-armenien-est-censuree_799353

Lafleur, Jean-Michel. *Transnational politics and the state: The external voting rights of diasporas*. Routledge, 2013.

Lagrou, Pieter. "Europe as a Place for Common Memories? Some Thoughts on Victimhood, Identity and Emancipation form the Past." *Clashes in European Memory: The Case of Communist Repression and the Holocaust*. Studienverlag, 2011: 281-288.

Lahneman, William J. *Impact of Diaspora Communities on National and Global Politics: Report on Survey of the Literature*. College Park, MD: CISSM, University of Maryland, 2005.

Lake, David A. & Rothchild, Donald. *The International Spread of Ethnic Conflict: Fear, Diffusion, and Escalation*. Princeton, NJ: Princeton University Press, 1998.

Lambert, Peter. "Myth, Manipulation and Violence: Relationships between National Identity and Political Violence." *Political Violence and the Construction of National Identity in Latin America*. New York: Palgrave, 2006.

Landau, Jacob M. "Ottoman Turkey." In *The Jews of the Middle East and North Africa in Modern Times*. Columbia University Press, 2003: 288-289.

Landau, Jacob M. *The" Young Turks" and Zionism: Some Comments*. Hebrew University of Jerusalem, Harry S. Truman Research Institute for the Advancement of Peace, 1983.

Lange-Akhund, Nadine. *The Macedonian Question, 1893-1908: From Western Sources*. NY: Columbia University Press, 1998.

Langer, William L. *The Diplomacy of Imperialism: 1890-1902.* New York: Alfred A. Knopf, 1935, 1.

Lauck, Jeffrey L. "Lost Cause in the Oval Office: Woodrow Wilson's Racist Policies and White-Washed Memory of the Civil War." *The Gettysburg Compiler: On the Front Lines of History.* Paper 136 (2015).

Lehmann, Maike. "Apricot Socialism: The National Past, the Soviet Project, and the Imagining of Community in Late Soviet Armenia." *Slavic Review* 74, no. 1 (2015): 9-31.

Levinson, B., Foley, D., and Holland, D. *The Cultural Production of the Educated Person: Critical Ethnographies of Schooling and Local Practice.* New York: State University of New York Press, 1996.

Lewis, Bernard. *The Emergence of Modern Turkey.* Oxford: Oxford University Press, 1968.

Lewy, Guenter. *The Armenian Massacres in Ottoman Turkey.* Salt Lake City, UT: University of Utah Press, 2005.

Libaridian, Gerard J. "The New Thinking Revisited." *Libaridian speaks at Princeton University*, May 9, 1998.

Lichtblau, Eric. "Arab Unrest Puts Their Lobbyists in Uneasy Spot." *New York Times* (March 1, 2011) http://www.nytimes.com/2011/03/02/world/middleeast/02lobby.html?scp=1&sq=arab%20lobby&st=cse

Linz, Juan, Stepan, Alfred, and Yadav, Yogendra. "'Nation State' Or 'State Nation'? India in Comparative Perspective." *Democracy and diversity: India and the American experience* (2007): 50-106.

Lis, Jonathan. "Foreign Ministry: Israel's Recognition of Armenian Genocide Could Threaten Turkey Ties," *Haaretz.* January 23, 2016. http://www.haaretz.com/israel-news/foreign-ministry-israel-s-recognition-of-armenian-genocide-could-threaten-turkey-ties-1.403687

Lowery, David. "Why Do Organized Interest Lobby? A Multi-Goal, Multi-Context Theory of Lobbying." *Polity* 39, no. 1 (January 2007), 29.

Lukyx, A. *The Citizen Factory: Schooling and Cultural Production in Bolivia.* New York: State University of New York Press, 1999.

Luterbacher, Celia, and Geiser, Urs. "European Court confirms Perinçek's right to freedom of speech." *SWI.* October 15, 2015. http://www.swissinfo.ch/eng/do%C4%9Fu-perin%C3%A7ek_european-court-confirms-perin%C3%A7ek-s-right-to-freedom-of-speech-/41720676

Lyons, Terrence and Mandaville, Peter. *Politics from Afar: Transnational Diasporas and Networks.* (2013)

MacDonald, David B. "America's Memory Problems: Diaspora Groups, Civil Society and the Perils of 'Chosen Amnesia.'" In *Japanese Wartime Medical Atrocities: Comparative Perspectives on Science, History and Ethics* (Routledge: 2010) pp. 166-182

Mack, John E. "The Psychodynamics of Victimization Among National Groups in Conflict." *The Psychodynamics of International Relationships, Volume 1: Concepts and Theories.* Toronto: Lexington Books, 1990, 124.

Madalian, James G. *Armenian Freedom Fighters: The Memoirs of Rouben der Minasian.* Boston: Hairenik Association, 1963.

Mamigonian, Marc A. *The Armenians of New England.* Belmont, MA: ArmenianHeritage Press/NAASR, 2004.

Mandel, Maud. *In the Aftermath of Genocide: Armenians and Jews in Twentieth-Century France.* Duke University Press, 2003.

Mandelbaum, Michael. *The New European Diasporas: National Minorities and Conflict in Eastern Europe.* New York: Council on Foreign Relations Press, 2000.

Mardin, Şerif. *The Genesis of Young Ottoman Thought: A Study in the Modernization of Turkish Political Ideas.* Syracuse University Press, 2000.

Mayall, B. *Children, Health and the Social Order.* Buckingham: Open University Press, 1996.

McCarthy, C., and Crichlow, W., eds. *Race, Identity and Representation in Education* (New York: Routledge), 1993.

McCarthy, Justin. *Death and Exile: The Ethnic Cleansing of Ottoman Muslims, 1821-1922.* Princeton, N.J: Darwin Press, 1995.

McCarthy, Justin; Esat, Arslan; Taşkıran, Cemalettin; and Turan, Ömer. *The Armenian Rebellion at Van.* Salt Lake City: University of Utah Press, 2006.

McCarthy, Justin. *The Ottoman Turks: An Introductory History to 1923.* London and New York: Longman, 1997.

McCarthy, Justin. *The Population of the Ottoman Armenians.* na, 2001.

McCarthy, Justin. "The Report of Niles and Sutherland: An American Investigation of Eastern Anatolia after World War I." *XI. Türk Tarih Kongresi, Ankara: 5–9 Eylül 1990* (1994): 1809-53.

Melson, Robert F. "The Armenian Genocide as Precursor and Prototype of Twentieth-Century Genocide." *Is the Holocaust Unique?* Boulder, CO: Westview Press, 1996.

Meray, Seha L. and Olcay, Osman. *Osmanlı İmparatorluğu Çöküş Belgeleri (Mondros Bırakışması, Sèvres Andlaşması ve İlgili Belgeler),* Ankara: SBF Yayınları, 1977.

Migliorino, Nicola. *(Re) constructing Armenia in Lebanon and Syria: Ethno-cultural Diversity and the State in the Aftermath of a Refugee Crisis.* Vol. 21. Berghahn Books, 2008.

Miller, Donald E. and Miller, Lorna Touryan. "Memory and Identity across the Generations: A Case Study of Armenian Survivors and Their Progeny." *Qualitative Sociology* Vol. 14, no. 1 (1991), 13-38.

"Military expenditure (% of GDP)." *The World Bank.* 2015. http://data.worldbank.org/indicator/MS.MIL.XPND.GD.ZS

Milton. Giles. *Paradise Lost: Smyrna 1922, The Destruction of a Christian City in the Islamic World.* New York: Basic Books, 2008, 69-88.

"Minister Oksanian Speaks on Genocide Remembrance in Brussels." *Ministry of Foreign Affairs of Armenia.* (Brussels: 25 April 2007).
http://www.mfa.am/en/speeches/item/2007/04/25/vo-genocide-brussels/

Mirak, Robert. *Torn Between Two Lands: Armenians in America 1890 to World War I.* Boston: Harvard University Press, 1984.

Morton, H. *Becoming Tongan: An Ethnography of Childhood.* Honolulu, HI: University of Hawaii Press, 1996.

Muchiri, Eliud Githiga. *Impact of remittances inflows on economic growth in Kenya.* PhD diss., University of Nairobi, 2014.

Muñoz, Jessica, "Mexican Identity Beyond Labels, Beyond Borders." *Sociology Honors Projects*. Paper 46, (2014).

Nalbandian, Louise. *The Armenian Revolutionary Movement: The Development of the Armenian Political Parties through the Nineteenth Century*. Berkeley, CA: University of California at Berkeley Press, 1963.

Narayanswamy, Anupama, Rosiak, Luke and LaFleur, Jennifer. "Opening the Window on Foreign Lobbying." *Pro Publica* (August 8, 2009).

"New Public Opinion Survey of Turkey." *Terror Free Tomorrow*, 2007. http://www.terrorfreetomorrow.org/template.php?section=PL

Nichol, Jim. "Armenian, Azerbaijan and Georgia: Political Developments and Implications for U.S. Interests." *CRS Report for Congress*. July 31, 2007. http://www.au.af.mil/au/awc/awcgate/crs/rl33453.pdf

Nie, Jing-Bao; Guo, Nanyan, and Kleinman, Arthur (eds). *Japanese Wartime Medical Atrocities: Comparative Perspectives on Science, History and Ethics* (Routledge: 2010).

Northrup, Terrel A. "The Dynamic of Identity in Personal and Social Conflict." *Intractable Conflicts and Their Transformation*. Syracuse: Syracuse University Press, 1989: 55-82.

Nygren, Bertil. *The rebuilding of Greater Russia: Putin's foreign policy towards the CIS countries*. Vol. 4. Routledge, 2007.

"Obama Budget Calls for Record Low Level of Aid to Armenia." *Asbarez*. February 3, 2015. http://asbarez.com/131444/obama-budget-calls-for-record-low-level-of-aid-to-armenia/

Oktay, Hasan. "On the Assassination of Mayor Kapamaciyan by the Tashnak Committee." *Review of Armenian Studies* I, no. 1 (2002): 79-89.

Öktem, Kerem. "A response to Norman Stone," *The Economist*, June 21-27, 2008, 24.

Oren, Neta. "The Jewish–Israeli Ethos of Conflict." In *A Social Psychology Perspective on The Israeli-Palestinian Conflict.* Springer International Publishing, 2016: 115-131.

Panossian, Razmik. "Between Ambivalence and Intrusion: Politics and Identity in Armenia-Diaspora Relations." *Diaspora: A Journal of Transnational Studies* 7, no. 2 (1998): 149-196.

Panossian, Razmik. "The Impact of the Genocide on Armenian National Identity." *Armenian Weekly* 73, no. 16 (2007).

Papava, Vladimir. "The Baku-Tbilisi-Ceyhan Pipeline: Implications for Georgia." *The Baku-Tbilisi-Ceyhan Pipeline: Oil Window to the West* (2005): 85-102.

Papian, Ara. "Recognition of the Armenian Genocide and territorial claims are two different fights." *Repair.* September 24, 2015.
http://www.repairfuture.net/index.php/en/armenian-genocide-recognition-and-reparations-standpoint-of-armenia/recognition-of-the-armenian-genocide-and-territorial-claims-are-two-different-fights

Parla, Taha. *The Social and Political Thought of Ziya Gökalp: 1876-1924.* Leiden: E.J. Brill, 1985.

Parla, Taha. *Türkiye'de Siyasal Kültürün Resmi Kaynakları* (İstanbul: İletişim Yayınları, 1991).

Parmar, Inderjeet. "Catalysing Events, Think Tanks and American Foreign Policy Shifts: A Comparative Analysis of the Impacts of Pearl Harbor 1941 and 11 September 2001." *Government and Opposition* 40, no. 1 (2005): 1-25.

Pattie, Susan. "At home in diaspora: Armenians in America." *Diaspora: A Journal of Transnational Studies* 3, no. 2 (1994): 185-198.

Pattie, Susan P. "Longing and belonging: Issues of homeland in Armenian diaspora." *PoLAR: Political and Legal Anthropology Review* 22, no. 2 (1999): 80-92.

Paul, Rachel Anderson. "Grassroots Mobilization and Diaspora Politics: Armenian Interest Groups and the Role of Collective Memory." *Nationalism and Ethnic Politics* 6, no. 1, (2000), 24-47.

Pecquet, Julian. "Turks link Armenia to US Foes in bid to derail Genocide Nod." *Al-Monitor.* April 16, 2015. http://www.al-monitor.com/pulse/originals/2015/04/turkey-armenian-genocide-congress-recognition-anniversary.html#

Phillips, Jenny. "Symbol, Myth, and Rhetoric: The Politics of Culture in an Armenian American Population." *Immigrant Communities and Ethnic Minorities in the United States and Canada,* 23. (New York: AMS Press, 1989).

Pisowicz, Andrzej. "Armenian Language." *Enyclopedia Brittanica.* http://www.britannica.com/EBchecked/topic/35305/Armenianlanguage#tab=active~checked%2Citems~checked&title=Armenian%20language%20%20Britannica%20Online%20Encyclopedial

Pleck, Elizabeth. "The making of the domestic occasion: The history of Thanksgiving in the United States." *Journal of Social History* (1999): 773-789.

"Pocket World in Figures, 2008 Edition." *The Economist* (London: Profile Books, 2007), 44.

Pope, Hugh. "Armenia Haunts Turkey Again." *Los Angeles Times.* January 23, 2007. http://www.latimes.com/news/la-oe-pope23jan23-story.html

"Poverty Rate in Armenia Nearly Doubles." *Asbarez.* November 23, 2013. http://asbarez.com/116670/poverty-rate-in-armenia-nearly-doubles/

Quinn-Judge, Paul. "Zhirinovsky vs. the Turks." *Middle East Quarterly* 1, no. 2 (June 1994).

"Recognition: States: Resolutions, Laws, and Declarations." *The Armenian Genocide Museum-Institute, National Academy of Sciences of the Republic of Armenia.* http://www.genocide-museum.am/eng/states.php

Reidel, James. "The Epic of Genocide." *The New York Review of Books*, April 24, 2015, http://www.nybooks.com/daily/2015/04/24/epic-armenian-genocide/

"Republic of Azerbaijan – Concluding Statement of the IMF Mission, 30 August – 06 September 2007." *International Monetary Fund*, 2007. http://www.imf.org/external/np/ms/2007/092607.htm

Richter, Heinz A. "The Grand Game and Britain's Acquisition of Cyprus." *Çanakkale Araştırmaları Türk Yıllığı* 12, no. 17 (2014): 85-96.

Robben, Antonius CGM, and Marcelo Su'arez-Orozco. *Cultures under siege: Collective Violence and Trauma.* Vol. 11. Cambridge University Press, 2000

Sahara, Tetsuya. "The Military Origins of the Teşkilat-ı Mahsusa: The IMRO and the Ottoman Special Force on the Eve of World War I." In *War and Collapse: World War I and the Ottoman State*. M. Hakan Yavuz and Feroz Ahmed, eds. (Salt Lake City: University of Utah Press, 2016).

Şahin, Erman. "Review Essay: A Scrutiny of Akçam's Version of History and the Armenian Genocide," *Journal of Muslim Minority Affairs*, Aug. 2008, p. 316.

Şahin, Erman. "Review Essay: The Armenian Question," *Middle East Policy*, Spring 2010, p. 157.

Salt, Jeremy. *Imperialism, Evangelism and the Ottoman Armenians, 1878-1896*. London: 1993.

Sammut, Dennis. "Armenia–Stuck between a rock and a hard place." *The South Caucasus* (2015): 44-52.

Sarafian, Ara. "The Issue of Access to Ottoman Archives." *Zeitschrift für Türkeistudien*. 1993.

Sargsyan, Serzh & Baghdasaryan, Arthur. "Moving Forward in Armenia." *The Washington Post*, March 17, 2008.
Sassounian, Harut. "Armenians Demand Justice, not Recognition." *The California Courier*, December 6, 2007. http://www.armeniapedia.org/wiki/Armenians_Demand_Justice,_Not_Recognition

Sassounian, Harut. "First Nationwide Turkish Survey Reveals Millions of Turks Support Genocide Bill." *Huffington Post*, May 25, 2011. http://www.huffingtonpost.com/harut-sassounian/first-nationwide-turkish-_b_74141.html

Sassounian, Harut. "TARC." *California Courier*. No date. http://www.armeniapedia.org/index.php?title=Turkish_Armenian_Reconciliation_Commission

Sassounian, Harut. "Those Who Want Reconciliation Versus Those Who Seek Justice." *Western Diocese of the Armenian Church*, December 11, 2007. http://www.armenianchurchwd.com/news/Those-Who-Want-Reconciliation-Versus-Those-Who-Seek-Justice/

Schrodt, Nikolaus. *Modern Turkey and the Armenian Genocide: An Argument About the Meaning of the Past.* Springer, 2014.

"Sealed Turkish archives could support genocide claims." *Times Higher Education*, April 27, 2001. https://www.timeshighereducation.com/news/sealed-turkish-archives-could-support-genocide-claims/159455.article

Sebald, W.G. *On the Natural History of Destruction.* New York: Modern Library, 2004.

"Secret life of professor Vahakn Dadrian." *Academic Integrity.* (April 15, 2013) http://academicintegrityresearch.blogspot.co.ke/2013/04/secret-life-of-professor-vahakn-dadrian.html

Şeyhun, Ahmet. "A Last Attempt to Solve the Armenian Question: The Reform of 1914." In *War and Collapse: World War I and the Ottoman State.* M. Hakan Yavuz and Feroz Ahmed, eds. (Salt Lake City: University of Utah Press, 2016).

Sezgin, Osman, and Biçer, Ramazan. "Foundations of tolerance in Turkish culture." *Kalem Eğitim ve İnsan Bilimleri Dergisi* 2012, 2 (1), 11-38.

Shain, Yossi, and Barth, Aharon. "Diasporas and International Relations Theory." *International Organization* 57 (2003): 449-479.

Shain, Yossi, and Bristman, Barry. "The Jewish Security Dilemma." *Orbis* 46, no. 1 (2002): 47-72

Shaw, Stanford, and Shaw, Ezel Kural. *History of the Ottoman Empire and the Turkish Republic*. Cambridge: Cambridge University Press, 1976-1977.

Silberstein, Gerard E. *The Troubled Alliance: German-Austrian Relations, 1914--1917*. University Press of Kentucky, 2015

Simon, Reeva S., Laskier, Michael M., and Reguer, Sara. *The Jews of the Middle East and North Africa in Modern Times*. Columbia University Press, 2003.

Singh, Milan, and Singh, Anita. "Diaspora, Political Action, and Identity: A Case Study of Canada's Indian Diaspora." *Diaspora: A Journal of Transnational Studies* 17, no. 2 (2014): 149-171

Smelser, Neil J. "Epilogue: September 11, 2001 as Cultural Trauma." In *Cultural Trauma and Collective Identity*. Berkeley, CA: University of California Press, 2004.

Smith, Anthony D. *The Ethnic Origins of Nations*. Cambridge, MA: Blackwell Publishing, 1996.

Socor, Vladimir. "The End of 'Complementarity' in Armenia's Foreign Policy." *Eurasia Daily Monitor* Volume: 10 Issue: 165, September 18, 2013.

Sonyel, Salahi R. "Mustafa Kemal and Enver in conflict, 1919–22." *Middle Eastern Studies* 25, no. 4 (1989): 506-515.

Sonyel, Salahi R. *The Ottoman Armenians: Victims of Great Power Diplomacy*. London: K. Rustem and Brothers, 1987.

Souleimanov, Emil. "The Politics of France's Criminalization of Genocide Denial," *Central Asia-Caucasus Institute*. http://old.cacianalyst.org/?q=node/4253

Spyrou, S. "Education, Ideology, and the National Self: The Social Practice of Identity Construction in the Classroom." *The Cyprus Review* 12: 61-81.

Spyrou, Spyros. "Images of 'the Other': 'the Turk' in Greek Cypriot Children's Imaginations." *Race, Ethnicity and Education* 5, no. 3, (2002), 255-272.

"Statement of President Barack Obama on Armenian Remembrance Day," *The White House, Office of the Press Secretary*, April 24, 2009, April 24, 2010, April 24, 2011, April 24, 2012, April 24, 2013, April 24,2014, April 24, 2015.

Stephens, S. *Children and the Politics of Culture.* Princeton, NJ: Princeton University Press, 1995.

Suny, R.G., Göçek, F.M., and Naimark, N.N. (eds.) *A Question of Genocide: Armenians and Turks at the End of the Ottoman Empire.* New York: Oxford University Press, 2011.

Suny, Ronald G. *Looking Toward Ararat: Armenia in Modern History.* Bloomington: Indiana University Press, 1993.

Suny, Ronald G., ed. *Transcaucasia, Nationalism and Social Change: Essays in the History of Armenia, Azerbaijan and Georgia* (Ann Arbor, MI: University of Michigan Press, 1999).

Suny, Ronald G. "Writing Genocide: The Fate of the Ottoman Armenians." In *A Question of Genocide: Armenians and Turks at the End of the Ottoman Empire.* Suny, R.G., Göçek, F.M., and Naimark, N.N. (eds.) New York: Oxford University Press, 2011

"Sweden Parliament Report." *The Armenian Genocide Museum-Institute, National Academy of Sciences of the Republic of Armenia,* (March 29, 2000). http://www.genocide-useum.am/eng/Sweden_Parliament_Report.php

Sztompka, Piotr. "Cultural Trauma." *European Journal of Social Theory*, no. 3 (2000): 449-67.

Tacar, Pulat, and Gauin, Maxime. "State Identity, Continuity, and Responsibility: The Ottoman Empire, the Republic of Turkey and the Armenian Genocide: A Reply to Vahagn Avedian." *European Journal of International Law* 23, no. 3 (2012): 821-835.

Takooshian, Harold. "Armenian Immigration to the United States from the Middle East." *Journal of Armenian Studies*, winter 1986-1987, 133-156.

Tanpınar, Ahmet Hamdi. *Huzur.* Vol. 97. Dergâh Yayınları, 2009.

Tanrıverdi, Mustafa. "Russian Military Mobilization in the Caucasus before World War I." In *War and Collapse: World War I and the Ottoman State.* M. Hakan Yavuz and Feroz Ahmed, eds. (Salt Lake City: University of Utah Press, 2016).

Tateossian, Steve. "April 24: Commemorative Date of Armenian Genocide." *Associated Content.*

Tavernise, Sabrina. "Turkey to Alter Speech Law." *New York Times*, January 25, 2008. http://www.nytimes.com/2008/01/25/world/europe/25turkey.html

"Text of the Chile Senate Resolution." *The Armenian Genocide Museum-Institute, National Academy of Sciences of the Republic of Armenia.* http://www.genocide-museum.am/Chile_Senate_Resolution.html

Tharoor, Ishaan. "Why Israel does not recognize the Armenian 'genocide.'" *The Washington Post*, April 24, 2015. https://www.washingtonpost.com/news/worldviews/wp/

2015/04/24/why-israel-does-not-recognize-the-armenian-genocide/

"The Armenian Genocide: Simplified." *Armenian Genocide 1915.* http://www.genocide1915.info/research/view.asp?ID=30

"The Economist Intelligence Unit's Index of Democracy 2014." *The Economist.* 2014

Ther, Philipp. *The Dark Side of Nation-States: Ethnic Cleansing in Modern Europe.* Vol. 19. Berghahn Books, 2014.

Thompson, Marilyn. "An Ex-Leader in Congress Is Now Turkey's Man in the Lobbies of Capitol Hill." *New York Times* (October 17, 2007). http://www.nytimes.com/2007/10/17/washington/17lobby.html?_r=0

Toker, Metin. *Şeyh Sait ve isyanı.* Akis Yayınları, 1968.

Toktaş, Şule and Aras, Bülent. "National Security Culture in Turkey: A Qualitative Study on Think Tanks." *Bilig* 61 (2012): 245-262.

Tölölyan, Khachig. "Cultural Narrative and the Motivation of the Terrorist." *Journal of Strategic Studies* 10, no. 4 (1987): 232.

Tölölyan, Khachig, and Papazian, Taline. "Armenian Diasporas and Armenia: Issues of Identity and Mobilization. An interview with Khachig Tölölyan." *Études Arméniennes Contemporaines* 3 (2014): 83-101.

"Top Novelist acquitted in Turkey," *BBC.* September 21, 2006. http://news.bbc.co.uk/1/hi/world/europe/5366446.stm

Topçu, E. Ümran. "The significance of neighborhood in Istanbul." *Conference Paper; 51st Congress of the European Regional Science Association: "New Challenges for European Regions and Urban Areas in a Globalised World", 30 August - 3 September 2011*, Barcelona, Spain.

Towards a Shared Vision of Normalization of Armenian-Turkish Relations: Draft Report. Caucasus Research Resource Center – Armenia: Yerevan, April 2015.

Trkulja, Jelena, and Lees, Christopher, "Armenians in Istanbul", 2008, *Encyclopaedia of the Hellenic World, Istanbul.* http://www.ehw.gr/l.aspx?id=12208.

Tsilimidis, Manos. "A Life in the Service of the Greek Diaspora." *Ekathimerini English Edition.* http://www.ekathimerini.com/4dcgi/news/content.asp?aid=74476

Tunaya, Tarık Zafer. *İslamcılık Akımı.* İstanbul: Simavi Yayınları, 1991.

"Turkish Armenian Reconciliation Commission." *American University*, 2003-2004. http://www1.american.edu/cgp/TARC/

Tuncel, Turgut Kerem. "Searching for the Right Approach to Solve the Turkish-Armenian Controversy." *Historians Without Borders: The Use and Abuse of History in Conflicts, Helsinki, 19-20 May 2016.*

Turkish Perceptions Survey 2015. The German Marshall Fund of the United States, 2015: 5. http://www.gmfus.org/listings/research/type/publication

"Turkish politician fined over genocide denial." *SWI.* March 9, 2007. http://www.swissinfo.ch/eng/turkish-politician-fined-over-genocide-denial/977094

Ülker, Erol. "Assimilation of the Muslim communities in the first decade of the Turkish Republic (1923-1934)." *European Journal of Turkish Studies. Social Sciences on Contemporary Turkey* (2008).

Ünal, Hasan. "Young Turk assessments of international politics, 1906–9."*Middle Eastern Studies* 32, no. 2 (1996): 30-44.

UN Whitaker Report on Genocide, 1985. *United Nations*, 1985. http://www.preventgenocide.org/prevent/UNdocs/whitaker/section5.htm

"United Nations Principles for the Nuremberg Tribunal, 1946." *United Nations*, December 11, 1946. https://www.icrc.org/applic/ihl/ihl.nsf/Treaty.xsp?documentId=53D11A6719F4627BC12563CD002D6ACA&action=openDocument

Uras, Esat. *Tarihte Ermeniler ve Ermeni Meselesi, 2. Baskı.* İstanbul: Belge Yayınları, 1987.

Uras, Umut. "Armenian immigrants look for a better life in Turkey." *Al-Jazeera* (April 20, 2015). http://www.aljazeera.com/news/2015/04/armenian-immigrants-life-turkey-150420070803126.html

Üstün, Kemal. *Menemen Olayı ve Kubilay Olayı.* İstanbul: Çağdaş Yayınları, 1990.

Uyar, Mesut. "The Ottoman Empire and the Early Modern World." *Agora* 50, no. 4 (2015): 22-28.

Valverde, Kieu-Linh Caroline. *Transnationalizing Viet Nam: Community, Culture, and Politics in the Diaspora.* Philadelphia, PA: Temple University Press, 2012.

Varjabedian, Hrag. *The Poetics of History and Memory: The Multiple Instrumentalities of Armenian Genocide Narratives*. PhD diss., University of Wisconsin-Madison, 2009.

Veerman, Alexander L., and Ganzevoort, R. Ruard. "Communities Coping with Collective Trauma." *International Association for the Psychology of Religion.* Soesterberg, The Netherlands. 2001. Conference Presentation.

Vetter, Anna R. "Press Release: Valadao, Forty House Members Introduce Bipartisan Resolution to Recognize the Armenian Genocide." *Congressman David G. Valadao*, March 18, 2015, http://www.valadao.house.gov/news/documentsingle.aspx?DocumentID=398000#sthash.aFeP3ISh.dpuf

Volkan, Vamık. *Blood Lines: From Ethnic Pride to Ethnic Terrorism.* Boulder, CO: Westview Press, 1997, 45.

Volkan, Vamık. *Killing in the Name of Identity.* Charlottesville, VA: Pitchstone Publishing, 2006.

Volkan, Vamık D. "Large group identity and chosen trauma." *Psyche. Zeitschrift für Psychoanalyse und ihre Anwendungen*, no. 9-10 (2000): 931-953.

Volkan, Vamık D.; Julius, Demetrios A. and Montville, Joseph V. (eds.) *The Psychodynamics of International Relationships, Volume 1: Concepts and Theories* (Toronto: Lexington Books, 1990)

Volkan, Vamık and Itzkowitz, Norman. *Turks and Greeks: Neighbors in Conflict.* Cambridgeshire, England: Eothen Press, 1994.

Voorhoof, Dirk. "Perinçek Judgment on Genocide Denial." *ECHR Blog*, January 7, 2014. https://biblio.ugent.be/publication/4227441/file/4227442

Voorwald, Alyssa. *The influence of Turkish ethnic interest groups on Dutch domestic policy towards the Turkish community in The Netherlands: A powerful lobby*? (2015). M.A Thesis: University of Leiden.

Vryonis, Speros. "Byzantium: The Social Basis of Decline in the Eleventh Century." *Greek, Roman and Byzantine Studies* 2, no. 2 (1959): 159-175.

Walker, Christopher J. *Armenia: The Survival of a Nation.* London: Croom Helm, 1980.

Walker, Christopher J. "World War I and the Armenian Genocide." In *Armenian People from Ancient to Modern Times, vol. II*. New York: Palgrave Macmillan, 2004.

Waller, James. *Becoming Evil: How Ordinary People Commit Genocide and Mass Killings*. Oxford: Oxford University Press, 2002.

Waters, Mary C. *Ethnic Options: Choosing Identities in America.* Berkeley: University of California Press, 1990.

"Waving Ataturk's Flag," *The Economist*. March 8, 2007: 45.

Werth, Paul. "Imperial Russia and the Armenian Catholicos at Home and Abroad." *Reconstruction and Interaction of Slavic Eurasia and Its Neighboring Worlds* (2006): 203-235.

White, Sam. *The climate of rebellion in the early modern Ottoman Empire*. Cambridge University Press, 2011.

"Why Will Russia Station 7,000 Soldiers on the Armenia-Turkey Border?" *Australia Network*. December 15, 2015. http://www.australianetworknews.com/will-russia-station-7000-soldiers-armenia-turkey-border/

Whyte, Murray. "Film: Facing the Pain of a Past Long Hidden," *New York Times*, November 17, 2002.

http://query.nytimes.com/gst/fullpage.html?res=9803E3D71131F934A25752C1A9649C8B63&scp=1&sq=egoyan&st=nyt

Wilson, James Q. *Political Organizations.* New York: Basic Books, 1973.

Yavuz, M. Hakan. "A Topography of Positions in the Turkish-Armenian Debate." In *War and Collapse: World War I and the Ottoman State.* M. Hakan Yavuz and Feroz Ahmed, eds. (Salt Lake City: University of Utah Press, 2016).

Yavuz, M. Hakan. "Contours of Scholarship on Armenian-Turkish Relations." *Middle East Critique* 20, no. 3 (2011): 231-251.

Yavuz, M. Hakan. *Islamic Political Identity in Turkey.* New York: Oxford University Press, 2003.

Yavuz, M. Hakan. "Orientalism, the 'Terrible Turk' and Genocide." *Middle East Critique* 23, no. 2 (2014): 111-126.

Yavuz, M. Hakan and Ahmed, Feroz (eds). *War and Collapse: World War I and the Ottoman State.* (Salt Lake City: University of Utah Press, 2016).

Yavuz, M. Hakan and Sluglett, Peter (eds). *War and Diplomacy: The Russo-Turkish War of 1877–78 and the Treaty of Berlin* (Salt Lake City: University of Utah Press, 2011).

Yiğit, Yücel. "The Teşkilat-ı Mahsusa and World War I." *Middle East Critique*23, no. 2 (2014): 157-174.

Young, Crawford. *The Politics of Cultural Pluralism* (Madison: University of Wisconsin Press, 1976).

Zarifian, Julien. "The Armenian-American lobby and its impact on US foreign policy." *Society* 51, no. 5 (2014): 503-512.

Zürcher, Erik Jan. "Between Death and Desertion: The Ottoman Army in World War I." *Turcica* 28 (1996): 235-258.

Zürcher, Erik Jan. "Ottoman Labour Battalions in World War I." In *Der Völkermord an den Armeniern und die Shoah*, (Zurich: Chronos, 2002).